M000023454

CONTENTS

Mediterranean Chicken Quinoa Bowl 29

Olive Chicken 29

Roasted Mediterranean Chicken 29

Lemon-Thyme Chicken 30

Mediterranean Chicken with Potatoes 30

Turkey with Cream Cheese Sauce 30

Healthy Marinara Chicken with Cauliflower Risotto 30

Buffalo Chicken Fingers with Nutty Kale Salad 31

Healthy Roasted Turkey with Low Carb Avocado Relish 31

Instant Pot Healthy Turkey Meat Balls 31

Delicious Turkey Sausage Patties with Lemon Tahini Sauce 32

Instant Pot Roast Chicken with Steamed Veggies 32

Healthy Chicken Curry 32

Low Carb Turkey Served with Creamy Sauce and Sautéed Capers 33

Tasty Instant Pot Thai Turkey Legs 33

Gingery Roasted Turkey 33

Herbed Instant Pot Turkey Breast 33

Tangy Instant Pot Turkey Meatballs 33

Pressure Roasted Chicken 34

Tasty Instant Pot Turkey Breast 34

Pressure Cooked Cajun Chicken with Lime Butter Steamed Veggies 34

Instant Pot Ginger Peach Chicken 34

Instant Pot Asian chicken lettuce wraps 35

Oregano Chicken with Sautéed Kale 35

Tasty Citric Chicken with Fried Button Mushrooms 35

Low Carb Turkey Ratatouille 35

Spiced Chicken Patties Low Carb Lemon Pesto 36

Vegetable & Chicken Stir-Fry 36

Turkey-Cauliflower Hash with Avocado and Hardboiled Egg 36

Instant Pot Chicken Curry 36

Healthy Turkey Loaf with Sautéed Button Mushrooms 37

Satisfying Turkey Lettuce Wraps 37

Lemon Olive Chicken 37

Instant Pot Turkey with Veggies 37

Instant Pot Crunchy Chicken Salad 37

Pressure Cooked Chicken Shawarma 38

Instant Pot Coconut Curry Turkey 38

Instant Pot Green Chile Chicken 38

Healthy Chicken Super Salad 38

Grilled Herb Marinade Chicken with Sautéed Mushrooms 39

Tropical Turkey Salad 39

Instant Pot Grilled Chicken & Green Onion 39

Healthy Turkey Chili 39

Pesto Chicken Casserole 40

Italian Turkey 40

Caprese Chicken 40

Roasted Chicken with Herbed Butter 40

Chicken Enchiladas 40

Turkey Balls 41

Chicken Zucchini Cutlets 41

Sour Grilled Turkey Breasts 41

Cheesy Chicken Tenders 41

Air Fried Chicken 41

Ham Wrapped Turkey Rolls 42

Stuffed Whole Chicken 42

Turkey with Mozzarella and Tomatoes 42

Boursin Stuffed Chicken 42

Mediterranean Turkey Cutlets 42

Cheesy Bacon Ranch Chicken 43

Garlic Turkey Breasts 43

Grilled Chicken Breast 43

Buffalo Skillet Turkey 43

Low Carb Chicken Nuggets 43

Turkey with Cream Cheese Sauce 44

Chicken Spinach Coconut Curry 44

Turkey Garlic Mushroom Sauté 44

Smokey Mountain Chicken 44

Cauliflower Turkey Casserole 44

Chicken Parmesan 45

Creamy Garlic Turkey Soup 45

Chicken Asparagus Sheet Pan 45

Turkey Breasts Stuffed with Pimiento Cheese 45

Beef Recipes 46

Healthy Italian Beef & Cabbage Stir-Fry 46

Instant Pot Beef Shred Rolls serve with Chilled Lemon Juice 46

Delicious Instant Pot Steak with Parsley & Arugula 46

Filet Mignon with Caramelized Onions 46

Healthy Beef Chili served with Avocado and Green Onions 47

Ground Beef with Veggies 47

Herbed London Broil with Lemon Garlic Butter Zucchini Noodles 47

Low Carb Beef & Sweet Potato Dish 48

Asparagus & Steak Bowl 48

Crunchy Steak Salad 48

Instant Pot Pork Rind Stuffed Peppers 68
Instant Spiced Pork Chops 69
Instant Pot Cheese Crusted Pork Chops 69
Pork Chops in Cream Sauce served with Avocado 69
Caramelized Onion Pork Chops with Steamed Green Beans and Avocado 69
Pork Filled Egg Muffins 70
Pork Bread 70
Garlic Creamy Pork Chops 70
Pork Fajitas 70
Jamaican Jerk Pork Roast 70
Pork Carnitas 71
Zesty Pork Chops 71
Greek Pork Gyros 71
Garlic Rosemary Pork Chops 71
Lemony Grilled Pork Chops 72
Cheddar Maple Squash 72
Spinach Pork Roll Ups 72
Stuffed Pork Chops 72
Pork with Butternut Squash Stew 72
Sweet Mustard Pork 73
Barbecue Dry Rub Ribs 73
Pork Enchilada Casserole 73
Cheesy Bacon Pork Chops 73
genic Easy Pork Briskets 73
Ground Pork with Zucchini 74
Creamy BBQ Pork 74
Broccoli Pork 74
Home Style Pork Meatloaf 74
Italian Pork with Veggies 74
Pork Taco Casserole 74
Slow Cooker Pork Stew 75
Buttered Chili Pork Chops 75
genic Pork in Gravy 75
Pork Asparagus Roll Ups 75

Fish and Seafood Recipes 75

Mixed Seafood Stew 75
Sauce Dipped Mussels 76
Squid Oyster Medley 76
Crusty Grilled Mussels 76
Seafood Garlic Couscous 77
Lobster Rice Paella 77
Fish and Vegetable Parcels 77
Seafood with Couscous Salad 77
Saffron Fish Gratins 78
Instant Pot Coconut Fishbowl 78
Instant Pot Shrimp Paella 78

Steamed Alaskan Crab Legs 79
Instant Pot Shrimp & Grits 79
Salmon with Gingery Orange Sauce 79
Instant Pot Mussels 79
Salmon w/ Chili-Lime Sauce 80
Instant Pot Tilapia 80
Pressure Cooked Coconut Curry Shrimp 80
Hot Lemony Tilapia w/ Asparagus 80
Tasty Citrus Tilapia 80
Pressure Steamed Salmon 81
Teriyaki Fish w/ Zucchini 81
Grilled Tuna w/ Bean & Tomato Salad 81
Steamed Bass with Fennel, Parsley, and Capers 81
Pressure Baked Salmon Salad with Mint Dressing 81
Spiced Mahi-Mahi with Creamed Sautéed Mushrooms 82
Instant Pot Seafood Cioppino 82
Instant Pot Shrimp Scampi 82
Instant Pot BBQ Shrimp 83
Spicy Grilled Cod 83
Coconut Fish & Vegetable Curry 83
Red Snapper in Hot Veggie Sauce 83
Pressure Grilled Salmon 84
Creamy Coconut Baked Salmon with Green Salad 84
Tilapia with Mushroom Sauce 84
Pressure Cooked Salmon with Herbs 84
Instant Pot White Fish Curry 85
Pressure Roasted Tilapia 85
Instant Pot Roasted Salmon 85
Instant Pot Tilapia in Coconut Cream Sauce 85
Garlic Butter Salmon 86
Tuscan Butter Salmon 86
Mahi Mahi Stew 86
Tilapia with Herbed Butter 86
Roasted Trout 86
Sour Fish with Herbed Butter 87
Cod Coconut Curry 87
Garlic Shrimp with Goat Cheese 87
Grain Free Salmon Bread 87
Buttered Mahi Mahi Slices 87
Salmon Stew 88
Paprika Shrimp 88
genic Butter Fish 88
Shrimp Magic 88
Sweet and Sour Cod 88
Buttered Scallops 89

900 Everyday Recipes!!!

This book will teach you how to create a variety of healthy, easy-to-make, delicious recipes in the easiest way possible.

We don't have to struggle anymore with the question: "We have no idea what to eat...What do we cook for breakfast or for dinner tonight?"

You will have dozens of mouth-watering delicious recipes, you can make everything, there's nothing you can't cook.

This cookbook is perfect for fans who wants to learn how to make the best dishes in the world.

In this Cookbook You will find recipes in various categories such as:

- Beans, Rice and Grains Recipes
- Breakfast Recipes
- Salads Recipes
- Poultry Recipes
- Beef Recipes
- Pork Recipes
- Fish and Seafood Recipes
- Vegetable Recipes
- Vegan Recipes
- Side Dishes Recipes
- Snacks Recipes
- Dessert Recipes
- Eggs and Dairy Recipes
- Soups Recipes
- Instant Pot Stews
- Sandwiches and Wraps Recipes
- Pizza and Pasta Recipes
- 3 Week Meal Plans and Shopping Lists

Making great cooking choices has never been easier! Get a copy of this 900 Everyday Recipes for the fast and healthy meals!

Beans, Rice and Grains Recipes

Spinach Beans

Serves: **2** | Prep Time: **30** mins

Ingredients

- 1 small onion, chopped
- 1 can (14½ ounces) diced tomatoes, undrained
- ¼ teaspoon salt
- 1 can (15 ounces) cannellini beans, rinsed and drained
- 6 ounces fresh baby spinach
- 1 tablespoon olive oil
- 2 garlic cloves, minced
- 2 tablespoons Worcestershire sauce
- ¼ teaspoon black pepper
- 1/8 teaspoon red pepper flakes, crushed
- 14 ounces bacon, chopped

Directions

1. Heat oil in a skillet and add bacon. Sauté until brown and stir in onions.
2. Sauté for about 5 minutes and add garlic to the pan.
3. Cook for about 1 minute and add Worcestershire sauce, seasonings, and tomatoes. Lower the heat and cook for another 8 minutes.
4. Toss in beans and spinach and cook for about 5 minutes.
5. Stir gently and serve immediately.

Meatballs Chickpea Medley

Serves: **6** | Prep Time: **25** mins

Ingredients

- ¼ cup whole wheat panko breadcrumbs
- ¼ cup fresh parsley, chopped
- 1 pound ground chicken
- 2 egg whites
- ¼ cup fat-free feta cheese, crumbled
- 2 tablespoons fresh rosemary, chopped
- 1 tablespoon olive oil
- ½ teaspoon salt
- 1 (15 ounces) can chickpeas, drained
- 3 garlic cloves, roughly chopped
- 1 cup cherry tomatoes

Directions

1. Preheat the oven to 400 degrees F and grease a baking sheet.
2. Whisk egg white in a bowl along with panko, parsley, chicken, feta and rosemary. Toss chickpeas with olive oil, salt, garlic, and tomatoes in a separate bowl. Spread the chickpea mixture on the baking sheet.
3. Use the chicken mince mixture to make 2-inch balls and place these balls over the chickpeas. Bake for about 20 minutes in the oven and immediately serve.

Lemony Mushroom and Herb Rice

Serves: **4** | Prep Time: **20** mins

Ingredients

- 1¼ cups chestnut mushrooms, diced
- 2 large garlic cloves, finely chopped
- 1 cup long grain rice
- 2 tablespoons olive oil
- 5 tablespoons parsley, chopped
- 1 lemon zest, finely grated
- 3 tablespoons chives, snipped

Directions

1. Boil water with salt in a pan and add rice.
2. Cook for about 10 minutes with constant stirring and drain them through a sieve. Sauté mushrooms for about 4 minutes and stir in garlic.
3. Sauté for about 1 minute and toss in lemon zest, chives, parsley, and drained rice. Serve to enjoy.

Citrus Garlic Beans

Serves: **2** | Prep Time: **25** mins

Ingredients

- 1 large onion, sliced
- 2 (14 oz.) cans beans, rinsed and drained
- 1 tablespoon olive oil
- 1 garlic clove, crushed
- 1 lemon zest
- 1 large bunch parsley, chopped
- 1 lemon, juiced

Directions

1. Heat oil in a pan and add onions. Sauté for about 3 minutes until soft and stir in the beans and garlic. Cook thoroughly and add lemon zest and lemon juice.
2. Garnish with parsley and serve to enjoy.

Cashew Rice

Serves: **4** | Prep Time: **30** mins

Ingredients

- 3 cups cooked basmati rice, cooled
- 4 oz. cashew nuts
- 1 green bell pepper, deseeded and finely sliced
- 1 small red onion, finely sliced
- 1 yellow bell pepper, deseeded and finely sliced

For the dressing

- 2 tablespoons light soy sauce
- 1 tablespoon brown sugar
- ½ lemon, juiced
- 3 tablespoons mango chutney
- 1 tablespoon oil
- 2 teaspoons curry powder

Directions

1. Put all the ingredients for dressing in a bowl. Toast the cashews until golden brown and transfer to the mixed dressing. Add rice, onions and bell peppers to serve.

Moroccan Couscous

Serves: **8** | Prep Time: **20** mins

Ingredients

- 1 orange zest
- 1/3 cup dried apricots, chopped
- ¼ teaspoon ground cinnamon
- 1½ cups vegetable stock
- 1 orange, juiced
- 1/3 cup dates, chopped
- 1/3 cup golden raisins
- ½ teaspoon ground cumin
- ½ teaspoon ground ginger
- 2 cups whole-wheat couscous
- ½ cup slivered almonds, toasted
- Salt, to taste
- ¼ teaspoon coriander
- ½ teaspoon turmeric
- 1 tablespoon butter
- ¼ cup mint, chopped

Directions

1. Boil stock in a medium saucepan and add the orange juice, zest, dates, apricots, raisins, couscous, and spices.
2. Remove the pan from the heat and allow the couscous to absorb the liquid for about 15 minutes. Stir in the butter, mint and almonds and season with salt to serve.

Greek Stock Beans

Serves: **2** | Prep Time: **35** mins

Ingredients

- 1 tablespoon red wine vinegar
- 2 tablespoons tomato purée
- 1 large onion, chopped
- 2 cups chicken stock
- 2 (14 oz.) can butter beans, drained
- 1 small bunch dill, chopped
- 2 tablespoons crumbled feta cheese

Directions

1. Heat oil in a skillet on medium heat and add garlic, onions, and seasonings.
2. Sauté for about 8 minutes and add tomato puree, beans, vinegar, stock, and dill. Let it simmer for about 15 minutes and garnish with dill leaves and feta cheese to serve.

Baked Mediterranean Rice

Serves: **8** | Prep Time: **50** mins

Ingredients

- 1½ cups arborio rice
- 2 tablespoons fresh oregano, chopped
- 1 pint cherry tomatoes, cut in half
- 2 tablespoons fresh basil, chopped
- ¼ cup Parmesan cheese, grated
- ½ cup sweet onion, diced
- 3 cups chicken broth
- 2 tablespoons butter, melted
- 1 teaspoon salt
- 8 ounces baby spinach, stem tips removed
- ¼ cup fresh parsley, chopped
- 1 cup mozzarella cheese, shredded

Directions

1. Preheat the oven to 370 degrees F and grease a casserole dish.
2. Layer the rice, onions and melted butter into the casserole.
3. Put basil, oregano and salt into the chicken broth and mix well.
4. Pour this mixture over the rice and top evenly with halved tomatoes.
5. Transfer into the oven and bake for about 30 minutes.
6. Remove from the oven and stir in the baby spinach and mozzarella cheese.
7. Top with parsley and grated Parmesan cheese to serve.

Bean Mash with Grilled Veggies

Serves: **2** | Prep Time: **20** mins

Ingredients
- 1 aubergine, sliced lengthwise
- 2 tablespoons olive oil

For the mash
- 1 garlic clove, crushed
- 1 tablespoon coriander, chopped
- 14 oz. can haricot bean, rinsed
- 1 red bell pepper, deseeded and quartered
- 2 zucchinis, sliced lengthwise
- ½ cup vegetable stock
- Lemon wedges, to serve

Directions
1. Preheat the grill and grease its grilling grate.
2. Arrange all the vegetables on the grates and grill them until golden from both sides.
3. Meanwhile, cook beans and garlic in the stock and let it simmer for 10 minutes.
4. Mash the beans in this mixture roughly with a masher.
5. Spread this beans mash in the serving plates and place the grilled vegetables over it.
6. Garnish with lemon wedges, coriander, oil and black pepper to serve.

Breakfast Recipes

Green Poached Egg Toasts

Serves: **2** | Prep Time: **15** mins

Ingredients
- 2 oz avocado flesh, mashed
- 2 bread slices, toasted
- ¼ teaspoon lemon juice
- 3.5 oz smoked salmon
- 1 teaspoon soy sauce
- 2 eggs
- Salt and black pepper, to taste

Directions
1. Boil water and create a whirlpool in it. Crack an egg in it and allow it to cook.
2. Repeat the same process with the other egg. Transfer both the eggs immediately to an ice bath for 10 seconds. Scoop out the fresh avocado flesh into a bowl and mash well.
3. Place 2 toasted slices in the serving plates and spread the avocado mash generously over them. Divide the smoked salmon over the bread slices.
4. Drizzle half of the soy sauce, lemon juice, salt and black pepper over each of the toasts.
5. Top each with one poached egg and serve.

Soufflé Omelet with Mushrooms

Serves: **6** | Prep Time: **25** mins

Ingredients
- 1 garlic clove, minced
- 1 tablespoon parsley, minced
- ½ teaspoon salt
- ¼ cup cheddar cheese, grated
- 1 teaspoon extra-virgin olive oil
- 8 ounces sliced mushrooms
- 3 large eggs, separated
- ½ teaspoon black pepper

Directions
1. Heat oil in a nonstick skillet over medium-high heat and add garlic.
2. Sauté for 1 minute and stir in the mushrooms.
3. Cook for about 10 minutes and drizzle parsley on top.
4. Beat egg yolks in a bowl and whisk the egg whites separately.
5. Season this mixture with salt, black pepper, and cheese.
6. Warm a large skillet on medium heat and pour in the egg batter.
7. Cover the lid and spread mushroom over one side of the egg.
8. Fold it over the mushrooms and dish out to serve.

Spinach Parmesan Baked Eggs

Serves: **4** | Prep Time: **25** mins

Ingredients
- 2 cloves garlic, minced
- ½ cup fat-free parmesan cheese, grated
- 1 small tomato, diced small
- 2 teaspoons olive oil
- 4 cups baby spinach
- 4 eggs

Directions
1. Preheat the oven to 350 degrees F and grease an 8-inch casserole dish.
2. Heat olive oil in a large skillet over medium heat and stir in garlic and spinach. Sauté until spinach is wilted and drain completely. Add parmesan cheese and transfer this mixture to the casserole dish.
3. Make four wells in the spinach mixture and crack one egg into each well.
4. Place the casserole dish in the oven and bake for about 15 minutes. Dish out and serve warm.

Red smoothie

Serves: **1** | Prep Time: **10** mins

Ingredients
- 3 tablespoons raspberry
- 4 plums, cored
- 3 tablespoons blueberry
- 1 teaspoon linseed oil
- 1 tablespoon lemon juice

Directions
Put all the ingredients in a blender and blend until smooth. Pour into a glass and immediately serve.

Sweet Potato Breakfast Hash

Serves: **6** | Prep Time: **30** mins

Ingredients
- 3 tablespoons olive oil
- ¼ teaspoon ground white pepper
- 2 cloves garlic, minced
- 2 sweet potatoes, peeled and cubed
- ½ teaspoon salt
- 1 tablespoon apple cider vinegar
- 1 teaspoon honey
- ¼ cup yellow onion, diced
- 8 ounces low sodium sulfate free ham, diced
- 1 tablespoon lemon juice
- ¼ cup green bell pepper, diced
- 1 avocado, peeled, pit removed, and diced

Directions
1. Preheat the oven to 450 degrees F and grease a baking sheet.
2. Season the sweet potatoes with black pepper and salt, and drizzle with a half tablespoon olive oil.
3. Arrange these seasoned potatoes in the baking sheet and transfer in the oven.
4. Bake for about 15 minutes and remove from the oven.
5. Combine apple cider vinegar, 1 tablespoon olive oil, garlic, and honey in a small bowl. Heat the skillet and add remaining olive oil in it. Stir in bell pepper and onion and sauté until soft.
6. Add baked potatoes and ham and cook until the meat turns golden.
7. Turn off the heat and season the mixture with vinegar sauce, lemon juice, and avocado. Dish out and serve warm.

Spinach and Feta Baked Egg

Serves: **4** | Prep Time: **25** mins

Ingredients
- 4 eggs
- 1 cup cooked spinach, squeezed
- ½ cup fat-free feta cheese

Directions
1. Preheat the oven to 370 degrees F and grease a muffin pan with muffin cups.
2. Divide the spinach into four muffin cups and press gently into the bottom.
3. Stir in whisked eggs and top with feta cheese. Bake for about 15 minutes and dish out to serve warm.

Cheesy Ham Souffle

Serves: **4** | Prep Time: **30** mins

Ingredients
- 1 cup cheddar cheese, shredded
- ½ cup heavy cream
- 6 large eggs
- 6 ounces ham, diced
- Salt and black pepper, to taste

Directions
1. Preheat the oven to 350°F and grease 4 ramekins gently.
2. Whisk together eggs in a medium bowl and add all other ingredients.
3. Mix well and pour the mixture into the ramekins.
4. Transfer into the ramekins and bake for about 18 minutes.
5. Remove from the oven and allow to slightly cool and serve.

Browned Butter Pumpkin Latte

Serves: **2** | Prep Time: **10** mins

Ingredients
- 2 shots espresso
- 2 tablespoons butter
- 2 scoops Stevia
- 2 cups hot almond milk
- 4 tablespoons pumpkin puree

Directions
1. Heat butter on low heat in a small pan and allow to lightly brown.
2. Brew two shots of espresso and stir in the Stevia.
3. Add browned butter along with pumpkin puree and hot almond milk.
4. Blend for about 10 seconds on high and pour into 2 cups to serve.

Breakfast Cheesy Sausage

Serves: **1** | Prep Time: **20** mins

Ingredients
- 1 pork sausage link, cut open and casing discarded
- Sea salt and black pepper, to taste
- ¼ teaspoon thyme
- ¼ teaspoon sage
- ½ cup mozzarella cheese, shredded

Directions
1. Mix sausage meat with thyme, sage, mozzarella cheese, sea salt and black pepper. Shape the mixture into a patty and transfer to a hot pan.
2. Cook for about 5 minutes per side and dish out to serve.

Avocado Toast

Serves: **2** | Prep Time: **20** mins

Ingredients
- 2 tablespoons sunflower oil
- ½ cup parmesan cheese, shredded
- 1 medium avocado, sliced
- Sea salt, to taste
- 4 slices cauliflower bread

Directions
1. Heat oil in a pan and cook cauliflower bread slices for about 2 minutes per side. Season avocado with sea salt and place on the cauliflower bread.
2. Top with parmesan cheese and microwave for about 2 minutes.

Cream Cheese and Chive Fold-Overs

Serves: **2** | Prep Time: **15** mins

Ingredients
- 6 tablespoons cream cheese
- 1 teaspoon lemon juice
- 4 coconut flour tortillas
- 3 tablespoons fresh chives, chopped
- 4 teaspoons olive oil

Directions
1. Whisk cream cheese thoroughly in a bowl and stir in chives and lemon juice.
2. Spread the cream cheese mixture evenly over the tortillas and fold into half-moon shapes.
3. Heat quarter of oil over medium high heat in a skillet and add a tortilla.
4. Cook until browned on both sides and repeat with the remaining tortillas. Serve warm.

Chocolate Chip Waffles

Serves: **2** | Prep Time: **30** mins

Ingredients
- 2 scoops vanilla protein powder
- 1 pinch pink Himalayan sea salt
- 50 grams sugar free chocolate chips
- 2 large eggs, separated
- 2 tablespoons butter, melted

Directions
1. Mix together egg yolks, vanilla protein powder and butter in a bowl.
2. Whisk together egg whites thoroughly in another bowl and transfer to the egg yolks mixture. Add the sugar free chocolate chips and a pinch of pink salt.
3. Transfer this mixture in the waffle maker and cook according to manufacturer's instructions.

Low Carb Cereal

Serves: **2** | Prep Time: **25** mins

Ingredients
- 2 tablespoons flaxseeds
- ¼ cup almonds, slivered
- 1 tablespoon chia seeds
- 1½ cups almond milk, unsweetened
- 10 grams cocoa nibs

Directions
Mix together flaxseeds, almonds, chia seeds and cocoa nibs in a bowl. Top with the almond milk and serve.

Low Carb Detox Tea

Serves: **1** | Prep Time: **10** mins

Ingredients
- 2 tablespoons apple cider vinegar
- 1 scoop Stevia
- 1 cup water
- 2 tablespoons lemon juice
- 1 teaspoon cinnamon

Directions
1. Boil water and add remaining ingredients. Pour into a cup and serve hot.

Iced Matcha Latte

Serves: **1** | Prep Time: **10** mins

Ingredients
- 1 tablespoon coconut oil
- 1 cup unsweetened cashew milk
- 1 teaspoon matcha powder
- 2 ice cubes
- 1/8 teaspoon vanilla bean

Directions
1. Mix together all the ingredients in a blender and blend until smooth. Pour into a glass to serve.

Low Carb Strawberry Jam

Serves: **8** | Prep Time: **1 hour 20** mins

Ingredients
- 1 tablespoon organic lemon juice
- 1 cup fresh organic strawberries, chopped
- ½ tablespoon grass fed gelatin
- 1 teaspoon Xylitol
- 1 tablespoon gelatin, dissolved in 1 tablespoon water

Directions
Put strawberries in a small saucepan over medium heat and add lemon juice and Xylitol. Mix well and cook for about 15 minutes, stirring occasionally. Mash the strawberries with a fork and stir in the gelatin mixture. Remove from heat and pour into a mason jar. Allow to cool and refrigerate for 1 hour until jelly-like.

Iced Matcha Latte

Serves: **1** | Prep Time: **10** mins

Ingredients
- 1 teaspoon matcha powder, high quality
- 1 cup water
- ½ tablespoon coconut oil
- ½ teaspoon Stevia powder
- 1 cup organic coconut milk, frozen into ice cubes

Directions
1. Put all the ingredients except collagen powder in a high powered blender.
2. Pulse until completely smooth and pour into a glass to serve.

Breakfast Wrap

Serves: **1** | Prep Time: **20** mins

Ingredients
- 1 organic nori sheet
- 1½ avocado, sliced
- 3 pastured eggs
- ¼ teaspoon salt
- ½ tablespoon butter

Directions
1. Whisk eggs and salt in a bowl until combined. Heat butter on medium heat in a frying pan and stir in whisked eggs. Cook for about 3 minutes on both sides and dish out.
2. Place the omelet on top of the nori sheet and top with avocado slices.
3. Roll up the breakfast wrap and slice in half to serve.

Egg Crepes with Avocados

Serves: **2** | Prep Time: **15** mins

Ingredients
- 4 eggs
- ¾ avocado, thinly sliced
- 2 teaspoons olive oil
- ½ cup alfalfa sprouts
- 4 slices turkey breast cold cuts, shredded

Directions
1. Heat olive oil over medium heat in a pan and crack in the eggs.
2. Spread the eggs lightly with the spatula and cook for about 3 minutes on both sides. Dish out the egg crepe and top with turkey breast, alfalfa sprouts and avocado. Roll up tightly and serve warm.

Breakfast Bacon Muffins

Serves: **6** | Prep Time: **30** mins

Ingredients
- 1 cup bacon bits
- 3 cups almond flour, organic
- ½ cup ghee, melted
- 1 teaspoon baking soda
- 4 eggs

Directions
1. Preheat the oven to 350°F and line muffin tins with muffin liners. Melt ghee in a bowl and stir in the almond flour and baking soda. Mix well and add the bacon bits and eggs.
2. Divide the mixture into the muffin tins and transfer into the oven.
3. Bake for about 20 minutes and remove from the oven to serve.

Non-Oatmeal Breakfast

Serves: **2** | Prep Time: **25** mins

Ingredients
- 1 cup organic coconut milk, full-fat
- 1 cup cauliflower, riced
- 3 tablespoons unsweetened coconut, shredded
- 1/3 cup fresh organic raspberries
- 3 drops liquid Stevia

Directions
1. Mix together cauliflower and coconut milk and pour in a pot.
2. Cook over medium heat until cauliflower warms up and add raspberries.
3. Mash the raspberries and stir in coconut and Stevia. Cover the lid and cook for about 10 minutes. Dish into a bowl and serve warm.

Spaghetti Squash Hash Browns

Serves: **3** | Prep Time: **25** mins

Ingredients
- Sea salt and black pepper, to taste
- 1½ cups spaghetti squash
- 3 tablespoons avocado oil, for frying
- ½ cup sour cream
- ½ cup green onions

Directions
1. Season the spaghetti squash with sea salt and black pepper.
2. Add green onions and sour cream and form into patties.
3. Heat avocado oil in a skillet over medium heat and add patties.
4. Fry until golden brown from both sides and dish out to serve.

Mini Bacon Guacamole Cups

Serves: **4** | Prep Time: **40** mins

Ingredients
- 1 ripe avocado
- 9 bacon slices, 6 slices halved, and 3 slices quartered
- 2 tablespoons onion, minced
- Kosher salt and black pepper, to taste
- 1 small jalapeno, seeded and minced

Directions
1. Preheat the oven to 400°F and turn 4 mini-muffin pans upside down on a baking sheet.
2. Spray the tops of the overturned muffin tins and place the quarter of the slice on top.
3. Wrap the sides of the mini-muffin pans with the longer portions of bacon and secure with a toothpick.
4. Bake for about 25 minutes and remove carefully from the mini muffin cups.
5. Meanwhile, mash avocado with a fork in a medium bowl and stir in the jalapeno, onions, salt and black pepper.
6. Put the guacamole in the bacon cups and serve warm.

Coconut Macadamia Bars

Serves: **6** | Prep Time: **10** mins

Ingredients
- ¼ cup coconut oil
- 10 drops Stevia drops
- 60 grams macadamia nuts, crushed
- ½ cup almond butter
- 6 tablespoons unsweetened coconut, shredded

Directions
1. Mix together coconut oil, almond butter and coconut in a bowl.
2. Stir in Stevia and macadamia nuts and mix well.
3. Pour this mixture into a baking dish and refrigerate overnight.
4. Slice and serve chilled.

Fried Radish, Bacon and Cauliflower Hash Browns

Serves: **4** | Prep Time: **30** mins

Ingredients
- 3 cups cauliflower, riced
- 1 pound radishes, shredded
- Paprika, sea salt and black pepper, to taste
- 6 strips bacon, cooked crisp and crumbled
- 3 tablespoons olive oil

Directions
1. Mix together cauliflower, radishes, paprika, sea salt and black pepper in a large bowl.
2. Heat olive oil over medium high heat in a large skillet and pour the mixture in a thin even layer. Add bacon strips and fry for about 20 minutes, stirring and flipping occasionally.
3. Dish out and season with more sea salt and black pepper to serve.

Cinnamon Bun Fat Bomb Bars

Serves: **2** | Prep Time: **30** mins

Ingredients
- ¼ teaspoon ground cinnamon
- 1 cup creamed coconut, cut into chunks
- ½ teaspoon ground cinnamon
- 1 tablespoon extra-virgin coconut oil
- 1½ tablespoons almond butter

Directions
1. Line 2 muffin pans with liners and keep aside. Meanwhile, mix together creamed coconut and ground cinnamon in a bowl. Pour this mixture into the muffin pans.
2. Whisk together coconut oil, almond butter and cinnamon in another bowl.
3. Divide this icing mixture into the muffin pans and place in the freezer for about 10 minutes. Remove from the freezer after 5 minutes and serve.

Zucchini Breakfast Hash

Serves: **2** | Prep Time: **30** mins

Ingredients
- 1 medium zucchini, diced
- 2 bacon slices
- 1 tablespoon ghee
- ¼ teaspoon pink Himalayan salt
- 1 large egg, fried

Directions
1. Heat ghee in a pan over medium heat and add bacon.
2. Cook for about 3 minutes until lightly browned and stir in the zucchini and pink salt.
3. Cook for about 15 minutes and dish out in a plate. Top with a fried egg and serve to enjoy.

Bulletproof Breakfast Bowl

Serves: **2** | Prep Time: **45** mins

Ingredients
- 2 Paleo sausages, precooked
- 2 pastured eggs, poached
- 1 cup cauliflower rice
- 2 handfuls organic leafy greens, lightly steamed
- 3 tablespoons grass fed ghee for cooking

Directions
1. Divide the leafy greens into 2 plates. Heat ghee in a pan over medium heat and add cauliflower rice.
2. Cook for about 4 minutes and transfer it to the plates alongside the leafy greens. Top with the poached eggs and keep aside. Meanwhile, put the sausages to the same pan and cook until done.
3. Transfer the sausages to the plate and serve.

Spaghetti Squash Patties with Avocado and Poached Egg

Serves: **4** | Prep Time: **55** mins

Ingredients
- 1 medium spaghetti squash, seeds removed
- 1 pasture raised egg
- ½ avocado
- 1 tablespoon avocado oil
- 2 teaspoons sea salt

Directions
1. Preheat the oven to 320°F and cut the spaghetti squash into a circular shape with biscuit cutter. Season the squash with sea salt and drizzle with avocado oil.
2. Transfer into the oven and bake for about 45 minutes. Boil water and crack the egg in it.
3. Cook for about 3 minutes and remove the egg to a plate.
4. Remove the squash patties from the oven and transfer onto the plate.
5. Mash the avocado and place it alongside the squash and poached egg.

Ham and Cheese Pockets

Serves: **2** | Prep Time: **30** mins

Ingredients
- 1 oz cream cheese
- ¾ cup mozzarella cheese, shredded
- 4 tablespoons flax meal
- 3 oz provolone cheese slices
- 3 oz ham

Directions
1. Preheat the oven to 400°F and line a baking sheet with parchment paper.
2. Microwave mozzarella cheese and cream cheese for about 1 minute.
3. Stir in the flax meal and combine well to make the dough.
4. Roll the dough and add provolone cheese slices and ham. Fold the dough like an envelope, seal it and poke some holes in it. Place on the baking sheet and transfer into the oven.
5. Bake for about 20 minutes until golden brown and remove from the oven.
6. Allow it to cool and cut in half while still hot to serve.

Tomato Parmesan Mini Quiches

Serves: **8** | Prep Time: **35** mins

Ingredients
- 2½ cups Roma tomatoes, seeded and chopped
- 24 (4 inch) round ham, cooked and thinly sliced
- Salt and black pepper, to taste
- 6 eggs, lightly beaten
- 1½ cups parmesan cheese, finely shredded

Directions
1. Preheat the oven to 350°F and grease the muffin cups. Place ham at the bottom of the muffin cups and top with tomatoes. Pour beaten eggs over tomato and season with salt and black pepper. Top with parmesan cheese and transfer into the oven.
2. Bake for about 20 minutes and then remove from the muffin cups. Serve warm.

Avocado and Smoked Salmon Omelet

Serves: **2** | Prep Time: **15** mins

Ingredients
- 4 large eggs
- 3 teaspoons extra virgin olive oil, divided
- 2 ounce smoked salmon
- Pinch of salt
- ½ avocado, sliced

Directions
1. Whisk together eggs and salt in a bowl.
2. Heat 2 teaspoons of oil over medium heat in a skillet and stir in the egg mixture. Cook for about 2 minutes until the center is still a bit runny and the bottom is set. Flip the omelet and cook for about 30 seconds. Transfer to a plate and top with smoked salmon and avocado
3. Sprinkle with the remaining olive oil and serve.

Cauliflower Bagels

Serves: **4** | Prep Time: **45** mins

Ingredients
- ½ cup sharp cheddar cheese, shredded
- 6 cups cauliflower florets, finely chopped
- ½ cup mozzarella cheese, shredded
- 2½ teaspoons everything bagel seasoning
- 1 large egg, lightly beaten

Directions
1. Preheat the oven to 425°F and line a baking sheet with parchment paper.
2. Transfer the cauliflower to a microwave oven and microwave for about 3 minutes. Allow it to cool slightly and transfer into a bowl.
3. Stir in the egg and sharp cheddar cheese until well combined.
4. Divide the mixture into 8 equal parts and transfer on the prepared baking sheet. Flatten into 3½ inch circles and make a hole in the center of each circle with a 1 inch biscuit cutter.
5. Top with mozzarella cheese and sprinkle with bagel seasoning.
6. Bake for about 25 minutes until browned around the edges and serve warm.

Banana Pancakes

Serves: **4** | Prep Time: **25** mins

Ingredients
- 1 medium banana
- 2 large eggs
- 2 tablespoons butter
- 1 tablespoon sugar free maple syrup
- 4 tablespoons ricotta cheese

Directions
1. Put the banana and eggs in a blender and blend until smooth.
2. Heat ½ tablespoon of butter over medium heat in a large nonstick pan and pour 2 tablespoons of the batter. Cook for about 2 minutes until bubbles appear on the surface.
3. Flip the pancakes gently with a spatula and cook for 2 more minutes.
4. Dish out the pancakes to a plate and repeat with the remaining batter.

Clementine and Pistachio Ricotta

Serves: **1** | Prep Time: **10** mins

Ingredients
- 2 teaspoons pistachios, chopped
- ⅓ cup ricotta
- 2 strawberries
- 1 tablespoon butter, melted
- 1 clementine, peeled and segmented

Directions
1. Put the ricotta into a serving bowl.
2. Top with clementine segments, strawberries, pistachios and butter to serve.

Salads Recipes

Mediterranean Sardine Salad

Serves: **4** | Prep Time: **20** mins

Ingredients
- ½ cup black olives, roughly chopped
- 2 (7 oz.) cans sardines in tomato sauce
- 1 tablespoon red wine vinegar
- 3 oz. salad leaves
- 1 tablespoon caper, drained and diced
- 1 tablespoon olive oil

Directions
1. Divide the salad leaves into 4 plates and top with capers and olives.
2. Drain the sardines and reserve the sauce. Roughly slice the sardines and divide it between the plates.
3. Drizzle with olive oil, vinegar and tomato sauce to serve.

Aubergine and Pepper Salad

Serves: **8** | Prep Time: **40** mins

Ingredients
- 3 aubergines
- 1¼ cups ready-roasted red pepper, soaked and drained
- 2 tablespoons olive oil
- ¼ cup thyme leaves
- 2 garlic cloves, sliced

Directions
1. Preheat the oven to 325 degrees F and grease a baking tray. Set the griddle pan over high heat and add oil and aubergines. Cook for about 3 minutes per side until grilled.
2. Add the grilled aubergines and red peppers to a baking tray.
3. Drizzle with olive oil and top with thyme leaves, seasoning and garlic slices.
4. Transfer the baking tray in the oven and bake for about 30 minutes.

Chickpeas Pepper Salad

Serves: **2** | Prep Time: **30** mins

Ingredients
- 2 cups water
- ¼ cup red wine vinegar
- 1 red bell pepper, diced
- 4 sun-dried tomatoes
- 2 garlic cloves, chopped
- 2 (14.5 ounce) cans chickpeas, drained and rinsed
- Salt, to taste
- 2 tablespoons extra-virgin olive oil
- ½ cup parsley, chopped

Directions
1. Preheat the oven to 350 degrees F and grease a baking tray.
2. Spread the red bell pepper slices in a baking tray with skin side up.
3. Bake for about 8 minutes and transfer the baked pepper to a ziplock bag.
4. Zip the bag and let it sit for 10 minutes then thinly slice the pepper.
5. Pour 2 cups of water in a bowl and microwave for about 4 minutes.
6. Soak sun-dried tomatoes to the hot water and let it sit for 10 minutes.
7. Drain these tomatoes and slice them thinly.
8. Toss garlic with olive oil and red wine vinegar in a bowl.
9. Add sliced bell pepper, salt, parsley, chickpeas, and sun-dried tomatoes to serve.

Cottage Cheese with Berries and Nuts

Serves: **3** | Prep Time: **10** mins

Ingredients
- ¼ cup blueberries
- ¾ cup cottage cheese
- ¼ cup blackberries
- 1 tablespoon almonds, chopped
- 1 tablespoon walnuts, chopped

Directions
1. Put the blueberries and blackberries in a bowl followed by cottage cheese.
2. Top with almonds and walnuts to serve.

Salami and Brie Cheese Salad

Serves: **4** | Prep Time: **10** mins

Ingredients
- 6 oz. salami
- 2 oz. lettuce
- ¼ cup olive oil
- 7 oz. Brie cheese
- ½ cup macadamia nuts

Directions
1. Put Brie cheese, lettuce, salami and macadamia nuts in a plate.
2. Sprinkle with olive oil and immediately serve.

Turkey Salad

Serves: **5** | Prep Time: **10** mins

Ingredients
- 6 oz. deli turkey
- 3 oz. cream cheese
- 2 avocados
- ¼ cup olive oil
- Salt and black pepper, to taste

Directions
1. Season the turkey with salt and black pepper.
2. Place the seasoned turkey on a plate and top with sliced avocados and cream cheese.
3. Drizzle with olive oil and serve immediately.

Salad in a Jar

Serves: **2** | Prep Time: **20** mins

Ingredients
- 1/6 oz. cherry tomatoes
- 4 oz. smoked salmon
- 1/6 oz. cucumber
- 4 tablespoons olive oil
- ½ scallion, chopped

Directions
1. Put cucumber, scallions and cherry tomatoes in a jar.
2. Top with smoked salmon and drizzle with olive oil to serve.

Tuna Salad with Capers

Serves: **4** | Prep Time: **10** mins

Ingredients
- ½ cup mayonnaise
- 4 oz. tuna in olive oil, drained
- 2 tablespoons crème fraiche
- Salt, black pepper and chili flakes, to taste
- 1 tablespoon capers

Directions
1. Mix together tuna, capers, mayonnaise and crème fraiche in a bowl.
2. Season with salt, black pepper and chili flakes to serve.

Roasted Fennel and Snow Pea Salad

Serves: **4** | Prep Time: **35** mins

Ingredients
- 3 tablespoons olive oil
- 2 tablespoons pumpkin seeds, toasted
- 1 pound fresh fennel, cut into small wedges
- Sea salt and black pepper, to taste
- 5 1/3 oz. snow peas

Directions
1. Preheat the oven to 425°F and lightly grease a baking dish.
2. Arrange the fennel wedges in a baking dish and sprinkle with olive oil, sea salt and black pepper. Transfer to the oven and bake for about 25 minutes until the fennel is golden in color. Meanwhile, put the pumpkin seeds in a pan and toast for about 2 minutes over medium heat.
3. Mix the roasted fennel, snow peas and pumpkin seeds in a bowl and serve.

Cauliflower Slaw

Serves: **5** | Prep Time: **10** mins

Ingredients
- 1 cup sour cream
- 1 tablespoon Dijon mustard
- 1 pound cauliflower, chopped
- ½ cup mayonnaise
- Salt, black pepper and garlic powder

Directions
1. Season the cauliflower with salt, black pepper and garlic powder.
2. Place the seasoned turkey in a bowl and stir in sour cream, Dijon mustard and mayonnaise. Mix well and immediately serve.

Cottage Cheese with Bacon, Avocado and Hot Pepper Salad

Serves: **2** | Prep Time: **15** mins

Ingredients
- 1 cup cottage cheese
- 2 bacon slices, crumbled
- 3 avocado slices
- Crushed red pepper, to taste
- 1 pinch salt

Directions
1. Put the bacon and avocado slices in a bowl followed by cottage cheese.
2. Season with salt and crushed red pepper to serve.

Swedish Shrimp Dill Salad

Serves: **6** | Prep Time: **10** mins

Ingredients

- 1 cup mayonnaise
- 10 oz. shrimp, peeled and cooked
- ¼ cup crème fraiche
- 2 tablespoons fresh dill
- Salt and black pepper, to taste

Directions

1. Mix together mayonnaise and crème fraiche in a bowl.
2. Stir in the shrimp and dill and season with salt and black pepper to serve.

Spinach Salad

Serves: **8** | Prep Time: **10** mins

Ingredients

- 4 oz. bacon, chopped
- 4 hardboiled eggs, chopped
- 2/3 cup parmesan cheese, finely grated
- 12 cups fresh spinach
- ½ cup olive oil

Directions

1. Divide the spinach into 8 salad plates evenly and add eggs and bacon.
2. Sprinkle with parmesan cheese and drizzle with olive oil to serve.

Chicken Salad

Serves: **6** | Prep Time: **15** mins

Ingredients

- 6 thin cut slices bacon, baked
- 2 boneless chicken breasts, cooked
- 1 large avocado, sliced
- 2 tablespoons ranch dressing
- 4 cups mixed leafy greens

Directions

1. Put the leafy greens in a bowl and top with bacon, chicken breasts, avocado and ranch dressing. Serve immediately.

Chicken Pecan Salad

Serves: **6** | Prep Time: **10** mins

Ingredients

- 3 ribs celery, diced
- 1½ pounds chicken breast, cooked
- ½ cup mayonnaise
- ¼ cup pecans, salted and chopped
- 2 teaspoons brown mustard

Directions

1. Toss the chicken with celery and pecans in a bowl.
2. Stir in the mayonnaise and brown mustard.
3. Transfer to refrigerator and serve chilled.

Turkey BLT Salad

Serves: **4** | Prep Time: **20** mins

Ingredients

- 1 oz. salted butter
- 1 pound boneless turkey, shredded
- 10 oz. Romaine lettuce
- ½ tablespoon garlic powder
- ¾ cup mayonnaise

Directions

1. Mix together mayonnaise and garlic powder in a bowl.
2. Divide lettuce in 4 plates and top with shredded turkey, salted butter and garlic mayonnaise to serve.

Sunflower Seed Salad

Serves: **6** | Prep Time: **20** mins

Ingredients

- ½ cup low carb Greek yogurt
- ½ cup sunflower seeds
- Salt and black pepper, to taste
- 2 cups fish, cooked and shredded
- ½ cup celery, minced

Directions

1. Place fish in a bowl and season with salt and black pepper.
2. Toss in rest of the ingredients and serve to enjoy.

Citrus Cheesy Brussels Sprout Salad

Serves: **8** | Prep Time: **12** mins

Ingredients
- 1¼ cups walnuts
- 1¼ pounds Brussels sprouts
- ¼ cup EVOO
- 1¼ cups parmesan cheese, freshly grated
- 1 lemon, juiced

Directions
1. Put walnuts and Brussels sprouts in a food processor and process until chopped.
2. Transfer into a bowl and drizzle with EVOO and lemon juice.
3. Top with parmesan cheese and serve immediately.

Caesar Dressing Beef Salad

Serves: **2** | Prep Time: **10** mins

Ingredients
- 1 large avocado, cubed
- 2 cups beef, cooked and cubed
- ¾ cup cheddar cheese, shredded
- Salt and black pepper, to taste
- ¼ cup Caesar dressing

Directions
1. Put avocado and beef in a bowl and season with salt and black pepper.
2. Top with cheese and Caesar dressing and refrigerate to serve chilled.

Cottage Cheese with Pineapple and Macadamia Nut Salad

Serves: **2** | Prep Time: **25** mins

Ingredients
- ½ cup pineapples, diced
- ½ cup cottage cheese
- 1 tablespoon macadamia nuts, chopped
- Salt and black pepper, to taste
- ¼ cup heavy whipping cream

Directions
1. Put the pineapples and macadamia nuts in a bowl followed by cottage cheese.
2. Top with heavy whipping cream and season with salt and black pepper to serve.

Strawberry Spinach Salad

Serves: **4** | Prep Time: **15** mins

Ingredients
- 200 g strawberries, sliced
- 200 g baby spinach
- 60 g pecans, lightly toasted and roughly chopped
- Salt and black pepper, to taste
- 40 g feta cheese

Directions
1. Mix together strawberries, baby spinach and pecans in a bowl.
2. Season with salt and black pepper and top with feta cheese to serve.

Greek Salad

Serves: **4** | Prep Time: **10** mins

Ingredients
- ½ cucumber, diced
- 12 olives
- 4 medium tomatoes, chopped
- 140 g feta cheese, crumbled
- 1 small green bell pepper, diced

Directions
1. Put the tomatoes, cucumber, feta cheese and bell pepper in a bowl.
2. Top with olives and serve to enjoy.

Mixed Green Spring Salad

Serves: **3** | Prep Time: **15** mins

Ingredients
- 2 tablespoons parmesan cheese, shaved
- 2 ounces mixed greens
- 3 tablespoons pine nuts, roasted
- Salt and black pepper, to taste
- 2 bacon slices, crispy and crumbled

Directions
1. Put the bacon along with rest of the ingredients in a bowl.
2. Serve and enjoy.

Cobb Salad

Serves: **2** | Prep Time: **10** mins

Ingredients
- 2 hardboiled eggs
- 8 cherry tomatoes
- 4 cups mixed green salad
- 4 oz. feta cheese, crumbled
- 4 oz. chicken breast, shredded

Directions
1. Place the mixed green salad, eggs and tomatoes into a large bowl.
2. Add chicken breast and top with feta cheese to serve.

Strawberry Cheesecake Salad

Serves: **4** | Prep Time: **15** mins

Ingredients
- ½ cup heavy cream
- ¼ cup almond flour
- 9 oz. fresh strawberries, hulled and chopped
- 8 oz. cream cheese
- 2 scoops Stevia

Directions
1. Whisk together heavy cream and cream cheese in a bowl until combined.
2. Stir in rest of the ingredients until well mixed.
3. Transfer into a serving dish and refrigerate until required. Serve chilled.

Lobster Roll Salad

Serves: **4** | Prep Time: **10** mins

Ingredients
- 1½ cups cauliflower florets, cooked until tender and chilled
- 2 cups lobster meat, cooked and chopped into bite sized pieces
- ½ cup mayonnaise
- ½ cup bacon, cooked and chopped
- 1 teaspoon fresh tarragon leaves, chopped

Directions
1. Mix together cooked lobster, bacon and cauliflower in a bowl.
2. Stir in mayonnaise and serve topped with fresh tarragon leaves.

Steak Salad

Serves: **3** | Prep Time: **12** mins

Ingredients
- 6 cups mixed green lettuce
- 1 cup feta cheese, crumbled
- 1 pound flank steak
- 2 avocados, sliced
- Salt and black pepper, to taste

Directions
1. Preheat a grill pan to medium high heat.
2. Season flank steak with salt and black pepper on both sides and transfer to the grill.
3. Cook for about 4 minutes per side and remove to a bowl. Add mixed green lettuce and avocados and mix well. Top with feta cheese and immediately serve.

Broccoli Cauliflower Salad

Serves: **6** | Prep Time: **40** mins

Ingredients
- 8 oz broccoli florets, cut into bite sized pieces
- 4 oz cheddar cheese, cubed
- 2 tablespoons purple onion
- 8 oz cauliflower florets, cut into bite sized pieces
- 1/3 pound bacon, cooked crisp and crumbled

Directions: Mix together broccoli, onion, cauliflower and bacon in a bowl. Top with cheddar cheese and serve instantly.

Italian Sub Salad

Serves: **6** | Prep Time: **30** mins

Ingredients
- ¼ cup pickled banana peppers, sliced
- 1 cup mixed Italian olives, pitted
- 6 cups Romaine lettuce, shredded
- 1 tablespoon Italian seasoning
- 6 ounces pepperoni, diced

Directions
1. Mix together pickled banana peppers, Italian olives, Romaine lettuce and pepperoni in a bowl. Sprinkle with Italian seasoning and serve instantly.

Israeli Salad

Serves: **4** | Prep Time: **10** mins

Ingredients
- 4 organic ripe tomatoes, finely chopped
- 3 large organic cucumbers, finely chopped
- 1/3 cup fresh Italian parsley, finely chopped
- Himalayan sea salt and black pepper, to taste
- 3 tablespoons extra-virgin olive oil

Directions
1. Mix together tomatoes, cucumbers and parsley in a medium bowl.
2. Season with sea salt and black pepper and drizzle with olive oil.
3. Cover and refrigerate to serve chilled.

Iceberg Wedge Salad

Serves: **4** | Prep Time: **15** mins

Ingredients
- 1/3 cup bacon, cooked and crumbled
- 1 Iceberg lettuce, cut into fourths
- 4 hardboiled eggs, chopped into pieces
- 4 tablespoons extra blue cheese, crumbled
- 4 grape tomatoes, sliced in half

Directions
1. Divide iceberg lettuce into 4 plates and top with bacon, eggs, tomatoes and blue cheese. Serve and enjoy.

Green Bean Summer Salad

Serves: **6** | Prep Time: **25** mins

Ingredients
- 1 pound green beans
- 2 cups cherry tomatoes, cut in half
- Salt and black pepper, to taste
- 1 cup fresh basil, thinly sliced
- 3 tablespoons olive oil

Directions
1. Steam green beans for 5 minutes in a boiling water and transfer in a bowl of ice water. Drain well and place in a serving bowl.
2. Add cherry tomatoes and basil and mix well.
3. Season with salt and black pepper and drizzle with olive oil to serve.

Cottage Cheese with Cherry Tomatoes and Basil Salad

Serves: **1** | Prep Time: **10** mins

Ingredients
- ¼ cup cherry tomatoes, quartered
- ½ cup cottage cheese
- 1 tablespoon basil, chopped
- Ground black pepper, to taste
- 2 tablespoons sour cream

Directions
1. Put the cherry tomatoes and basil in a bowl followed by cottage cheese.
2. Top with sour cream and season with black pepper to serve.

Poultry Recipes

Mediterranean Chicken and Orzo

Serves: **4** | Prep Time: **2 hours 40** mins

Ingredients
- 1 cup low-sodium chicken broth
- 1 medium onion, halved and sliced
- 1 pound boneless, skinless chicken breasts, trimmed
- 2 medium tomatoes, chopped
- 1 lemon, zested and juiced
- ½ teaspoon salt
- ¾ cup whole-wheat orzo
- 2 tablespoons fresh parsley, chopped
- 1 teaspoon herbs de Provence
- ½ teaspoon black pepper
- ⅓ cup black olives, quartered

Directions
1. Put chicken, tomatoes, onion, lemon zest, juice, broth, salt, black pepper, and herbs de Provence in a slow cooker.
2. Cover the lid and cook on High for about 2 hours.
3. Mix well and add orzo and olives to the dish.
4. Allow it to cook for about 30 more minutes more on High.
5. Garnish with parsley and serve warm.

Greek Chicken with Roasted Spring Vegetables

Serves: **4** | Prep Time: **20** mins

Ingredients

- 1 tablespoon olive oil
- ½ teaspoon honey
- ¼ cup light mayonnaise
- 1 lemon
- 1 tablespoon feta cheese, crumbled
- 2 (8 ounces) chicken breast, cut in half lengthwise
- 6 garlic cloves, minced
- ½ cup panko bread crumbs

- ½ teaspoon salt
- 2 cups (1-inch pieces) asparagus
- 1½ cups tomatoes, chopped
- Fresh dill, snipped
- 3 tablespoons Parmesan cheese, grated
- ½ teaspoon black pepper
- 1½ cups fresh cremini mushrooms, sliced
- 1 tablespoon olive oil

Directions

1. Preheat the oven to 470 degrees F and grease a baking pan.
2. Flatten the chicken pieces in a plastic wrap with a mallet.
3. Season with mayonnaise and 2 garlic cloves.
4. Mix bread crumbs with salt, black pepper and cheese in a bowl.
5. Dip the seasoned chicken into the crumbs mixture to coat well.
6. Transfer the pieces to the baking sheet and bake for about 20 minutes, flipping once in between.
7. Sauté remaining garlic with oil, salt and black pepper in a saucepan.
8. Cook for about 1 minute and add tomatoes.
9. Cook for about 5 minutes and stir in mushrooms and asparagus.
10. Toss the chicken into the saucy asparagus and serve warm.

Chicken with Tomato Sauce

Serves: **4** | Prep Time: **25** mins

Ingredients

- ½ teaspoon salt, divided
- 2 (8-ounce) chicken breasts, boneless and skinless, sliced into 4 equal sized pieces
- ½ teaspoon black pepper, divided
- 3 tablespoons olive oil, divided
- 2 tablespoons shallots, sliced
- ¼ cup balsamic vinegar

- 1 tablespoon garlic, minced
- 1 tablespoon butter
- ¼ cup white whole-wheat flour
- ½ cup cherry tomatoes, halved
- 1 cup low-sodium chicken broth
- 1 tablespoon fennel seeds, toasted and lightly crushed

Directions

1. Season the chicken pieces with salt and black pepper.
2. Spread flour in a dish and dredge the chicken through it.
3. Shake off the excess flour and keep aside.
4. Heat 2 tablespoons of cooking oil in a large skillet and add 2 pieces of chicken at a time.
5. Sear for about 3 minutes on each side and transfer this chicken to a plate.
6. Cover with a foil and heat the remaining oil in the same pan.
7. Add tomatoes and shallots and cook for about 2 minutes until soft.
8. Pour in the vinegar and cook for about 45 seconds.
9. Add broth, garlic, fennel seeds, salt and black pepper and cook for about 5 minutes. Stir in the butter and serve warm.

Hasselback Caprese Chicken

Serves: **4** | Prep Time: **35** mins

Ingredients

- ½ teaspoon salt, divided
- 3 ounces fresh mozzarella, halved and sliced
- 2 chicken breasts, boneless and skinless
- ½ teaspoon black pepper, divided

- 1 medium tomato, sliced
- ¼ cup prepared pesto
- 2 tablespoons extra-virgin olive oil
- 8 cups broccoli florets

Directions

1. Preheat the oven to 370 degrees F and grease a baking sheet.
2. Season the chicken with salt and black pepper.
3. Insert mozzarella and tomato slices in the chicken cuts.
4. Brush with pesto and transfer the chicken breasts on the baking sheet.
5. Toss broccoli with oil, salt and black pepper in a large bowl.
6. Spread the broccoli mixture around the chicken and bake for about 25 minutes.
7. Dish out and serve warm.

Mediterranean Chicken Quinoa Bowl

Serves: **4** | Prep Time: **25** mins

Ingredients

- ¼ teaspoon salt
- ¼ cup slivered almonds
- 1 small garlic clove, crushed
- 1-pound boneless, skinless chicken breasts, trimmed
- ¼ teaspoon black pepper
- 1 (7-ounce) jar roasted red peppers, rinsed
- 4 tablespoons extra-virgin olive oil, divided
- 1 teaspoon paprika
- ¼ teaspoon crushed red pepper
- ¼ cup pitted Kalamata olives, chopped
- 1 cup cucumber, diced
- 2 tablespoons fresh parsley, finely chopped
- ½ teaspoon ground cumin
- 2 cups cooked quinoa
- ¼ cup red onions, finely chopped
- ¼ cup feta cheese, crumbled

Directions

1. Preheat the oven on broiler setting and grease a baking sheet. Season the chicken with salt and black pepper. Transfer it on the baking sheet and broil for about 15 minutes.
2. Allow the chicken to cool for 5 minutes and transfer it to a cutting board.
3. Shred the chicken and keep aside.
4. Blend almonds, paprika, black pepper, garlic, 1 tablespoon of oil, red pepper, and cumin in a blender.
5. Toss quinoa, red onions, 2 tablespoons oil, quinoa, and olives in a bowl.
6. Divide the quinoa mixture in the serving bowls and top with cucumber, red pepper sauce, and shredded chicken. Garnish with feta cheese and parsley to serve.

Olive Chicken

Serves: **6** | Prep Time: **45** mins

Ingredients

- 2 tablespoons white wine
- 3 garlic cloves, minced
- 2 teaspoons olive oil
- 6 chicken breast halves, skinless and boneless
- ½ cup onions, diced
- ½ cup white wine
- 1 tablespoon fresh basil, chopped
- 2 fennel bulbs, sliced in half
- Salt and black pepper, to taste
- 3 cups tomatoes, chopped
- 2 teaspoons fresh thyme, chopped
- ½ cup kalamata olives
- ¼ cup fresh parsley, chopped

Directions

1. Heat oil with 2 tablespoons white wine in a large skillet on medium heat.
2. Add chicken and cook for about 6 minutes per side. Transfer the chicken to a plate and stir in garlic. Sauté for about 30 seconds and add onions.
3. Sauté for about 3 minutes and stir in fennel and tomatoes.
4. Allow it to boil and lower the heat. Add half cup white wine and cook for about 10 minutes. Stir in basil and thyme and cook for about 5 minutes.
5. Return the cooked chicken to the skillet. Cover the cooking pan and cook on low heat.
6. Stir in parsley and olives and cook for about 1 minute.
7. Adjust seasoning with salt and black pepper to serve.

Roasted Mediterranean Chicken

Serves: **4** | Prep Time: **55** mins

Ingredients

- 1 tablespoon fresh oregano
- 1 teaspoon fresh rosemary, chopped
- 1½ pounds chicken thighs, boneless and skinless
- 1 red onion, sliced
- 2 garlic cloves, minced
- 1-pound asparagus spears, trimmed and cut
- 1 cup cherry tomatoes, diced
- 2 tablespoons balsamic vinegar
- 2 tablespoons fresh parsley, chopped
- 1 tablespoon fresh basil, chopped
- ¼ teaspoon salt
- ¼ teaspoon black pepper
- 8 oz. mushrooms, diced
- ½ cup green bell pepper, chopped
- 1 tablespoon olive oil
- 1 (16 ounces) can cannellini beans
- 10 pitted kalamata olives, sliced

Directions

1. Preheat the oven to 425 degrees F and grease a baking pan
2. Mix rosemary, oregano, basil, salt, pepper, and parsley in a bowl.
3. Place the chicken in the baking pan and season with herbs mixture.
4. Toss mushrooms with garlic, bell pepper, onions and oil. Add this mixture to the pan around the chicken and roast for about 30 minutes. Add asparagus, beans, tomatoes, olives and balsamic vinegar and basil mixture to the chicken pans. Bake for 15 minutes and dish out to serve warm.

Lemon-Thyme Chicken

Serves: **4** | Prep Time: **30** mins

Ingredients
- 1 teaspoon crushed dried thyme, divided
- ¼ teaspoon black pepper
- 4 small skinless, boneless chicken breast halves
- 1 lemon, thinly sliced
- 4 teaspoons extra-virgin olive oil, divided
- ½ teaspoon salt
- 1-pound fingerling potatoes halved lengthwise
- 2 garlic cloves, minced

Directions
1. Heat 2 teaspoons of oil in a skillet over medium heat and add ½ teaspoon thyme, potatoes, salt, and black pepper.
2. Cook for about 1 minute and cook, covered for about 12 minutes, stirring occasionally. Push the potatoes to a side and add rest of the oil and chicken.
3. Sear the chicken pieces for 5 minutes on each side and sprinkle with thyme.
4. Arrange lemon slices over the chicken and cover the pan again.
5. Cook for about 10 minutes and dish out to serve warm.

Mediterranean Chicken with Potatoes

Serves: **6** | Prep Time: **50** mins

Ingredients
- 1 tablespoon olive oil
- ¼ teaspoon dried thyme
- 12 small red potatoes, halved
- 4 teaspoons garlic, minced and divided
- 1 teaspoon salt, divided
- ½ teaspoon black pepper, divided
- 2 pounds chicken breast, cut into bite-sized pieces
- ¾ cup dry white wine
- ½ cup pepperoncini peppers, chopped
- 2 cups plum tomatoes, chopped
- 1 (14-ounce) can artichoke hearts, quartered
- 3 thyme sprigs
- 1 cup red onion, sliced
- ¾ cup chicken broth
- ¼ cup pitted kalamata olives, halved
- 2 tablespoons fresh basil, chopped
- ½ cup fresh Parmesan cheese, grated

Directions
1. Preheat the oven to 400 degrees F and grease a baking sheet.
2. Toss garlic, salt, oil, thyme, potatoes, and black pepper in a bowl.
3. Transfer to a baking sheet and bake for about 30 minutes.
4. Grease a Dutch oven with cooking spray and warm it over medium heat.
5. Season the chicken with salt and black pepper. Sear this chicken for 5 minutes on each side.
6. Cook the chicken in two batches and transfer the chicken into a plate.
7. Add onions to the same pan and stir in wine.
8. Deglaze the pan and cook the mixture until reduced to 1/3.
9. Add broth, chicken, potatoes, pepperoncini and olives.
10. Sauté for about 3 minutes and add salt, basil, garlic, artichokes, and tomatoes.
11. Cook for another 3 minutes and garnish with thyme sprigs and cheese to serve.

Turkey with Cream Cheese Sauce

Serves: **4** | Prep Time: **30** mins

Ingredients
- 20 oz. turkey breast
- 2 tablespoons butter
- 2 cups heavy whipping cream
- Salt and black pepper, to taste
- 7 oz. cream cheese

Directions
1. Season the turkey generously with salt and black pepper.
2. Heat butter in a skillet over medium heat and cook turkey for about 5 minutes on each side.
3. Stir in the heavy whipping cream and cream cheese.
4. Cover the skillet and cook for about 15 minutes on medium low heat.
5. Dish out to serve hot.

Healthy Marinara Chicken with Cauliflower Risotto

Yield: 4 | Total Time: 75 Mins | Prep Time: 10 Mins | Cook Time: 65 Mins

Ingredients
- 2 pounds boneless skinless chicken breast
- 3 tablespoons olive oil
- 4 small tomatoes, diced
- 4 cloves garlic
- 1 teaspoon oregano
- 1 teaspoon basil
- ½ teaspoon chili powder
- Dash garlic powder
- Dash pepper
- 1 cup chicken broth

Cauliflower Risotto

- 1/4 cup butter
- 8 ounces mushrooms, chopped
- 2 cloves garlic minced
- 12 ounces riced cauliflower
- 1/4 cup dry white wine
- 1/2 cup chicken broth
- 4 tablespoons heavy cream
- 1 cup grated parmesan cheese
- Salt & pepper

Directions:

1. **Prepare Risotto:** Melt butter in a large pan; sauté garlic and mushrooms until tender and lightly brown. Season with salt and pepper and lower heat to medium low. Stir in cauliflower and then add white wine. Cook for a few Mins or until liquid is evaporated. Stir in broth and cook for about 3 Mins. Stir in cream and cook, covered, until cauliflower is tender. Stir in parmesan until melted and remove from heat. Serve sprinkled with more parmesan.
2. Set your instant pot to manual high and heat the oil. Sprinkle chicken with garlic powder, salt and pepper; fry in the pot for 2 Mins per side or until browned. Add in the remaining ingredients and lock lid. Cook on high for 20 Mins and then let pressure come down on its own. Serve warm.

Buffalo Chicken Fingers with Nutty Kale Salad

Yield: 4 | Total Time: 35 Mins | Prep Time: 10 Mins | Cook Time: 25 Mins

Ingredients

- 2 pounds chicken, sliced into strips
- 4 tablespoons fresh lemon juice
- 2 tablespoons hot sauce
- Breadcrumbs
- Pinch of salt & black pepper
- ½ cup chicken broth

Salad

- 2 tablespoons extra virgin olive oil
- 1 pound Lacinato kale, sliced into thin strips
- 1/2 cup roasted almonds
- Pinch of sea salt
- Pinch of pepper

Directions:

1. Prepare salad: Place kale in a bowl and add olive oil; massage olive oil with hands into kale until kale is tender; sprinkle with salt and pepper and toss with toasted almonds.
2. Marinate chicken in fresh lemon juice and salt for a few hours and then coat with crushed crumbs; fry in an instant pot set on sauté mode for about 5 Mins or until browned. Stir in broth and lock lid. Cook on high for 20 Mins and let pressure come down naturally. Toss with black pepper and hot sauce and serve with raw celery, garnish with parsley.

Healthy Roasted Turkey with Low Carb Avocado Relish

Yield: 6 | Total Time: 1 Hour 40 Mins | Prep Time: 10 Mins | Cook Time: 1 Hour 30 Mins

Ingredients:

- 3 tablespoons extra-virgin olive oil
- ½ cup apple cider vinegar
- 3 cloves garlic, minced
- 2-3 tablespoons minced ginger
- 2 pounds whole turkey
- 1-pound chopped carrots
- handful of rosemary
- Pinch of sea salt
- Pinch of pepper

Avocado Relish

- ½ avocado, diced, 1 seedless grapefruit cut into segments discarding the membranes
- 1 small Vidalia onion, minced
- 1 tsp. red wine vinegar
- 1 tbsp. fresh cilantro, chopped
- 1 tsp natural honey

Directions:

1. Place turkey in aluminum foil. In a bowl, whisk together olive oil, apple cider vinegar, garlic, and ginger until well combined; pour over the turkey and top with carrots and rosemary. Sprinkle with salt and pepper and fold to wrap well. Add water to an instant pot and insert a metal trivet. Place the foil over the trivet and cook on high for 1 ½ hours. Let pressure come down naturally.
2. **Prepare Relish:** Combine the avocado, grapefruit segments, onion, honey, vinegar and cilantro and toss well to combine.
3. Serve turkey with the avocado relish.

Instant Pot Healthy Turkey Meat Balls

Yield: 4 | Total Time: 20 Mins | Prep Time: 10 Mins | Cook Time: 10 Mins

Ingredients

- 2 tablespoons olive oil
- 1-pound ground turkey
- 1/2 cup crushed cheese crackers
- 1 teaspoon minced onion
- 1 tablespoon red pepper flakes
- 1 tablespoon garlic powder
- 1 egg

Directions

1. In a bowl, mix together all ingredients until well combined; form four large patties from the mixture. Set your instant pot on manual high and add in oil; cook the patties for 5 Mins per side or until cooked through. Lock lid and cook the patties for 5 Mins. Let pressure come down naturally.

Delicious Turkey Sausage Patties with Lemon Tahini Sauce
Yield: 8 | Total Time: 26 Mins | Prep Time: 10 Mins | Cook Time: 16 Mins

Ingredients
- 2 pounds ground turkey
- 1/4 teaspoon cayenne pepper
- 3/4 teaspoon ground ginger
- 1 teaspoon dried sage

- 1 1/2 teaspoons salt
- 1 1/2 teaspoons pepper
- 4 cups of green salad for serving

Low Carb Lemon Tahini Sauce
- 4 tablespoons lemon juice
- ½ cup organic tahini
- 1 tablespoon olive oil

- 2 cloves garlic
- ⅓ cup water
- A pinch sea & pepper

Directions

1. Prepare Tahini: in a blender, blend together all ingredients until very smooth. Refrigerate until ready to use.
2. Mix together ground turkey, cayenne pepper, sage, ginger, salt and pepper in a bowl until well blended. Form patties from the mixture and place on a plate.
3. Set your instant pot on manual high and add in oil; cook the patties for 5 Mins per side or until cooked through. Lock lid and cook the patties for 5 Mins. Let pressure come down naturally. Serve the turkey patties with green salad drizzled with lemon tahini.

Instant Pot Roast Chicken with Steamed Veggies
Yield: 4 | Total Time: 1 Hour 40 Mins | Prep Time: 10 Mins | Cook Time: 1 Hour 30 Mins

Ingredients
- 1.5 kg chicken
- 3 heads garlic, cut in half across
- 3 brown onions, cut into wedges
- 200g cauliflower
- 2 tbsp. chicken seasoning blend: Mix together ½ tsp. each of crushed dried rosemary, paprika, dry mustard powder, garlic powder, ground dried thyme, ground black pepper, 1 tsp. dried basil, 1 ½ tsp. sea salt, ¼ tsp. celery seeds, ¼ tsp. dried parsley, 1/8 tsp. each of cayenne pepper, ground cumin, and chicken bouillon granules.

- 200g broccoli
- 200g green beans
- 1 pouch cheese sauce

Directions

1. Add water to an instant pot and insert a metal trivet.
2. On aluminum foil, combine garlic and onion; sprinkle with olive oil.
3. Rub the chicken seasoning blend into the chicken and place it on top of the bed of garlic and onion; fold the foil to wrap the contents and place over the trivet. Lock lid and cook on high for 90 Mins. Release pressure naturally. Place the beans into a steamer and add cauliflower and broccoli; steam for about 10 Mins or until tender. Serve the chicken and steamed veggies on a plate; heat the cheese sauce and pour over the veggies. Enjoy!

Healthy Chicken Curry
Yield: 1 Serving | Total Time: 30 Mins | Prep Time: 10 Mins | Cook Time: 20 Mins

Ingredients
- 1 tablespoon olive oil
- 100 grams chicken, diced
- ¼ cup chicken broth
- Pinch of turmeric
- Dash of onion powder
- 1 tablespoon minced red onion
- Pinch of garlic powder
- ¼ teaspoon curry powder

- Pinch of sea salt
- Pinch of pepper
- Stevia
- Pinch of cayenne
- 1 cup riced cauliflower
- 1 tablespoon butter
- 1 red onion

Directions

1. Prepare cauliflower by melting butter in a skillet and then sautéing red onion. Stir in cauliflower and cook for about 4 Mins or until tender. Set aside until ready to serve.
2. Set an instant pot on sauté mode, heat oil and sauté onion and garlic; stir in chicken and cook until browned. Stir spices in chicken broth and Stevia and add to the pot. Lock lid and cook on high for 15 Mins. Release the pressure naturally and serve hot over sautéed cauliflower.

Low Carb Turkey Served with Creamy Sauce and Sautéed Capers

Yield: 4 | Total Time: 40 Mins | Prep Time: 15 Mins | Cook Time: 25 Mins

Ingredients
- 2 pounds turkey breast
- 1/3 cup small capers
- 1 cup cream cheese
- 2 cups sour cream
- 2 tbsp. butter
- 1 tbsp. tamari sauce
- A pinch of sea salt
- A pinch of pepper

Directions
1. Set your instant pot on manual high; heat half of the butter; season turkey with salt and pepper and fry until golden brown. Add in cream cheese and sour cream; bring to a gentle boil and then simmer until the sauce is thick. Season the sauce with tamari, salt and pepper; lock lid and cook on high for 5 Mins. Let pressure come down naturally.
2. Melt the remaining butter in a pan and sauté the capers over high heat until crispy. Serve the turkey meat with the fried capers and creamy sauce. Enjoy!

Tasty Instant Pot Thai Turkey Legs

Yield: 4 | Total Time: 1 Hour 12 Mins | Prep Time: 7 Mins | Cook Time: 1 Hour 5 Mins

Ingredients
- 1-pound turkey legs
- 2 cups coconut milk
- 1 tbsp. lime juice
- 1½ tsp. lemon garlic seasoning
- Lime wedges
- ¼ cup fresh cilantro
- 1 tsp. ghee

Directions
1. Set your instant pot to manual high and melt in ghee; sauté turkey until browned and then stir in coconut milk, lime juice, lime wedge, lemon garlic seasoning, and cilantro. Add the turkey legs and lock lid. Cook on high for 1 hour and then let pressure come down on its own.

Gingery Roasted Turkey

Yield: 6 | Total Time: 1 Hour 10 Mins | Prep Time: 10 Mins | Cook Time: 1 Hour

Ingredients:
- 3 tablespoons extra-virgin olive oil
- ½ cup apple cider vinegar
- 3 cloves garlic, minced
- 2-3 tablespoons minced ginger
- 2 pounds whole turkey
- 1 pound chopped carrots
- handful of rosemary
- Pinch of sea salt
- Pinch of pepper

Directions:
1. Set your instant pot to high sauté setting and add in turkey; In a bowl, whisk together olive oil, apple cider vinegar, garlic, and ginger until well combined; pour over the turkey and top with carrots and rosemary. Sprinkle with salt and pepper and lock lid; select manual and set pressure to high for 1 hour. When ready, release the pressure naturally. Serve warm.

Herbed Instant Pot Turkey Breast

Yield: 2 | Total Time: 1Hour 10 Mins | Prep Time: 10 Mins | Cook Time: 1 Hour

Ingredients
- 1-pound turkey breast
- ¼ cup whipped cream cheese, spread with garden veggies
- 2 tbsp. softened butter
- 1 tbsp. soy sauce
- ½ tsp. dried basil
- 1 tbsp. minced parsley
- ½ tsp. dried thyme
- ½ tsp. dried sage
- ¼ tsp. garlic powder
- ¼ tsp sea salt
- ¼ tsp. ground black pepper

Directions
1. In a small bowl, combine all the ingredients, except turkey, until well blended; brush the mixture over the turkey breast and place in your instant pot. Lock lid and cook on high setting for 1 hour. Naturally release the pressure and then serve.

Tangy Instant Pot Turkey Meatballs

Yield: 6 | Total Time: 1 Hours 30 Mins | Prep Time: 30 Mins | Cook Time: 1 Hour

Ingredients
For meatballs
- 1-pound ground turkey
- ½ cup panko breadcrumbs
- ½ tsp. onion powder
- ½ tsp. chili powder
- ½ tsp. garlic salt
- 1 egg

For sauce
- 2 ½ tbsp. raw honey
- 1 cup tomato sauce
- 2 tbsp. white vinegar
- 2 tbsp. Worcestershire sauce
- ½ tsp. onion powder
- ½ tsp. chili powder
- ½ tsp. garlic salt

Directions
1. In a bowl, mix ground turkey, breadcrumbs, onion powder, garlic salt, chili powder, and egg until well combined; roll the mixture into 1-inch balls and arrange them on a greased heatproof dish that fits in your pot. Add water to your instant pot and put in a metal trivet; place the dish with the meatballs over the trivet and lock lid. Cook on high setting for 1 hour and then naturally release the pressure.

Pressure Roasted Chicken

Yield: 6 | Total Time: 1 Hour 40 Mins | Prep Time: 10 Mins | Cook Time: 1 Hour 30 Mins

Ingredients:
- 1 tablespoon extra-virgin olive oil
- ½ cup apple cider vinegar
- 3 cloves garlic, minced
- 2-3 tablespoons minced ginger
- 2 pounds whole chicken
- 1 pound chopped carrots
- handful of rosemary
- Pinch of sea salt
- Pinch of pepper

Directions
1. Place chicken in your instant pot. In a bowl, whisk together olive oil, apple cider vinegar, garlic, and ginger until well combined; pour over the chicken and top with carrots and rosemary. Sprinkle with salt and pepper and lock lid. Cook on high setting for 1 ½ hours and then let pressure come down on its own. Serve warm over steamed veggies.

Tasty Instant Pot Turkey Breast

Yield: 2 | Total Time: 1 Hour 10 Mins | Prep Time: 10 Mins | Cook Time: 1 Hour

Ingredients
- 1-pound turkey breast (bone-in)
- 1-ounce dry onion soup mix

Directions
1. Rinse turkey and pat it dry; rub the soup mix under and outside the skin and place it in your instant pot. Lock lid and cook on high setting for 1 hour. Let pressure come down on its own.

Pressure Cooked Cajun Chicken with Lime Butter Steamed Veggies

Yield: 2 | Total Time: 30 Mins | Prep Time: 10 Mins | Cook Time: 20 Mins

Ingredients
- 12 ounces boneless skinless chicken breast
- 2 teaspoons water
- 1 tablespoon cayenne pepper
- ½ teaspoon sea salt
- ¼ teaspoon pepper
- ½ teaspoon onion powder
- ½ teaspoon garlic powder

Lime Butter Steamed Veggies
- 3 cups cut-up fresh assorted vegetables (cauliflower, broccoli florets, and sliced carrots)
- 1 tbsp. fresh lime juice
- 1 tsp. chopped jalapeño pepper
- 1 small clove garlic, chopped
- 2 tbsp. butter
- 1 tsp. grated lime peel
- ½ tsp. salt

Directions:
1. **Prepare Veggies:** In a saucepan, melt butter over medium low heat; add garlic and sauté for about 1 minute or until fragrant. Stir in lime juice, lime peel, jalapeño pepper, and salt; mix well and set aside. Place steamer in a large saucepan and add a cup of water; bring to a boil. Add the veggies to the steamer and cook, covered, for about 5 Mins or until crisp and tender. Place the steamed veggies in a serving bowl and pour over the butter sauce; toss to coat well and serve.
2. Stir all spices into water and rub onto chicken; let marinate for at least 1hour. Heat a tablespoon of oil in the instant pot and fry the chicken until browned. Remove the chicken and add in broth. Insert a metal trivet into the pot and place the chicken over the trivet. Lock lid and cook on manual high for 10 Mins. Let pressure come down on its own. Serve grilled chicken over steamed veggies. Enjoy!

Instant Pot Ginger Peach Chicken

Yield: 2 | Total Time: 1 Hour 10 Mins | Prep Time: 10 Mins | Cook Time: 1 Hour

Ingredients
- 1-pound chicken thighs, boneless, skinless
- 2 cloves garlic, minced
- 2 tablespoons olive oil
- 1-inch fresh ginger root, grated
- 1 tbsp. low-sodium soy sauce
- 2 tablespoons peach jam

Directions
1. Place the chicken thighs in your instant pot.
2. In a small bowl, mix ginger, garlic, olive oil, peach jam, and soy sauce until well blended; spoon the sauce over the chicken and cover the pot with lid; cook on high setting for 1 hour and then let pressure come down on its own. Remove the chicken from the pot and shred. Return and let sit for a few Mins to mix with juice. Serve with steamed veggies.

Instant Pot Asian chicken lettuce wraps

Yields: 2 | Total Time: 1 Hour 5 Mins | Prep Time: 5 Mins | Cook Time: 1 Hour

Ingredients
- 1-pound ground chicken
- 2 minced cloves garlic
- 2 large carrots, grated
- 1 medium red bell pepper, diced
- 1 teaspoon Stevia
- 1/4 cup low-sodium soy sauce
- 1/4 tsp. crushed red pepper flakes
- 1/4 cup ketchup

Directions
1. Combine all ingredients in your instant pot and cook on high setting for 1 hour. Shred the chicken and return to the pot. Stir to mix well and divide among lettuce leaves. Roll to form wraps and serve.

Oregano Chicken with Sautéed Kale

Yield: 4 | Total Time: 30 Mins | Prep Time: 10 Mins | Cook Time: 20 Mins

Ingredients
- 2 pounds chicken breast
- 3 tablespoons olive oil
- 1 cup chicken broth
- 1 teaspoon dried oregano
- ¼ teaspoon onion powder
- ¼ teaspoon garlic powder
- Pinch of salt & pepper
- ½ cup breadcrumbs
- 4 cups kale, chopped
- 2 tablespoons butter
- 2 red onions, chopped

Directions:
1. Mix dry spices with crumbs; dip chicken in olive oil and dust with bread crumb mix.
2. Add broth to the instant pot and then insert a metal trivet. Place the chicken over the trivet and lock lid; cook on manual high for 20 Mins. Add butter to a skillet over medium heat and sauté red onion until fragrant; stir in kale and cook for about 3 Mins or until just wilted; season with salt and pepper. Serve the chicken over the fried kale.

Tasty Citric Chicken with Fried Button Mushrooms

Yield: 4 | Total Time: 1 Hour 10 Mins | Prep Time: 10 Mins | Cook Time: 1 Hour

Ingredients
- 2 pounds chicken breast
- 1 red onion, minced
- Juice of ½ lemon
- Pinch of lemon zest
- 2 red onions, chopped
- Pinch of saffron
- Pinch of ground coriander
- Pinch of ginger
- Pinch of salt & pepper
- Lemon slices
- 2 cups button mushrooms
- 2 tablespoons butter

Directions:
1. Soak saffron in fresh lemon juice; crush into paste and then add dry spices.
2. Dip in chicken and rub remaining spices into chicken; sprinkle with salt and pepper and wrap in foil. Add water to an instant pot and insert a trivet; place the chicken over the trivet, lock lid and cook on manual high for 1 hour.
3. Add butter to a skillet over medium heat and sauté red onion until fragrant; stir in mushrooms and cook for about 6 Mins or until tender. Season with salt and pepper. Serve the chicken over the mushrooms.

Low Carb Turkey Ratatouille

Yield: 4 | Total Time: 40 Mins | Prep Time: 15 Mins | Cook Time: 25 Mins

Ingredients
- 4 tablespoons extra-virgin olive oil
- 2 pounds boneless turkey cutlet
- 1 cup mushrooms
- 1 sweet red pepper
- 1 medium zucchini
- 1 eggplant
- 1/2 cup tomato puree
- 1 tsp garlic
- 1 tsp leaf basil
- 1/8 tsp salt
- 1/2 teaspoon sweetener
- 1/8 tsp black pepper

Directions
1. Set your instant pot to manual high and heat oil; sprinkle the meat with salt and pepper and sauté for about 3 Mins per side; transfer to a plate and add the remaining oil to the pot. Sauté red pepper, zucchini and eggplant for about 5 Mins. Stir in garlic, mushrooms, basil, tomato puree. Cook for 5 Mins and then stir in turkey, salt and pepper. Lock lid and cook on high for 15 Mins. Let pressure come down on its own. Serve hot.

Spiced Chicken Patties Low Carb Lemon Pesto

Yield: 4 | Total Time: 40 Mins | Prep Time: 10 Mins | Cook Time: 30 Mins

Ingredients
- 4 tablespoons olive oil
- 400 grams ground chicken breast
- 1 clove garlic, minced
- ½ red onion, minced

- Dash of garlic powder
- Dash of onion powder
- Pinch of cayenne pepper
- Pinch of salt & pepper

Low Carb Lemon Pesto
- 1 tablespoon fresh lemon juice
- 2 tablespoons lemon zest, chopped
- 1/2 cup grated parmesan cheese
- 5 cloves garlic, chopped

- 1/4 cup pine nuts
- 1/2 cup extra virgin olive oil
- 2 cups basil leaves, packed
- Pinch of salt & pepper

Directions:
1. Prepare pesto: blend together all ingredients in a blender until very smooth; refrigerate until ready to use.
2. In a small bowl, mix all ingredients until well combined; form patties and set aside. Set your instant pot to manual high and heat in oil; fry in a saucepan, deglazing with water to keep chicken moist. Lock lid and cook the patties for 5 Mins on high setting. Let pressure come down on its own. Serve with lemon pesto.

Vegetable & Chicken Stir-Fry

Yield: 4 | Total Time: 20 Mins | Prep Time: 10 Mins | Cook Time: 10 Mins

Ingredients
- 4 chicken breasts (butterfly), marinate in egg white overnight
- 2 cups red pepper
- 2 cups mange tout
- 2 cups grated carrot
- 2 cups broccoli
- 2 cups almonds

- 2 cloves of garlic
- ½ tsp. ginger
- 2 tbsp. soya sauce
- 125ml chicken stock.
- 2 tbsp. coconut oil

Directions
1. Heat coconut oil in your instant pot. Sauté the garlic and ginger until fragrant.
2. Cook the chicken breast in the oil until browned and then add the vegetables. Toss and cook until almost done. Add 2 tbsp. soya sauce and chicken stock. Lock lid and cook on manual high for 5 Mins. Let pressure come down on its own.

Turkey-Cauliflower Hash with Avocado and Hardboiled Egg

Yield: 4 | Total Time: 40 Mins | Prep Time: 20 Mins | Cook Time: 20 Mins

Ingredients
- 2 tablespoons butter stick
- 2 pounds turkey meat
- 1 small onion
- 3 cups cauliflower

- 1 tsp thyme
- 1/4 cup heavy cream
- 1/2 tsp salt
- 1/8 tsp pepper

- 4 hardboiled eggs, chopped
- 1 avocado, diced

Directions
1. Bring a pot of salted water to a rolling boil; add cauliflower and cook for 4 Mins or until tender; drain and let cool before chopping coarsely.
2. In the meantime, melt butter in an instant pot and sauté onion and thyme; season with salt and pepper; add cauliflower and cook for 2 Mins. Stir in turkey meat; cook for about 6 Mins or until browned. Stir in cream and lock lid. Cook for 10 Mins and let pressure come down on its own. Serve topped with chopped boiled eggs and avocado.

Instant Pot Chicken Curry

Yield: 1 Serving | Total Time: 35 Mins | Prep Time: 10 Mins | Cook Time: 25 Mins

Ingredients
- 4 tbsp. coconut oil
- 100 grams chicken, diced
- ¼ cup chicken broth
- Pinch of turmeric
- Dash of onion powder

- 1 tablespoon minced red onion
- Pinch of garlic powder
- ¼ teaspoon curry powder
- Pinch of sea salt

- Pinch of pepper
- Stevia
- Pinch of cayenne

Directions
1. Set your instant pot to manual high, melt coconut oil and then stir in garlic and onion. Cook until fragrant and stir in chicken. In a small bowl, stir together spices, Stevia, and chicken broth until dissolved, stir into the chicken and lock lid. Cook for 20 Mins and then naturally release the pressure. Serve hot.

Healthy Turkey Loaf with Sautéed Button Mushrooms

Yield: 2 | Total Time: 45 Mins | Prep Time: 15 Mins | Cook Time: 30 Mins

Ingredients
- 2 eggs
- 1-pound ground turkey
- 1/2 cup chopped onion
- 1/4 cup chopped yellow bell pepper
- 1/4 cup chopped red bell pepper
- 1/2 cup salsa
- 1/4 cup dry breadcrumbs
- A pinch of lemon pepper
- 1 cup button mushrooms
- 1 tablespoon olive oil
- 1 red onion

Directions
1. In a bowl, mix together bell peppers, breadcrumbs, salsa, egg, turkey, onion and lemon pepper until well blended. Roll the mixture to form a loaf. Add water to an instant pot and insert a metal trivet; place the meatloaf over the trivet and lock lid. Cook on high setting for 25 Mins and then transfer the meatloaf to oven. Bake at 450 degrees for 5 Mins or until golden browned.
2. Meanwhile, heat olive oil in a skillet; sauté red onion until fragrant; stir in button mushrooms and cook until tender. Serve the meatloaf topped with sautéed mushrooms for a healthy satisfying meal.

Satisfying Turkey Lettuce Wraps

Yields: 4 | Total Time: 50 Mins | Prep Time: 15 Mins | Cook Time: 35 Mins

Ingredients
- 1/2 lb. ground turkey
- 1/2 small onion, finely chopped
- 1 garlic clove, minced
- 2 tablespoons extra virgin olive oil
- 1 head lettuce
- 1 teaspoon cumin
- 1/2 tablespoon fresh ginger, sliced
- 2 tablespoons apple cider vinegar
- 2 tablespoons freshly chopped cilantro
- 1 teaspoon freshly ground black pepper
- 1 teaspoon sea salt

Directions
1. Add oil to your instant pot and set it on sauté mode; add in garlic and onion and cook until fragrant and translucent. Add turkey and lock lid; cook for about 5 Mins. Stir in the remaining ingredients and lock lid; cook on high for 30 Mins and then quick release the pressure.
2. To serve, ladle a spoonful of turkey mixture onto a lettuce leaf and wrap. Enjoy!

Lemon Olive Chicken

Yield: 4 | Total Time: 30 Mins | Prep Time: 10 Mins | Cook Time: 20 Mins

Ingredients
- 4 boneless skinless chicken breasts
- 1/2 cup coconut oil
- 1/4 tsp. black pepper
- 1/2 tsp. cumin
- 1 tsp. sea salt
- 1 cup chicken bone broth
- 2 tbsp. fresh lemon juice
- 1/2 cup red onion, sliced
- 1 can pitted green olives
- 1/2 lemon, thinly sliced

Directions
1. Generously season chicken breasts with cumin, pepper and salt; set your instant pot on sauté mode and heat the coconut oil; add chicken and brown both sides. Stir in the remaining ingredients; bring to a gentle simmer and then lock lid.
2. Cook on high for 10 Mins and then use quick release method to release pressure.

Instant Pot Turkey with Veggies

Yield: 4 | Total Time: 20 Mins | Prep Time: 15 Mins | Cook Time: 5 Mins

Ingredients
- 1 tablespoon extra-virgin olive oil
- 6 ounces turkey
- 1/4 cup capers
- 1/4 cup diced fresh tomatoes
- Steamed green beans for serving

Directions
1. Heat oil in your instant pot; add turkey and lock lid. Cook on high for 5 Mins and then let pressure come down.
2. Remove the cooked turkey from the pot and transfer to a plate; add capers and tomatoes to the pan and cook until juicy. Spoon the caper mixture over the turkey and serve with steamed green beans.

Instant Pot Crunchy Chicken Salad

Yield: 2 | Total Time: 45 Mins | Prep Time: 10 Mins | Cook Time: 35 Mins

Ingredients
- 250g chicken
- 1/4 cup Tamari soy sauce
- 1 tablespoon avocado oil
- 1 tablespoon Olive oil
- 1/2 tablespoon lemon juice, freshly squeezed
- 4 Radishes, sliced
- 6 cherry tomatoes, halved
- 1/2 red bell pepper, sliced
- 2 cups salad greens
- 1/2 teaspoon salt

Directions
1. Pour tamari sauce in a large bowl; add in steak and toss to coat well; cover and let marinate for a few hours before cooking.
2. In another bowl, combine green salad, radishes, tomatoes, bell peppers, lemon juice, olive oil and salt; toss to coat well and set aside.
3. Set your instant pot to high sauté setting and add in oil; place the chicken in the pot and cook for about 4 Mins per side or until evenly browned. Remove the chicken and place a metal trivet in your pot and add in chicken broth; place the chicken over the trivet and lock lid; select manual and set pressure to high for 25 Mins. When ready, release the pressure naturally and then remove chicken from the pot; let cool for a minute before slicing to serve. Divide the salad between two plates and top each with chicken slices.

Pressure Cooked Chicken Shawarma

Yield: 6 | Total Time: 25 Mins | Prep Time: 10 Mins | Cook Time: 15 Mins

Ingredients
- 1-pound chicken thighs
- 1-pound chicken breasts, sliced
- 1/8 tsp. cinnamon
- 1/4 tsp. chili powder
- 1 tsp. ground cumin
- 1/4 tsp. ground allspice
- 1/4 tsp. granulated garlic
- 1/2 tsp. turmeric
- 1 tsp. paprika
- Pinch of salt
- Pinch of pepper
- 1 cup chicken broth

Directions
1. Mix all ingredients in your instant pot and lock lid; cook on poultry setting for 15 Mins and then release pressure naturally.
2. Serve chicken with sauce over mashed sweet potato drizzled with tahini sauce.

Instant Pot Coconut Curry Turkey

Yield: 4 | Total Time: 20 Mins | Prep Time: 5 Mins | Cook Time: 15 Mins

Ingredients
- 1-pound turkey
- 15 ounces water
- 30 ounces light coconut milk
- ½ cup Thai red curry sauce
- ¼ cup cilantro
- 2½ tsp. lemon garlic seasoning

Directions
1. In an instant pot, combine turkey, water, coconut milk, red curry paste, cilantro, and lemon garlic seasoning; stir to mix well and lock lid; cook on high pressure for 15 Mins and then release pressure naturally. Serve garnished with cilantro.

Instant Pot Green Chile Chicken

Yield: 6 | Total Time: 30 Mins | Prep Time: 10 Mins | Cook Time: 20 Mins

Ingredients
- 3 pounds chicken thighs
- 3 to 4 tomatillos, husked and diced
- 1 tsp black pepper
- 1 tsp ground coriander
- 2 tsp cumin
- 1-1/2 tsp sea salt
- 3 cloves garlic, chopped finely
- 1/2-pound diced chilies
- 1 medium red onion, diced
- chopped cilantro, garnish
- Fresh lime wedges, garnish

Directions
1. Lay chicken in the bottom of your instant pot; sprinkle with spices and toss until well coated. Add garlic, green chilies, red onion and tomatillos. Lock lid and cook on high for 20 Mins and then let pressure come down naturally. Remove chicken and shred with fork to serve.

Healthy Chicken Super Salad

Yield: 1 | Total Time: 30 Mins | Prep Time: 10 Mins | Cook Time: 20 Mins

Ingredients
- 1 red onion, sliced
- 2 tbsp. extra virgin olive oil
- 1 large date, chopped
- 1 tbsp. capers
- ¼ cup rocket
- 1/4 avocado, peeled, stoned and sliced
- 150g chicken slices
- ¼ cup chicory leaves
- 2 tbsp. chopped walnuts
- 1 tbsp. fresh lemon juice
- ¼ cup chopped parsley
- ¼ cup chopped celery leaves

Directions
1. Add water to your instant pot and insert a metal trivet; season chicken with salt and pepper and place it over the trivet. Lock lid and cook on high setting for 20 Mins. Let pressure come down naturally. Arrange salad leaves in a large bowl or a plate; mix the remaining ingredients well and serve over the salad leaves.

Grilled Herb Marinade Chicken with Sautéed Mushrooms

Yield: 4 | Total Time: 40 Mins | Prep Time: 10 Mins | Cook Time: 30 Mins

Ingredients

- 1 cup chopped mixed fresh herb leaves (basil, parsley, cilantro)
- 2 large garlic cloves, chopped
- 1/4 cup apple cider vinegar
- 1/4 cup extra-virgin olive oil
- 3 teaspoons sea salt
- 1/4 teaspoon pepper
- 2 lbs. chicken breasts, boneless, skinless, sliced in half lengthwise
- 4 cups button mushrooms
- 1 1/2 tablespoons butter
- 2 red onions, chopped

Directions

1. In a food processor, process together herbs, garlic, vinegar, oil, salt and pepper until smooth; transfer to a Ziploc bag and add chicken. Shake to coat chicken well and refrigerate for about 30 Mins.
2. Set your instant pot on manual high and heat in oil; add chicken and cook for 5 Mins per side or until browned. Remove chicken and add water to the pot; insert a trivet and place the chicken over the trivet. Lock lid and cook for 30 Mins. Let pressure come down naturally.
3. Add butter to a skillet over medium heat and sauté red onion until fragrant; stir in mushrooms and cook for about 6 Mins or until tender; season with salt and pepper. Serve grilled chicken over the sautéed mushrooms.

Tropical Turkey Salad

Yield: 6 | Total Time: 50 Mins | Prep Time: 20 Mins | Cook Time: 30 Mins

Ingredients

- 2 cups chopped cooked turkey
- 1/2 cup chopped green onion
- 1 cup chopped orange segments
- 1 cup diced red bell pepper
- 1 cup pineapple chunks
- 1 cup diced celery
- 1 tablespoon fresh lemon juice
- 1 teaspoon liquid Stevia
- 2 tablespoons mango chutney
- 1/3 cup sour cream
- 1/4 teaspoon curry powder

Directions

1. Add water to an instant pot and insert a trivet; season turkey with salt and pepper and place over the trivet. Lock lid and cook for 30 Mins. Let pressure come down naturally.
2. In a small bowl, whisk together lemon juice, sour cream, Stevia, and curry powder until well blended; refrigerate until ready to use.
3. In a bowl, mix the turkey with the remaining ingredients; drizzle with dressing and toss until well coated. Refrigerate for at least 1 hour before serving.

Instant Pot Grilled Chicken & Green Onion

Yield: 1 Serving | Total Time: 50 Mins | Prep Time: 10 Mins | Cook Time: 40 Mins

Ingredients

- 3 ounces chicken breast
- 1 tablespoon olive oil
- 1 green onion, chopped
- Pinch of garlic powder
- Pinch of sea salt
- Pinch of pepper
- 1 cup steamed green beans

Directions:

1. Set your instant pot on manual high and heat in oil; add chicken and cook for 5 Mins per side or until browned. Remove chicken and add water to the pot; insert a trivet. Place the chicken in aluminum foil and top with onion slices. Sprinkle with garlic powder, salt and pepper and wrap the foil; place over the trivet. Lock lid and cook for 30 Mins. Let pressure come down naturally.
2. Serve chicken over steamed green beans.

Healthy Turkey Chili

Yield: 2 | Total Time: 1 Hour 10 Mins | Prep Time: 10 Mins | Cook Time: 1 Hour

Ingredients

- 1-pound lean ground turkey
- 2 tablespoons olive oil
- 1 garlic clove, minced
- 1 large red onion, chopped
- 1 (15-ounces) can black beans
- 1 (8-ounces) can tomato sauce
- 1 (28-ounces) can crushed tomatoes
- 1 green bell pepper, chopped
- 1 red bell pepper, chopped
- 1 package (1 1/4-oz.) chili seasoning mix
- 1/2 teaspoon sea salt

Directions

1. Set your instant pot on manual high, cook ground turkey, garlic and onion until turkey is no longer pink. Stir in the remaining ingredients. Lock lid and cook for 1 hour. Let pressure come down on its own. Serve hot with your favorite toppings.

Pesto Chicken Casserole

Serves: **3** | Prep Time: **45** mins

Ingredients
- 1½ pounds boneless chicken thighs, cut into bite sized pieces
- Salt and black pepper, to taste
- 2 tablespoons butter
- 3 oz. green pesto
- 5 oz. feta cheese, diced

Directions
1. Preheat the oven to 400 F and grease a baking dish. Season the chicken with salt and black pepper.
2. Heat butter in a skillet over medium heat and cook chicken for about 5 minutes on each side. Dish out in the greased baking dish and add feta cheese and pesto.
3. Transfer the baking dish to the oven and bake for about 30 minutes.
4. Remove from the oven and serve hot.

Italian Turkey

Serves: **6** | Prep Time: **25** mins

Ingredients
- 1½ cups Italian dressing
- Salt and black pepper, to taste
- 2 tablespoons butter
- 1 (2 pound) bone-in turkey breast
- 2 garlic cloves, minced

Directions
1. Preheat the oven to 350°F and grease a baking dish with butter.
2. Mix together minced garlic cloves, salt and black pepper and rub the turkey breast with this mixture.
3. Arrange turkey breast in the baking dish and top evenly with Italian dressing.
4. Bake for about 2 hours, coating with pan juices occasionally. Dish out and serve immediately.

Caprese Chicken

Serves: **4** | Prep Time: **30** mins

Ingredients
- 1 pound chicken breasts, boneless and skinless
- ¼ cup balsamic vinegar
- 1 tablespoon extra-virgin olive oil
- Kosher salt and black pepper, to taste
- 4 mozzarella cheese slices

Directions
1. Season the chicken with salt and black pepper.
2. Heat olive oil in a skillet over medium heat and cook chicken for about 5 minutes on each side.
3. Stir in the balsamic vinegar and cook for about 2 minutes.
4. Add mozzarella cheese slices and cook for about 2 minutes until melted.
5. Dish out in a plate and serve hot.

Roasted Chicken with Herbed Butter

Serves: **6** | Prep Time: **30** mins

Ingredients
- 1 tablespoon garlic paste
- 6 chicken legs
- 4 cups water
- Salt, to taste
- 4 tablespoons herbed butter

Directions
1. Season the chicken legs with salt and mix with garlic paste.
2. Put a rack in an electric pressure cooker and add water.
3. Place the marinated pieces of chicken on the rack and lock the lid.
4. Cook on high pressure for about 15 minutes.
5. Naturally release the pressure and dish out in a platter.
6. Spread herbed butter on the chicken legs and serve.

Chicken Enchiladas

Serves: **2** | Prep Time: **25** mins

Ingredients
- 2 ounces chicken, shredded
- ½ tablespoon olive oil
- 2 ounces shiitake mushrooms, chopped
- Sea salt and black pepper, to taste
- ½ teaspoon apple cider vinegar

Directions
1. Heat olive oil in a skillet and add mushrooms. Sauté for about 30 seconds and stir in chicken.
2. Cook for about 2 minutes and pour in apple cider vinegar.
3. Season with sea salt and black pepper and cover the lid.
4. Cook for about 20 minutes on medium low heat. Dish out and serve hot.

Turkey Balls

Serves: **6** | Prep Time: **35** mins

Ingredients
- 1 cup broccoli, chopped
- 1 pound turkey, boiled and chopped
- 2 teaspoons ginger-garlic paste
- Salt and lemon pepper seasoning, to taste
- ½ cup olive oil

Directions
1. Preheat the oven to 360°F and grease a baking tray.
2. Mix together turkey, olive oil, broccoli, ginger-garlic paste, salt and lemon pepper seasoning in a bowl.
3. Make small balls out of this mixture and arrange on the baking tray.
4. Transfer to the oven and bake for about 20 minutes.
5. Remove from the oven and serve with the dip of your choice.

Chicken Zucchini Cutlets

Serves: **6** | Prep Time: **20** mins

Ingredients
- 3 zucchinis, boiled and mashed
- 3 tablespoons lemon pepper seasoning
- ½ pound chicken, boiled and chopped
- ½ cup avocado oil
- Salt and black pepper, to taste

Directions
1. Mix together chicken, zucchinis, lemon pepper seasoning, salt and black pepper in a bowl.
2. Make cutlets out of this mixture and set aside. Heat avocado oil in a pan and put the cutlets in it.
3. Fry for about 2-3 minutes on each side and dish out to serve.

Sour Grilled Turkey Breasts

Serves: **3** | Prep Time: **40** mins

Ingredients
- ½ onion, chopped
- 2 garlic cloves, minced
- 1 pound pastured turkey breasts
- ½ cup sour cream
- Salt and black pepper, to taste

Directions
1. Preheat the grill to medium high heat.
2. Mix together sour cream, onion, garlic, salt and black pepper in a bowl.
3. Add turkey breasts to this mixture and marinate for about an hour.
4. Transfer the marinated turkey breasts to the grill.
5. Grill for about 25 minutes and transfer to a plate to serve.

Cheesy Chicken Tenders

Serves: **6** | Prep Time: **35** mins

Ingredients
- 1 cup cream
- 4 tablespoons butter
- 2 pounds chicken tenders
- Salt and black pepper, to taste
- 1 cup feta cheese

Directions
1. Preheat the oven to 350°F and grease a baking dish.
2. Season chicken tenders with salt and black pepper.
3. Heat butter in a skillet and add chicken tenders.
4. Cook for about 3 minutes on each side and transfer to the baking dish.
5. Top with cream and feta cheese and place in the oven.
6. Bake for about 25 minutes and remove from the oven to serve.

Air Fried Chicken

Serves: **2** | Prep Time: **20** mins

Ingredients
- 1 tablespoon olive oil
- 4 skinless, boneless chicken tenderloins
- 1 egg
- Salt and black pepper, to taste
- ½ teaspoon turmeric powder

Directions
1. Preheat the air fryer to 370°F and coat the fryer basket with olive oil.
2. Beat the egg and dip the chicken tenderloins in it.
3. Mix together turmeric powder, salt and black pepper in a bowl and dredge chicken tenderloins.
4. Arrange the chicken tenderloins in the fryer basket and cook for about 10 minutes.
5. Dish out on a platter and serve with salsa.

Ham Wrapped Turkey Rolls

Serves: **4** | Prep Time: **40** mins

Ingredients
- 2 tablespoons fresh sage leaves
- Salt and black pepper, to taste
- 4 ham slices
- 4 (6 ounce) turkey cutlets
- 1 tablespoon butter, melted

Directions
1. Preheat the oven to 350°F and grease a baking dish. Season the turkey cutlets with salt and black pepper.
2. Roll the turkey cutlets and tightly wrap with ham slices.
3. Coat each roll with butter and sprinkle evenly with the sage leaves.
4. Arrange the rolls on the baking dish and transfer to the oven.
5. Bake for about 25 minutes, flipping halfway in between. Remove from the oven and serve immediately.

Stuffed Whole Chicken

Serves: **6** | Prep Time: **1 hour 15** mins

Ingredients
- 1 cup mozzarella cheese
- 4 garlic cloves, peeled
- 1 (2 pound) whole chicken, cleaned, pat dried
- Salt and black pepper, to taste
- 2 tablespoons fresh lemon juice

Directions
1. Preheat the oven to 360°F and grease a baking dish.
2. Season the chicken with salt and black pepper.
3. Stuff the chicken cavity with garlic cloves and mozzarella cheese.
4. Transfer the chicken to oven on the baking dish and drizzle with lemon juice.
5. Bake for about 1 hour and remove from the oven to serve.

Turkey with Mozzarella and Tomatoes

Serves: **2** | Prep Time: **1 hour 30** mins

Ingredients
- 1 tablespoon butter
- 2 large turkey breasts
- ½ cup fresh mozzarella cheese, thinly sliced
- Salt and black pepper, to taste
- 1 large Roma tomato, thinly sliced

Directions
1. Preheat the oven to 375°F and grease the baking tray with butter.
2. Make some deep slits in the turkey breasts and season with salt and black pepper.
3. Stuff the mozzarella cheese slices and tomatoes in the turkey slits.
4. Put the stuffed turkey breasts on the baking tray and transfer to the oven.
5. Bake for about 1 hour 15 minutes and dish out to serve warm.

Boursin Stuffed Chicken

Serves: **4** | Prep Time: **50** mins

Ingredients
- 4 chicken breasts, boneless and skinless
- 4 oz. Boursin cheese
- 4 prosciutto slices
- Kosher salt and black pepper, to taste
- ½ cup mozzarella cheese, shredded

Directions
1. Preheat the oven to 400°F and grease a baking dish.
2. Season the chicken with salt and black pepper and top with Boursin and mozzarella cheese.
3. Wrap chicken breasts with prosciutto slices and transfer into a baking dish.
4. Place in the oven and bake for about 35 minutes. Remove from the oven and serve hot.

Mediterranean Turkey Cutlets

Serves: **6** | Prep Time: **45** mins

Ingredients
- 2 teaspoons Greek seasoning
- 2 pounds turkey cutlets
- 4 tablespoons olive oil
- 2 teaspoons turmeric powder
- 1 cup almond flour

Directions
1. Mix together almond flour, Greek seasoning and turmeric powder in a bowl.
2. Dredge the turkey cutlets and set aside for about 15 minutes.
3. Heat olive oil in a skillet and transfer half of the turkey cutlets.
4. Cover the lid and cook on medium low heat for about 20 minutes.
5. Dish out in a serving platter and repeat with the remaining batch.

Cheesy Bacon Ranch Chicken

Serves: **4** | Prep Time: **35** mins

Ingredients
- 4 boneless skinless chicken breasts
- 4 slices thick cut bacon, cooked and crisped
- Kosher salt and black pepper, to taste
- 1½ cups mozzarella cheese, shredded
- 2 teaspoons ranch seasoning

Directions
1. Preheat the oven to 390°F and grease a baking dish.
2. Season the chicken breasts with kosher salt and black pepper.
3. Cook chicken breasts in a nonstick skillet for about 5 minutes per side.
4. Top the chicken with mozzarella cheese and ranch seasoning and transfer to the oven.
5. Bake for about 15 minutes and dish out on a platter.
6. Crumble the crispy bacon and sprinkle over the chicken to serve.

Garlic Turkey Breasts

Serves: **4** | Prep Time: **35** mins

Ingredients
- ½ teaspoon garlic powder
- 4 tablespoons butter
- ½ teaspoon dried oregano
- Salt and black pepper, to taste
- 1 pound turkey breasts, boneless

Directions
1. Preheat the oven to 450°F and grease a baking dish.
2. Sprinkle garlic powder, dried oregano, salt and black pepper on both sides of the turkey. Heat butter in a skillet and add seasoned turkey. Cook for about 5 minutes on each side and dish out. Arrange the turkey on the baking dish and transfer to the oven. Bake for about 15 minutes and dish out in a platter.

Grilled Chicken Breast

Serves: **4** | Prep Time: **45** mins

Ingredients
- 3 tablespoon extra-virgin olive oil
- ¼ cup balsamic vinegar
- 2 teaspoons dried rosemary and thyme
- Kosher salt and black pepper, to taste
- 4 chicken breasts

Directions
1. Preheat grill to medium high heat. Whisk together balsamic vinegar, olive oil, dried rosemary, dried thyme, kosher salt and black pepper in a bowl.
2. Reserve about one fourth of the marinade and add chicken breasts in the marinade. Mix well and allow it to marinate for about 30 minutes. Transfer chicken to the grill and cook for about 6 minutes on each side, basting with reserved marinade. Remove from the grill and serve on a platter.

Buffalo Skillet Turkey

Serves: **4** | Prep Time: **25** mins

Ingredients
- 4 boneless skinless turkey breasts
- 3 tablespoons butter
- 8 slices muenster cheese
- Garlic powder, cayenne pepper, kosher salt and black pepper
- 1 cup buffalo sauce

Directions
1. Heat half of the butter over medium heat in a large skillet and add turkey.
2. Season with garlic powder, kosher salt and black pepper.
3. Cook for about 5 minutes on each side until golden and dish out on a plate.
4. Heat the rest of the butter in the same skillet and add cayenne pepper and buffalo sauce. Return the turkey to the skillet and top with 2 slices of muenster cheese on each breast.
5. Cover with a lid and cook for about 3 minutes until the cheese is melted.

Low Carb Chicken Nuggets

Serves: **6** | Prep Time: **25** mins

Ingredients
- ¼ cup mayonnaise
- 2 medium chicken breasts
- 1 cup blanched almond flour
- 2 tablespoons olive oil
- Sea salt and black pepper, to taste

Directions
1. Put the chicken in the salted water for about 10 minutes.
2. Drain it and cut the chicken into nugget sized pieces.
3. Put mayonnaise in one bowl and mix almond flour, sea salt and black pepper in another bowl.

4. Coat each chicken nugget with mayonnaise and dredge in the almond flour mixture.
5. Heat oil over medium high heat in a skillet and add chicken nuggets in a single layer.
6. Cook for about 3 minutes per side until golden and dish out to serve.

Turkey with Cream Cheese Sauce

Serves: **8** | Prep Time: **35** mins

Ingredients
- 20 oz. turkey breast
- Salt and black pepper, to taste
- 2 tablespoons butter
- 3 cups cream cheese
- 1 tablespoon tamari soy sauce

Directions
1. Season the turkey generously with salt and black pepper.
2. Heat butter in a large pan over medium heat and add turkey breasts.
3. Cook for about 6 minutes on each side and stir in cream cheese and tamari soy sauce.
4. Cook for about 15 minutes on medium low heat and dish out to serve hot.

Chicken Spinach Coconut Curry

Serves: **6** | Prep Time: **5 hours 10** mins

Ingredients
- 2 tablespoons curry paste
- 1 onion, finely sliced
- 1 pound chicken, cubed
- 800 g fresh spinach, chopped
- 400 ml coconut cream

Directions
1. Put all the ingredients in a slow cooker and stir well.
2. Lock the lid and cook on High Pressure for about 5 hours. Dish out in a serving bowl and serve hot.

Turkey Garlic Mushroom Sauté

Serves: **4** | Prep Time: **30** mins

Ingredients
- 1 cup mushrooms, sliced
- 3 tablespoons butter, divided in half
- 1½ pounds turkey thighs, skinless and boneless
- Sea salt and black pepper, to taste
- 3 garlic cloves, minced

Directions
1. Season the turkey with sea salt and black pepper.
2. Heat half of butter over medium high heat in a large skillet and add turkey.
3. Cook for about 6 minutes on each side and dish out on a plate.
4. Heat the rest of the butter in the skillet and add garlic and mushrooms.
5. Sauté for about 5 minutes and stir in the cooked turkey. Sauté for about 3 minutes and dish out to serve.

Smokey Mountain Chicken

Serves: **8** | Prep Time: **30** mins

Ingredients
- 1 cup low carb Barbecue sauce
- 1½ cups provolone cheese, sliced
- 2 pounds chicken breast, boneless and skinless
- ½ pound bacon, cooked
- ½ cup mozzarella cheese, shredded

Directions
1. Preheat the grill to medium high heat. Grill chicken for about 8 minutes over medium heat. Drizzle with barbecue sauce and flip the chicken.
2. Baste the other side with the barbecue sauce and layer with bacon strips, mozzarella and provolone cheese slices. Cover the grill and cook for about 2 more minutes until the cheese is melted. Remove from the grill and serve hot.

Cauliflower Turkey Casserole

Serves: **4** | Prep Time: **35** mins

Ingredients
- 1 tablespoon Italian seasoning
- 2 cups cauliflower rice, uncooked
- 2 cups cooked turkey, diced
- ¼ cup heavy whipping cream
- ½ cup parmesan and garlic cheese

Directions
1. Preheat the oven to 360°F and grease a casserole dish with nonstick cooking spray. Mix together cauliflower rice, Italian seasoning and turkey in a large bowl.
2. Transfer this mixture into the prepared casserole dish.

3. Combine cream, parmesan and garlic cheese in another bowl until mixed.
4. Pour over the cauliflower rice mixture and transfer to the oven.
5. Bake for about 20 minutes and remove from the oven to serve hot.

Chicken Parmesan

Serves: **3** | Prep Time: **55** mins

Ingredients
- ¾ cup parmesan cheese
- 1 oz. pork rinds
- 1 pound chicken breasts
- Salt, black pepper, oregano and garlic powder
- ½ cup marinara sauce

Directions
1. Preheat the oven to 360°F.
2. Put half of parmesan cheese and the pork rinds in a food processor and process until coarse. Transfer this mixture into a dish and dredge the chicken breasts.
3. Season the chicken breasts with salt, black pepper, oregano and garlic powder.
4. Transfer into the oven and bake for about 25 minutes until golden brown in color. Remove from the oven and pour marinara sauce over each chicken breast.
5. Top with the remaining parmesan cheese and return to the oven.
6. Bake for about 15 more minutes and dish out to serve warm.

Creamy Garlic Turkey Soup

Serves: **4** | Prep Time: **30** mins

Ingredients
- 2 cups turkey, shredded
- 2 tablespoons butter, melted
- 1 cup heavy cream
- Garlic seasoning and salt, to taste
- 14.5 oz chicken broth

Directions
1. Heat butter over medium heat in a saucepan and add shredded turkey.
2. Coat with melted butter and add heavy cream, chicken broth and garlic seasoning. Mix well and bring to a boil.
3. Reduce heat to low and simmer for about 4 minutes. Season with salt and serve hot.

Chicken Asparagus Sheet Pan

Serves: **8** | Prep Time: **40** mins

Ingredients
- ½ pound asparagus, trimmed
- 2 pounds chicken breasts, cut in half to make 4 thin pieces
- 4 sundried tomatoes, cut into strips
- 8 provolone cheese slices
- Salt and black pepper, to taste

Directions
1. Preheat the oven to 400°F and grease a large sheet pan.
2. Arrange chicken breasts and asparagus on the sheet pan and top with sundried tomatoes. Season with salt and black pepper and transfer to the oven.
3. Bake for about 25 minutes and remove from the oven.
4. Top with provolone cheese slices and bake for about 3 more minutes.
5. Dish out and serve hot.

Turkey Breasts Stuffed with Pimiento Cheese

Serves: **4** | Prep Time: **40** mins

Ingredients
- 1 tablespoon pimientos, sliced and chopped
- Paprika, salt and black pepper, divided
- ½ cup Gouda cheese, smoked and shredded
- 4 small boneless, skinless turkey breasts, trimmed
- 1 tablespoon extra-virgin olive oil

Directions
1. Preheat the oven to 400°F.
2. Mix together pimientos, Gouda cheese and paprika in a bowl.
3. Cut slits in the turkey breasts horizontally and add the pimientos mixture inside the slits.
4. Season the turkey breasts with paprika, salt and black pepper.
5. Heat oil over medium high heat in a large ovenproof skillet and add turkey.
6. Cook for about 2 minutes on each side until browned and transfer to the oven.
7. Bake for about 15 minutes and remove from the oven to serve hot.

Beef Recipes

Healthy Italian Beef & Cabbage Stir-Fry

Yield: 4 | Total Time: 30 Mins | Prep Time: 10 Mins | Cook Time: 20 Mins

Ingredients

- 2 pounds ground beef
- 4 tablespoons butter
- 4 cups green cabbage, shredded
- 2 garlic cloves, finely chopped
- ½ cup leeks, thinly sliced
- 1 tsp onion powder
- ½ cup fresh basil
- 1 tbsp. tomato paste
- 1 tbsp. white wine vinegar
- 1 tsp salt
- ¼ tsp pepper
- 1 cup sour cream
- 4 cups green salad to serve

Directions

1. Heat half the butter in an instant pot and sauté the cabbage for about 10 Mins or until tender; stir in onion powder, vinegar, salt and pepper and cook for 3 Mins. Transfer the sautéed cabbage to a bowl and set aside.
2. Heat the remaining butter in the pot and sauté leeks and garlic for 1 minute or until fragrant; stir in meat and fry for about 5 Mins. Stir in tomato paste and lock lid. Cook on high for 5 Mins and then let pressure come down on its own. Stir in basil and sautéed cabbage cook on manual high for 2 Mins and then remove from heat. Serve drizzled with sour cream and green salad on the side.

Instant Pot Beef Shred Rolls serve with Chilled Lemon Juice

Yield: 3 | Total Time: 30 Mins | Prep Time: 10 Mins | Cook Time: 20 Mins

Ingredients

- 300g beef steak
- 1 yellow pepper, sliced thin lengthwise
- 1 white onion, sliced lengthwise
- 6 pcs. butter lettuce
- 2 tsp. mayo
- 1/8 tsp. chili flakes
- 3 glasses freshly squeezed chilled lemon juice to serve

Directions

1. Place the butter lettuce on a serving plate.
2. Set your instant pot on manual high and heat oil; fry beef for 5 Mins per side. Add broth and lock lid; cook on high for 10 Mins and then remove beef. Shred thinly. Spread mayo on the lettuce and top with the shredded beef.
3. Place pepper slices and onions on top and season with chili flakes. Fold to form the rolls, securing with toothpicks. Serve with fresh lemon juice.

Delicious Instant Pot Steak with Parsley & Arugula

Yield: 3 | Total Time: 25 Mins | Prep Time: 10 Mins | Cook Time: 15 Mins

Ingredients

- 2 (10-ounce) boneless steaks
- 2 tbsp. extra virgin olive oil, and extra for drizzling
- 2 tbsp. fresh lemon juice
- 2 ounces shaved Parmesan
- 4 ounces caper berries, halved if large
- 1 red chili, thinly sliced
- ¼ medium red onion, thinly sliced
- 1 bunch arugula, tough stems removed
- Kosher salt and pepper
- 1 cup parsley

Directions

Heat oil in an instant pot set on manual high; sprinkle steaks with salt and pepper and add to the pot. Cook for about 5 Mins per side or until browned. Lock lid and cook for 3 Mins on high. Let pressure come down naturally.

In a medium bowl, toss together caper berries, chili, onion, arugula, parsley and Parmesan cheese; drizzle with lemon juice and toss to coat well. Season to taste.

Drizzle the grilled steaks with extra virgin olive oil and season with more salt and pepper. Serve the steaks with the salad.

Filet Mignon with Caramelized Onions

Yield: 3 | Total Time: 1 Hour | Prep Time: 45 Mins | Cook Time: 15 Mins

Ingredients

- 3 filet mignon steaks
- ¼ cup olive oil
- 1 tbsp. Dijon mustard
- ¼ cup aged balsamic vinegar
- 2 cups medium sliced onions
- 100g goat cheese or your favourite cheese, crumbled
- 1 tbsp. butter
- 1 tsp. sugar
- 2 tsp. dried rosemary
- Cracked black pepper
- Seasoned salt

Directions

1. Generously season the steaks with the cracked black pepper and seasoned salt then place them in a dish in a single layer. In a medium bowl, combine the vinegar, olive oil, rosemary and mustard until well incorporated. Pour this over the filets and coat both sides. Cover the dish with cling wrap and transfer to your fridge to marinate for 30 Mins.
2. Meanwhile, melt the butter in an instant pot set on manual high and cook the onion slices for 5 Mins until the onions become caramelized.
3. Add in the steak and cook for about 5 Mins per side or until golden browned. Top with cheese and lock lid for 2 Mins. Let pressure come down naturally and then serve the cheesy steak hot. Enjoy!

Healthy Beef Chili served with Avocado and Green Onions

Yields: 6 | Total Time: 45 Mins | Prep Time: 10 Mins | Cook Time: 35 Mins

Ingredients

- 2 lb. ground beef
- 3 slices bacon, cut into thin strips
- ¼ yellow onion, chopped
- 2 cloves garlic, minced
- 1 green bell pepper, chopped
- 2 celery stalks, chopped
- 1/2 cup sliced baby Bellas
- 2 tbsp. smoked paprika
- 2 tsp. dried oregano
- 2 tsp. ground cumin
- 2 tbsp. chili powder
- 2 cup low-sodium beef broth
- 2 avocados, sliced avocado
- 2 cups sliced green onions
- 1 cup shredded cheddar
- 1 cup sour cream
- A pinch of salt
- A pinch of pepper

Directions

1. Cook bacon in an instant pot on manual high setting until crispy; remove bacon from the pot and add in onion, mushrooms, celery and pepper. Cook for about 6 Mins and then stir in garlic for about 1 minute. Push the veggies on the side and add in beef. Cook until it is no longer pink. Stir in paprika, oregano, cumin, chili powder, salt and pepper. Cook for about 2 Mins and then stir in broth; lock lid and cook on high setting for 20 Mins. Let pressure come down on its own. Ladle the chili into serving bowls and top each serving with reserved bacon, cheese, sour cream avocado and green onions.

Ground Beef with Veggies

Yields: 4 | Total Time: 30 Mins | Prep Time: 5 Mins | Cook Time: 25 Mins

Ingredients

- 1 lb. lean ground beef
- 2 medium (6 to 8 inches each) zucchinis, diced
- 1 tbsp. coconut oil
- 1-2 cloves garlic, minced
- 2 medium tomatoes, diced
- 2 tbsp. dried oregano
- 1/2 yellow onion, diced

Directions

1. Rinse and prepare the veggies. Set your instant pot on manual high and melt coconut oil; stir in onions and sauté for about 4 Mins or until translucent.
2. Roll ground beef into small balls and add to the pot along with oregano and garlic; cook for about 5 Mins. Add tomatoes and zucchini and lock lid. Cook on high for 20 Mins and then let pressure come down on its own. Serve and enjoy!

Herbed London Broil with Lemon Garlic Butter Zucchini Noodles

Yield: 4 | Total Time: 40 Mins | Prep Time: 10 Mins | Cook Time: 30 Mins

Ingredients

- 2 pounds lean London broil, sliced thinly into strips
- 2 clove garlic, minced
- 2 red onion, minced
- 1 cup beef broth or water
- Chopped Italian parsley
- Pinch of rosemary
- 1 teaspoon thyme
- Pinch of salt & pepper

Lemon Garlic Butter Zucchini Noodles

- 3 tablespoons butter
- 4 cloves garlic, minced
- ½ teaspoon red chili pepper flakes
- 4 medium zucchinis, spiralized
- 1 tablespoon hot sauce
- 1 cup chopped cilantro
- Juice of 1/2 lemon

Directions:

1. **Prepare the Zucchini noodles:** Melt butter in a large skillet; stir in garlic for 2 Mins or until fragrant. Stir in red pepper flakes, hot sauce and lemon juice. Cook for 1 minute and then stir in zucchini and cook for about 3 Mins until well coated with butter sauce. Season with salt and pepper and remove from heat. Coat beef with salt and pepper and add to an instant pot along with beef broth and
2. herbs; lock lid and cook on high for 30 Mins. Naturally release the pressure and then serve beef with zucchini noodles garnished with parsley.

Low Carb Beef & Sweet Potato Dish
Yield: 6 | Total Time: 35 Mins | Prep Time: 10 Mins | Cook Time: 25 Mins

Ingredients
- 4 tablespoons olive oil
- 2 pounds ground beef
- 3 cups beef stock
- 2 sweet potatoes, peeled and diced
- 1 clove garlic, minced
- 1 onion, diced
- 1 (14-oz) can petite minced tomatoes
- 1 (14-oz) can tomato sauce
- 3-4 tbsp. chili powder
- ¼ tsp. oregano
- 2 tsp. salt
- ½ tsp. black pepper
- Cilantro, optional, for garnish

Directions
1. Brown the beef in a pan over medium heat; drain excess fat and then transfer it to an instant pot. Stir in the remaining ingredients and lock lid; cook on high for 25 Mins and then release pressure naturally. Garnish with cilantro and serve warm.

Asparagus & Steak Bowl
Yield: 4 | Total Time: 25 Mins | Prep Time: 10 | Cook Time: 15 Mins

Ingredients
- Olive oil cooking spray
- ¾ pound beef top sirloin steak, diced
- 1/2 tsp. low-sodium steak seasoning
- 1/2 cup chopped red bell pepper
- 1/2 cup chopped red onion
- 1 cup frozen asparagus cuts
- 2 ½ tbsp. soy sauce
- 1 avocado, sliced

Directions
1. Coat an instant pot with cooking spray and set on manual high; sprinkle beef with the steak seasoning and cook in the pot for about 3 Mins; add bell pepper and red onion and cook for 3 Mins more or until beef is browned. Add asparagus and lock lid. Cook on high for 5 Mins and then let the pressure come down on its own.
2. Stir soy sauce in the beef mixture and serve with avocado.

Crunchy Steak Salad
Yield: 2 | Total Time: 15 Mins | Prep Time: 10 Mins | Cook Time: 5 Mins

Ingredients
- 250g steak
- 1/4 cup tamari soy sauce
- 1 tablespoon avocado oil
- 1 tablespoon olive oil
- 1/2 tablespoon lemon juice
- 4 radishes, sliced
- 6 cherry tomatoes, halved
- 1/2 red bell pepper, sliced
- 2 cups salad greens
- ¼ teaspoon salt

Directions
1. Pour tamari sauce in a large bowl; add in steak and toss to coat well; cover and let marinate for a few hours before cooking. In another bowl, combine green salad, radishes, tomatoes, bell peppers, lemon juice, olive oil and salt; toss to coat well and set aside.
2. Heat avocado oil in an instant pot on manual high setting; cook the steak for about 8 Mins per side or until cooked through and browned on the outside. Lock lid and cook for 4 Mins and then quick release pressure and then slice.
3. Divide the salad between two plates and top each with steak slices.

Mango Chili Beef Stir Fry
Yield: 4 | Total Time: 30 Mins | Prep Time: 15 Mins | Cook Time: 5 Mins

Ingredients
- ½ tablespoon sesame oil
- 1 tablespoon low-sodium soy sauce
- 1 tablespoon cornstarch
- 1 pound beef steak, diced
- ½ tablespoon peanut oil
- 1 tablespoon minced fresh ginger
- 1 red onion, chopped
- 2 cups snow peas
- 1 tablespoon chili garlic sauce
- 1 mango, peeled, chopped
- 1/8 teaspoon sea salt
- 1/8 teaspoon black pepper
- 2 cups brown rice
- 4 cups water
- Salt

Directions
1. In a mixing bowl, combine sesame oil, soy sauce, cornstarch and chicken; let sit for at least 20 Mins. Set your instant pot on manual high and heat peanut oil and then sauté ginger and onion for about 2 Mins; add snow peas and stir fry for about 1 minute. Add beef with the marinade and stir fry for about 2 Mins or until chicken is browned. Add chili sauce, mango and pepper and lock lid. Cook for 5 Mins on high and then quick release the pressure.

Creamy Beef, Red Pepper & Cucumber Salad

Yield: 4 | Total Time: 34 Mins | Prep Time: 5 Mins | Cook Time: 29 Mins

Ingredients
- 400g beef steak
- 1 red onion, sliced
- 3 cucumbers, sliced
- 2 tablespoons fresh chopped chives
- 2 tablespoons mayonnaise
- 1/2 cup sour cream
- Salt & black pepper

Directions
1. Rub beef steak with olive oil, salt and pepper; add to an instant pot and fry on manual high for 7 Mins per side. Transfer to a plate. Add water to the pot and insert a trivet. Place the beef on the trivet and lock lid. Cook on high for 15 Mins and then let pressure come down on its own.
2. Remove beef and shred. In a bowl, combine shred beef, red onion and cucumber. In a small bowl, whisk together mayonnaise, sour cream, chives and pepper until well blended; stir into the cucumber salad until well coated; sprinkle with salt and serve.

Instant Pot Lemon Beef Steak

Yield: 4 | Total Time: 1 Hour 10 Mins | Prep Time: 10 Mins | Cook Time: 1 Hour

Ingredients
- 2 pounds beef steak
- 1 red onion, minced
- Juice of ½ lemon
- Pinch of lemon zest
- Pinch of saffron
- Pinch of ground coriander
- Pinch of ginger
- Pinch of salt & pepper

Directions:
1. Soak saffron in fresh lemon juice; crush into paste and then add dry spices.
2. Dip beef steak in mixture and rub remaining spices into steak; sprinkle with salt and pepper and wrap in foil. Add water to an instant pot and insert a trivet; place the beef over the trivet and lock lid and cook on manual high for 1 hour.

Instant Pot Beef Curry

Yield: 3 | Total Time: 40 Mins | Prep Time: 10 Mins | Cook Time: 30 Mins

Ingredients
- 4 tbsp. coconut oil
- 300 grams beef steak, diced
- ¼ cup beef broth
- Pinch of turmeric
- Dash of onion powder
- 1 tablespoon minced red onion
- Pinch of garlic powder
- ¼ teaspoon curry powder
- Pinch of sea salt
- Pinch of pepper
- Stevia
- Pinch of cayenne

Directions
1. Set your instant pot to manual high, melt in coconut oil and then stir in garlic and onion. Cook until fragrant and stir in beef. In a small bowl, stir together spices, Stevia, and beef broth until dissolved; stir into the beef and lock lid. Cook for 30 Mins and then naturally release the pressure. Serve hot.

Steak Salad with Spiced Avocado Dressing

Yield: 2 | Total Time: 39 Mins | Prep Time: 10 Mins | Cook Time: 29 Mins

Ingredients
Salad:
- ¾ pound grilled ribeye, sliced
- 1 cup salad greens
- 1/2 cup sliced cucumber
- ½ cup sliced black olives
- 1 avocado
- 1/2 cup grape tomatoes, halved

Dressing:
- 1 avocado
- 2 tablespoons avocado oil
- 2 tablespoons balsamic vinegar
- 2 tablespoons lime juice
- ¼ teaspoon red pepper flakes
- 1 cup fresh cilantro
- 1 clove garlic minced
- 1/2 teaspoon sea salt

Directions
1. Rub beef steak with olive oil, salt and pepper; add to an instant pot and fry on manual high for 7 Mins per side. Transfer to a plate. Add water to the pot and insert a trivet. Place the beef on the trivet and lock lid. Cook on high for 15 Mins and then let pressure come down on its own.
2. Remove beef and shred.
3. In a bowl, mix all salad ingredients and set aside.
4. In a blender, blend together all dressing ingredients until very smooth; pour over the salad and toss to coat well. Divide between serving bowls and enjoy!

Healthy Zucchini Beef Sauté with Avocado

Yield: 2 | Total Time: 25 Mins | Prep Time: 5 Mins | Cook Time: 20 Mins

Ingredients
- 300g beef, sliced into thin strips
- 1 zucchini, sliced into thin strips
- 1/4 cup cilantro, chopped
- 3 cloves of garlic, diced or minced
- 2 tablespoons gluten-free tamari sauce
- 2 tablespoons avocado oil
- 1 avocado, diced

Directions
1. Heat oil in an instant pot set on manual high setting; add in beef and sauté for about 10 Mins or until browned. Stir in zucchini and cook for 5 Mins more or until zucchini is tender. Stir in garlic, cilantro and tamari sauce and lock lid. Cook on high for 5 Mins and then serve right away topped with avocado.

Low Carb Ground Beef Tacos with Salsa

Yield: 4 | Total Time: 35 Mins | Prep Time: 10 Mins | Cook Time: 25 Mins

Ingredients
- 500 grams lean ground beef
- 2 clove garlic, minced
- 2 red onions, minced
- 8 lettuce leaves
- A pinch of cayenne pepper
- Fresh chopped cilantro
- Pinch of dried oregano
- Dash of onion powder
- Dash of garlic powder
- Pinch of salt & pepper

Directions:
1. Fry beef in olive oil in an instant pot set on manual high setting until browned; add garlic, onion and spices, and water; lock lid and cook on high for 10 Mins and then release the pressure naturally. Season with salt and serve taco style in romaine lettuce or butter lettuce or with a side of salsa.

Pepper Crusted Steak with Garlic Creamed Sautéed Spinach

Yield: 2 | Total Time: 25 Mins | Prep Time: 10 Mins | Cook Time: 15 Mins

Ingredients
- 300 grams lean steak
- 1 tablespoon olive oil
- Dash of Worcestershire sauce
- Pinch of salt & pepper
- ½ cup beef broth
- 1 cup of green salad for serving.

Garlic Creamed Sautéed Spinach
- 2 tablespoons melted butter
- 4 cloves garlic, thinly sliced
- 2 cups fresh spinach, rinsed
- ¼ cup coconut cream
- 1 teaspoon lemon juice
- Sea salt & pepper

Directions
1. Prepare spinach: Melt butter in a skillet and sauté garlic until fragrant. Stir in spinach, lemon juice and coconut cream and cook for about 3 Mins. Stir in salt and pepper and remove from heat.
2. Pound meat until tender and flat; rub with salt and pepper. Heat olive oil in an instant pot set on manual high setting; add meat and cook for about 3 Mins per side. Stir in broth and lock lid; cook on high for 10 Mins and then let pressure come down on its own. Serve over a bowl of creamed spinach topped with Worcestershire sauce and garnished with caramelized onions. Enjoy!

Steak Frites with Rocket & Peppercorn Sauce

Yield: 4 | Total Time: 30 Mins | Prep Time: 15 Mins | Cook Time: 15 Mins

Ingredients
- 4 x 200g beef eye-fillet steaks
- 2 tbsp. extra virgin olive oil
- 1/4 cup red wine
- 55g can green peppercorns, rinsed, drained
- 1/2 cup beef stock
- 1/2 cup crème fraiche
- Handfuls of rocket and chopped parsley

Directions
1. Combine wine and peppercorns in a large bowl; let stand for about 5 Mins.
2. Season steaks with sea salt and black pepper.
3. Heat oil in an instant pot set on manual high and add the steaks; cook for about 3 Mins per side or until cooked to your desired doneness. Add in the wine mixture and stir in crème fraiche and stock; lock lid. Cook on high for 15 Mins and then let pressure come down on its own. Season and serve with rocket and parsley.

Lean Steak with Oregano-Orange Chimichurri & Arugula Salad

Yield: 4 | Total Time: 15 Mins | Prep Time: 5 Mins | Cook Time: 10 Mins

Ingredients

- 1 teaspoon finely grated orange zest
- 1 teaspoon dried oregano
- 1 small garlic clove, grated
- 2 teaspoon vinegar (red wine, cider, or white wine)
- 1 tablespoon fresh orange juice
- 1/2 cup chopped fresh flat-leaf parsley leaves
- 1 ½ pound lean steak, cut into 4 pieces
- Sea salt and pepper
- 1/4 cup and 2 teaspoons extra virgin olive oil
- 4 cups arugula
- 2 bulbs fennel, shaved
- 2 tablespoons whole-grain mustard

Directions

1. Make chimichurri: In a medium bowl, combine orange zest, oregano and garlic. Mix in vinegar, orange juice and parsley and then slowly whisk in ¼ cup of olive oil until emulsified. Season with sea salt and pepper.
2. Sprinkle the steak with salt and pepper; heat the remaining olive oil in an instant pot and set on manual high; cook steak for about 6 Mins per side or until browned. Add water to an instant pot and insert a trivet; place beef over the trivet and lock lid. Cook on high for 10 Mins and then let pressure come down on its own. Let rest and slice.
3. Toss steak, greens, and fennel with mustard in a medium bowl; season with salt and pepper.
4. Serve steak with chimichurri and salad. Enjoy!

Instant Pot Paleo Meatballs

Yield: 4 | Total Time: 30 Mins | Prep Time: 15 Mins | Cook Time: 15 Mins

Ingredients

- 1 ½ pounds ground beef
- ¼ cups almond flour
- 2 beat eggs
- ⅔ cups diced red onion
- 5 teaspoons minced garlic
- ½ cups chopped basil
- ¾ cups tomato paste
- ½ cups grate carrot
- 2 cups dice tomato
- 1 teaspoon dried oregano
- 4 teaspoons minced garlic
- 1 teaspoon salt
- ½ cups water

Directions

1. In a bowl, mix garlic, basil leaves, tomato paste, and diced tomatoes.
2. In another bowl, mix together almond flour, garlic, carrot, onion, oregano, egg and salt until well blended; add ground beef and mix well. Roll out ¼ cup of the mixture into balls and brown them in an instant pot under sauté mode. Pour water and tomato mixture over the meat balls and lock lid. Cook on manual for 6 Mins and then let pressure come down on its own. Serve.

Beef and Zucchini Lasagna

Yield:4 | Total Time: 48 Mins | Prep Time: 15 Mins | Cook Time: 33 Mins

Ingredients

- 1 large zucchini, spiralized into thin strips
- 1 cup marinara
- 16 oz. ground beef
- 10 oz. ricotta cheese
- 4 oz. shredded mozzarella cheese

Directions

1. Add water to your instant pot and insert a trivet. Sprinkle the zucchini noodles with salt and let sit for about 15 Mins. Brown the ground beef in a frying pan and stir in marinara, and salt and pepper.
2. In a casserole dish, layer the beef mixture, zucchini, ricotta cheese, tofu mixture, zucchini, ricotta cheese and top with mozzarella cheese; cover the dish with foil and place the dish on the trivet; lock lid and cook for 20 Mins and then quick release pressure. Uncover and broil for about 3 Mins or until the top is browned. Remove from oven and serve.

Instant Pot Barbacoa

Yield: 6 | Total Time: 1 Hour 10 Mins | Prep Time: 10 Mins

Ingredients

- 4 tablespoons olive oil
- 2 pounds grass-fed chuck roast, diced into large chunks
- 6 garlic cloves
- 1 large onion, chopped
- 2-4oz cans of green chilies
- 3 dried chipotle peppers, chopped
- 3 tbsp. coconut vinegar
- 1 cup fresh lime juice
- 1/2 cup water
- 1 tsp. salt
- 1 tsp. pepper
- 1 tbsp. cumin
- 1 tbsp. oregano

Directions

1. Combine all ingredients in your instant pot; lock lid and cook on high for 60 Mins. When done, release pressure naturally and shred before serving.

Pressure Cooked Italian Beef

Yield: 6 | Total Time: 1 Hours 40 Mins | Prep Time: 10 Mins | Cook Time: 1 Hour 30 Mins

Ingredients
- 2 pound grass-fed chuck roast
- 6 cloves garlic
- 1 tsp. marjoram
- 1 tsp. basil
- 1 tsp. oregano
- 1/2 tsp. ground ginger
- 1 tsp. onion powder
- 2 tsp. garlic powder
- 1 tsp. salt
- 1/4 cup apple cider vinegar
- 1 cup beef broth

Directions
1. Cut slits in the roast with a sharp knife and then stuff with garlic cloves.
2. In a bowl, whisk together marjoram, basil, oregano, ground ginger, onion powder, garlic powder, and salt until well blended; rub the seasoning all over the roast and place it in your instant pot.
3. Add vinegar and broth and lock lid; cook on high for 90 Mins. Release pressure naturally and then shred meat with a fork.
4. Serve along with cooking juices.

Roast Red Wine Beef Steak with Chili Olive Salsa

Yield: 6 | Total Time: 1 Hour 45 Mins | Prep Time: 15 Mins | Cook Time: 1 Hour 30 Mins

Ingredients
- 2kg leg of beef
- 2 tbsp. balsamic vinegar
- 3 red onions, each cut into 6 wedges
- 4 garlic cloves, sliced
- 3 cups hot lamb stock
- 2 tbsp. fresh lemon zest
- 8 good sprigs thyme
- 1/2 cup red wine
- 5 tbsp. extra virgin olive oil

Chili Olive Salsa
- 3 large tomatoes, finely chopped
- 1 cup olives, finely chopped
- 1 bird's eye chili, finely chopped
- Juice of 1 lemon
- 1/2 cup parsley, finely chopped

Directions
1. **Make salsa:** mix chopped tomato, olives, chili, lemon juice, and parsley in a large bowl.
2. With a knife, cut holes all over beef and push a garlic slice into each.
3. Mix lemon zest, wine, 3 tablespoons of olive oil, thyme and pepper in a freezer bag and add in the lamb, seal and refrigerate for about 4 hours or overnight. Set your instant pot on manual high and heat oil; add in the remaining thyme and cook in steak for 5 Mins per side.
4. In the meantime, strain the marinade through a fine mesh into the pot. Lock lid and cook for 20 Mins and then naturally release pressure.
5. Transfer the steak to a cutting board and wrap in foil. Place onions in a bowl and set aside.
6. Set your instant pot to manual high and add in balsamic vinegar and a splash of stock; cook, scraping all the bits from the base and add to the jug with gravy. Serve the steak drizzled with the gravy.

Instant Pot Chipotle Shredded Beef

Yield: 2 | Total Time: 1 Hour 30 Mins | Prep Time: 20 Mins | Cook Time: 1 Hour 10 Mins

Ingredients
- 2 tbsp. olive oil
- 2 pounds beef chuck roast
- 1 tbsp. adobo sauce
- 1 chipotle in adobo, chopped
- 1/2 tsp. chili powder
- 2 tsp. dried oregano
- 2 tsp. dried cumin
- 1 tsp. black pepper
- 2 tsp. salt
- 1 cup fresh cilantro, chopped
- 1 green bell pepper, diced
- 1 onion, chopped
- 1 cup water

Directions
1. Generously season the roast with salt and pepper.
2. Add olive oil to your instant pot and press the sauté button; add the roast and brown on both sides; spread adobo sauce and chipotle pepper over the roast and sprinkle with seasoning and cilantro; add bell pepper and onions and pour water around the edges of meat. Lock lid; cook on high for 60 Mins and then release pressure naturally. Shred meat and serve with cooking sauce.

Instant Pot AIP Beef

Yield: 6 | Total Time: 1 Hours 40 Mins | Prep Time: 10 Mins | Cook Time: 1 Hour 30 Mins

Ingredients
- 2 pound grass-fed chuck roast
- 6 cloves garlic
- 1 tsp. marjoram
- 1 tsp. basil
- 1 tsp. oregano
- 1/2 tsp. ground ginger
- 1 tsp. onion powder
- 2 tsp. garlic powder
- 1 tsp. salt
- 1/4 cup apple cider vinegar
- 1 cup beef broth

Directions
1. Cut slits in the roast with a sharp knife and then stuff with garlic cloves.
2. In a bowl, whisk together marjoram, basil, oregano, ground ginger, onion powder, garlic powder, and salt until well blended; rub the seasoning all over the roast and place it in your instant pot.
3. Add vinegar and broth and lock lid; cook on high for 90 Mins. Release pressure naturally and then shred meat with a fork. Serve along with cooking juices.

Beef & Sweet Potato Enchilada Casserole

Yield: 6 | Total Time: 40 Mins | Prep Time: 20 Mins | Cook Time: 20 Mins

Ingredients
- 2 small sweet potatoes
- 2 tablespoons olive oil
- 1-pound ground beef
- 1 can black beans, drained
- 1 cup frozen corn
- 1 can red enchilada sauce
- 4 tablespoon chopped fresh cilantro
- 2 teaspoon ground cumin
- 1 teaspoon garlic powder
- 1 teaspoon onion powder
- 1 small can diced olives
- 1 cup shredded parmesan cheese

Directions
1. Peel and cook the sweet potatoes; mash and mix with 2 tablespoons of cilantro.
2. In an instant pot set on manual high, cook the ground beef until browned. Stir in beans, corn, sauce and spices until well combined; sprinkle with half of the cheese and top with sweet potatoes, olives and cilantro. Cover with the remaining cheese and lock lid. Cook on high for 20 Mins and then let pressure come down on its own.

Instant Pot Beef Roast

Yield: 6 | Total Time: 1 Hour 30 Mins | Prep Time: 20 Mins | Cook Time: 1 Hour 10 Mins

Ingredients
- 2 tbsp. olive oil
- 2 pounds beef chuck roast
- 1 tbsp. adobo sauce
- 1 chipotle in adobo, chopped
- ½ tsp. chili powder
- 2 tsp. dried oregano
- 2 tsp. dried cumin
- 1 tsp. black pepper
- 2 tsp. salt
- 1 cup fresh cilantro, chopped
- 1 green bell pepper, diced
- 1 onion, chopped
- 1 cup water

Directions
1. Generously season the roast with salt and pepper.
2. Add olive oil to your instant pot and press the sauté button; add the roast and brown on both sides; spread adobo sauce and chipotle pepper over the roast and sprinkle with seasoning and cilantro; add bell pepper and onions and pour water around the edges of meat. Lock lid; cook on high for 60 Mins and then release pressure naturally.
3. Shred meat and serve with cooking sauce.

Paleo Instant Pot Beef Jalapeno Chili

Yield: 2 | Total Time: 1 Hour 55 Mins | Prep Time: 25 Mins | Cook Time: 1 Hour 30 Mins

Ingredients
- 2 tablespoons olive oil
- 1/2 pound ground beef
- 1 red bell pepper, chopped
- 1 green bell pepper, chopped
- 2 jalapeños, finely diced
- 1/2 acorn squash, diced
- 1 zucchini, sliced
- 2 small carrots, sliced
- 2 green onions, thinly sliced
- 1 cup canned tomatoes
- 4 tbsp. chili powder
- 4 tbsp. tomato paste
- 4 tbsp. can tomato sauce

Directions
1. Set your instant pot on manual high and heat oil; brown ground beef and then stir in, bell peppers, jalapeños, zucchinis, carrots, onions, and squash. Add whole tomatoes and stir with a spatula to mix well. Stir in chili powder along with the remaining ingredients and lock lid. Cook on high for 1 ½ hours and then release the pressure naturally.

Low Carb Cheese Steak Casserole with Fresh Lemon Juice

Yield: 6 | Total Time 50 Mins | Prep Time 5 Mins | Cook Time 45 Mins

Ingredients
- 4 tablespoons olive oil
- 1 ½ pounds lean ground beef
- 1 clove garlic
- 1/2 yellow onion
- 2 bell peppers
- 4 slices Provolone cheese
- 1 teaspoon Worcestershire sauce
- 1 teaspoon hot sauce
- 1/4 cup heavy cream
- 4 large eggs
- 1 teaspoon seasoned salt
- 6 glasses freshly squeezed lemon juice

Directions

1. Set your instant pot on manual high and heat oil; add in beef and cook, crumbling; stir in garlic, onion, peppers and salt. Cook until beef is browned. Top with cheese pieces. In a bowl, whisk together cream, egg, Worcestershire sauce and hot sauce until well blended; pour over the beef mixture and lock lid. Cook on high for 15 Mins and then let pressure come down naturally. Serve with a glass of freshly squeezed lemon juice.

Tasty Lime Steak with Green Salad

Yield: 6 | Total Time: 20 Mins | Prep Time: 10 Mins | Cook Time: 10 Mins

Ingredients

- 1-pound flank steak
- 3 tbsp. toasted sesame oil
- 1 tsp. hot pepper sauce
- 2 tbsp. fresh lime juice
- 1 garlic clove, chopped
- 6 scallions, thinly sliced
- 3 tbsp. olive oil
- 1/3 cup soy sauce
- 1 tsp liquid Stevia
- Kosher salt
- 4 cups green salad

Directions

1. In a resealable plastic bag, combine scallions, garlic, lime juice, olive oil, sesame oil, Stevia, and soy sauce; add steak and seal the bag. Shake to coat the steak well and refrigerate for at least 8 hours.
2. Add oil to an instant pot and set to manual high; remove steak from the bag and shake off excess marinade; season with salt and fry the meat for about 6 Mins per side or until browned. Remove meat from the pot and add in water; insert a metal trivet and place the beef on it. Lock lid and cook on high for 10 Mins. Let pressure come down.
3. Transfer the steak to a chopping board and let rest for at least 10 Mins; slice thinly and serve with green salad.

Loaded Low Carb Flank Steak with Steamed Asian Veggies

Yield: 6 | Total Time: 30 Mins | Prep Time: 15 Mins | Cook Time: 15Mins

Ingredients

- 2 pounds beef flank steak
- 1/2 cup softened butter
- 2 tbsp. salad dressing mix

Steamed Asian Veggies

- 1 bunch broccoli, trimmed
- 1 bunch baby choy sum, trimmed
- 3 green onions, chopped
- 6 cooked and crumbled bacon strips
- 1/2 tsp. pepper
- 1/2 tsp. sesame seeds, toasted

Directions

1. **Prepare Veggies:** Separate the leaves from the stems of choy sum. Place a steamer over a large saucepan or wok of simmering water; place broccoli and choy sum stems in the steamer and cover. Cook for about 4 Mins or until tender; add the choy sum leaves and continue cooking, covered, for about 2 Mins or until wilted.
2. Beat butter, salad dressing mix, onions, bacon strips, and pepper in a small bowl. Horizontally cut a small pocket in the steak and fill with the butter mixture.
3. Add oil to an instant pot and set to manual high; fry in the meat for about 7 Mins per side or until browned. Remove meat from the pot and add in water; insert a metal trivet and place the beef on it. Lock lid and cook on high for 10 Mins. Let pressure come down.
4. Transfer to a chopping board and slice across the grain. Serve.

Beef Stir Fry with Red Onions & Cabbage

Yield: 4 | Total Time: 20 Mins | Prep Time: 10 Mins | Cook Time: 10 Mins

Ingredients:

- 550g grass-fed flank steak, thinly sliced strips
- 1 tablespoon rice wine
- 2 teaspoons balsamic vinegar
- Pinch of sea salt
- Pinch of pepper
- 4 tablespoons extra-virgin olive oil
- 1 large yellow onion, thinly chopped
- 1/2 red bell pepper, thinly sliced
- 1/2 green bell pepper, thinly sliced
- 1 tablespoon toasted sesame seeds
- 1 teaspoon crushed red pepper flakes
- 4 cups cabbage
- 1 ½ avocados, diced

Directions:

1. Place meat in a bowl; stir in rice wine and vinegar, sea salt and pepper. Toss to coat well.
2. Heat a tablespoon of olive oil in an instant pot set on manual high; add meat and cook for about 2 Mins or until meat is browned; stir for another 2 Mins and then remove from heat. Sauté the onions for about 2 Mins or until caramelized; stir in pepper and cook for 2 Mins more. Stir in cabbage and cook for 2 Mins; stir in sesame seeds and red pepper flakes. Lock lid and cook for 5 Mins on high setting. Let pressure come down on its own. Serve hot topped with diced avocado!

Chili Fried Steak with Toasted Cashews & Sautéed Spinach

Yields: 4 | Total Time: 35 Mins | Prep Time: 10 Mins | Cook Time: 25 Mins

Ingredients

- 3 tbsp. extra virgin olive oil or canola oil
- 1 pound sliced lean beef
- 2 tablespoons apple cider vinegar
- 2 teaspoon fish sauce
- 2 teaspoons red curry paste
- 1 cup green capsicum, diced
- 24 toasted cashews
- 1 teaspoon arrowroot
- 1 teaspoon liquid Stevia
- ½ cup water
- 2 cups spinach
- 1 tablespoon butter
- 1 red onion, chopped

Directions

1. Prepare spinach: melt butter in a skillet and sauté onion until fragrant; stir in kale for 3 Mins or until wilted.
2. Add oil to an instant pot set on manual high; add beef and fry until it is no longer pink inside. Stir in red curry paste and cook for a few more Mins.
3. Stir in Stevia, vinegar, fish sauce, capsicum and water. Lock lid and cook on high for 10 Mins. Naturally release the pressure.
4. Mix cooked arrowroot with water to make a paste; stir the paste into the sauce and cook on manual high until the sauce is thick. Stir in toasted cashews and serve with sautéed spinach.

Protein-Rich Beef & Veggie Stew

Yield: 4 | Total Time: 3 Hours 10 Mins | Prep Time: 10 Mins | Cook Time: 3 Hours

Ingredients

- 2 cups zucchini, cubed
- 2 lb. beef (chuck), cubed
- 1 cup eggplant, cubed
- 1 can tomato sauce
- 1/2 cup onion, chopped
- 4 tbsp. extra virgin olive oil
- 1 clove garlic, chopped
- ½ cup vegetable broth
- 1 carrot, thinly sliced
- 1 tomato, chopped
- ¼ tsp paprika
- ½ tsp Cumin, ground
- ½ tsp turmeric, ground
- ¼ tsp cinnamon, ground
- ¼ tsp red pepper, crushed

Directions

1. Combine everything in an instant pot, cover and cook on high for 3 hours. Let pressure come down on its own. Serve with steamed cauliflower rice. Enjoy!

Peppered Steak with Cherry Tomatoes

Yield: 4 | Total Time: 25 Mins | Prep Time: 10 Mins | Cook Time: 10 Mins

Ingredients

- 4 (250g each) beef sirloin steaks, trimmed
- 4 tbsp. extra virgin olive oil
- 2 tsp. cracked black pepper
- 1 bunch rocket, trimmed
- 2 cups cherry tomatoes
- 4 cups green salad, to serve
- olive oil cooking spray

Directions

1. Brush the steak with oil. Place the pepper on a large plate and press the steaks into the pepper until well coated.
2. Set your instant pot to manual high; add oil and heat. Add in steaks and cook for 5 Mins per side. Lock lid and cook on high for 3 Mins and the let pressure come down on its own. In the meantime, spray the tomatoes with oil and barbecue them, turning occasionally, for about 5 Mins or until tender.
3. Arrange the rocket on serving plates and add steaks and tomatoes; serve with green salad.

Ground Beef Chili served with Avocado

Yield: 1 Serving | Total Time: 25 Mins | Prep Time: 10 Mins | Cook Time: 15 Mins

Ingredients

- 180 grams lean ground beef
- 1 ½ tablespoons olive oil
- 1 tablespoon chopped red onion
- 2 cloves garlic, minced
- 1 cup chopped tomatoes
- ½ cup water
- Pinch of garlic powder
- ¼ avocado, chopped tomato and green onion to serve
- ¼ teaspoon chili powder
- Pinch of oregano
- Pinch of onion powder
- Pinch of cayenne pepper
- Pinch of salt
- Pinch of pepper

Directions:

1. Set your instant pot on manual high setting, cook beef in olive oil until browned; stir in garlic, onion, tomatoes, water and spices. Lock lid and cook on high setting for 10 Mins and then let pressure come down naturally. Season with salt and pepper. Serve topped with diced avocado, chopped tomato and green onion.

Loaded Flank Steak with Salsa

Yield: 1 Serving | Total Time: 34 Mins | Prep Time: 10 Mins | Cook Time: 24 Mins

Ingredients
- 150g beef flank steak
- 1 tablespoon softened butter
- 2 tbsp. salad dressing mix
- 3 green onions, chopped

- 1 cooked and crumbled bacon strip
- 1/2 tsp. pepper
- ½ cup broth

For the salsa
- 1 large tomato, finely chopped
- 1 tablespoon capers, finely chopped
- 1 bird's eye chili, finely chopped

- Juice of ¼ lemon
- ½ cup parsley, finely chopped

Directions
1. Make salsa: mix chopped tomato, capers, chili, lemon juice, and parsley in a large bowl.
2. Beat butter, salad dressing mix, onions, bacon strips, and pepper in a small bowl. Horizontally cut a small pocket in the steak and fill with the butter mixture.
3. Set your instant pot on manual high; heat oil and fry the steak for about 7 Mins per side or until well cooked. Add in broth and lock lid. Cook on high setting for 10 Mins and then let pressure come down naturally. Transfer to a chopping board and slice across the grain. Serve with salsa.

Instant Pot Beef & Zucchini

Yield: 1 Serving | Total Time: 25 Mins | Prep Time: 10 Mins | Cook Time: 15 Mins

Ingredients
- 100g lean ground beef
- 1 medium zucchini, diced
- 1 tbsp. coconut oil

- 1-2 cloves garlic, minced
- 2 medium tomatoes, diced
- 2 tbsp. dried oregano

- 1/2 yellow onion, diced

Directions
1. Rinse and prepare the veggies.
2. Set your instant pot and melt coconut oil; stir in onions and sauté for about 4 Mins or until translucent.
3. Roll ground beef into small balls and add to the pot along with oregano and garlic; cook for about 5 Mins. Add tomatoes and zucchini and lock lid. Cook on high for 3 Mins and then let pressure come down on its own. Serve and enjoy!

Coriander & Buttermilk Steak with Salad

Yield: 6 | Total Time: 25 Mins | Prep Time: 15 Mins | Cook Time: 10 Mins

Ingredients
- 4 tbsp. extra virgin olive oil
- 2 cups buttermilk
- 3 lb. beef skirt steak
- 3 cloves garlic, chopped
- 1 lime, zested, juiced
- 1 long green chilli, sliced

- 1 bunch coriander, chopped
- 3 cucumbers, cut into wedges
- 1 bunch radish, quartered
- 3 avocados, diced
- baby lettuce, outer leaves removed

Directions
1. In a food processor, combine garlic, zest, chili, and coriander; pulse to a coarse paste; add buttermilk and continue pulsing until well combined. Reserve a cup of the dressing.
2. Place the steak in a bowl; pour over the remaining dressing. Refrigerate, covered, for about 1 hour.
3. Set your instant pot to manual high; add oil and heat. Remove the steak from the marinade and brush with oil. Add in steaks and cook for 5 Mins per side. Lock lid and cook on high for 3 Mins and the let pressure come down on its own.
4. Slice the steak into thin strips and serve with the salad, drizzled with the buttermilk dressing. Divide the lettuce leaves and place in a bowl; add radishes, cucumber and avocado. Whisk lime juice, salt and pepper into the reversed dressing.

Cheese Stuffed Meatloaf Stuffed

Yield: 6 | Total Time: 50 Mins | Prep Time: 5 Mins | Cook Time: 45 Mins

Ingredients
- 1 egg
- 1-pound ground Chorizo
- 1-pound ground beef
- 1/2 cup coconut flour
- 2 garlic cloves, minced
- 1/4 red onion, minced
- 1/2 tablespoon smoked paprika

- 1/2 tablespoon onion powder
- 1/2 tablespoon garlic powder
- ¾ cup sliced cheddar cheese
- 1/2 teaspoon salt
- 1/2 teaspoon pepper
- 6 cups tomato salsa

Directions
1. In a large bowl, mix all ingredients except salsa and cheese. Press half of the meat mixture in a loaf pan that fits into your instant pot; top with cheese and add the remaining meat mixture, pressing it down to slightly compress. Add water to your instant pot and insert a trivet. Place the dish over the trivet and lock lid. Cook on high for 45 Mins and then let pressure come down naturally. Let rest for at least 10 Mins before serving.
2. Serve the meatloaf with salsa.

Hamburger Patties
Serves: **6** | Prep Time: **30** mins

Ingredients
- 1 egg
- 25 oz. ground beef
- 3 oz. feta cheese, crumbled
- 2 oz. butter, for frying
- Salt and black pepper, to taste

Directions
1. Mix together egg, ground beef, feta cheese, salt and black pepper in a bowl.
2. Combine well and form equal sized patties. Heat butter in a pan and add patties.
3. Cook on medium low heat for about 3 minutes per side. Dish out and serve warm.

Buttery Beef Curry
Serves: **2** | Prep Time: **30** mins

Ingredients
- ½ cup butter
- ½ pound grass fed beef
- ½ pound onions
- Salt and red chili powder, to taste
- ½ pound celery, chopped

Directions
1. Put some water in a pressure cooker and add all the ingredients.
2. Lock the lid and cook on High Pressure for about 15 minutes.
3. Naturally release the pressure and dish out the curry to a bowl to serve.

Cheesy Beef
Serves: **6** | Prep Time: **40** mins

Ingredients
- 1 teaspoon garlic salt
- 2 pounds beef
- 1 cup cream cheese
- 1 cup mozzarella cheese, shredded
- 1 cup low carb Don Pablo's sauce

Directions
1. Season the meat with garlic salt and add to the instant pot.
2. Put the remaining ingredients in the pot and set the instant pot on low.
3. Cook for about 2 hours and dish out.

Beef Quiche
Serves: **3** | Prep Time: **30** mins

Ingredients
- ¼ cup grass fed beef, minced
- 2 slices bacon, cooked and crumbled
- ¼ cup goat cheddar cheese, shredded
- ¼ cup coconut milk
- 3 large pastured eggs

Directions
1. Preheat the oven to 365°F and grease 3 quiche molds.
2. Whisk together eggs and coconut milk in a large bowl.
3. Put beef in quiche molds and stir in the egg mixture. Top with the crumbled bacon and cheddar cheese.
4. Transfer quiche molds to the oven and bake for about 20 minutes.
5. Remove from the oven and serve warm.

Chili Beef
Serves: **8** | Prep Time: **50** mins

Ingredients
- 3 celery ribs, finely diced
- 2 pounds grass fed beef, ground
- 2 tablespoons chili powder
- 2 tablespoons avocado oil, divided
- 2 cups grass fed beef broth

Directions
1. Heat avocado oil in a skillet on medium heat and add beef.
2. Sauté for about 3 minutes on each side and stir in broth and chili powder. Cover the lid and cook for about 30 minutes on medium low heat. Add celery and dish out in a bowl to serve.

Smoked Brisket with Maple Syrup

Serves: **8** | Prep Time: **40** mins

Ingredients
- 1 tablespoon sugar free maple syrup
- 3 pounds grass fed beef briskets
- 3 tablespoons almond oil
- 2 cups bone broth
- 4 tablespoons liquid smoke

Directions
1. Heat almond oil in a skillet on medium heat and add beef briskets.
2. Sauté for about 4 minutes per side and stir in the bone broth and liquid smoke.
3. Cover the lid and cook for about 30 minutes on medium low heat.
4. Dish out in a platter and drizzle with sugar free maple syrup to serve.

Beef Sirloin Steak

Serves: **3** | Prep Time: **45** mins

Ingredients
- 3 tablespoons butter
- ½ teaspoon garlic powder
- 1 pound beef top sirloin steaks
- Salt and black pepper, to taste
- 1 garlic clove, minced

Directions
1. Heat butter in a large grill pan and add beef top sirloin steaks.
2. Brown the steaks on both sides by cooking for about 3 minutes per side.
3. Season the steaks with garlic powder, salt and black pepper and cook for about 30 minutes, flipping once.
4. Dish out the steaks to a serving platter and serve hot.

Bacon Swiss Beef Steaks

Serves: **4** | Prep Time: **25** mins

Ingredients
- ½ cup Swiss cheese, shredded
- 4 beef top sirloin steaks
- 6 bacon strips, cut in half
- Salt and black pepper, to taste
- 1 tablespoon butter

Directions
1. Season the beef steaks generously with salt and black pepper.
2. Put butter in the skillet and heat on medium low heat.
3. Add beef top sirloin steaks and cook for about 5 minutes per side.
4. Add bacon strips and cook for about 15 minutes.
5. Top with Swiss cheese and cook for about 5 minutes on low heat.
6. Remove from heat and dish out on a platter to serve.

Mexican Taco Casserole

Serves: **3** | Prep Time: **35** mins

Ingredients
- ½ cup cheddar cheese, shredded
- ½ cup low carb salsa
- ½ cup cottage cheese
- 1 pound ground beef
- 1 tablespoon taco seasoning

Directions
1. Preheat the oven to 425ºF and lightly grease a baking dish.
2. Mix together the taco seasoning and ground beef in a bowl.
3. Stir in the cottage cheese, salsa and cheddar cheese.
4. Transfer the ground beef mixture to the baking dish and top with cheese mixture.
5. Bake for about 25 minutes and remove from the oven to serve warm.

Mustard Beef Steaks

Serves: **4** | Prep Time: **40** mins

Ingredients
- 2 tablespoons butter
- 2 tablespoons Dijon mustard
- 1 tablespoon fresh rosemary, coarsely chopped
- 4 beef steaks
- Salt and black pepper, to taste

Directions
1. Marinate the beef steaks with Dijon mustard, fresh rosemary, salt and black pepper for about 2 hours.
2. Put the butter and marinated beef steaks in a nonstick skillet.
3. Cover the lid and cook for about 30 minutes on medium low heat.
4. Dish out when completely cooked and serve hot.

Beef Roast

Serves: **6** | Prep Time: **55** mins

Ingredients
- 2 pounds beef
- Salt and black pepper, to taste
- 1 cup onion soup
- 2 teaspoons lemon juice
- 1 cups beef broth

Directions
1. Put the beef in a pressure cooker and stir in the beef broth, lemon juice, onion soup, salt and black pepper. Lock the lid and cook at High Pressure for about 40 minutes.
2. Naturally release the pressure and dish out on a platter to serve.

Minced Meat

Serves: **4** | Prep Time: **30** mins

Ingredients
- 1 pound ground lamb meat
- 1 cup onions, chopped
- 2 tablespoons ginger garlic paste
- 3 tablespoons butter
- Salt and cayenne pepper, to taste

Directions
1. Put the butter in a pot and add garlic, ginger and onions.
2. Sauté for about 3 minutes and add ground meat and all the spices.
3. Cover the lid and cook for about 20 minutes on medium high heat.
4. Dish out to a large serving bowl and serve hot.

Taco Casserole

Serves: **8** | Prep Time: **55** mins

Ingredients
- 2 pounds ground beef
- 1 tablespoon extra-virgin olive oil
- Taco seasoning mix, kosher salt and black pepper
- 2 cups Mexican cheese, shredded
- 6 large eggs, lightly beaten

Directions
1. Preheat the oven to 360ºF and grease a 2 quart baking dish.
2. Heat oil over medium heat in a large skillet and add ground beef.
3. Season with taco seasoning mix, kosher salt and black pepper.
4. Cook for about 5 minutes on each side and dish out to let cool slightly.
5. Whisk together eggs in the beef mixture and transfer the mixture to the baking dish. Top with Mexican cheese and bake for about 25 minutes until set. Remove from the oven and serve warm.

Ice-Burgers

Serves: **4** | Prep Time: **30** mins

Ingredients
- 4 slices bacon, cooked and crisped
- 1 large head iceberg lettuce, sliced into 8 rounds
- 1 pound ground beef
- 4 slices cheddar cheese
- Kosher salt and black pepper, to taste

Directions
1. Make 4 large patties out of ground beef and season both sides with salt and black pepper.
2. Grill for about 10 minutes per side and top with cheddar cheese slices.
3. Place one iceberg round on a plate and layer with grilled beef. Place a slice of bacon and close with second iceberg round. Repeat with the remaining ingredients and serve warm.

Beef in Cheese Taco Shells

Serves: **4** | Prep Time: **30** mins

Ingredients
- 2 cups cheddar cheese, shredded
- 1 tablespoon olive oil
- 1 tablespoon taco seasoning
- Freshly ground black pepper, to taste
- 1 pound ground beef

Directions
1. Preheat the oven to 375ºF and grease a baking dish.
2. Arrange cheddar cheese on the baking sheet and season with black pepper.
3. Bake for about 7 minutes until cheese melts and becomes slightly crispy.
4. Form shells with the help of a wooden spoon and allow them to cool.
5. Meanwhile, heat oil in a large skillet over medium heat and add ground beef.
6. Cook for about 10 minutes and season with taco seasoning. Place beef in the shells and serve.

Mexican Ground Beef

Serves: **3** | Prep Time: **30** mins

Ingredients
- 1 pound ground beef
- ½ cup cheddar cheese, shredded
- 2 tablespoons organic Mexican seasoning
- ¼ cup water
- Salt and black pepper, to taste

Directions
1. Put beef in a nonstick pan and season with salt and black pepper.
2. Cook for about 8 minutes until brown and pour in the water and Mexican seasoning. Cook for about 5 minutes and dish out in a bowl to serve.

Cheesesteak Stuffed Peppers

Serves: **4** | Prep Time: **55** mins

Ingredients
- 16 oz. cremini mushrooms, sliced
- 4 bell peppers, halved
- Italian seasoning, kosher salt and black pepper
- 16 provolone cheese slices
- 1½ pounds sirloin steak, thinly sliced

Directions
1. Preheat the oven to 325ºF and grease a large baking dish.
2. Arrange bell peppers in the baking dish and transfer to the oven.
3. Bake for about 30 minutes until tender and dish out.
4. Grease a nonstick pan and add mushrooms, Italian seasoning, kosher salt and black pepper. Cook for about 6 minutes and add sirloin steak.
5. Cook for about 3 minutes, stirring occasionally and dish out.
6. Put provolone cheese to the bottom of baked bell peppers and top with steak mixture.
7. Top with the rest of provolone cheese and broil for about 3 minutes until golden. Serve .

Beef with Green Olives and Prunes

Serves: **4** | Prep Time: **40** mins

Ingredients
- 2 tablespoons salted butter
- 1¼ pounds beef
- 1 cup reduced sodium chicken broth
- ¼ cup prunes, pitted and chopped
- ¼ cup green olives, pitted and chopped

Directions
1. Heat butter in a large nonstick skillet over medium high heat and add beef.
2. Cook for about 2 minutes per side until browned and add broth.
3. Bring to a simmer, stirring occasionally and add olives and prunes.
4. Reduce heat to low and cover with lid.
5. Cook until the beef is tender and no longer pink in the center, 12 to 15 minutes.
6. Transfer beef to a plate and serve hot.

Stir Fried Spicy Beef Steaks

Serves: **7** | Prep Time: **30** mins

Ingredients
- Cayenne pepper, paprika, salt and black pepper
- 3 tablespoons olive oil
- 1 scoop Stevia
- 1½ pounds top round steaks
- 1 (16 ounce) package frozen bell pepper and onion mix

Directions
1. Mix together Stevia, cayenne pepper, paprika, salt and black pepper in a bowl.
2. Add top round steaks and toss to coat well. Cover and refrigerate overnight.
3. Heat olive oil in a large nonstick skillet over high heat and add bell pepper and onion mix.
4. Cook for about 7 minutes, stirring occasionally and add the spice rubbed steaks.
5. Cook for about 15 minutes and dish out to serve hot.

Sausage Balls

Serves: **6** | Prep Time: **35** mins

Ingredients
- 1 cup blanched almond flour
- 1 pound bulk Italian sausage
- 1¼ cups sharp cheddar cheese, shredded
- 2 teaspoons baking powder
- 1 large egg

Directions

1. Preheat the oven to 350°F and place a wire rack on the baking sheet.
2. Mix together all the ingredients in a large bowl until well incorporated.
3. Form small meatballs out of the meat mixture and arrange them on the wire rack.
4. Bake for about 20 minutes until golden brown and remove from the oven to serve hot.

Cumin Spiced Beef Wraps

Serves: **6** | Prep Time: **25** mins

Ingredients

- 2 pounds ground beef
- Salt and black pepper, to taste
- 8 large cabbage leaves, boiled for 20 seconds and plunged in cold water
- 3 tablespoons coconut oil
- 2 teaspoons cumin

Directions

1. Heat coconut oil in a pan on medium heat and add the ground beef.
2. Sauté for about 5 minutes and add cumin, salt and black pepper.
3. Place the cabbage leaves on a plate and spoon the ground beef mixture on it.
4. Fold into a roll and serve warm.

Creamy Mexican Beef

Serves: **6** | Prep Time: **9 hours 5** mins

Ingredients

- ½ cup beef stock
- 2 tablespoons homemade taco seasoning
- 1 cup sour cream
- 1 (14 oz) can diced tomatoes and green chilies
- 2 pounds boneless beef

Directions

1. Put all the ingredients in a slow cooker and close the lid.
2. Cover and cook on LOW for about 9 hours. Dish out and serve hot.

Beef with Carrots

Serves: **8** | Prep Time: **8 hours 10** mins

Ingredients

- 1 large onion, thinly sliced
- 2 pounds beef, boneless
- 4 medium carrots, peeled and sliced lengthwise
- Salt and black pepper, to taste
- 1 teaspoon dried oregano, crushed

Directions

1. Season the beef with dried oregano, salt and black pepper.
2. Transfer beef to a bowl and set aside for at least 3 hours.
3. Place onion and carrots at the bottom of a slow cooker and top with beef.
4. Cover the lid and cook on LOW for about 8 hours. Dish out and serve hot.

Creamy Garlic Beef Soup

Serves: **8** | Prep Time: **40** mins

Ingredients

- 2 cups beef meat, shredded
- 2 cups chicken broth
- Salt, to taste
- 1 cup cream cheese, cubed
- ¼ cup heavy cream

Directions

1. Put beef along with all other ingredients in a pressure cooker.
2. Cover the lid and cook on High Pressure for about 30 minutes.
3. Naturally release the pressure and dish out to serve hot.

Paprika Mushroom Beef

Serves: **8** | Prep Time: **45** mins

Ingredients

- 2 tablespoons butter
- 2 pounds beef
- ¾ cup sour cream
- Paprika, salt and black pepper, to taste
- 1 cup white mushrooms

Directions

1. Season the beef with paprika, salt and black pepper.
2. Put butter in a skillet and add seasoned beef.
3. Sauté for about 4 minutes and add mushrooms and sour cream.
4. Cover the lid and cook for about 30 minutes. Dish out and serve hot.

Pesto Parmesan Beef Steaks

Serves: **6** | Prep Time: **8 hours 10** mins

Ingredients
- 1 cup parmesan cheese, shredded
- 6 beef steaks
- 6 tablespoons pesto sauce
- Salt and black pepper, to taste
- ½ cup parsley, chopped

Directions
1. Season the beef steaks with salt and black pepper. Drizzle with pesto sauce and put in the slow cooker.
2. Cover and cook on Low for about 7 hours. Top with Parmesan cheese and parsley.
3. Cook again on Low for about 1 hour and dish out to serve.

Bacon Garlic Beef Tenderloins

Serves: **6** | Prep Time: **40** mins

Ingredients
- 2 pounds beef tenderloins
- 6 garlic cloves, minced
- 1 tablespoon canola oil
- 6 slices bacon, thick cut
- Salt and black pepper, to taste

Directions
1. Rub the beef tenderloins with garlic, salt and black pepper.
2. Wrap the beef tenderloins with the bacon slices. Put the canola oil and wrapped beef in a skillet.
3. Cook on all sides for about 30 minutes on medium low heat. Dish out and serve hot.

Italian Beef Steaks

Serves: **5** | Prep Time: **50** mins

Ingredients
- ¾ cup cream cheese
- 1½ pounds beef steaks
- 1 tablespoon butter
- 1 teaspoon Italian seasoning
- ¾ cup mozzarella cheese, grated

Directions
1. Mix the mozzarella cheese, Italian seasoning and cream cheese in a bowl.
2. Heat butter in a skillet and add beef steaks.
3. Sauté for about 3 minutes on each side and stir in the cheese mixture.
4. Cover and cook for about 30 minutes on medium low heat. Dish out and serve hot.

BLT Burgers

Serves: **4** | Prep Time: **35** mins

Ingredients
- 1 pound ground beef
- 1 pound bacon slices, halved
- Kosher salt and black pepper, to taste
- 4 butterhead lettuce, for serving
- ½ cup mayonnaise

Directions
1. Preheat a grill pan to medium high heat.
2. Season the ground beef with kosher salt and black pepper. Make large patties out of this mixture and transfer to the grill pan. Grill for about 4 minutes on each side and dish out.
3. Place bacon slices at the bottom of a plate and spread with mayonnaise.
4. Top with beef and lettuce and close with the bacon slices. Serve immediately.

Pork Recipes

Feta & Spinach Stuffed Pork

Yield: 4 | Total Time: 30 Mins | Prep Time: 10 Mins | Cook Time: 20 Mins

Ingredients
- 4 (6-ounce) pork chops, butterflied
- 1/3 cup crumbled feta
- 1/2 cup frozen spinach
- 2 tablespoons coconut oil
- 1/4 teaspoon dried parsley
- 1/4 teaspoon dried oregano
- 1/4 teaspoon garlic powder
- 1 cup water
- 1/4 teaspoon pepper
- 11/4 teaspoons salt, divided

Directions
1. Pound the pork chops to ¼-inch thickness. In a large bowl, mix together feta cheese, spinach and salt; divide the mixture onto the pork chops and close the chops with butcher's string or toothpicks. Set your instant pot on sauté mode and heat coconut oil; sear the pork chops for about 7 Mins per side or until golden browned. Press the cancel button. Remove the pork chops and pour in water; insert a metal trivet and place the chops on the trivet. Lock lid and cook on high for 15 Mins. Quick release the pressure and then serve chops with favorite low carb sauce.

Pressure Cooked Sour Cream Pork Chops

Yield: 4 | Total Time: 30 Mins | Prep Time: 10 Mins | Cook Time: 20 Mins

Ingredients
- 4 boneless pork chops
- 2 medium onions, chopped
- 1 coconut oil
- 1/3 cup sour cream
- 1 teaspoon arrowroot
- 1 teaspoon Worcestershire sauce
- 1 cup beef stock
- salt and pepper

Directions

Set your instant pot on sauté mode and heat in oil; sauté onions until tender. Add in pork chops and stir in salt and pepper. Switch to the pot and then stir in Worcestershire sauce and beef stock. Lock lid and cook on high for 8 Mins and then let pressure come down on its own. Set the pot on simmer and stir in a mix of arrowroot and water. Cook for 5 Mins and then stir in sour cream. Serve hot.

Four-Ingredient Pork Chops

Yield: 4 | Total Time: 20 Mins | Prep Time: 10 Mins | Cook Time: 10 Mins

Ingredients
- 4 medium pork chops
- 2 tablespoons olive oil
- 1/2 cup water
- 2 tablespoons BBQ sauce

Directions
1. Set your instant pot on sauté mode and heat in oil; brown in the meat and transfer to a plate.
2. Stir in water and then add in BBQ sauce; return the meat and lock lid. Cook on high for 5 Mins and the let pressure come down on its own. Serve hot.

Instant Pot Low Lime Carb Pork Carnitas

Yield: 4 | Total Time: 1 Hour 40 Mins | Prep Time: 10 Mins | Cook Time: 1 Hour 10 Mins

Ingredients
- 2 tablespoons olive oil
- 4 pounds boneless pork shoulder, diced
- 4 garlic cloves diced
- 1/2 onion diced
- 1 jalapeño pepper, chopped
- 1/2 cup chicken stock
- 1 tablespoon orange zest
- 2 tablespoons fresh orange juice
- 2 tablespoons lime zest
- ½ cup fresh lime juice
- 1/2 teaspoon dried oregano
- 2 teaspoons smoked paprika
- 2 teaspoons ground cumin
- 1 dried bay leaf
- salt and pepper

Directions

Set your instant pot on sauté mode and heat oil; brown the meat and transfer to a plate. Add onions, salt and pepper to the pot and cook for 2 Mins and then stir in garlic for 20 seconds. Stir in the remaining ingredients and return the pork meat. Lock lid and cook on high for 90 Mins. Let pressure come down on its own. Serve the pork in lettuce leaves drizzled with lime juice. Enjoy!

Low Carb Pork Tenderloin

Yield: 4 | Total Time: 35 Mins | Prep Time; 10 Mins | Cook Time: 25 Mins

Ingredients:
- 4 tablespoons olive oil, divided
- 6 cloves garlic
- 1 ½ pounds pork tenderloin
- ½ teaspoon Italian herbs
- 1 teaspoon salt
- ½ teaspoon pepper
- 1 head broccoli
- 1 medium onion

Directions
1. Set your instant pot on manual high. Poke holes all over pork tenderloin with a folk; stuff the holes with minced garlic and rub the pork with a tablespoon of olive oil, herbs, salt and pepper. Heat another tablespoon of olive oil in the pot and then add the pork tenderloin; cook for about 6 Mins or until browned on all sides. Add in the remaining oil and then stir in onions and broccoli. Lock lid and cook on high for 20 Mins. Let pressure come down on its own.
2. Remove the pork from the pot and let rest for at least 10 Mins before serving.

Pressure Cooked Parmesan Dijon Crusted Pork Chops

Yield: 4 | Total Time: 45 Mins | Prep Time: 15 Mins | Cook Time: 30 Mins

Ingredients
- 4 boneless pork loin chops
- 2 tablespoons olive oil
- 1/4 teaspoon Italian seasoning
- 2 tablespoons spiced brown mustard
- 1/4 cup Dijon mustard
- 1/4 teaspoon dried oregano
- 1/4 teaspoon onion powder
- 1/2 teaspoon dried thyme
- 1/2 teaspoon garlic powder
- 1/4 teaspoon dried basil
- 1/4 teaspoon sea salt
- 1/4 teaspoon black pepper
- 1 cup grated Parmesan cheese
- 4 cups kale, chopped
- 2 tablespoons butter
- 2 red onions

Directions

1. Rub the pork chops with sea salt and pepper. In a bowl, mix together olive oil, spicy brown mustard, Italian seasoning, Dijon mustard, oregano, onion powder, thyme, garlic powder, and basil. Dust the pork chops with the spice mixture until well coated. Set your instant pot on manual high; add oil and cook in the pork chops for 5 Mins per side. Add water to the pot and insert a metal trivet.
2. Spread cheese in a single layer on a plate; coat the chops generously with the cheese. Arrange the chops on aluminum foil and place over the trivet. Lock the pot and cook on high for 20 Mins and then quick release the pressure. Transfer the pork to the oven and broil on high for about 5 Mins or until crispy and golden brown.
3. Meanwhile, heat butter in a skillet over medium heat; sauté onions until fragrant and stir in kale. Cook for 3 Mins or until wilted. Serve the pork chops with sautéed kale.

Shredded Pressure-Cooked Pork with Green Salad and Avocado

Yield: 6 | Total Time: 2 Hours 10 Mins | Prep Time: 10 Mins | Cook Time: 2 Hours

Ingredients

- 1/4 cup butter
- 3 pounds pork roast
- 2 cups chicken stock
- 1 batch taco seasoning
- 8 cups green salad
- 2 avocados, diced

Directions

1. Set your instant pot on manual high and melt butter; brown pork roast and add in chicken stock and taco seasoning; lock lid and cook on high for 2 hours. Let pressure come down on its own. When ready, shred the meat with fork. Serve with green salad topped with diced avocado.

Instant Pot Pork Chops with Bacon & Caramelized Onions

Yield: 4 | Total Time: 50 Mins | Prep Time: 10 Mins | Cook Time: 40 Mins

Ingredients

- 4 large boneless pork chops
- 4 slices bacon, diced
- 4 tablespoons butter
- 1 large onion, sliced
- salt and pepper to taste
- 1/2 cup chicken broth
- 1/4 cup heavy cream
- 1 tablespoon water
- 1 teaspoon arrowroot

Directions

1. Set your instant pot on manual high; add bacon and cook until crispy; transfer to a plate and keep warm. Add butter to the pot and sauté onions until fragrant; stir in salt and cook onions until caramelized. Transfer the onions to another plate and keep warm.
2. Sprinkle the pork chops with sea salt and pepper; add to pot and cook for about 3 Mins per side.
3. In a bowl, stir together arrowroot powder and water; whisk in cream and chicken broth until smooth. Add to the pork chops and lock lid. Cook on high for 20 Mins and then quick release the pressure. Top with bacon and caramelized onions and cook on manual high for about 10 Mins. Serve hot!

Instant Pot BBQ Pork Wraps

Yield: 2 | Total Time: 2 Hours 15 Mins | Prep Time: 15 Mins | Cook Time: 2 Hours

Ingredients

- 2 (200-gram) boneless pork ribs
- 1 1/2 cups beef broth
- 2 tbsp. barbeque sauce
- 4 lettuce leaves

Directions

1. Combine pork ribs and bone broth in your instant pot and cook on high setting for 1 ½ hours. Let pressure come down naturally. Shred pork and transfer to a baking dish; stir in barbecue sauce and bake at 350°F for about 30 Mins. Divide the pork among lettuce leaves and roll to form wraps. Serve.

Pork & Mushroom Dumplings

Yield: 6 | Total Time: 12 Mins | Prep Time: 10 Mins | Cook Time: 2 Mins

Ingredients

- 1 ¾ pounds ground pork
- 1 egg, beaten
- 3 tbsp. sesame oil
- 4 tbsp. soy sauce
- 2 tbsp. sliced green onion
- 4 cloves garlic, minced
- 1 cup mushrooms, minced
- 1 tbsp. minced ginger
- 100 wonton wrappers, sliced into circles
- Sliced green onions

Directions

1. In a bowl, mix together pork, egg, sesame oil, soy sauce, green onion, ginger, and garlic until well combined. Lay down the wonton wrapper and wet the edges; add three teaspoons of the mixture in the center and roll up to wrap. Insert a steamer basket in your instant pot and add a cup of water; arrange the shumai in the basket in a single layer and then lock lid. Cook on manual high for 2 Mins. Let pressure come down naturally and then remove the shumai. Serve garnished with more green onions.

Instant Pot Low Carb Spiced Pork Chops

Yield: 4 | Total Time: 1 Hour 40 Mins | Prep Time: 10 Mins | Cook Time: 1 Hour 30 Mins

Ingredients
- 2 pounds pork chops
- 3 heads garlic, cut in half across
- 3 brown onions, cut into wedges
- 200g cauliflower
- 200g broccoli
- 200g green beans
- 1 pouch cheese sauce
- 2 tbsp. seasoning blend

Directions
1. Add water to an instant pot and insert a metal trivet.
2. On an aluminum foil, combine garlic and onion; sprinkle with olive oil.
3. Rub the pork chops seasoning blend into the pork and place it on top of the bed of garlic and onion; fold the foil to wrap the contents and place over the trivet. Lock lid and cook on high for 90 Mins. Release pressure naturally.
4. Transfer the chops to the oven and broil for about 20 Mins or until browned and crisp on the outside.

Barbecued Pork Chops with Broccoli

Yield: 4 | Total Time: 1 Hour 5 Mins | Prep Time: 10 Mins | Cook Time: 55 Mins

Ingredients
- 1 tsp. bottled BBQ sauce
- ½ tsp. garlic powder
- 4 pork chops, 1-inch thick
- 1 cup non-fat milk
- Salt and pepper
- 5 cups frozen broccoli florets (450g)

Directions
1. Generously sprinkle pork chops with BBQ sauce and garlic powder. Set your instant pot on manual high and add in the pork chops, cook turning once, for about 10 Mins or until cooked through. Add in milk and lock lid. Cook on high for 30 Mins and then quick release the pressure.
2. Place broccoli in a microwave-safe pot and cover; microwave on high for about 5 Mins; remove from heat and let stand. Microwave again for 2 Mins and serve with the pork chops.

Bone-In Pork Chops

Yield: 6 | Total Time: 35 Mins | Prep Time: 15 Mins | Cook Time: 20 Mins

Ingredients
- 3 ¾ inch thick bone-in pork chops
- 3 russet potatoes
- 1/4 cup butter,
- 3 tbsp. Worcestershire sauce
- 1 cup vegetable broth
- 1 onion, chopped
- 1 cup baby carrots
- Salt & pepper

Directions
1. Season the pork chops with salt and pepper.
2. Melt two tablespoons of butter in your instant pot set on sauté mode; brown the pork chops in batches and then transfer to a platter.
3. Add the remaining butter to the pot and cook onion and carrots for about 2 Mins; stir in Worcestershire sauce and then add in the pork chops. Add potatoes in a steamer basket and place it in the pot; lock lid and cook on high for 13 Mins. Let pressure come down naturally and then slice the potatoes. Serve with pork chops.

Pork Roast w/ Cauliflower Gravy

Yield: 6 | Total Time: 1 Hour 45 Mins | Prep Time: 15 Mins | Cook Time: 1 Hour 30 Mins

Ingredients
- 3-pound pork roast
- 4 cloves garlic
- 1 red onion, chopped
- 4 cups chopped cauliflower
- 2 ribs celery
- 2 tbsp. organic coconut oil
- 1 cup sliced portabella mushrooms
- 1 tsp. sea salt
- ½ tsp. black pepper
- 2 cups filtered water

Directions
1. Add garlic, onion, cauliflower, water and celery to your instant pot; add pork and season with salt and pepper; lock lid and cook on high for 1 hour and then let pressure come down on own.
2. Transfer pork to a baking dish and bake at 400⁰F for about 15 Mins.
3. Meanwhile, transfer cooked veggies along with broth to a blender and blend until very smooth.
4. Add coconut oil to your pot and set on sauté mode; add mushrooms and cook for about 5 Mins or until tender; stir in veggie puree and cook until thick.
5. Serve shredded pork with mushroom gravy.

Italian Pulled Pork Ragu

Yield: 6 | Total Time: 1 Hour | Prep Time: 10 Mins | Cook Time: 50 Mins

Ingredients:
- 1 pound pork tenderloin
- 1 tsp. kosher salt
- black pepper, to taste
- 4 tablespoons olive oil
- 5 cloves garlic, minced
- 4 cups crushed tomatoes
- 1 cup roasted red peppers
- 2 sprigs fresh thyme
- 2 bay leaves
- 1 tbsp. chopped fresh parsley, divided

Directions:
1. Season the pork with salt and pepper.
2. Set your instant pot on sauté mode and add oil; sauté garlic for about two Mins until tender and then add pork; brown for about two Mins per side and then stir in the remaining ingredients.
3. Lock lid and cook on high for 45 Mins. Release the pressure naturally and serve.

Instant Pot Herbed Pork

Yield: 4 | Total Time: 45 Mins | Prep Time: 10 Mins | Cook Time: 35 Mins

Ingredients
- 8 pork chops
- 2 Italian sausages removed from casings
- 1 medium red bell pepper, diced
- 1 small onion, thinly sliced
- 4 cloves garlic, pressed
- 2 tablespoons dry vermouth
- ¼ cup fresh parsley, chopped
- 1 teaspoon corn starch
- ¼ tsp coarsely ground pepper
- ½ tsp dried oregano
- 2 tsps. dried rosemary
- 2 tbsp. cold water
- Salt

Directions
1. Combine onion, garlic, bell pepper, rosemary and oregano in your instant pot. Crumble the sausages over the mixture, casings removed. Arrange the pork in a single layer over the sausage and sprinkle with pepper. Add the vermouth and lock lid; cook on high for 30 Mins. Naturally release the pressure.
2. Move the pork to a warm, deep platter and cover.
3. Mix the corn starch with the water in a small bowl and add this to the liquid in the pot. Lock lid and cook on high for 2 Mins; season with salt. Pour the soup over the pork and garnish with parsley.Enjoy!

Pressure Cooked Jamaican Jerk Pork Roast

Yield: 6 | Total Time: 55 Mins | Prep Time: 10 Mins | Cook Time: 45 Mins

Ingredients
- 2-pound pork shoulder
- 1 tbsp. extra-virgin olive oil
- 1/4 cup Jamaican Jerk spice blend
- 1/2 cup beef stock

Directions
1. Thoroughly rub pork roast with oil and coat with spice blend. Brown the meat in your instant pot under sauté mode and then add in beef broth. Lock lid and cook on manual for 45 Mins and then release pressure naturally. Serve.

Instant Pot Crisp Chinese pork with Yummy Broccoli Mash

Yield: 4 | Total Time: 50 Mins | Prep Time: 10 Mins | Cook Time: 40 Mins

Ingredients
- 1-pound piece boned pork
- 3 tablespoons olive oil
- 2 tsp. Chinese five-spice powder

For dipping sauce
- 1 spring onion, finely chopped
- 1 tbsp. Thai sweet chilli sauce
- 1 tbsp. minced ginger
- 4 tbsp. soy sauce

Yummy Broccoli Mash
- 600g fresh/ frozen broccoli
- 4 tablespoons butter
- 1 tsp sea salt
- Freshly ground pepper to taste
- 1/4 cup full fat extra virgin coconut milk

Directions
Make the Broccoli Mash: Pour about an inch of water in a medium pot and bring it to a boil, add a steamer basket or colander and steam the broccoli for 5 Mins. Drain and pulse the broccoli in a food processor or blender. Add in butter, salt, pepper and coconut milk and continue pulsing to make a mash.
1. Rub pork with two teaspoons salt and 5-spice and chill, uncovered, in the fridge for at least 2 hours.
2. When ready, add water to your instant pot and insert a metal trivet. Drizzle pork with olive oil and season with salt and pepper; place over the trivet and lock lid. Cook on high for 40 Mins and let pressure come down on its own. Remove from the pot and place it over a chopping board and let it rest for at least 10 Mins before serving. Mix all dipping ingredients and stir in two tablespoons of water. Serve pork with sauce and broccoli mash. Enjoy!

Instant Pot Pork Salad

Yield: 4 | Total Time: 40 Mins | Prep Time: 10 Mins | Cook Time: 30 Mins

Ingredients
For the salads
- Salad greens
- 2 plum tomatoes, sliced
- 1 pound pork
- 3 tablespoons olive oil
- ½ cup chopped nuts

Dressing
- 2/3 cup buttermilk
- half of an avocado
- 8-10 chives
- 1 clove of garlic, chopped
- 4 fresh basil leaves
- 1 teaspoon dried minced red onion
- A sprig fresh rosemary
- 1/2 teaspoon dried dill
- A few leaves of fresh parsley
- 1/2 liquid Stevia
- pinch of chicory powder
- 1/4 teaspoon sea salt
- Pinch of pepper

Directions
1. Drizzle pork with olive oil and season with salt and pepper. Add water to an instant pot and insert a trivet; place pork over the trivet and lock lid. Cook on high for 30 Mins and then let pressure come down on its own. Transfer the pork to the oven and cook at 350 degrees for 10 Mins or until crispy.
2. Slice the pork to serve. Mix salad ingredients and divide among serving plates; top each with steak slices, tomato, and mango.
3. In a food processor or blender, blend together dressing ingredients until very smooth; pour over salad and toss to coat well. Enjoy!

Instant Pot Citrus Pork

Yield: 4 | Total Time: 1 Hour 25 Mins | Prep Time: 10 Mins | Cook Time: 1 Hour 15 Mins

Ingredients
- 2 pounds pork
- 1 red onion, minced
- Juice of ½ lemon
- Pinch of lemon zest
- Pinch of saffron
- Pinch of ground coriander
- Pinch of ginger
- Pinch of salt & pepper

Directions:
1. Soak saffron in fresh lemon juice; crush into paste and then add dry spices.
2. Dip in pork and rub remaining spices into pork; sprinkle with salt and pepper and wrap in foil.
3. Heat oil in the instant pot on manual high and cook pork for 5 Mins per side or until browned. Remove and transfer to foil. Wrap and set aside. Add water to an instant pot and insert a trivet; place the pork over the trivet and lock lid and cook on manual high for 1 hour.

Instant Pot BBQ Pork Ribs

Yield: 5 | Total Time: 2 Hours | Prep Time: 30 Mins | Cook Time: 1 Hour 30 Mins

Ingredients
- 4 tablespoons olive oil
- 2 ½ pounds pork ribs
- 1 cup barbeque sauce
- 1 tablespoon garlic powder
- 2 tablespoons sea salt
- 1 teaspoon ground black pepper
- 5 cups steamed broccoli

Directions
1. Add oil to an instant pot and set on sauté mode, but not smoking. Add in the pork ribs and cook until seared on both sides. Add in enough water to cover the pork ribs and season with salt, garlic powder and pepper. Lock lid and cook on meat/stew for 20 Mins and the quick release the pressure.
2. Preheat your oven to 325 degrees.

Transfer the ribs to a baking dish and pour over the barbecue sauce. Cover with foil and bake for about 1 hour 30 Mins. Remove and let rest for at least 10 Mins before serving. Serve with steamed broccoli. Enjoy!

Instant Pot Spiced Pork Chops

Yield: 4 | Prep Time: 5 Mins | Cook Time: 10 Mins | Total Time: 15 Mins

Ingredients
Pork Chops
- 4 (100g each) boneless pork chops
- ½ tsp garlic paste
- 1 tsp lemon juice
- 1 tbsp. Worcestershire sauce
- 4 tbsp. olive oil
- ½ tsp ground cumin
- ½ tsp onion powder
- 1 tsp paprika
- A pinch of salt
- A pinch of pepper

Steamed Veggies
- 1 head broccoli, cut into florets
- 1 head cauliflower, cut into florets
- 2 zucchinis, halved and sliced
- 5 ginger-lemongrass tea bags
- A two-inch ginger root, chopped roughly
- Freshly ground pepper to taste

Directions

1. **Prepare the Veggies:** Add the water to the bottom of an instant pot and add the chopped ginger. Add the tea bags once the water boils together with the pepper and a pinch of salt. Let the tea steep for 5 Mins. Add the steamer basket or colander start by placing the broccoli and cauliflower at the bottom. Season with salt and pepper and top with zucchini. Lock lid and cook on high for 5 Mins and then quick release the pressure.
2. **For the Pork Chops:** Combine all ingredients in a bag; add in the pork chops and massage the marinade around the meat. Remove the meat from the marinade and discard the marinade; season the meat with salt and pepper. Cook the pork in the pot on manual high 5 Mins per side or until cooked through.
3. Serve the pork chops with the steamed veggies. Enjoy!

Instant Pot Pork Chops

Yield: 2 | Total Time: 15 Mins | Prep Time: 5 Mins | Cook Time: 10 Mins

Ingredients

- 2 boneless pork chops
- 4 slices tomato
- 2 slices of fresh mozzarella
- 1 tbsp. olive oil
- 1 tbsp. butter
- A pinch of sea salt
- A pinch of pepper
- 2 cups green salad to serve

Directions

1. Rub the pork chops with salt and pepper; melt butter and olive oil in an instant pot. Add the pork chops and sear for about 3 Mins per side.
2. Transfer the pork chops to a baking sheet and place tomato slices and mozzarella cheese on top. Broil the meat on high for 5 Mins or until cheese is melted. Serve with a green salad.

Lemon & Herb Pork Chops

Yield: 4 | Total Time: 35 Mins | Prep Time: 5 Mins | Cook Time: 30 Mins

Ingredients

- 4 large bone in thick pork chops
- 1 tbsp. Italian seasoning
- 1/3 cup lemon juice
- 1 tbsp. minced garlic
- 3 tbsp. extra virgin olive oil
- 1 teaspoon salt

Steamed Spring Veggies

- 3 small zucchinis, quartered lengthways
- 1 bunch asparagus, woody ends removed
- 1 bunch baby carrots, trimmed
- 1 tbsp. white balsamic vinegar
- 2 tsp. fresh lemon zest
- 40g butter

Directions

1. **Prepare the Veggies:** Place the baby carrots in a steamer set over a saucepan of boiling water; cover and cook for about 5 Mins. Add zucchini and asparagus and cook, covered, for 2 Mins more or until the veggies are tender crisp. In a large frying pan, heat butter until melted and foamy; add the lemon zest and cook for about 30 seconds. Stir in the steamed veggies and vinegar; toss until well coated. Season with salt and pepper and serve.
2. **For the Pork Chops:** In a small bowl, whisk together olive oil, lemon juice, Italian seasoning, garlic and salt until well combined. In a plastic bag, combine the pork chops and marinade; seal and shake to coat the chops well and then refrigerate overnight. When ready, set your instant pot on manual high and add in oil. Cook the pork chops for 10 Mins per side and remove from the pot. Add water to the pot and insert a trivet. Place the chops on the trivet and cook on meat setting for 10 Mins. Let pressure come down on its own.

Instant Pot Pork Rind Stuffed Peppers

Yield: 4 | Total Time: 30 Mins | Prep Time: 10 Mins | Cook Time: 20 Mins

Ingredients

- 1 tablespoon butter
- 3 Green/red/yellow peppers, top parts cut off
- 1/2 cup celery, chopped
- 2 tablespoons onion, chopped
- 5 ounces pork rinds, crushed
- 2 eggs
- 2 ounces chicken broth
- 2 tablespoons heavy cream
- Pepper
- 1 teaspoon granular Splenda
- Poultry seasoning

Directions

1. Melt butter in a skillet and sauté onion, celery and seasonings until onion is tender. Transfer to a bowl and mix in all ingredients, except the peppers. Stuff the mixture into each pepper and arrange them on a foil. Add water to an instant pot and insert a metal trivet; place the peppers over the trivet and lock lid. Cook on high for 20 Mins and then let pressure come down on its own.

Instant Spiced Pork Chops

Yield: 4 | Total Time: 2 Hours 10 Mins | Prep Time: 10 Mins | Cook Time: 2 Hours

Ingredients

- 2 pounds pork chops
- 4 tbsp. olive oil
- 1 tbsp. fennel seeds
- 1 tbsp. chives chopped, fresh
- 1 tbsp. curry powder dried
- 1 tbsp. thyme dried
- 1 tbsp. rosemary dried
- 1 tbsp. ground cumin
- 1 tsp salt
- 4 cups chopped cauliflower, steamed

Directions

1. In a bowl, mix together fennel seeds, chives, curry powder, thyme, rosemary, half of olive oil, cumin and salt until well combined; rub the pork chops with the oil-spice mixture until well coated.
2. Heat the remaining oil in the instant pot and add in pork meat. Cover and cook on high for at least 2 hours. Serve the pork chops with steamed cauliflower.

Instant Pot Cheese Crusted Pork Chops

Yield: 4 | Total Time: 46 Mins | Prep Time: 6 Mins | Cook Time: 40 Mins

Ingredients

- 4 (1 ¼ pound) boneless pork chops
- 2 tbsp. olive oil
- ½ teaspoon sea salt
- ½ teaspoon pepper
- 2 tsp water
- 1 large egg, beaten
- 1/2 cup crushed pork rinds
- 1/2 tsp lemon zest
- 1/2 cup grated parmesan cheese
- 1/2 tsp minced fresh garlic
- 1 tbsp. minced fresh parsley
- 4 cups spinach
- 1 tablespoon butter
- 2 red onions, chopped

Directions

1. Using a paper towel, pat pork dry and then season with salt and pepper.
2. In a shallow bowl, whisk together the egg and water until well combined.
3. In a bowl, mix together parmesan cheese with crushed pork rinds, parsley, lemon zest, minced garlic until well combined.
4. Add oil to an instant pot and set on sauté mode; dip the pork chops into the egg mix and then coat well with the cheese mixture. Place the coated pork chops in the pot and cook for about 3 Mins; flip over to cook the other side for 3 Mins more or until cooked through and crispy on the outside. Transfer the cooked chops to foil and wrap well. Add water to the pot and insert a trivet. Place the pork on the trivet and lock lid. Set your pot on meat/stew setting for 20 Mins. Quick release the pressure and remove the pork. Let rest for about 10 Mins before serving.
5. Heat butter in a skillet over medium heat; sauté red onions until fragrant. Stir in spinach for about 3 Mins or until wilted; season with salt and pepper and serve with pork chops.

Pork Chops in Cream Sauce served with Avocado

Yield: 6 | Total Time: 25 Mins | Prep Time: 10 Mins | Cook Time: 15 Mins

Ingredients

- 2 lb. boneless pork chops
- 4 tablespoons butter
- 4 cups sliced fresh mushrooms
- 2 cups heavy cream
- 3/4 cup white wine
- A pinch of sea salt
- A pinch of pepper
- 4 avocados, diced

Directions

1. Set your instant pot on manual high and melt in butter. Season the pork chops with sea salt and pepper; arrange the chops in the pot and fry for about 2 Mins per side or until browned. Stir in wine and cook for 6 Mins; remove the pork chops from the pot and place on a plate. Stir the cream in the pot and stir in mushrooms and pork chops and lock lid. Cook on high for 6 Mins and press venting button to release the pressure. Serve hot topped with Avocado slices. Enjoy!

Caramelized Onion Pork Chops with Steamed Green Beans and Avocado

Yield: 6 | Total Time: 45 Mins | Prep Time: 5 Mins | Cook Time: 40 Mins

Ingredients

- 4 tablespoon vegetable oil
- 2 cups sliced onions
- 2 lb. pork loin chops
- 3 teaspoons seasoning salt
- 2 teaspoons ground black pepper
- 1 onion, cut into strips
- 1 cup water
- 2 cups chopped green beans, steamed
- 3 avocados, diced

Directions

1. Season the chops with salt and pepper; heat oil in an instant pot set on manual high and brown the chops for about 5 Mins per side. Stir in onions and water and lock lid. Cook on high for 20 Mins and then quick release the pressure.
2. Meanwhile, add the remaining oil to a skillet set over medium-low heat; add in onions and cook, stirring, for about 10 Mins or until caramelized.
3. Serve the chops with caramelized onions and steamed green beans topped with avocado slices. Enjoy!

Pork Filled Egg Muffins

Serves: **6** | Prep Time: **25** mins

Ingredients

- 4 eggs
- 4 slices pork, precooked
- ½ teaspoon lemon pepper seasoning
- 4 tablespoons goat cheddar cheese, shredded
- 1 green onion, diced

Directions

1. Preheat the oven to 375ºF and grease 6 muffin molds lightly.
2. Mix together eggs, onion, pork, lemon pepper seasoning and cheddar cheese in a bowl. Pour the batter into the muffin molds and transfer to the oven.
3. Bake for about 15 minutes and take the muffins from oven to serve.

Pork Bread

Serves: **6** | Prep Time: **35** mins

Ingredients

- ½ cup almond milk
- ½ cup almond oil
- 2 pastured eggs
- ½ pound pork, precooked and shredded
- ¼ teaspoon baking soda

Directions

1. Preheat the oven to 375ºF and grease a baking dish with almond oil.
2. Mix eggs, almond milk, baking soda and pork in a bowl.
3. Pour the batter into the baking dish and transfer the oven.
4. Bake for about 20 minutes and remove from the oven. Slice and serve hot.

Garlic Creamy Pork Chops

Serves: **8** | Prep Time: **45** mins

Ingredients

- ½ cup butter
- Salt and black pepper, to taste
- 4 garlic cloves, minced
- 2 pounds pork chops
- 1½ cups heavy cream

Directions

1. Rub the pork chops with garlic, salt and black pepper.
2. Marinate the chops with butter and cream and set aside for 1 hour.
3. Preheat the grill to medium high heat and transfer the steaks to it.
4. Grill for about 15 minutes on each side and transfer to a plate and serve hot.

Pork Fajitas

Serves: **4** | Prep Time: **40 minutes**

Ingredients

- 1 tablespoon butter
- 1 bell pepper, sliced
- 1 pound pork tenderloins, sliced
- 1 tablespoon fajita seasoning
- 1 onion, sliced

Directions

1. Put the butter in the bottom of a skillet and add onions.
2. Sauté for about 3 minutes and add bell pepper.
3. Cook for about 2 minutes and stir in pork tenderloins and fajita seasoning.
4. Cover with lid and cook for about 25 minutes on medium low heat.
5. Dish out the delicious pork fajitas and serve hot.

Jamaican Jerk Pork Roast

Serves: **3** | Prep Time: **35** mins

Ingredients

- 1 tablespoon butter
- 1/8 cup beef broth
- 1 pound pork shoulder
- 1/8 cup Jamaican jerk spice blend
- Salt, to taste

Directions
1. Season the pork with Jamaican jerk spice blend.
2. Heat the butter in the pot and add seasoned pork.
3. Cook for about 5 minutes and add beef broth.
4. Cover with lid and cook for about 20 minutes on low heat.
5. Dish out on a serving platter and serve hot.

Pork Carnitas
Serves: **3** | Prep Time: **40** mins

Ingredients
- 1 pound pork shoulder, bone-in
- Salt and black pepper, to taste
- 1 tablespoon butter
- 1 orange, juiced
- ½ teaspoon garlic powder

Directions
1. Season the pork with salt and black pepper.
2. Put butter in the pressure cooker and add garlic powder.
3. Sauté for 1 minute and add seasoned pork.
4. Sauté for 3 minutes and pour orange juice.
5. Lock the lid and cook on high pressure for about 20 minutes.
6. Naturally release the pressure and dish out.
7. Shred the pork with a fork and transfer back to the cooker.
8. Sauté for about 3 minutes and serve warm.

Zesty Pork Chops
Serves: **4** | Prep Time: **50** mins

Ingredients
- 4 tablespoons butter
- 3 tablespoons lemon juice
- 4 pork chops, bone-in
- 2 tablespoons low carb flour mix
- 1 cup picante sauce

Directions
1. Coat the pork chops with low carb flour mix.
2. Mix picante sauce and lemon juice in a bowl.
3. Heat oil in a skillet on medium heat and add the chops and picante mixture.
4. Cook covered for about 35 minutes and dish out to serve hot.

Greek Pork Gyros
Serves: **4** | Prep Time: **40** mins

Ingredients
- 4 garlic cloves
- 3 teaspoons ground marjoram
- 1 pound pork meat, ground
- Salt and black pepper, to taste
- ½ small onion, chopped

Directions
1. Preheat the oven to 400°F and grease a loaf pan lightly.
2. Put onions, garlic, marjoram, salt and black pepper in a food processor and process until well combined. Add ground pork meat and process again.
3. Press meat mixture into the loaf pan until compact and very tight.
4. Tightly cover with tin foil and poke some holes in the foil.
5. Bake in the oven for about 25 minutes and dish out to serve warm.

Garlic Rosemary Pork Chops
Serves: **4** | Prep Time: **30** mins

Ingredients
- 1 tablespoon rosemary, freshly minced
- 2 garlic cloves, minced
- 4 pork loin chops
- ½ cup butter, melted
- Salt and black pepper, to taste

Directions
1. Preheat the oven to 375°F and season pork chops with salt and black pepper.
2. Mix together ¼ cup butter, rosemary and garlic in a small bowl.
3. Heat the rest of the butter in an oven safe skillet and add pork chops.
4. Sear for about 4 minutes per side until golden and brush pork chops generously with garlic butter.
5. Place skillet in the oven and bake for about 15 minutes until cooked through.
6. Dish out and serve hot.

Lemony Grilled Pork Chops

Serves: **4** | Prep Time: **20** mins

Ingredients
- 2 tablespoons extra-virgin olive oil
- 4 pork chops
- 2 tablespoons butter
- Kosher salt and black pepper, to taste
- 2 lemons, sliced

Directions
1. Preheat the grill to high heat.
2. Brush pork chops with olive oil and season with salt and black pepper.
3. Put the pork chops on grill and top with lemon slices.
4. Grill for about 10 minutes per side until lemons are charred and chops are cooked through. Dish out on a platter and serve hot.

Cheddar Maple Squash

Serves: **4** | Prep Time: **30** mins

Ingredients
- 1½ pounds summer squash, peeled, halved, seeded, and cut into 1½ inch cubes
- 1 cup aged white cheddar cheese, coarsely grated
- 1 tablespoon sugar free maple syrup
- 1 tablespoon fresh sage, chopped and crushed
- 2 slices pork bacon, cooked and chopped

Directions
1. Boil the summer squash for about 15 minutes and mash with a potato masher.
2. Stir in cheddar cheese, sage and maple syrup and top with cooked pork bacon to serve.

Spinach Pork Roll Ups

Serves: **8** | Prep Time: **15** mins

Ingredients
- 2 teaspoons honey mustard
- 8 thin slices bacon, smoked
- 1 cup Monterey Jack cheese, cut lengthwise into quarters
- 1 cup fresh baby spinach leaves
- ½ medium red bell pepper, seeded and cut into thin strips

Directions
1. Spread the honey mustard over bacon slices.
2. Divide spinach leaves among 8 plates and place bacon slices on it.
3. Top with red bell pepper and cheese to serve.

Stuffed Pork Chops

Serves: **6** | Prep Time: **40** mins

Ingredients
- 4 garlic cloves, minced
- 2 pounds cut boneless pork chops
- 2 cups baby spinach
- 1½ teaspoons salt
- 8 oz. provolone cheese

Directions
1. Preheat the oven to 350°F and grease a baking sheet.
2. Mix garlic with salt and rub on one side of the pork chops.
3. Place half of the pork chops garlic side down on a baking sheet and top with spinach and provolone cheese.
4. Top with rest of the pork chops garlic side up and place in the oven.
5. Bake for about 30 minutes and dish out to serve hot.

Pork with Butternut Squash Stew

Serves: **4** | Prep Time: **40** mins

Ingredients
- ½ pound butternut squash, peeled and cubed
- 1 pound lean pork
- 2 tablespoons butter
- Salt and black pepper, to taste
- 1 cup beef stock

Directions
1. Put the butter and lean pork in a skillet and cook for about 5 minutes.
2. Add butternut squash, beef stock and season with salt and black pepper.
3. Cover with lid and cook for about 25 minutes on medium low heat. Dish out to a bowl and serve hot.

Sweet Mustard Pork

Serves: **4** | Prep Time: **40** mins

Ingredients
- ¼ cup Dijon mustard
- 4 pork chops
- 1 tablespoon granular Erythritol
- 2 tablespoons olive oil
- ½ cup sour cream

Directions
1. Preheat the oven to 350°F.
2. Mix together Dijon mustard, Erythritol and sour cream in a bowl.
3. Combine the pork chops and half of the mustard dressing in a bowl.
4. Marinate the pork chops overnight in the refrigerator.
5. Heat olive oil over medium high heat in a large oven proof skillet and add pork. Cook for about 4 minutes on both sides until brown and pour in the remaining mustard dressing.
6. Place the skillet into the oven and bake for about 20 minutes. Dish out and serve hot.

Barbecue Dry Rub Ribs

Serves: **8** | Prep Time: **2 hours 50** mins

Ingredients
- 2 tablespoons olive oil
- 2 pounds pork baby back ribs
- Garlic powder, onion powder, chili powder and sea salt
- 1½ tablespoons smoked paprika
- 1 tablespoon Erythritol

Directions
1. Preheat the oven to 300°F and line a baking sheet with aluminum foil.
2. Mix together garlic powder, onion powder, chili powder, sea salt, Erythritol and smoked paprika in a bowl. Place the pork baby back ribs on the baking sheet and brush with olive oil.
3. Sprinkle the dry rub over both sides of the ribs and place in the oven.
4. Bake for about 2 hours until the ribs are juicy and tender. Dish out onto a platter and serve hot.

Pork Enchilada Casserole

Serves: **5** | Prep Time: **1 hour**

Ingredients
- 1 pound boneless pork
- 1½ cups enchilada sauce
- 3 cups cheddar cheese, shredded
- Salt and black pepper, to taste
- ½ cup fresh cilantro, minced

Directions
1. Preheat the oven to 450°F and grease a casserole dish with olive oil.
2. Season pork with salt and black pepper. Put the pork and 1 cup enchilada sauce in a saucepan and cook on medium low heat for about 30 minutes. Dish out the pork and shred with a fork. Combine shredded pork, ½ cup enchilada sauce and cilantro in the casserole dish and top with cheddar cheese.
3. Transfer to the oven and bake for about 15 minutes. Dish out and serve hot.

Cheesy Bacon Pork Chops

Serves: **6** | Prep Time: **50** mins

Ingredients
- ½ pound bacon, cut strips in half
- 6 pork chops
- 1 cup cheddar cheese, shredded
- Salt and black pepper, to taste
- 2 tablespoons paprika, smoked

Directions
1. Preheat the oven to 360°F and grease a baking dish. Season the pork chops with paprika, salt and black pepper. Put the pork chops in the baking dish and top with bacon.
2. Sprinkle the cheese over the pork chops and bacon and transfer to the oven.
3. Bake for about 35 minutes and dish out to serve hot.

genic Easy Pork Briskets

Serves: **6** | Prep Time: **7 hours 10** mins

Ingredients
- 1 tablespoon butter
- 2 pounds pork briskets
- 2 garlic cloves, minced
- Salt and black pepper, to taste
- 1 small onion, sliced

Directions
1. Put all the ingredients in a large slow cooker and cover the lid.
2. Cook on low for about 7 hours and dish out the pork briskets onto a cutting board. Slice with a knife into desired slices to serve.

Ground Pork with Zucchini

Serves: **6** | Prep Time: **35** mins

Ingredients
- 2 large zucchinis, chopped
- 2 pounds lean ground pork
- 3 tablespoons butter
- Salt and black pepper, to taste
- ½ cup homemade bone broth

Directions
1. Put the butter and pork in a skillet and cook for about 5 minutes.
2. Add the bone broth, zucchini, salt and black pepper.
3. Cook for about 20 minutes and dish out to serve hot.

Creamy BBQ Pork

Serves: **6** | Prep Time: **55** mins

Ingredients
- ½ cup BBQ sauce
- 2 pounds pork, boneless
- 4 tablespoons butter
- Salt, to taste
- 1 cup cream

Directions
1. Heat butter in a skillet and add pork and salt.
2. Cook for about 5 minutes and stir in the BBQ sauce and cream.
3. Cover and cook for about 35 minutes. Dish out in a bowl and serve hot.

Broccoli Pork

Serves: **4** | Prep Time: **45** mins

Ingredients
- 3 cups broccoli florets
- 1 pound pork, thinly sliced and chopped into 2 inch pieces
- 2 tablespoons butter
- 2 tablespoons cornstarch + 4 tablespoons cold water
- 1 cup bone broth

Directions
1. Heat butter on medium heat in a skillet and add pork.
2. Sauté for about 3 minutes on each side and add broccoli and bone broth.
3. Cook for about 30 minutes and stir in the cornstarch with water.
4. Cover the skillet and cook for about 4 minutes. Dish out and serve hot.

Home Style Pork Meatloaf

Serves: **4** | Prep Time: **30** mins

Ingredients
- 1 large onion, sliced
- 1 cup tomato sauce
- 1 pound ground pork
- 1 egg
- Salt and black pepper, to taste

Directions
1. Put the ground pork, salt, black pepper, egg and onion in a grinder and grind well. Mold the ground mixture into loaves. Put the tomato sauce and loaves in the pressure cooker.
2. Cook on High Pressure for about 20 minutes and dish out to serve.

Italian Pork with Veggies

Serves: **5** | Prep Time: **40** mins

Ingredients
- 2 bell peppers, sliced
- 1½ pounds pork, sliced
- 2 tablespoons butter
- 1 onion, sliced
- 2 tablespoons Italian seasoning

Directions
1. Heat butter on medium heat in a skillet and add pork.
2. Sauté for about 3 minutes and add bell pepper, onion, and Italian seasoning.
3. Cover with lid and cook for about 25 minutes. Dish out and serve hot.

Pork Taco Casserole

Serves: **6** | Prep Time: **40** mins

Ingredients
- 1 cup cottage cheese
- 2 pounds ground pork
- 2 tablespoons taco seasoning
- 1 cup salsa
- ½ cup cheddar cheese, shredded

Directions

1. Preheat the oven to 375°F and grease a casserole dish.
2. Mix the ground pork and taco seasoning in a bowl.
3. Mix together the cottage cheese, cheddar cheese and salsa.
4. Put the ground pork mixture in the casserole dish and top with the cheese mixture. Transfer to the oven and bake for about 30 minutes. Remove from the oven and serve hot.

Slow Cooker Pork Stew

Serves: **6** | Prep Time: **7 hours 10** mins

Ingredients

- 2 medium onions, chopped
- 2 pounds salmon fillet, cubed
- 2 tablespoons butter
- 2 cups homemade fish broth
- Salt and black pepper, to taste

Directions

1. Put all the ingredients in the slow cooker and mix well.
2. Cover the lid and cook on low for about 7 hours. Dish out to a bowl and serve hot.

Buttered Chili Pork Chops

Serves: **6** | Prep Time: **40** mins

Ingredients

- 6 green chilies, chopped
- 2 pounds pork chops
- 1½ cups butter
- Salt and black pepper, to taste
- 1 teaspoon paprika

Directions

1. Season the pork chops evenly with paprika, salt and black pepper.
2. Put 3 tablespoons of butter in a skillet and add pork chops.
3. Cook for about 4 minutes on each side and top with butter and chilies.
4. Cover the skillet and cook on medium low heat for about 25 minutes. Dish out and serve hot.

genic Pork in Gravy

Serves: **6** | Prep Time: **45** mins

Ingredients

- 4 tablespoons butter
- Salt and black pepper, to taste
- 2 pounds pork, cubed
- 1 large onion, sliced
- 1 cup homemade tomato puree

Directions

1. Heat butter on medium heat in a skillet and add onions.
2. Sauté for about 3 minutes and add pork, tomato puree, salt and black pepper.
3. Cover the skillet and cook for about 30 minutes on medium low heat. Dish out and serve hot.

Pork Asparagus Roll Ups

Serves: **1** | Prep Time: **20** mins

Ingredients

- 1 tablespoon mozzarella cheese
- 2 teaspoons cream cheese
- 2 thin slices pork meat, smoked
- 2 asparagus spears, boiled
- Ground black pepper, to taste

Directions

1. Mix together cream cheese and mozzarella cheese in a bowl.
2. Put the cheese mixture between pork slices and season lightly with black pepper. Place an asparagus spear on each pork slice and roll up to serve.

Fish and Seafood Recipes

Mixed Seafood Stew

Serves: **4** | Prep Time: **20** mins

Ingredients

- 1 medium onion, finely chopped
- 1 tablespoon olive oil
- 1½ teaspoons garlic, minced and divided
- ½ pound plum tomatoes, seeded and diced
- 1 teaspoon lemon peel, grated
- ¼ teaspoon red pepper flakes, crushed
- 1/3 cup white wine
- 1 tablespoon tomato paste
- Salt, to taste
- 1 oz. red snapper fillets, cut into 1-inch cubes
- 1 pound shrimp, peeled and deveined
- ½ pound sea scallops
- 1 cup clam juice
- 1/3 cup fresh parsley, minced
- 1/3 cup mayonnaise, reduced-fat

Directions

1. Heat cooking oil in a Dutch oven on medium heat and stir in garlic and onions.
2. Sauté until soft and add tomatoes, lemon peel and pepper flakes.
3. Sauté for 2 minutes and stir in wine, salt, tomato paste, and clam juice.
4. Boil this mixture then reduce it to a simmer. Cover the lid and cook for 10 minutes.
5. Gently toss in shrimps, scallops, parsley and fish.
6. Cook, covered for 10 more minutes and garnish with garlic and mayonnaise to serve.

Sauce Dipped Mussels

Serves: **2** | Prep Time: **35** mins

Ingredients

- 2 tablespoons olive oil
- 1 red or green chili, deseeded and chopped
- 2 ripe tomatoes, soaked, drained and diced
- 1 garlic clove, minced
- 1 shallot, finely diced
- 1 glass dry white wine
- 1 pinch sugar
- 1 handful basil leaves
- 1 teaspoon tomato paste
- 1 pound mussels, cleaned

Directions

1. Heat olive oil in a wok and stir in garlic, chili, and shallots.
2. Sauté for about 3 minutes and add seasonings, sugar, wine, and tomatoes.
3. Cook for about 2 minutes and add mussels.
4. Cover with a lid and cook for about 4 minutes. Garnish with basil leaves to serve.

Squid Oyster Medley

Serves: **4** | Prep Time: **55** mins

Ingredients

- 4 garlic cloves, minced
- 1½ cups chicken stock
- 10 baby squids, cleaned
- 1½ cups milk
- 1 large carrot, chopped
- ¼ cup tomato paste
- ¼ bunch tarragon, fresh
- 4 tablespoons olive oil, divided
- 1 tomato, chopped
- ¼ bunch parsley, fresh
- ½ teaspoon black peppercorns
- 3 baby fennel bulbs, halved
- 10 fresh mussels
- 3 sprigs parsley, for garnish
- ½ tablespoon saffron threads, loosely packed
- ¼ bunch fresh thyme, chopped
- 3 (6 ounce) fillets fresh sea bass
- 1 small onion, chopped
- ½ cup dry white wine
- ¼ bunch fresh thyme
- 3 cloves garlic, minced
- 5 fresh oysters in shells, scrubbed well
- Salt and black pepper, to taste
- 1 bay leaf
- ¼ cup oil-packed sun-dried tomatoes, drained and cut into strips
- 10 clams

Directions

1. Soak the squids in the milk for 5 hours and drain the milk. Heat half of oil in a cooking pan and add tomatoes, half of the fennels, carrots, garlic, and onions. Sauté for about 8 minutes and stir in tomato paste. Cook for about 10 minutes and pour in the wine.
2. Bring to a boil and add saffron, tarragon, thyme, stock, bay leaves, parsley, and peppercorns. Cook for about 12 minutes and strain the stock. Discard all the vegetables and dish out in a bowl.
3. Heat the remaining oil in the same pot and add garlic.
4. Sauté for about 30 seconds and stir in the tomatoes and remaining fennel.
5. Cook for about 2 minutes and bring to a boil. Add the oysters to the pot and cook, covered for about 5 minutes. Stir in the mussels and clams and cook for about 3 minutes.
6. Add drained squid and cook for another 1 minute.
7. Meanwhile, sear the fish fillets in a skillet for about 4 minutes on each side.
8. Serve topped with fish fillets and garnished with parsley.

Crusty Grilled Mussels

Serves: **2** | Prep Time: **15** mins

Ingredients

- 1 cup toasted bread crumbs
- 2 tablespoons garlic and parsley butter
- Fresh herbs, to garnish
- 1 pound mussels, rinsed and debearded
- 1 lemon zest
- Chopped tomato, to garnish

Directions

1. Boil mussels in a water in a large pot for about 3 minutes. Preheat the grill and grease a baking sheet.
2. Mix zest and bread crumbs in a bowl. Drizzle butter on top of the mussels and arrange them shell side down on the baking sheet. Top the mussels with bread crumbs mixture and transfer on the grill.
3. Cover the grill for about 4 minutes and allow to cook. Garnish with tomato and parsley to serve.

Seafood Garlic Couscous

Serves: **4** | Prep Time: **30** mins

Ingredients

- ½ pound raw shrimp, peeled, deveined and coarsely chopped
- 4 scallions, sliced
- ½ cup fresh parsley, chopped
- 2 tablespoons olive oil
- 2 (5.4-oz.) boxes garlic-flavored couscous, boiled and drained
- 1 pound codfish, cut into 1-inch pieces
- ½ pound bay scallops
- ½ cup fresh chives, chopped
- Salt and black pepper, to taste
- Hot sauce, to taste

Directions

1. Mix shrimps with codfish, scallions, scallops, parsley, chives, salt, and black pepper in a bowl. Heat oil in a deep wok and add seafood mixture.
2. Sauté until golden and stir in hot sauce. Lower the heat and cover with a lid.
3. Divide the couscous into the serving plates and top evenly with the fish mixture.

Lobster Rice Paella

Serves: **2** | Prep Time: **40** mins

Ingredients

- 1 small onion, chopped
- 2 garlic cloves, chopped
- ½ teaspoon sweet Spanish paprika
- 1½ tablespoons olive oil
- 3 oz. French green beans
- ¼ cup fresh parsley, chopped
- Water, as required
- 2 small lobster tails
- 1 cup Spanish rice, soaked overnight and drained
- 1 large pinch of Spanish saffron threads soaked in ½ cup water
- ½ teaspoon cayenne pepper
- ¼ teaspoon Aleppo pepper flakes
- 1 large Roma tomato, finely chopped
- ½ pound prawns, peeled and deveined
- Salt, to taste

Directions

1. Boil lobster in water for 2 minutes and transfer to an ice bath immediately.
2. Remove the meat from its shell and cut into small sized chunks.
3. Heat 3 tablespoons of oil in a skillet and add onions. Sauté for about 2 minutes and add rice.
4. Cook for about 3 minutes and add garlic and lobsters.
5. Stir in paprika, saffron, salt and black pepper and add tomatoes and green beans. Cover with a lid and reduce the heat to low. Allow it to cook for about 18 minutes and add shrimps.
6. Cover again and cook for about 14 minutes. Stir in parsley and lobster chunks to serve immediately.

Fish and Vegetable Parcels

Serves: **2** | Prep Time: **35** mins

Ingredients

- 1 teaspoon olive oil
- 1 small lemon zest, finely grated
- 10 black olives
- 2 fresh rosemary sprigs
- 1¼ cups baby potatoes, scrubbed
- 2 (6 oz.) firm haddock fillets
- 2 teaspoons sun-dried tomato paste
- 2 teaspoons lemon juice
- 1 tablespoon capers, rinsed

Directions

1. Preheat the oven to 325 degrees F and grease 2 baking sheets.
2. Boil potatoes in a salt mixed water in a large pot and transfer in a colander to drain well.
3. Place one fish fillet in each of the baking sheet and drizzle with lemon juice, tomato paste, seasonings and lemon zest.
4. Arrange capers, potatoes and olives on the sides of fillets and cover the fillets with rosemary sprigs.
5. Transfer in the oven and bake for about 25 minutes. Dish out and serve immediately.

Seafood with Couscous Salad

Serves: **2** | Prep Time: **35** mins

Ingredients

- 2 lemons, 1 zested and juiced and the other cut into wedges
- 7 oz. cherry tomatoes
- 2 tablespoons balsamic vinegar
- 2 tablespoons pitted black olives, halved
- ½ cucumber, diced
- 2 white fish fillets
- 1 red chili, sliced
- 1 small bunch basil, shredded
- 4 oz. couscous

Directions
1. Preheat the oven to 375 degrees F and grease a baking sheet.
2. Place the fish in the baking sheet and add basil, seasonings, sliced chilies and half of the lemon juice and zest.
3. Surround the fillets with tomatoes and transfer in the oven.
4. Bake for about 20 minutes and dish out.
5. Meanwhile, soak couscous in boiled water for about 20 minutes and drain well.
6. Mix together couscous, basil, tomatoes, cucumber, olives, lemon zest and juice in a bowl.
7. Serve the baked fish with the couscous salad and enjoy.

Saffron Fish Gratins

Serves: **6** | Prep Time: **45** mins

Ingredients
- 1 large onion, thinly sliced
- 3 large garlic cloves, finely sliced
- ½ cup white wine
- 3 tablespoons olive oil
- 1 fennel bulb, trimmed and thinly sliced
- 1 heaped teaspoon coriander seeds, lightly crushed
- 2 (14 oz.) cans chopped tomatoes with herbs
- 1 pinch saffron
- 1 tablespoon lemon juice
- 2 pounds mixed skinless fish fillets, cut into chunks
- ¼ cup parmesan cheese, finely grated
- Green salad, to serve
- 2 tablespoons tomato purée
- 1 bay leaf
- 1 bunch parsley, leaves roughly chopped
- 1¾ cups raw king prawns, peeled
- ¼ cup panko breadcrumbs

Directions
1. Preheat the oven to 375 degrees F and grease a baking dish.
2. Heat oil in a large nonstick pan and add fennel, garlic, onions and coriander seeds.
3. Sauté for about 5 minutes and pour in wine, saffron, tomatoes, tomato puree and bay leaf.
4. Cook for about 15 minutes and add tomatoes mixture, prawns, and fish chunks.
5. Cook for about 5 minutes and transfer the mixture a baking dish.
6. Mix together breadcrumbs, parsley, cheese and black pepper and top it on the fish mixture.
7. Transfer in the oven and bake for about 20 minutes to serve.

Instant Pot Coconut Fishbowl

Yield: 8 | Total Time: 20 Mins | Prep Time: 5 Mins | Cook Time: 15 Mins

Ingredients
- 1 ½ pounds fish fillets, sliced into bite-size pieces
- 2 cups coconut milk
- 1 tbsp. freshly grated ginger
- 2 garlic cloves, minced
- 2 medium onions, chopped
- 2 green chilies, sliced into strips
- 1 tomato, chopped
- 6 curry leaves
- 3 tbsp. curry powder mix
- 2 tbsp. fresh lemon juice
- 2 tsp. salt

Directions
1. Set your instant pot on sauté mode and add oil; sauté curry leaves for 1 minute and then add ginger, garlic and onion; cook until tender; stir in curry powder mix and cook for 2 Mins or until fragrant.
2. Add coconut milk and then stir in fish, tomatoes, and green chilies until well combined; lock lid and cook on high for 5 Mins. Let pressure come down naturally and then stir in lemon juice and salt.

Instant Pot Shrimp Paella

Yield: 4 | Total Time: 20 Mins | Prep Time: 10 Mins | Cook Time: 10 Mins

Ingredients
- 1-pound jumbo shrimp
- 4 tbsp. butter
- 1 red pepper chopped
- 4 cloves garlic chopped
- 1 onion chopped
- 1/2 cup white wine
- 1 cup chicken broth
- 1/4 cup cilantro
- 1/4 tsp red pepper flakes
- 1 pinch saffron threads
- 1 tsp turmeric
- 1 tsp paprika
- 1/2 tsp salt
- 1/4 tsp black pepper

Directions
1. Set your instant pot on sauté mode and melt in butter; stir in onion until tender and then add in garlic; cook for 1 minute and then stir in spices. Cook for 1 minute and then add red peppers. Stir in wine and chicken broth. Add in shrimp and lock lid; cook on manual for 5 Mins. Let pressure come down naturally; stir in cilantro and serve.

Steamed Alaskan Crab Legs

Yield: 6 | Total Time: 10 Mins | Prep Time: 5 Mins | Cook Time: 5 Mins

Ingredients
- 3 pounds crab legs
- 1 cup water
- 1/2 tbsp. salt
- melted butter

Directions
1. Place a steamer basket in your instant pot and add a cup of water and salt to the pot; add crab legs to the basket and lock lid; cook on manual high for 5 Mins. Quick release pressure and then serve the steamed crab legs with melted butter.

Instant Pot Shrimp & Grits

Yield: 4 | Total Time: 40 Mins | Prep Time: 15 Mins | Cook Time: 25 Mins

Ingredients

Shrimp Ingredients
- 3 strips smoked bacon, diced
- 1-pound shrimp, peeled and deveined
- 1 tbsp. garlic, minced
- 1/2 cup bell peppers, chopped
- 1/3 cup onion, chopped
- 1 1/2 cups diced tomatoes
- 2 tsp. Old Bay seasoning
- 1/4 tsp hot sauce
- 2 tbsp. lemon juice
- 1/4 cup chicken broth
- 2 tbsp. dry white wine
- 1/2 tsp salt
- 1/4 tsp pepper
- 1/4 cup heavy cream
- 1/4 cup scallions, sliced

Grits Ingredients
- 1/2 cup grits
- 1 tbsp. butter
- 1 cup milk
- salt & pepper
- 1 cup water

Directions
1. Season shrimp with Old Bay seasoning and set aside.
2. Set your instant pot on sauté mode and cook bacon for 3 Mins or until crisp; transfer to a plate. Add bell peppers and onions to the pot and cook for about 3 Mins; stir in garlic and cook for 1 minute.
3. Turn off your pot and then stir in white wine to deglaze; stir in hot sauce, broth, lemon juice, tomatoes, salt and pepper and then add in a trivet.
4. In a heat-proof bowl, mix together milk, grits, salt, water and pepper and place it over the trivet; lock lid and cook on manual for 10 Mins; let pressure come down on its own. Remove the grits and trivet and the stir in shrimp; lock lid and let shrimp cook. Fluff grits and add butter. Stir the shrimp and then turn the pot on sauté mode; stir in cream and serve with grits garnished with bacon and scallions.

Salmon with Gingery Orange Sauce

Yield: 4 | Total Time: 15 Mins | Prep Time: 10 Mins | Cook Time: 5 Mins

Ingredients
- 1-pound salmon
- 1 tbsp. dark soy sauce
- 2 tbsp. marmalade
- 1 tsp. minced garlic
- 2 tsp. minced ginger
- 1 tsp. salt
- 1 ½ tsp pepper

Directions
1. Add fish to a Ziplock bag; mix all remaining ingredients and add to the bag; let marinate for at least 15 Mins.
2. Add two cups of water to your instant pot and add in a steamer rack. Place the bag with fish on the rack and lock lid; cook on high for 5 Mins and then let pressure come down on its own.

Instant Pot Mussels

Yield: 4 | Total Time: 25 Mins | Prep Time: 15 Mins | Cook Time: 10 Mins

Ingredients
- 2 pounds mussels, cleaned
- 2 tbsp. butter
- 4 garlic cloves, minced
- 2 shallots, chopped
- 1/2 cup white wine
- 1/2 cup broth
- 1 tbsp. fresh lemon juice
- 1 tbsp. chopped parsley

Directions
1. Melt butter in your instant pot under sauté mode and cook onion until tender; stir in garlic and cook for 1 minute; stir in wine and broth and then turn off the pot.
2. Add the mussels and lock lid; cook on manual for 5 Mins and then release pressure naturally. Serve with fresh lemon juice and parsley.

Salmon w/ Chili-Lime Sauce

Yield: 2 | Total Time: 15 Mins | Prep Time: 10 Mins | Cook Time: 5 Mins

Ingredients
For steaming salmon:
- 2 salmon fillets
- 1 cup water
- sea salt & pepper

For chili-lime sauce:
- 1 jalapeno seeds removed and diced
- 1 tbsp. olive oil
- 1 tbsp. liquid Stevia
- 2 cloves garlic minced
- 1 tbsp. chopped parsley
- 1 tbsp. hot water
- 2 tbsp. lime juice
- 1/2 tsp. cumin
- 1/2 tsp. paprika

Directions
1. In a bowl, mix all sauce ingredients and set aside.
2. Add water to your instant pot and place salmon in a steamer basket inside the pot; sprinkle fish with salt and pepper and then lock lid; cook on high for 5 Mins and then let pressure come down naturally. Transfer fish to a plate and drizzle with sauce to serve.

Instant Pot Tilapia

Yield: 6 | Total Time: 2 Hours 15 Mins | Prep Time: 15 Mins | Cook Time: 15 Mins

Ingredients
- 6 tilapia filets
- Lemon pepper seasoning
- 1 bundle of asparagus
- 3 tbsp. melted coconut oil
- 12 tbsp. lemon juice

Directions
1. Divide asparagus into equal amounts per each fillet.
2. Place each fillet in the center of a piece of foil and sprinkle with about 1 tsp. lemon pepper seasoning; drizzle with about 2 tbsp. lemon juice and about ½ tbsp. melted coconut oil. Top each filet with the asparagus and fold the foil to form a packet. Repeat with the remaining ingredients and then place the packets into an instant pot. Lock lid and cook on high for 15 Mins.

Pressure Cooked Coconut Curry Shrimp

Yield: 4 | Total Time: 15 Mins | Prep Time: 5 Mins | Cook Time: 10 Mins

Ingredients
- 1 pound shelled shrimp
- ½ cup Thai red curry sauce
- 15 ounces water
- ¼ cup cilantro
- 4 cups coconut milk
- 2½ tsp. garlic-lemon seasoning

Directions
1. In your instant pot, combine water, coconut milk, red curry paste, cilantro, and lemon garlic seasoning; stir to mix well and lock lid; cook on high for 10 Mins and then release the pressure quickly. Add shrimp and continue cooking for another five Mins and then release pressure naturally.
2. Serve garnished with cilantro.

Hot Lemony Tilapia w/ Asparagus

Yield: 6 | Total Time: 30 Mins | Prep Time: 15 Mins | Cook Time: 15 Mins

Ingredients
- 6 tilapia filets
- 12 tbsp. lemon juice
- 3 tbsp. melted coconut oil
- 1 bundle of asparagus
- Lemon pepper seasoning

Directions
1. Divide asparagus into equal amounts per each fillet.
2. Place each fillet in the center of a piece of foil and sprinkle with about 1 tsp. lemon pepper seasoning; drizzle with about 2 tbsp. lemon juice and about ½ tbsp. melted coconut oil. Top each filet with the asparagus and fold the foil to form a packet. Repeat with the remaining ingredients and then place the packets into an instant pot. Lock lid and cook on high for 15 Mins.

Tasty Citrus Tilapia

Yield: 4 | Total Time: 25 Mins | Prep Time: 10 Mins | Cook Time: 15 Mins

Ingredients
- 4 tilapia filets
- 3 tbsp. coconut oil
- 1-10-ounce can mandarin oranges
- Sea salt and pepper
- 2 tbsp. minced garlic

Directions
1. Arrange fish side by side on a large piece of aluminum foil and sprinkle with garlic and coconut oil evenly. Top the fish with oranges and season with salt and pepper; fold the foil to wrap the contents well. Place in an instant pot and lock lid; cook on high for 15 Mins.

Pressure Steamed Salmon

Yield: 4 | Total Time: 21 Mins | Prep Time: 15 Mins | Cook Time: 6 Mins

Ingredients
- 1 tablespoon extra-virgin olive oil
- 6 ounces wild salmon fillets, skinless
- Fennel fronds
- 1 tablespoon chopped parsley
- 1 tablespoon chopped dill
- 1 tablespoon chopped chives
- 1 tablespoon chopped tarragon
- 1 tablespoon chopped basil
- 1 tablespoon chopped shallot
- 1 tablespoon lemon juice

Directions
1. Add water to an instant pot and insert a trivet; place salmon and fennel wedges over the trivet and lock lid. Cook on high for 6 Mins. In a bowl, combine the chopped herbs, extra virgin olive oil, and shallot and lemon juice; stir until well combined. Season and spoon over cooked fish.

Teriyaki Fish w/ Zucchini

Yields: 2 | Total Time: 40 Mins | Prep Time: 10 Mins | Cook Time: 30 Mins

Ingredients
- 2 (6-ounce) salmon fillets
- 7 tablespoons teriyaki sauce (low sodium)
- 2 tablespoons sesame seeds
- 2 teaspoons canola oil
- 4 scallions, chopped
- 2 small zucchinis, thinly sliced

Directions
1. Mix fish with 5 tablespoons of teriyaki sauce in a zip-top bag and marinate for at least 20 Mins.
2. Set your instant pot on manual high, toast sesame seeds; set aside. Drain the marinated fish and discard the marinade.
3. Add fish to the pot and cook for about 5 Mins per side; remove fish from skillet and keep warm.
4. Add oil, scallions and zucchini to the skillet and sauté for about 4 Mins or until browned.
5. Stir in the remaining teriyaki sauce and lock lid. Cook on high for 5 Mins and then let pressure come down. Sprinkle with toasted sesame seeds and serve with fish.

Grilled Tuna w/ Bean & Tomato Salad

Yields: 4 | Total Time: 23 Mins | Prep Time: 10 Mins | Cook Time: 13 Mins

Ingredients
- 1 ½ tablespoons extra virgin olive oil
- 3 scallions, thinly sliced
- 1 tablespoon fresh lemon juice
- 1/4 cup fresh tarragon leaves
- 1 (15 ounces) can beans, drained, rinsed
- 1 pound heirloom tomatoes, cored, diced
- Sea salt
- 4 (8 ounce) tuna steaks

Directions
1. In a bowl, mix together oil, scallions, lemon juice, tarragon, beans, tomatoes, and salt; set aside.
2. Set your instant pot on manual high and heat in oil; add in tuna and cook for 4 Mins per side. Add in coconut milk and cook on high for 5 Mins. Let pressure come down. Serve tuna with bean salad.

Steamed Bass with Fennel, Parsley, and Capers

Yields: 2 | Total Time: 30 Mins | Prep Time: 15 Mins | Cook Time: 15 Mins

Ingredients
- 2- 5-ounce portions of striped bass
- 2 tablespoons extra-virgin olive oil
- 1/2 lemon, juiced
- 1 fennel bulb, sliced
- 1/4 medium onion, sliced
- 1/4 cup chopped parsley
- 1 tablespoon capers, rinsed
- 1/2 teaspoon sea salt
- Chopped parsley and olive oil, for garnish

Directions
1. Add lemon juice, fennel and onion to an instant pot and cover with 1-inch water; bring the mixture to a gentle boil on manual high. Add seasoned fish and sprinkle with parsley and capers; lock lid and cook on high for 10 Mins. Let pressure come down on its own.
2. Transfer to a serving bowl and drizzle with extra virgin olive oil and top with more parsley to serve.

Pressure Baked Salmon Salad with Mint Dressing

Yield: 1 Serving | Total Time: 30 Mins | Prep Time: 10 Mins | Cook Time: 20 Mins

Ingredients
- 130g salmon fillet
- 1 tablespoon olive oil
- 2 red onions, thinly sliced
- 1 cucumber (50g) cucumber, sliced
- 2 radishes, thinly sliced
- ¼ cup baby spinach
- ½ cup mixed salad leaves
- ½ cup chopped parsley

The dressing:
- 1 tbsp. rice vinegar
- 1 tablespoon olive oil
- 1 tbsp. natural yogurt
- 1 tsp. mayonnaise
- 1 tbsp. finely chopped mint leaves
- salt and black pepper

Directions
1. Set your instant pot to manual high and heat olive oil; add in fish and cook for 3 Mins per side; remove the fish to a plate. Add water to the pot and insert a trivet; place the fish over the trivet and lock lid. Cook on high for 10 Mins and then naturally release the pressure.
2. In a bowl, mix together rice wine vinegar, yogurt, oil, mayonnaise, mint, salt and pepper; let stand for at least 5 Mins for flavors to blend.
3. Arrange salad leaves and spinach on a plate and top with red onions, cucumber, radishes, and parsley. Flake the fish and place onto the salad; drizzle with the mint dressing and serve.

Spiced Mahi-Mahi with Creamed Sautéed Mushrooms

Yield: 2 | Total Time: 35 Mins | Prep Time: 15 Mins | Cook Time: 20 Mins

Ingredients
- 1 ¾ tsps. ground cumin
- 1/2 tsp. garlic powder
- 1/2 tsp. dried oregano
- 1/4 tsp. ground ginger
- 1/4 tsp. smoked paprika
- 1/4 tsp. kosher salt
- 1/4 tsp. ground black pepper
- 1/8 tsp. ground red pepper
- 1 tbsp. olive oil
- 2 Mahi Mahi fillets
- Grilling Spray
- 1 cup cream cheese
- 4 cups button mushrooms
- 2 tablespoons butter
- 1 red onion, chopped

Directions
1. Mix ¾ tsp. cumin, garlic powder, dried oregano, ground ginger, smoked paprika, salt and red and black pepper in a small bowl. Add in olive oil to make a spicy paste; divide mixture in half and set one portion aside.
2. Rub half of the spice mix on the fish fillets then put aside. Set your instant pot to manual high and then add the fish; cook for 3-4 Mins per side, turning once.
3. Remove grilled fish as soon as it easily flakes when pierced with a fork. Brush the remaining fish with the remaining spice rub.
4. Add butter to the pot and sauté red onion until fragrant; stir in mushrooms, whipping cream, salt and pepper. Lock lid and cook for 5 Mins on high. Let pressure come down naturally. Serve the fish over the creamed mushrooms.

Instant Pot Seafood Cioppino

Yield: 2 | Total Time: 50 Mins | Prep Time: 10 Mins | Cook Time: 40 Mins

Ingredients
- 3 ounces lump crabmeat
- 3 ounces chopped clams
- 3 ounces shrimp, peeled, deveined
- 3 ounces haddock fillets, sliced
- 1 tbsp. olive oil
- 3 celery ribs, chopped
- ¼ cup chopped onions
- 2 garlic cloves, minced
- 1 cup canned tomatoes
- 4 tbsp. tomato paste
- ½ cup clam juice
- 1 tbsp. red wine vinegar
- 1/2 cup vegetable broth
- 2 tsp. Italian seasoning
- 2 tbsp. minced fresh parsley
- 1/2 tsp. sugar
- 1 bay leaf

Directions
1. In an instant pot, combine all ingredients except seafood and parsley. Cook for 10 Mins and then stir in seafood. Cook on high for about 30 Mins. Let pressure come down and then discard bay leaf and stir in parsley. Serve.

Instant Pot Shrimp Scampi

Yield: 2 | Total Time: 1 Hours 10 Mins | Prep Time: 10 Mins | Cook Time: 1 Hour

Ingredients
- ½ pound shrimp, peeled, deveined
- 2 tbsp. butter
- 2 tbsp. olive oil
- 1 tbsp. minced garlic
- 1/4 cup chicken broth
- 2 tbsp. parsley
- 1/2 squeezed lemon
- salt & pepper

Directions
1. Combine all ingredients in your instant pot; lock lid and cook on high for about 1 hour. Let pressure come down on its own. Serve over steamed veggies.

Instant Pot BBQ Shrimp

Yield: 2 | Total Time: 40 Mins | Prep Time: 10 Mins | Cook Time: 30 Mins

Ingredients
- 2 tbsp. butter
- ½ pound peeled, deveined shrimp
- 2 tsp minced garlic
- 1/4 cup BBQ sauce
- 2 tbsp. Worcestershire sauce
- Salt & pepper
- Lemon wedges,

Directions
1. Add shrimp to your instant pot and add the remaining ingredients except lemon wedge; lock lid and cook on high for 30 Mins. Naturally release the pressure. Serve warm, garnished with lemon wedge and a side dish of veggies.

Spicy Grilled Cod

Yields: 4 | Total Time: 35 Mins | Prep Time: 15 Mins | Cook Time: 20 Mins

Ingredients
- 1-pound cod filets
- 2 tablespoons extra virgin olive oil
- 2 minced garlic cloves
- 1/8 teaspoon cayenne pepper
- 3 tablespoons fresh lime juice
- 1 ½ teaspoon fresh lemon juice
- ¼ cup freshly squeezed orange juice
- 1/3 cup water
- 1 tablespoon chopped fresh thyme
- 2 tablespoon chopped fresh chives

Healthy Steamed Vegetables
- 1 head broccoli
- 2 red bell peppers, sliced in bite-sized lengths
- ¼ cup zucchini, sliced into rounds
- 2 baby carrots, sliced into rounds

Direction
1. **Prepare Veggies:** Add water to an instant pot, up to 1 ½ inches from the bottom; set the steamer inside the pot and heat over medium high heat or until the water boils.
2. Add the veggies to the steamer and season with salt and garlic powder. Lock lid and cook for 5 Mins on high setting. Let pressure come down naturally
3. In a bowl, mix together lemon juice, lime juice, orange juice, cayenne pepper, extra virgin olive oil, garlic and water. Place fish in a dish and add the marinade, reserving ¼ cup; marinate in the refrigerator for at least 30 Mins. Broil or grill the marinated fish for about 4 Mins per side, basting regularly with the marinade. Serve the grilled fish on a plate with steamed veggies topped with chives, thyme and the reserved marinade.

Coconut Fish & Vegetable Curry

Yield: 2 | Total Time: 25 Mins | Prep Time: 5 Mins | Cook Time: 20 Mins

Ingredients
- 300g firm white fish, cubed
- 450g spinach, roughly chopped
- 100g coconut cream
- 2 ½ tbsp. Thai curry paste
- 2 tbsp. coconut oil
- 100ml water
- Kosher salt and pepper, to taste

Directions
1. Add the oil to an instant pot set on manual high. Stir in the curry paste and cook for 3 Mins to bring the spices to life.
2. Pour in the coconut cream and water and bring the sauce to a boil.
3. Add in the fish cubes and lock lid. Cook on high for 15 Mins and then let pressure come down on its own. Gently stir in the spinach and cook for 3 Mins until it wilts. Serve hot!

Red Snapper in Hot Veggie Sauce

Yields: 4 | Total Time: 35 Mins | Prep Time: 15 Mins | Cook Time: 20 Mins

Ingredients
- 2-pounds red snapper filets
- ¼ cup canola or extra virgin olive oil
- ½ red bell pepper, chopped
- ½ green bell pepper, chopped
- 4 scallions, thinly sliced
- 2 tomatoes, diced
- 2 cloves garlic
- 2 tablespoon fresh lemon juice
- ½ cup freshly squeezed lime juice
- 1 teaspoon cayenne pepper
- 1 teaspoon pepper
- Cilantro for garnish

Directions
1. Add extra virgin olive oil to an instant pot set on manual high and sauté garlic for about 4 Mins or until golden brown. Place fish in the oil and drizzle with lemon and lime juice. Sprinkle with black pepper and cayenne pepper and top with green and red bell peppers, scallions, and tomatoes.
2. Lock lid and cook on high for 15 Mins and then quick release the pressure.
3. To serve, garnish with cilantro.

Pressure Grilled Salmon

Yields: 6 | Total Time: 4 Hours 27 Mins | Prep Time: 4 Hours 15 Mins | Cook Time: 12 Mins

Ingredients
- 6 (180 grams each) Atlantic salmon fillets, with skin on
- 1/4 cup extra virgin olive oil
- 1 bunch roughly chopped lemon thyme
- 1/3 cup finely chopped dill leaves
- 2 tablespoons drained and chopped capers
- 2 fresh lemons, juiced
- 2 garlic cloves, finely chopped
- A pinch of sea salt
- Lemon wedges, to garnish

Directions
1. In a large jug, mix together lemon thyme, dill, capers, vinegar, garlic, extra virgin olive oil, sea salt and pepper. Arrange salmon fillets, in a single layer, in a ceramic dish and pour over half of the marinade. Turn it over and pour over the remaining marinade. Refrigerate, covered, for about 4 hours.
2. Remove the fish from the refrigerator at least 30 Mins before cooking.
3. Spray the instant pot with oil and cook the fish, skin side down, for about 3 Mins. Turn and continue barbecuing, basting occasionally with the marinade until browned on both sides. Add a splash of the marinade and lock lid. Cook on high for 6 Mins and then quick release the pressure. Serve garnished with lemon wedges.

Creamy Coconut Baked Salmon with Green Salad

Yields: 2 | Total Time: 45 Mins | Prep Time: 15 Mins | Cook Time: 20 Mins

Ingredients
For Salmon
- 15-ounce salmon filet
- 1 tablespoon mustard
- A pinch of sea salt
- ½ cup coconut milk
- 2 tablespoons coconut cream

For Salad
- 2 tablespoon dried cranberries
- 2 tablespoon chopped pecans
- 1/2 cup chopped baby spinach
- 1 cup chopped arugula

Directions
1. Preheat your oven to 350°F. Grease a baking sheet with extra virgin olive oil and place on salmon filet; pat dry with paper towels and sprinkle with ground mustard, covering the entire top of fish.
2. Bake for about 15 Mins or until fish flakes easily with a fork.
3. Place the fish in an instant pot and add in coconut milk and coconut cream. Lock lid and cook on high for 10 Mins and then let pressure come down on its own.
4. Meanwhile, whisk together the dressing ingredients and set aside.
5. Combine together the salad ingredients in a mixing bowl.
6. Serve the fish with coconut sauce on plates and top each with the salad. Enjoy!

Tilapia with Mushroom Sauce

Yields: 4 | Total Time: 45 Mins | Prep Time: 15 Mins | Cook Time: 30 Mins

Ingredients
- 6 ounces tilapia fillets
- 2 teaspoon arrowroot
- 1 cup mushrooms, sliced
- 1 clove garlic, finely chopped
- 1 small onion, thinly sliced
- 2 tablespoons extra virgin olive oil
- ½ cup fresh parsley, roughly chopped
- 1 teaspoon thyme leaves, finely chopped
- ½ cup water
- A pinch of freshly ground black pepper
- A pinch of sea salt

Directions
1. Add extra virgin olive oil to an instant pot and set on manual high; sauté onion, garlic and mushrooms for about 4 Mins or until mushrooms are slightly tender.
2. Stir in arrowroot, sea salt, thyme and pepper and cook for about 1 minute.
3. Stir in water until thickened; stir in parsley and cook for 1 minute more.
4. Place the fillets in the pot and cover with mushroom sauce, lock lid and cook on high for 20 Mins. Let pressure come down on its own.

Pressure Cooked Salmon with Herbs

Yield: 4 | Total Time: 21 Mins | Prep Time: 15 Mins | Cook Time: 6 Mins

Ingredients
- 8 ounces wild salmon fillets
- Fennel fronds
- 1 tablespoon chopped parsley
- 1 tablespoon chopped dill
- 1 tablespoon chopped chives
- 1 tablespoon chopped tarragon
- 1 tablespoon chopped basil
- 1 tablespoon extra virgin olive oil
- 1 tablespoon chopped shallot
- 1 tablespoon lemon juice

Directions

1. Lightly oil a steamer basket with olive oil; add salmon and fennel wedges. Add water to an instant pot and insert a metal trivet; place the steamer over the trivet and cook for 6 Mins.
2. In a bowl, combine the chopped herbs, extra virgin olive oil, shallot and lemon juice; stir until well combined. Season and spoon over cooked fish.

Instant Pot White Fish Curry

Yield: 2 | Total Time: 30 Mins | Prep Time: 10 Mins | Cook Time: 20 Mins

Ingredients

- 2 tablespoons olive oil
- 200g white fish filet, diced
- ¼ cup fish broth
- Pinch of turmeric
- Dash of onion powder
- 1 tablespoon minced red onion
- Pinch of garlic powder
- ¼ teaspoon curry powder
- Pinch of sea salt
- Pinch of pepper
- Stevia

Directions

1. Set an instant pot on sauté mode, heat oil and sauté onion and garlic; stir in fish filet and cook until browned. Stir spices in fish broth and Stevia and add to the pot. Lock lid and cook on high for 15 Mins. Release the pressure naturally and serve hot over steamed veggies.

Pressure Roasted Tilapia

Yield: 6 | Total Time: 1 Hour 40 Mins | Prep Time: 10 Mins | Cook Time: 1 Hour 30 Mins

Ingredients:

- 4 tablespoons extra virgin olive oil
- ½ cup apple cider vinegar
- 3 cloves garlic, minced
- 2-3 tablespoons minced ginger
- 2 pounds Tilapia Fillets
- 1-pound chopped carrots
- handful of rosemary
- Pinch of sea salt
- Pinch of pepper

Directions:

1. Place Tilapia in aluminum foil. In a bowl, whisk together olive oil, apple cider vinegar, garlic, and ginger until well combined; pour over the fish and top with carrots and rosemary. Sprinkle with salt and pepper and fold to wrap well. Add water to an instant pot and insert a metal trivet. Place the foil over the trivet and cook on high for 1 ½ hours. Let pressure come down naturally.

Instant Pot Roasted Salmon

Yield: 6 | Total Time: 1 Hour 40 Mins | Prep Time: 10 Mins | Cook Time: 1Hour 30 Mins

Ingredients:

- 1 tablespoon extra virgin olive oil
- ½ cup apple cider vinegar
- 3 cloves garlic, minced
- 2-3 tablespoons minced ginger
- 2 pounds salmon fillets
- 1 pound chopped carrots
- handful of rosemary
- Pinch of sea salt
- Pinch of pepper

Directions

1. Place salmon in your instant pot. In a bowl, whisk together olive oil, apple cider vinegar, garlic, and ginger until well combined; pour over the fish and top with carrots and rosemary. Sprinkle with salt and pepper and lock lid. Cook on high setting for 1 ½ hours and then let pressure come down on its own. Serve warm over steamed veggies.

Instant Pot Tilapia in Coconut Cream Sauce

Yields: 2 | Total Time: 25 Mins | Prep Time: 5 Mins | Cook Time: 20 Mins

Ingredients

- 2 tablespoons olive oil
- 2 tilapia filets
- 2 red onions
- 2 minced cloves garlic
- 1 medium red bell pepper, diced
- 1/4 cup low-sodium soy sauce
- 1/4 tsp. crushed red pepper flakes
- ¼ cup coconut cream

Directions

1. Set your instant pot on sauté mode and heat olive oil; sauté the red onion and garlic until fragrant and then cook tilapia filets until browned on both sides. Stir in the remaining ingredients and lock lid; cook on high setting for 10 Mins. Quick release the pressure and serve.

Garlic Butter Salmon

Serves: **8** | Prep Time: **40** mins

Ingredients

- Kosher salt and black pepper, to taste
- 1 pound (3 pounds) salmon fillet, skin removed
- 4 tablespoons butter, melted
- 2 garlic cloves, minced
- ¼ cup parmesan cheese, freshly grated

Directions

1. Preheat the oven to 350°F and lightly grease a large baking sheet.
2. Season the salmon with salt and black pepper and transfer to the baking sheet.
3. Mix together butter, garlic and parmesan cheese in a small bowl.
4. Marinate salmon in this mixture for about 1 hour. Transfer to the oven and bake for about 25 minutes.
5. Additionally, broil for about 2 minutes until top becomes lightly golden.
6. Dish out onto a platter and serve hot.

Tuscan Butter Salmon

Serves: **4** | Prep Time: **35** mins

Ingredients

- 4 (6 oz) salmon fillets, patted dry with paper towels
- 3 tablespoons butter
- ¾ cup heavy cream
- Kosher salt and black pepper
- 2 cups baby spinach

Directions

1. Season the salmon with salt and black pepper.
2. Heat 1½ tablespoons butter over medium high heat in a large skillet and add salmon skin side up. Cook for about 10 minutes on both sides until deeply golden and dish out onto a plate. Heat the rest of the butter in the skillet and add spinach.
3. Cook for about 5 minutes and stir in the heavy cream. Reduce heat to low and simmer for about 3 minutes. Return the salmon to the skillet and mix well with the sauce.
4. Allow to simmer for about 3 minutes until salmon is cooked through. Serve hot.

Mahi Mahi Stew

Serves: **3** | Prep Time: **45** mins

Ingredients

- 2 tablespoons butter
- 2 pounds Mahi Mahi fillets, cubed
- 1 onion, chopped
- Salt and black pepper, to taste
- 2 cups homemade fish broth

Directions

1. Season the Mahi Mahi fillets with salt and black pepper. Heat butter in a pressure cooker and add onion.
2. Sauté for about 3 minutes and stir in the seasoned Mahi Mahi fillets and fish broth. Lock the lid and cook on High Pressure for about 30 minutes.
3. Naturally release the pressure and dish out to serve hot.

Tilapia with Herbed Butter

Serves: **6** | Prep Time: **35** mins

Ingredients

- 2 pounds tilapia fillets
- 12 garlic cloves, chopped finely
- 6 green broccoli, chopped
- 2 cups herbed butter
- Salt and black pepper, to taste

Directions

1. Season the tilapia fillets with salt and black pepper.
2. Put the seasoned tilapia along with all other ingredients in an Instant Pot and mix well. Cover the lid and cook on High Pressure for about 25 minutes. Dish out in a platter and serve hot.

Roasted Trout

Serves: **4** | Prep Time: **45** mins

Ingredients

- ½ cup fresh lemon juice
- 1 pound trout fish fillets
- 4 tablespoons butter
- Salt and black pepper, to taste
- 1 teaspoon dried rosemary, crushed

Directions

1. Put ½ pound trout fillets in a dish and sprinkle with lemon juice and dried rosemary. Season with salt and black pepper and transfer into a skillet.
2. Add butter and cook, covered on medium low heat for about 35 minutes.
3. Dish out the fillets in a platter and serve with a sauce.

Sour Fish with Herbed Butter

Serves: **3** | Prep Time: **45** mins

Ingredients
- 2 tablespoons herbed butter
- 3 cod fillets
- 1 tablespoon vinegar
- Salt and black pepper, to taste
- ½ tablespoon lemon pepper seasoning

Directions
1. Preheat the oven to 375°F and grease a baking tray.
2. Mix together cod fillets, vinegar, lemon pepper seasoning, salt and black pepper in a bowl. Marinate for about 3 hours and then arrange on the baking tray.
3. Transfer into the oven and bake for about 30 minutes.
4. Remove from the oven and serve with herbed butter.

Cod Coconut Curry

Serves: **6** | Prep Time: **35** mins

Ingredients
- 1 onion, chopped
- 2 pounds cod
- 1 cup dry coconut, chopped
- Salt and black pepper, to taste
- 1 cup fresh lemon juice

Directions
1. Put the cod along with all other ingredients in a pressure cooker.
2. Add 2 cups of water and cover the lid. Cook on High Pressure for about 25 minutes and naturally release the pressure. Open the lid and dish out the curry to serve hot.

Garlic Shrimp with Goat Cheese

Serves: **4** | Prep Time: **30** mins

Ingredients
- 4 tablespoons herbed butter
- Salt and black pepper, to taste
- 1 pound large raw shrimp
- 4 ounces goat cheese
- 4 garlic cloves, chopped

Directions
1. Preheat the oven to 375°F and grease a baking dish.
2. Mix together herbed butter, garlic, raw shrimp, salt and black pepper in a bowl. Put the marinated shrimp on the baking dish and top with the shredded cheese. Place in the oven and bake for about 25 minutes.
3. Take the shrimp out and serve hot.

Grain Free Salmon Bread

Serves: **6** | Prep Time: **35** mins

Ingredients
- ½ cup olive oil
- ¼ teaspoon baking soda
- ½ cup coconut milk
- 2 pounds salmon, steamed and shredded
- 2 pastured eggs

Directions
1. Preheat the oven to 375°F and grease a baking dish with olive oil.
2. Mix together coconut milk, eggs, baking soda and salmon in a bowl.
3. Pour the batter of salmon bread in the baking dish and transfer into the oven.
4. Bake for about 20 minutes and remove from the oven to serve hot.

Buttered Mahi Mahi Slices

Serves: **3** | Prep Time: **30** mins

Ingredients
- ½ cup butter
- 1 pound Mahi Mahi, steamed and shredded
- ½ onion, chopped
- Salt and black pepper, to taste
- 1 mushroom, chopped

Directions
1. Preheat the oven to 375°F and grease a baking dish.
2. Mix together butter, onion, mushrooms, salt and black pepper in a bowl.
3. Make slices from the batter and place them on the baking dish.
4. Transfer to the oven and bake for about 20 minutes.
5. Remove from the oven and serve with a sauce.

Salmon Stew

Serves: **3** | Prep Time: **20** mins

Ingredients
- 1 cup homemade fish broth
- 1 medium onion, chopped
- 1 pound salmon fillets, cubed
- Salt and black pepper, to taste
- 1 tablespoon butter

Directions
1. Season the salmon with salt and black pepper.
2. Heat butter in a skillet on medium heat and add onions.
3. Sauté for about 3 minutes and add seasoned salmon.
4. Cook about 2 minutes on each side and stir in the fish broth.
5. Cover with lid and cook for about 7 minutes. Dish out and serve hot.

Paprika Shrimp

Serves: **6** | Prep Time: **25** mins

Ingredients
- 1 teaspoon smoked paprika
- 6 tablespoons butter
- 2 pounds tiger shrimp
- Salt, to taste
- 2 tablespoons sour cream

Directions
1. Preheat the oven to 400ºF and grease a baking dish with butter.
2. Mix together all the ingredients with tiger shrimp in a large bowl and marinate well.
3. Place the seasoned shrimp on the baking dish and transfer to the oven.
4. Bake for about 15 minutes and dish out on a platter to serve hot.

genic Butter Fish

Serves: **3** | Prep Time: **40** mins

Ingredients
- 2 tablespoons ginger garlic paste
- 3 green chilies, chopped
- 1 pound salmon fillets
- Salt and black pepper, to taste
- ¾ cup butter

Directions
1. Season the salmon fillets with ginger garlic paste, salt and black pepper.
2. Place the salmon fillets in the pot and top with green chilies and butter.
3. Cover the lid and cook on medium low heat for about 30 minutes.
4. Dish out in a platter to serve hot.

Shrimp Magic

Serves: **3** | Prep Time: **25** mins

Ingredients
- 2 tablespoons butter
- ½ teaspoon smoked paprika
- 1 pound shrimp, peeled and deveined
- Lemongrass stalks
- 1 red chili pepper, seeded and chopped

Directions
1. Preheat the oven to 390ºF and grease a baking dish.
2. Mix together all the ingredients in a bowl except lemongrass and marinate for about 3 hours. Thread the shrimp onto lemongrass stalks and place in the baking dish.
3. Bake for about 15 minutes and dish out to serve immediately.

Sweet and Sour Cod

Serves: **3** | Prep Time: **35** mins

Ingredients
- ¼ cup butter
- 2 drops liquid Stevia
- 1 pound cod, chunked
- Salt and black pepper, to taste
- 1 tablespoon vinegar

Directions
1. Heat butter in a large skillet and add cod chunks.
2. Sauté for about 3 minutes and stir in liquid Stevia, vinegar, salt and black pepper. Cook for about 20 minutes at medium low heat, stirring continuously.
3. Dish out to a serving bowl and serve hot.

Buttered Scallops

Serves: **6** | Prep Time: **15** mins

Ingredients
- 4 tablespoons fresh rosemary, chopped
- 4 garlic cloves, minced
- 2 pounds sea scallops
- Salt and black pepper, to taste
- ½ cup butter

Directions
1. Season the sea scallops with salt and black pepper.
2. Put butter, rosemary and garlic on medium high heat in a skillet.
3. Sauté for about 2 minutes and stir in the seasoned sea scallops.
4. Cook for about 3 minutes per side and dish out to serve hot.

Buffalo Fish

Serves: **3** | Prep Time: **20** mins

Ingredients
- 3 tablespoons butter
- 1/3 cup Franks Red Hot sauce
- 3 fish fillets
- Salt and black pepper, to taste
- 1 teaspoon garlic powder

Directions
1. Heat butter in a large skillet and add fish fillets.
2. Cook for about 2 minutes on each side and add salt, black pepper and garlic powder.
3. Cook for about 1 minute and add Franks Red Hot sauce.
4. Cover with lid and cook for about 6 minutes on low heat.
5. Dish out on a serving platter and serve hot.

Garlicky Lemon Scallops

Serves: **6** | Prep Time: **30** mins

Ingredients
- 2 pounds scallops
- 3 garlic cloves, minced
- 5 tablespoons butter, divided
- Red pepper flakes, kosher salt and black pepper
- 1 lemon, zest and juice

Directions
1. Heat 2 tablespoons butter over medium heat in a large skillet and add scallops, kosher salt and black pepper. Cook for about 5 minutes per side until golden and transfer to a plate.
2. Heat remaining butter in a skillet and add garlic and red pepper flakes.
3. Cook for about 1 minute and stir in lemon juice and zest.
4. Return the scallops to the skillet and stir well. Dish out on a platter and serve hot.

Garlic Parmesan Cod

Serves: **6** | Prep Time: **35** mins

Ingredients
- 1 tablespoon extra-virgin olive oil
- 1 (2½) pound cod fillet
- ¼ cup parmesan cheese, finely grated
- Salt and black pepper, to taste
- 5 garlic cloves, minced

Directions
1. Preheat the oven to 400°F and grease a baking dish with cooking spray.
2. Mix together olive oil, garlic, parmesan cheese, salt and black pepper in a bowl.
3. Marinate the cod fillets in this mixture for about 1 hour.
4. Transfer to the baking dish and cover with foil.
5. Place in the oven and bake for about 20 minutes. Remove from the oven and serve warm.

Energetic Cod Platter

Serves: **6** | Prep Time: **40** mins

Ingredients
- 1 pound cherry tomatoes, halved
- 6 (4 ounce) cod fillets
- 3 garlic cloves, minced
- Salt and black pepper, to taste
- 2 tablespoons olive oil

Directions
1. Preheat the oven to 375°F and grease a baking dish.
2. Put half the cherry tomatoes in the baking dish and layer with cod fillets.
3. Season with garlic, salt and black pepper and drizzle with olive oil.
4. Arrange remaining tomatoes on the cod fillets and transfer to the oven.
5. Bake for about 30 minutes and dish out to serve hot.

Dinner Mussels

Serves: **6** | Prep Time: **20** mins

Ingredients
- 4 tablespoons olive oil
- 2 pounds mussels, cleaned and debearded
- 2 garlic cloves, minced
- Salt and black pepper, to taste
- 1 cup homemade chicken broth

Directions
1. Heat olive oil in a skillet over medium heat and add garlic.
2. Sauté for about 1 minute and add mussels.
3. Cook for about 5 minutes and stir in the broth, salt and black pepper.
4. Cover with lid and cook for about 5 minutes on low heat.
5. Dish out to a bowl and serve hot.

3 Cheese Mussels

Serves: **6** | Prep Time: **15** mins

Ingredients
- 1 tablespoon salted butter
- 2 pounds mussels, cleaned and debearded
- ¼ cup mozzarella cheese
- ¼ cup parmesan cheese
- ¼ cup cheddar cheese

Directions
1. Heat butter in a skillet on medium heat and add mussels.
2. Cover with lid and cook for about 5 minutes.
3. Stir in all the cheeses and cook for about 3 minutes. Dish out to a bowl to serve hot.

Buttered Lobster

Serves: **6** | Prep Time: **20** mins

Ingredients
- 2 pounds lobster tails, cut in half
- ½ cup unsalted butter, melted
- 1 garlic clove, minced
- Salt, to taste
- ¼ cup parsley

Directions
1. Preheat the oven to 375°F and lightly grease a baking tray.
2. Place the lobster tails, shell side on the baking tray and season with salt.
3. Top with garlic, butter and parsley and transfer to the oven.
4. Bake for about 15 minutes and dish out to serve hot.

Creamed Crab Legs

Serves: **4** | Prep Time: **25** mins

Ingredients
- 2 tablespoons butter, melted
- 2 pounds crab legs, frozen
- 1 medium onion, thinly sliced
- Salt, to taste
- 1 cup sour cream

Directions
1. Heat butter in a skillet over medium heat and add onion.
2. Sauté for about 3 minutes and add crab legs and salt.
3. Cook for about 3 minutes per side and stir in the sour cream.
4. Cook for about 2 minutes and dish out to serve hot.

Prosciutto Wrapped Salmon Skewers

Serves: **4** | Prep Time: **20** mins

Ingredients
- 1 pound salmon, frozen in pieces
- ¼ cup fresh basil, finely chopped
- Black pepper, to taste
- 1 tablespoon olive oil
- 3 oz. prosciutto, in slices

Directions
1. Soak 4 skewers in water and season the salmon fillets with black pepper.
2. Mount the salmon fillets lengthwise on the skewers.
3. Roll the skewers in the chopped basil and wrap with prosciutto slices.
4. Drizzle with olive oil and fry in a nonstick pan for about 5-10 minutes on all sides. Dish out and immediately serve.

Garlic Butter Broiled Lobster Tails

Serves: **4** | Prep Time: **25** mins

Ingredients
- 10 tablespoons butter
- 2 lemons, juiced
- 4 lobster tails, top removed and deveined
- ½ cup garlic, minced
- Sea salt, smoked paprika and white pepper

Directions
1. Preheat the broiler to high and grease a baking sheet.
2. Heat 4 tablespoons butter in a medium skillet and add garlic. Sauté for about 2 minutes and set aside.
3. Mix together sea salt, smoked paprika and white pepper in a bowl.
4. Arrange the lobster tails on the baking sheet and sprinkle with the spice mixture.
5. Drizzle with half the garlic butter and transfer to the oven. Bake for about 10 minutes, drizzling rest of the garlic butter in between. Remove from the oven and serve warm.

5 Ingredient Clam Chowder

Serves: **6** | Prep Time: **30** mins

Ingredients
- 1 pound cauliflower florets, cut into small pieces
- 2 (6.5 oz) cans clams, finely chopped and liquid retained
- 2½ cups almond milk, unsweetened
- Sea salt and black pepper, to taste
- 1½ cups chicken broth

Directions
Put cauliflower florets, clams, almond milk, chicken broth, sea salt and black pepper in a skillet and mix well. Bring to a boil and lower the heat. Allow to simmer for about 20 minutes and dish out in a bowl to serve hot.

Ginger Butter Prawns

Serves: **1** | Prep Time: **20** mins

Ingredients
- ¼ pound prawns
- 2 tablespoons butter
- ½ lemon, juiced
- Salt, black pepper, cayenne pepper
- 2 tablespoons ginger

Directions
1. Marinate the prawns with salt, black pepper, and cayenne pepper and mix well.
2. Heat butter in a pan on medium low heat and add ginger and lemon juice.
3. Cook for about 8 minutes and dish out to a bowl and serve hot.

Grilled Shrimp with Creole Butter

Serves: **4** | Prep Time: **20** mins

Ingredients
- ½ cup salted butter, softened
- 1 pound shrimp, threaded onto skewers
- 2 teaspoons fresh garlic, minced
- 2 tablespoons fresh parsley, chopped
- 1 tablespoon Creole seasoning

Directions
1. Preheat the grill to about 400°F.
2. Mix together butter, parsley, Creole seasoning and garlic in a bowl until well combined. Place the skewers shrimp side down over the grill and grill for about 3 minutes. Flip over the shrimp and baste generously with the Creole butter. Cook for 4 more minutes and dish out to serve.

Vegetable Recipes

Griddled Vegetable and Feta Tart

Serves: **4** | Prep Time: **40** mins

Ingredients
- 1 aubergine, sliced
- 2 red onions, chunked
- 2 tablespoons olive oil
- 2 zucchinis, sliced
- 3 large sheets filo pastry
- 1 tablespoon balsamic vinegar
- 1 teaspoon dried oregano
- 12 cherry tomatoes, halved
- ½ cup feta cheese, crumbled

Directions
1. Preheat the oven to 375 degrees F and line a baking dish with filo pastry.
2. Heat oil into a griddle pan and add aubergines. Grill until charred and dish out in a plate. Grill the onions and zucchinis in the pan. Place the charred vegetables, tomatoes, and seasonings in the baking dish. Sprinkle with feta cheese and oregano and transfer in the oven.
3. Bake for about 20 minutes and remove from the oven to serve.

Mediterranean Gnocchi

Serves: **4** | Prep Time: **15** mins

Ingredients

- 7 oz. chargrilled vegetables (aubergines, peppers, semi-dried tomatoes, and artichokes)
- 1 handful basil leaves
- 14 oz. gnocchi, boiled and drained
- 2 tablespoons red pesto
- Parmesan cheese, to serve

Directions

1. Put the gnocchi to a pan along with a splash of water.
2. Stir in charred vegetables, red pesto, basil leaves, and parmesan cheese.Dish out .

Parmesan Roasted Broccoli

Serves: **4** | Prep Time: **35** mins

Ingredients

- 2 tablespoons olive oil
- ½ cup Parmesan cheese, grated
- 1 lemon, zested
- Pinch of flaky sea salt
- 1 pound broccoli florets, cut into bite-sized pieces
- Salt, to taste
- 2 tablespoons balsamic vinegar
- Pinch of red pepper flakes

Directions

1. Preheat the oven to 400 degrees F and grease a baking sheet.
2. Season the broccoli florets with salt and arrange on the baking sheet.
3. Bake for about 15 minutes and sprinkle with parmesan cheese.
4. Bake these florets again for 10 minutes and season with lemon zest, salt, red pepper flakes, and balsamic vinegar to serve.

Baked Goat Cheese with Tomato Sauce

Serves: **4** | Prep Time: **30** mins

Ingredients

- ½ cup white onions, finely chopped
- 1¼ tablespoons fresh basil, chopped
- 1½ teaspoons white wine vinegar
- ½ teaspoon salt
- Whole grain baguette, to serve
- 1 tablespoon olive oil
- 2 medium garlic cloves, pressed or minced
- ¼ teaspoon red pepper flakes
- ¼ teaspoon dried oregano
- 1 can (15 ounces) crushed tomatoes
- Black pepper, to taste
- 4 ounces goat cheese

Directions

1. Preheat the oven to 375 degrees F and grease 4 ramekins.
2. Pour oil in a pan and add onions.
3. Sauté for about 3 minutes and add basil, red pepper flakes, oregano, and garlic.
4. Cook for about 1 minute and add white wine vinegar, tomatoes, salt, and black pepper.
5. Cover with a lid and cook for about 10 minutes.
6. Divide this mixture into the ramekins and sprinkle with cheese.
7. Arrange the ramekins in a baking tray and transfer in the oven.
8. Bake for about 15 minutes and top with olive oil and basil to serve.

Roasted Vegetable Tabbouleh

Serves: **4** | Prep Time: **35** mins

Ingredients

- 3 medium carrots, chopped
- 1 (16-ounce) can garbanzo beans, rinsed and drained
- ¾ cup bulgur, boiled and drained
- 1 small red onion, chopped
- ½ cup fresh parsley, chopped
- 3 tablespoons lemon juice
- 2 tablespoons olive oil
- ¼ teaspoon black pepper
- ⅛ teaspoon salt
- ½ teaspoon lemon peel, finely shredded
- 2 tablespoons water
- 2 teaspoons fresh thyme, snipped
- 1 medium tomato, chopped

Directions

1. Preheat the oven to 400 degrees F and grease a baking dish.
2. Arrange carrots and onions in a baking dish and drizzle with olive oil.
3. Bake for about 25 minutes and dish out in a bowl.
4. Add bulgur, lemon peel, pepper, salt, parsley, lemon juice, and garbanzo to the baked veggies bowl to serve.

Vegan Pesto Spaghetti Squash

Serves: **4** | Prep Time: **1 hour**

Ingredients
- 4 tablespoons extra-virgin olive oil, divided
- ½ cup sun-dried tomatoes, julienned
- 1 (3-pounds) spaghetti squash, halved lengthwise and seeded
- 8 ounces cremini mushrooms, sliced
- ½ teaspoon salt, divided
- 2 garlic cloves, coarsely chopped
- 3 tablespoons lemon juice
- ½ teaspoon black pepper
- 1 cup packed fresh basil leaves
- ⅓ cup unsalted raw cashews
- 2 teaspoons nutritional yeast

Directions
1. Preheat the oven to 400 degrees F and grease a baking sheet.
2. Arrange the squash on the baking sheet and bake for about 45 minutes.
3. Sauté mushrooms, tomatoes and salt in 1 tablespoon oil in a pan for about 5 minutes.
4. Blend 3 tablespoons of oil with basil, cashews, yeast, lemon juice, garlic, salt, and black pepper. Scrape the flesh of the baked squash to get thin spaghetti.
5. Place the spaghetti in a colander to drain all the liquid.
6. Divide the squash spaghetti into the serving plates and top with mushrooms and basil sauce to serve.

Smoky Roasted Vegetables

Serves: **8** | Prep Time: **1 hour 40** mins

Ingredients
- 2 small red onions, sliced into rounds and separated
- 1 small orange bell pepper, sliced
- 1 small summer squash, cut into 3-inch sticks
- 1 teaspoon sea salt, divided
- 1 bay leaf
- ⅓ cup extra-virgin olive oil
- 1 tablespoon red-wine vinegar
- 3 medium tomatoes, sliced
- 1 small eggplant, cut into 3-inch sticks
- 1 small yellow bell pepper, sliced
- 1 small zucchini, cut into 3-inch sticks
- 3 sprigs fresh parsley
- 2 sprigs fresh thyme
- 4 cloves garlic, divided
- 1 tablespoon balsamic vinegar

Directions
1. Preheat the oven to 350 degrees F and grease a baking dish.
2. Season vegetables with salt and transfer to the baking dish.
3. Tie parsley, thyme, and bay leaf with a kitchen string, and place them at the center of the vegetables.
Top with garlic cloves and some oil and bake for about 1 hour and 15 minutes. Drizzle with vinegar and serve.

Baked Goat Cheese with Tomato Sauce

Serves: **4** | Prep Time: **30** mins

Ingredients
- ½ cup white onions, finely chopped
- 1¼ tablespoons fresh basil, chopped
- 1½ teaspoons white wine vinegar
- ½ teaspoon kosher salt
- 4 ounces goat cheese
- 1 tablespoon olive oil
- 2 medium garlic cloves, pressed or minced
- ¼ teaspoon red pepper flakes
- ¼ teaspoon dried oregano
- 1 can (15 ounces) crushed tomatoes
- Black pepper, to taste

Directions
1. Preheat the oven to 375 degrees F and grease 4 ramekins. Heat olive oil in a pan and add onions.
2. Sauté for about 3 minutes and add garlic, basil, red pepper flakes, and oregano.
3. Sauté for about 1 minute and add white wine vinegar, tomatoes, salt, and black pepper.
4. Lower the heat, cover and allow to simmer for about 10 minutes.
5. Divide this mixture into the ramekins and top with goat cheese.
6. Transfer into the oven and bake for about 15 minutes. Top with basil and olive oil to serve.

Charred Green Beans with Mustard

Serves: **4** | Prep Time: **20** mins

Ingredients
- 3 tablespoons extra-virgin olive oil, divided
- 2 teaspoons whole-grain mustard
- 1 pound green beans, trimmed
- 1 tablespoon red-wine vinegar
- ¼ teaspoon salt
- ¼ cup toasted hazelnuts, chopped
- ¼ teaspoon black pepper

Directions
1. Preheat a grill on high heat. Mix green beans with 1 tablespoon of olive oil in a pan.
2. Transfer to the grill and grill the beans for about 7 minutes.
3. Mix the beans with mustard, oil, vinegar, salt, and black pepper. Garnish with hazelnuts and serve hot.

Sage-Infused Butternut Squash Zucchini Noodles

Yield: 4 | Total Time: 25 Mins | Prep Time: 10 Mins | Cook Time: 15 Mins

Ingredients
- 3 large zucchinis, spiralized or julienned into noodles
- 3 cups cubed butternut squash
- 2 cloves garlic, finely chopped
- 1 yellow onion, chopped
- 2 tablespoons olive oil
- 2 cups homemade vegetable broth
- ¼ teaspoon red pepper flakes
- Freshly ground black pepper
- 1 tablespoon fresh sage, finely chopped
- Salt, to taste and smoked salt for garnish

Directions
1. Add the oil to a pan over medium heat and sauté the sage once it's hot until it turns crisp. Transfer to a small bowl and season lightly with salt then set aside.
2. Add the onion, butternut, garlic, broth, salt and pepper flakes to in instant pot and lock the lid; cook on high pressure for 10 Mins and then release pressure naturally.
3. Meanwhile, steam the zucchini noodles in your microwave or steamer until crisp-tender.
4. Once the butternut mixture is ready, remove from heat and let cool off slightly then transfer to a blender and process until smooth. Combine the zucchini noodles and the butternut puree in the skillet over medium heat and cook until heated through and evenly coated for 2 Mins.
5. Sprinkle with fried sage and smoked salt and serve hot.

Instant Pot Coconut Curry Tofu

Yield: 4 | Total Time: 20 Mins | Prep Time: 5 Mins | Cook Time: 15 Mins

Ingredients
- 1-pound tofu
- 15 ounces water
- 30 ounces light coconut milk
- ½ cup Thai red curry sauce
- ¼ cup cilantro
- 2½ tsp. lemon garlic seasoning

Directions
1. In an instant pot, combine tofu, water, coconut milk, red curry paste, cilantro, and lemon garlic seasoning; stir to mix well and lock lid; cook on high pressure for 15 Mins and then release pressure naturally. Serve garnished with cilantro.

Asian Saag Aloo

Yield: 4-6 | Total Time: 20 Mins | Prep Time: 10 Mins | Cook Time: 10 Mins

Ingredients
- 500g fresh spinach, roughly chopped
- 200g fresh baby spinach
- 2 tbsp. ginger root, crushed
- 4 cloves garlic, crushed
- 350ml coconut milk
- ¼ cup frozen peas
- 2 pkts marinated tofu
- 1 cup tomato sauce
- 2 tbsp. tomato ketchup
- 1 tbsp. ground coriander
- 1 tbsp. ground cumin
- 1 tbsp. garam masala
- 1 pinch cayenne pepper
- 2 tbsp. cilantro, chopped
- Salt to taste

Directions
1. First, set aside the baby spinach. Combine all the remaining ingredients in your instant pot and lock lid; cook on high pressure for 10 Mins and then release the pressure naturally.
2. Use an immersion blender to puree the entire mixture. (You can omit the blending part if you don't like your food mushy). Fold in the baby spinach and cover the pot until spinach is wilted. Serve hot with roast potatoes.

Creamy Cauliflower 'Mashed Potatoes'

Yield: 4 | Total Time: 20 Mins | Prep Time: 10 Mins | Cook Time: 10 Mins

Ingredients
- 1 whole cauliflower, cut into florets
- 4 cloves garlic, peeled and roughly chopped
- 2 tbsp. butter
- 2 tbsp. cream cheese
- 1 bay leaf
- 3 cups water
- 1 cup low-fat milk
- Salt and pepper to taste

Directions
1. Combine the cauliflower florets in your instant pot with all the ingredients apart from the milk and cream cheese. Lock lid and cook on high pressure for 10 Mins. Release the pressure naturally and then discard the bay leaf and garlic cloves and drain off the water. Mash the cauliflower using a potato masher or an immersion blender if you want it very creamy. If you are adding milk, do so a tablespoon at a time, until you get the desired consistency. Blend in the coconut cream.
2. Season with salt and pepper and garnish with chopped chives or chopped green onions and serve with your favorite stew. Enjoy!

Instant Pot Spanish Tortilla

Yield: 4 | Total Time: 25 Mins | Prep Time: 10 Mins | Cook Time: 15 Mins

Ingredients
- 6 large eggs
- 1/4 cup milk
- 1 tablespoon butter melted
- 4 oz. raw potatoes, sliced thinly into strips
- 1/4 cup diced red onions
- 1 clove fresh garlic, minced
- 1/2 teaspoon sea salt
- 1/4 teaspoon pepper
- 1 teaspoon tomato paste
- 2 tablespoons baking mix
- 1 teaspoon seasoning
- 4 oz. grated parmesan cheese
- 1 ½ cups water
- 1 cup spinach
- 1 cup chopped green bell pepper

Directions
1. Soak the potato strips in water for at least 20 Mins. Whisk eggs and seasoning in a bowl until frothy.
2. In another bowl, whisk together milk, baking mix and tomato paste until well blended and then whisk into the egg mixture; stir in garlic and onion. Grease your casserole dish.
3. Drain the potato strips and dry with paper towel; add to the casserole dish and pour in the melted butter. Pour in the egg mixture, chopped green pepper and spinach; top with grated cheese. Add water to your instant pot and insert a trivet; place the casserole dish over the trivet and lock lid. Cook on high for 15 Mins and then let pressure come down on its own. Serve warm.

Sage-Infused Butternut Squash Zucchini Noodles

Yield: 4 | Total Time: 25 Mins | Prep Time: 10 Mins | Cook Time: 15 Mins

Ingredients
- 3 large zucchinis, spiralized or julienned into noodles
- 3 cups cubed butternut squash
- 2 cloves garlic, finely chopped
- 1 yellow onion, chopped
- 2 tbsp. olive oil
- 2 cups homemade vegetable broth
- ¼ tsp. red pepper flakes
- Freshly ground black pepper
- 1 tbsp. fresh sage, finely chopped
- Salt, to taste and smoked salt for garnish

Directions
1. Add the oil to a pan over medium heat. Once it's hot, sauté the sage until crisp. Transfer to a small bowl, season lightly with salt, then set aside. Add the onion, butternut, garlic, broth, salt, and pepper flakes to an instant pot and lock the lid; cook on high pressure for 10 Mins and then release pressure naturally.
2. Meanwhile, steam the zucchini noodles in your microwave or steamer until crisp-tender.
3. Once the butternut mixture is ready, remove from heat; let it cool off slightly, then transfer to a blender and process until smooth. Combine the zucchini noodles and the butternut puree in the skillet over medium heat and cook until heated through and evenly coated for two Mins.
4. Sprinkle with fried sage and smoked salt and serve hot.

Coconut Porridge

Yield: 6 | Total Time: 15 Mins | Prep Time: 5 Mins | Cook Time: 10 Mins

Ingredients
- ¼ cup almond flour
- 1/4 cup dried shredded coconut (unsweetened)
- 2 2/3 cups water
- 2 cups coconut milk
- 1/4 cup psyllium husks
- 2 tsp. liquid Stevia
- 1/4 tsp. nutmeg
- 1/2 tsp. cinnamon
- 1 tsp. vanilla extract

Directions
1. Add coconut to your instant pot and set it on sauté setting; cook, stirring until toasted; stir in water and coconut milk; lock lid and cook on high for 5 Mins and then quick release the pressure; stir in the remaining ingredients.

Instant Pot Coconut Cabbage

Yield: 6 | Total Time: 25 Mins | Prep Time: 15 Mins | Cook Time: 10 Mins

Ingredients
- 2 tbsp. coconut oil
- 2 tbsp. olive oil
- 1/4 cup desiccated unsweetened coconut
- 2 tbsp. lemon juice
- 1 medium carrot, sliced
- 1 medium yellow onion, sliced
- 1 medium cabbage, shredded
- 1 tbsp. turmeric powder
- 1 tbsp. mild curry powder
- 1 tsp. mustard powder
- ½ long red chili, sliced
- 2 large cloves of garlic, diced
- 1½ tsp. salt
- ⅓ cup water

Directions
Turn your instant pot on sauté mode and add coconut oil; stir in onion and salt and cook for about four Mins. Stir in spices, chili, and garlic for about 30 seconds. Stir in the remaining ingredients and lock the lid; set on manual high for 5 Mins. When done, naturally release the pressure and stir the mixture. Serve with beans or rice.

Yummy Brussels Sprouts

Yield: 4 | Total Time: 16 Mins | Prep Time: 10 Mins | Cook Time: 6 Mins

Ingredients
- 2 pounds Brussels sprouts, halved
- 1 tbsp. chopped almonds
- 1 tbsp. rice vinegar
- 2 tbsp. sriracha sauce
- 1/4 cup soy sauce
- 4 tbsp. sesame oil
- 1/2 tbsp. cayenne pepper
- 1 tbsp. smoked paprika
- 1 tsp. onion powder
- 2 tsp. garlic powder
- 1 tsp. red pepper flakes
- Salt and pepper

Directions
1. Set your pot to sauté and add in almond; cook for about 3 Mins and then stir in all the seasonings and liquid ingredients. Stir in Brussels sprouts and set on manual high for 3 Mins. When done, quick release pressure and serve over rice.

Peperonata (Tasty Pepper Salad)

Yield: 4 | Total Time: 15 Mins | Prep Time: 5 Mins | Cook Time: 10 Mins

Ingredients:
- 2 red capsicums, sliced into strips
- 2 yellow capsicums, sliced into strips
- 1 green capsicum, sliced into strips
- 2 tbsp. olive oil
- 1 red onion
- 2 garlic cloves
- 3 tomatoes, chopped
- basil, chopped
- salt and pepper

Directions
1. Add oil to your instant pot and sauté onions until tender; add one garlic clove and capsicums and cook until browned. Add the chopped tomatoes, salt, and pepper and stir to mix; lock lid and cook on high pressure for 5 Mins and then release pressure naturally.
2. Press the remaining garlic clove and set aside. Remove capsicums into a bowl and add olive oil, garlic and chopped basil; mix well and serve.

Instant Pot Korean Breakfast Eggs

Yield: 1 Serving | Total time: 10 Mins | Prep time: 5 Mins | Cook time: 5 Mins

Ingredients
- 1 large egg
- pinch of sesame seeds
- 1 tsp. chopped scallions
- 1/3 cup cold water
- pinch of garlic powder
- pinch of salt
- pinch of pepper

Directions
1. In a small bowl, whisk together water and eggs until frothy; strain the mixture through a fine mesh into a heatproof bowl. Whisk in the remaining ingredients until well combined; set aside.
2. Add a cup of water to an instant pot and place a steamer basket or trivet in the pot; place the bowl with the mixture over the basket and lock lid. Cook on high for 5 Mins and then naturally release pressure. Serve hot with a glass of freshly squeezed orange juice.

Arugula, Orange & Kamut Salad

Yield: 6 | Total Time: 28 Mins | Prep Time: 10 Mins | Cook Time: 18 Mins

Ingredients
- 1 cup whole Kamut grains, rinsed
- 1 teaspoon vegetable oil
- 2 cups water
- 1 teaspoon sea salt
- ½ lemon
- ¼ cup chopped walnuts
- 3 tablespoons extra virgin olive oil
- 2 medium blood oranges, sliced
- 2 cups rocket Arugula

Directions
1. In a bowl, combine kamut grains, lemon juice and 4 cups of water; soak overnight.
2. Strain the kamut and add to an instant pot along with oil, salt and water; lock the lid and cook on high pressure for 18 Mins. Release the pressure naturally and then transfer to a serving bowl; stir in olive oil, walnuts, orange pieces and arugula. Serve right away.

Creamy Cauliflower Mash

Yield: 4 | Total Time: 20 Mins | Prep Time: 10 Mins | Cook Time: 10 Mins

Ingredients
- 1 whole cauliflower, cut into florets
- 4 cloves garlic, peeled and roughly chopped
- 1 tbsp. coconut oil
- 2 tbsp. coconut cream
- 1 bay leaf
- 3 cups water
- 1 cup coconut milk
- Salt and pepper to taste

Directions

1. Combine the cauliflower florets in your instant pot with all the ingredients apart from the milk and cream. Lock lid and cook on high pressure for 10 Mins. Release the pressure naturally and then discard the bay leaf and garlic cloves and drain off the water. Mash the cauliflower using a potato masher or an immersion blender if you want it very creamy. If you are adding milk, do so a tablespoon at a time, until you get the desired consistency. Blend in the coconut cream.
2. Season with salt and pepper and garnish with chopped chives or chopped green onions and serve with your favorite stew. Enjoy!

Delicious Sage-Infused Butternut Squash Zucchini Noodles

Yield: 4 | Total Time: 25 Mins | Prep Time: 10 Mins | Cook Time: 15 Mins

Ingredients

- 3 large zucchinis, spiralized or julienned into noodles
- 3 cups cubed butternut squash
- 2 cloves garlic, finely chopped
- 1 yellow onion, chopped
- 2 tablespoons olive oil
- 2 cups homemade vegetable broth
- ¼ teaspoon red pepper flakes
- Freshly ground black pepper
- 1 tablespoon fresh sage, finely chopped
- Salt, to taste and smoked salt for garnish

Directions

1. Add the oil to a pan over medium heat and sauté the sag until it turns crisp. Transfer to a small bowl and season lightly with salt then set aside.
2. Add the onion, butternut, garlic, broth, salt and pepper flakes to in instant pot and lock the lid; cook on high pressure for 10 Mins and then release pressure naturally.
3. Meanwhile, steam the zucchini noodles in your microwave or steamer until crisp-tender.
4. Once the butternut mixture is ready, remove from heat and let cool off slightly then transfer to a blender and process until smooth. Combine the zucchini noodles and the butternut puree in the skillet over medium heat and cook until heated through and evenly coated for 2 Mins.
5. Sprinkle with fried sage and smoked salt and serve hot.

Tasty Coconut Cabbage

Yield: 6 | Total Time: 25 Mins | Prep Time: 15 Mins | Cook Time: 10 Mins

Ingredients

- 2 tablespoons coconut oil
- 2 tablespoons olive oil
- ½ cup desiccated unsweetened coconut
- 2 tablespoons lemon juice
- 1 medium carrot, sliced
- 1 medium brown onion, sliced
- 1 medium cabbage, shredded
- 1 tablespoon turmeric powder
- 1 tablespoon mild curry powder
- 1 teaspoon mustard powder
- ½ long red chili, sliced
- 2 large cloves of garlic, diced
- 1 + ½ teaspoons salt
- ⅓ cup water

Directions

1. Turn your instant pot on sauté mode and add coconut oil; stir in onion and salt and cook for about 4 Mins. Stir in spices, chili and garlic for about 30 seconds. Stir in the remaining ingredients and lock the lid; set on manual high for 5 Mins. When done, naturally release the pressure and stir the mixture. Serve with beans or rice.

Instant Pot Freekeh & Roasted Cauliflower w/ Tahini Sauce

Yield: 4-6 | Total Time: 30 Mins | Prep Time: 15 Mins | Cook Time: 15 Mins

Ingredients

For the freekeh:

- 1 ¼ - 1 ½ cups cracked freekeh
- ¼ cup sliced almonds
- 2 cloves garlic, minced
- 1 tablespoon olive oil
- ¼ teaspoon coriander
- ½ teaspoon salt
- ¼ teaspoon cumin
- 3 ½ cups homemade vegetable stock

For the cauliflower:

- 1 large cauliflower, cut into florets
- 3 tablespoons olive oil
- Black pepper and salt to taste

Tahini sauce:

- 1/3 cup tahini
- 2 cloves garlic, minced
- 3 tablespoons freshly squeezed lime juice
- 1/3 cup water
- A large pinch of red pepper flakes
- Black pepper and salt to taste

Toppings:

- Sesame seeds
- Chopped cilantro
- Raisins

Directions

1. Preheat your oven to 425 degrees F. Arrange the cauliflower on a baking sheet and toss with salt, pepper and olive oil. Spread them in one layer and roast for half an hour, until they start turning golden, turning them halfway through cook time.
2. Meanwhile, add a tablespoon of olive oil to an instant pot set on sauté mode and cook the almonds for 3 Mins or until they start browning. Toss in the freekeh and cook for 2 Mins then add the remaining dry ingredients and cook for a minute. Add broth, salt and pepper and lock the lid; cook on high pressure for 10 Mins and then release the pressure naturally. Remove from heat and fluff with a fork. Whisk the dressing ingredients until smooth then set aside. To serve, start with the freekeh followed by the roasted cauliflower and top with the tahini sauce. Garnish with the desired toppings and serve immediately.

Yummy Refried Beans

Yield: 6 | Total Time: 35 Mins | Prep Time: 5 Mins | Cook Time: 30 Mins

Ingredients

- 4 tablespoons olive oil
- 2 pounds dried pinto beans, sorted and soaked, rinsed
- 5 garlic cloves, roughly chopped
- 1 1/2 cups chopped onion
- 3 tablespoons vegetable shortening
- 1 1/2 teaspoons ground cumin
- 2 teaspoons dried oregano
- 1 jalapeno, seeded and chopped
- 4 cups vegetable broth
- 1-2 teaspoons sea salt
- 4 cups water
- 1/2 teaspoon ground black pepper

Directions

1. Mix all the ingredients in an instant pot and lock the lid; press the chili or bean button for 30 Mins. When done, let pressure release naturally.
2. Stir in sea salt and transfer the mixture to a blender; blend to your desired consistency and serve.

Pressure Cooked Navy Beans, Split Pea & Sweet Potatoes Bowl

Yield: 4-6 | Total Time: 40 Mins | Prep Time: 10 Mins | Cook Time: 30 Mins

Ingredients

- 3 tablespoons coconut oil
- ½ cup dried navy beans
- 1 cup split peas
- 1 medium sweet potato, diced
- 1/2 cup nutritional yeast
- ½ teaspoon liquid smoke
- bay leaves
- Pinch of pepper
- Pinch of sea salt
- 5 cups water

Directions

1. In an instant pot, mix coconut oil, navy beans, split peas, sweet potatoes, water and liquid smoke; cook on high pressure for 20 Mins. Naturally release pressure and stir in salt, pepper and nutritional yeast. Serve.

Healthy Italian Mushrooms

Yield: 4 | Total Time: 25 Mins | Prep Time: 10 Mins | Cook Time: 15 Mins

Ingredients

- 1-pound Portobello mushrooms, cleaned and sliced
- 2 tbsp. garlic infused ghee
- 1 ½ cups grated Parmesan cheese
- 1 ½ cups chopped tomatoes
- 1 tsp. dried oregano
- 1 tbsp. chopped fresh parsley
- 2 tbsp. chopped fresh basil
- salt and pepper

Directions:

1. Add water to your instant pot and insert a trivet.
2. In a nonstick pan set over medium heat, heat garlic infused ghee; stir in mushrooms, salt and pepper and cook for about 5 Mins.
3. Remove the pan from heat and transfer the cooked mushrooms to a baking pan.
4. In a bowl, mix canned tomatoes, parsley, basil and herbs; season with salt and pour the mixture over the mushrooms. Top with grated cheese and place the pan over the trivet; lock lid and cook on manual for 10 Mins. Quick release pressure and let cool for a few Mins before serving.

Instant Pot Low Carb Veggie Dish

Yield: 4 | Total Time: 15 Mins | Prep Time: 5 Mins | Cook Time: 10 Mins

Ingredients

- 1.5 cups dry Soy Curls
- 2 tsp. minced ginger
- 6 cloves garlic, minced
- 2 cups diced tomatoes
- 1 tsp. paprika
- ½ tsp. cayenne pepper
- 1 tsp. turmeric
- 1 tsp. ground cumin
- 1 tsp. graham masala
- 4 ounces heavy cream
- 4 ounces butter
- ¼-1/2 cup chopped cilantro
- 1 tsp. salt
- 1 cup water

Directions

1. In your instant pot, combine soy curls, tomatoes, spices and water and lock lid; cook on high for 6 Mins; let pressure come down on its own and then turn the pot on sauté mode and then add in cream and butter; stir until melted and crush the tomatoes with a spoon.
2. Stir in cilantro and more graham masala and serve right away.

Instant Pot Ham & Greens

Yield: 4 | Total Time: 14 Mins | Prep Time: 10 Mins | Cook Time: 4 Mins

Ingredients

- 2 cups tofu chopped
- 6 cloves garlic, chopped
- 1 red onion, chopped
- 8 cups chopped collard greens
- 1 tsp. dried thyme
- 2 bay leaves
- 1 tsp red pepper flakes
- ½ tsp. Salt
- ½ tsp. Pepper
- ¼ cups water
- 1 tsp. liquid smoke
- 2 tsp. hot sauce
- 1 tbsp. apple cider vinegar

Directions

1. Combine all ingredients, except liquid smoke, apple cider vinegar and hot sauce, in your instant pot; cook on high for 4 Mins and then let pressure come down on its own. Stir in hot sauce, liquid smoke and apple cider vinegar. Serve.

Mixed Veggie Pot Pie

Yield: 1 9-inch pie | Total Time: 1 Hour 20 Mins | Prep Time: 20 Mins | Cook Time: 1 Hour

Ingredients

For the pie crust:

- ¾ cup coconut flour
- 2 eggs
- ½ cup salted butter, chilled

For the pie filling:

- ½ cup frozen spinach, separated
- 2 cups, cauliflower florets, cut into smaller chunks
- 1/3 cup frozen peas
- ¼ cup win sauce
- ½ cup cheddar cheese, shredded

Directions

1. Add water to your instant pot and insert a trivet.
2. Prepare the pie crust as in the crusty spinach pie recipe and spread it on a 9-inch pie pan.
3. Add the cauliflower to an oven proof pan and roast until they start browning for 30 Mins.
4. Combine the roast cauliflower with the peas. Spinach, win sauce. and cheese in a mixing bowl. Spread the filling on the crust and place the pan on the trivet; lock lid and cook on manual for 20 Mins. Release pressure naturally.
5. Remove from pot and let stand for 5 Mins before serving.

Instant Pot Pepper Salad

Yield: 4 | Total Time: 15 Mins | Prep Time: 5 Mins | Cook Time: 10 Mins

Ingredients:

- 2 red capsicums, sliced into strips
- 2 yellow capsicums, sliced into strips
- 1 green capsicum, sliced into strips
- ½ teaspoon olive oil
- 1 red onion
- 2 garlic cloves
- 3 tomatoes, chopped
- basil, chopped
- salt and pepper

Directions

1. Add oil to your instant pot and sauté onions until tender; add 1 garlic clove, and capsicums and cook until browned. Add the chopped tomatoes, salt and pepper and stir to mix; lock lid and cook on high pressure for 5 Mins and then release pressure naturally.
2. Press the remaining garlic clove and set aside.
3. Remove capsicums to a bowl and add olive oil, garlic and chopped basil; mix well.

Egg- Sauerkraut Salad

Yield: 3-4 | Total Time: 20 Mins | Prep Time: 10 Mins | Cook Time: 10 Mins

Ingredients

- 6 eggs
- ½ - ¾ cup sauerkraut
- ¼ cup mayonnaise
- Freshly ground pepper to taste

Directions

1. In your instant pot, boil the eggs for 10 Mins.
2. Add the sauerkraut to a bowl and peel the hardboiled eggs and chop them up finely in the bowl. Add in the sauerkraut and mayonnaise and combine well until evenly mixed.
3. Season with pepper and salt and serve. Enjoy!

Broccoli & Cauliflower Mash

Yield: 4 | Total Time: 15 Mins | Prep Time: 10 Mins | Cook Time: 5 Mins

Ingredients
- 4 cups broccoli and cauliflower florets
- 2 tsp butter
- 3 cloves garlic
- ½ tsp freshly ground pepper
- ½ tsp salt

Directions
1. Melt the butter in your instant pot and sauté the broccoli and cauliflower. Sprinkle with salt and lock lid; cook on high for 1 minute and then quick release the pressure.
2. Turn your pot on sauté mode and cook until the veggies lose all of their water to give them a roasty finish.
3. Combine the cooked veggies with garlic and pepper in your food processor and process until you get a mashed potato texture. Serve with more butter, if desired. Serve immediately.

Cheese & Broccoli Casserole

Yield: 3-4 | Total Time: 25 Mins | Prep Time: 15 Mins | Cook Time: 10 Mins

Ingredients
- 3 cups frozen broccoli
- 1 cup almond milk
- ½ cup shredded cheddar cheese
- 8 eggs
- Freshly ground pepper and salt to taste

Directions
1. Add two cups of water to your instant pot and insert a trivet.
2. Grease a large pie dish or casserole dish.
3. Combine all ingredients in a bowl, reserving a little cheese for topping.
4. Scoop into the prepared dish and top with the reserved cheese.
5. Place the dish on the trivet and lock lid; cook on manual for 5 Mins and then quick release pressure. Transfer the dish to the oven and bake for about 5 Mins or until top is browned. Enjoy!

Gluten-Free Coconut Breakfast Cereal

Yield: 5 | Total Time: 10 Mins | Prep Time: 5 Mins | Cook Time: 5 Mins

Ingredients
- 1 cup golden flax meal
- 1 cup coconut flour
- 1 cup coconut milk
- 2 tbsp. butter
- 4 large eggs, beaten
- 1 cup water
- ¼ tsp. salt
- 1 tbsp. liquid Stevia

Directions
1. Add in flax meal, coconut flour, water and salt to your instant pot; lock lid and cook on manual for 5 Mins; quick release pressure and then set it on sauté mode; beat in beaten egg, one at a time, until the mixture is thick. Whisk in coconut milk, butter and sweetener and then serve.

Low Carb Oatmeal

Yield: 4 | Total Time: 15 Mins | Prep Time: 5 Mins | Cook Time: 10 Mins

Ingredients
- 1/3 cup flaked coconut
- 1/3 cup flaked almonds
- 1/4 cup chia Seeds
- 1/2 cup coconut milk
- 1/4 cup shredded coconut
- 1 tsp. vanilla Extract
- 1 tsp. liquid Stevia
- 1 cup water

Directions
1. Set your instant pot on sauté mode and toast flaked almonds and coconut for about 5 Mins; add in the remaining ingredients and lock lid; cook on high for 5 Mins and then quick release the pressure.

Tasty Spiced Pecans

Yield: 6 | Total Time: 25 Mins | Prep Time: 10 Mins | Cook Time: 15 Mins

Ingredients
- 3 cups raw pecans
- 1/8 tsp. cayenne pepper
- 1/8 tsp. ground ginger
- 1/2 tsp. ground nutmeg
- 1 tsp. ground cinnamon
- 1/8 tsp. sea salt
- 1 tbsp. water

Directions
1. Combine all ingredients in your instant pot and lock lid; cook on manual for 10 Mins and then quick release the pressure.
2. Transfer the mixture to a baking sheet and spread it out; bake at 350 degrees for about 5 Mins.

Crusty Spinach Pie

Yield: 4 | Total Time: 30 Mins | Prep Time: 10 Mins | Cook Time: 20 Mins

Ingredients
For the pie crust:
- ¾ cup almond flour
- 4 eggs
- 3/4 cup butter

For the pie filling:
- ½ cup marinated artichoke hearts, chopped
- 1 cup frozen spinach, thawed and thoroughly drained
- 1 cup feta, crumbled
- dash of pepper

Directions
1. Add water to your instant pot and insert a trivet.
2. Combine the drained spinach and artichoke hearts and drain any present liquid then set aside.
3. Combine the almond flour and butter using a fork until you get a coarse texture. Mix in the eggs until you get a nice and thick dough. If, however the dough is too dry, add a tablespoon or two of cold water and continue kneading.
4. Press the dough into a 9-inch pie pan. Add the feta and pepper to the spinach and artichokes and toss well to combine.
5. Spread over the pie crust and place the pan on the trivet; lock lid and cook on manual for 20 Mins. Release pressure naturally.
6. Remove from pot and let stand for 5 Mins then serve.

Browned Butter Cauliflower Mash

Serves: 4 | Prep Time: 35 mins

Ingredients
- 1 yellow onion, finely chopped
- ¾ cup heavy whipping cream
- 1½ pounds cauliflower, shredded
- Sea salt and black pepper, to taste
- 3½ oz. butter

Directions
1. Heat 2 tablespoons butter in a skillet on medium heat and add onions.
2. Sauté for about 3 minutes and dish out to a bowl.
3. Mix together cauliflower, heavy whipping cream, sea salt and black pepper in the same skillet.
4. Cover with lid and cook on medium low heat for about 15 minutes.
5. Season with salt and black pepper and stir in sautéed onions.
6. Dish out to a bowl and heat the rest of the butter in the skillet.
7. Cook until the butter is brown and nutty and serve with cauliflower mash.

Cauliflower Gratin

Serves: 6 | Prep Time: 35 mins

Ingredients
- 20 oz. cauliflower, chopped
- 2 oz. salted butter, for frying
- 5 oz. cheddar cheese, shredded
- 15 oz. sausages in links, precooked and chopped into 1 inch pieces
- 1 cup crème fraiche

Directions
1. Preheat the oven to 375°F and grease a baking dish lightly.
2. Heat 1 oz. butter in a pan on medium low heat and add chopped cauliflower.
3. Sauté for about 4 minutes and transfer to the baking dish.
4. Heat the rest of the butter in a pan on medium low heat and add sausage links.
5. Sauté for about 3 minutes and transfer to the baking dish on top of cauliflower.
6. Pour the crème fraiche in the baking dish and top with cheddar cheese.
7. Transfer into the oven and bake for about 15 minutes. Dish out to a bowl and serve hot.

Beefless Ground Tofu

Serves: 2 | Prep Time: 20 mins

Ingredients
- 2 tablespoons tamari
- 1 (16 ounce) package extra firm tofu, drained, crumbled and patted dry
- ½ teaspoon garlic powder
- 1 tablespoon extra-virgin olive oil
- ½ teaspoon paprika

Directions
1. Mix together tofu, garlic powder, tamari and paprika in a bowl.
2. Heat olive oil over medium high heat in a nonstick skillet and add the tofu mixture.
3. Cook for about 10 minutes until nicely browned, stirring occasionally.
4. Dish out to a bowl and serve hot.

Browned Butter Asparagus

Serves: **4** | Prep Time: **25** mins

Ingredients
- ½ cup sour cream
- 25 oz. green asparagus
- 3 oz. parmesan cheese, grated
- Salt and cayenne pepper, to taste
- 3 oz. butter

Directions
1. Season the asparagus with salt and cayenne pepper.
2. Heat 1 oz. butter in a skillet over medium heat and add seasoned asparagus.
3. Sauté for about 5 minutes and dish out to a bowl.
4. Heat the rest of the butter in a skillet and cook until it is light brown and has a nutty smell. Add asparagus to the butter along with sour cream and parmesan cheese.
5. Dish out to a bowl and serve hot.

Baked Mini Bell Peppers

Serves: **4** | Prep Time: **30** mins

Ingredients
- 1 oz. chorizo, air dried and thinly sliced
- 8 oz. mini bell peppers, sliced lengthwise
- 8 oz. cream cheese
- 1 cup cheddar cheese, shredded
- 1 tablespoon mild chipotle paste

Directions
1. Preheat the oven to 400ºF and grease a large baking dish.
2. Mix together cream cheese, chipotle paste, bell peppers and chorizo in a small bowl. Stir the mixture until smooth and transfer to the baking dish.
3. Top with cheddar cheese and place in the oven.
4. Bake for about 20 minutes until the cheese is golden brown and dish onto a platter.

Lemon Cream Bok Choy

Serves: **4** | Prep Time: **45** mins

Ingredients
- 28 oz. bok choy
- 1 large lemon, juice and zest
- ¾ cup heavy whipping cream
- 1 cup parmesan cheese, freshly grated
- 1 teaspoon black pepper

Directions
1. Preheat the oven to 350ºF and lightly grease a baking dish.
2. Pour the cream over the bok choy evenly and drizzle with the lemon juice.
3. Mix well and transfer to the baking dish.
4. Top with parmesan cheese, lemon zest and black pepper and place in the oven.
5. Bake for about 30 minutes until lightly browned and remove from the oven to serve hot.

Butter Fried Green Cabbage

Serves: **4** | Prep Time: **30** mins

Ingredients
- 3 oz. butter
- Salt and black pepper, to taste
- 25 oz. green cabbage, shredded
- 1 tablespoon basil
- ¼ teaspoon red chili flakes

Directions
1. Heat butter in a large skillet over medium heat and add cabbage.
2. Sauté for about 15 minutes, stirring occasionally, until the cabbage is golden brown.
3. Stir in basil, red chili flakes, salt and black pepper and cook for about 3 minutes.
4. Dish out to a bowl and serve hot.

Broccoli and Cheese

Serves: **4** | Prep Time: **20** mins

Ingredients
- 5½ oz. cheddar cheese, shredded
- 23 oz. broccoli, chopped
- 2 oz. butter
- Salt and black pepper, to taste
- 4 tablespoons sour cream

Directions
1. Heat butter in a large skillet over medium high heat and add broccoli, salt and black pepper.
2. Cook for about 5 minutes and stir in the sour cream and cheddar cheese.
3. Cover with lid and cook for about 8 minutes on medium low heat.
4. Dish out to a bowl and serve hot.

Broccoli Gratin

Serves: **4** | Prep Time: **35** mins

Ingredients
- 2 oz. salted butter, for frying
- 5 oz. parmesan cheese, shredded
- 20 oz. broccoli, in florets
- 2 tablespoons Dijon mustard
- ¾ cup crème fraiche

Directions
1. Preheat the oven to 400°F and grease a baking dish lightly.
2. Heat half the butter in a pan on medium low heat and add chopped broccoli.
3. Sauté for about 5 minutes and transfer to the baking dish.
4. Mix the rest of the butter with Dijon mustard and crème fraiche.
5. Pour this mixture in the baking dish and top with parmesan cheese.
6. Transfer to the oven and bake for about 18 minutes. Dish out to a bowl and serve hot.

Fried Mac and Cheese

Serves: **4** | Prep Time: **25** mins

Ingredients
- 1½ cups cheddar cheese, shredded
- 1 medium cauliflower, riced
- 3 large eggs
- 1 tablespoon olive oil
- 2 teaspoons paprika

Directions
1. Microwave cauliflower rice for about 5 minutes and dry completely on a kitchen towel.
2. Mix cheddar cheese, eggs, turmeric and paprika with the cauliflower rice.
3. Make small patties out of the cauliflower mixture. Heat olive oil in a pan on medium heat and add patties.
4. Fry on each side for about 3 minutes until crisp and dish onto a platter to serve.

Low Carb Cauliflower Rice

Serves: **4** | Prep Time: **20** mins

Ingredients
- 25 oz. cauliflower, riced in a processor
- ½ teaspoon turmeric powder
- 3 oz. coconut oil
- ½ teaspoon salt
- ¼ teaspoon paprika

Directions
1. Heat coconut oil on medium heat in a skillet and add cauliflower rice.
2. Cook for about 10 minutes and season with salt, paprika and turmeric powder.
3. Dish out to a bowl and serve warm.

Creamed Green Cabbage

Serves: **4** | Prep Time: **20** mins

Ingredients
- 25 oz. green cabbage, shredded
- 2 oz. butter
- 1¼ cups heavy whipping cream
- ½ cup fresh parsley, finely chopped
- Salt and black pepper, to taste

Directions
1. Heat butter over medium high heat in a pan and add the cabbage.
2. Sauté for about 6 minutes until soft and golden brown and stir in the cream.
3. Reduce the heat and season with salt and black pepper.
4. Cook for about 3 minutes and add parsley.
5. Dish out to a bowl and serve warm.

Roasted Brussels Sprouts

Serves: **5** | Prep Time: **30** mins

Ingredients
- 4 tablespoons olive oil
- 23 oz. Brussels sprouts
- 1 teaspoon dried rosemary
- 4 oz. parmesan cheese, shaved
- Salt and black pepper, to taste

Directions
1. Preheat the oven to 450°F and grease a baking dish with 2 tablespoons of olive oil.
2. Season the Brussels sprouts with dried rosemary, salt and black pepper.
3. Arrange the seasoned Brussels sprouts in a baking dish and sprinkle with olive oil and parmesan cheese.
4. Roast in the oven for about 20 minutes and remove from the oven to serve.

Baked Rutabaga Wedges

Serves: **4** | Prep Time: **35** mins

Ingredients
- 4 tablespoons olive oil
- 15 oz. rutabaga, peeled and cut into wedges
- 1 teaspoon chili powder
- ½ cup sour cream
- Salt and black pepper, to taste

Directions
1. Preheat the oven to 400°F and grease a baking sheet.
2. Arrange the wedges on a baking sheet and season with chili powder, salt and black pepper.
3. Drizzle with olive oil and transfer to the oven.
4. Bake for about 20 minutes and remove from the oven to serve with sour cream.

Zucchini Fettuccine

Serves: **1** | Prep Time: **15** mins

Ingredients
- 1 oz. olive oil
- 1 zucchini, spiralized into noodles
- ¼ cup parmesan cheese
- Salt and black pepper, to taste
- ¼ teaspoon red chili flakes

Directions
1. Boil the zucchini noodles and dish out in a microwave safe serving bowl.
2. Season with red chili flakes, salt and black pepper and drizzle with olive oil.
3. Top with parmesan cheese and microwave for about 5 minutes.
4. Remove from the oven and serve hot.

Low Carb Cauliflower Mash

Serves: **4** | Prep Time: **12** mins

Ingredients
- 3 oz. parmesan cheese, grated
- 1 pound cauliflower, cut into florets
- 4 oz. salted butter
- ½ lemon, juice and zest
- 2 tablespoons olive oil

Directions
1. Boil the cauliflower in salted water until tender and drain well.
2. Put the cauliflower in a food processor along with rest of the ingredients.
3. Pulse until smooth and dish out in a bowl to serve.

Whipped Lemon Butter Artichokes

Serves: **5** | Prep Time: **45** mins

Ingredients
- 1½ lemons, juice and zest
- ½ teaspoon red chili flakes
- 7 oz. butter
- Salt and black pepper, to taste
- 2 fresh artichokes

Directions
1. Boil the artichokes in salted water for about 35 minutes with ½ a lemon.
2. Melt the butter in a microwave oven and beat until fluffy.
3. Season with red chili flakes, salt and black pepper and squeeze in juice from 1 lemon. Mix in lemon zest and whip well.
4. Dip the artichokes in this lemon butter and serve warm.

Low Carb Cauliflower Cheese

Serves: **8** | Prep Time: **1 hour 10** mins

Ingredients
- 8 oz. cream cheese
- 1 cup heavy whipping cream
- Garlic powder, salt and black pepper, to taste
- 2¾ pounds cauliflower, cut into small florets
- 2 cups cheddar cheese, shredded

Directions
1. Preheat the oven to 350°F and grease a baking dish.
2. Boil the cauliflower in water for about 20 minutes until tender and drain well. Add the heavy whipping cream, cream cheese, garlic powder, salt and black pepper to an immersion blender.
3. Blend until smooth and transfer into a baking dish. Top with cheddar cheese and place in the oven.
4. Bake for about 40 minutes until the cauliflower is golden brown and dish out to serve hot.

Brussels Sprouts with Caramelized Red Onions

Serves: **4** | Prep Time: **30** mins

Ingredients

- 4 oz. butter
- 1 red onion, cut into wedges
- 1 tablespoon red wine vinegar
- 15 oz. Brussels sprouts
- Salt and black pepper, to taste

Directions

1. Heat butter in a medium skillet on low heat and add onions.
2. Sauté for about 10 minutes until the onions are caramelized.
3. Stir in the Brussels sprouts, vinegar, salt and black pepper and cover the skillet. Cook on medium low heat for about 15 minutes and dish out to a bowl to serve hot.

Stuffed Mushrooms

Serves: **3** | Prep Time: **35** mins

Ingredients

- 4 oz. bacon, cooked and crisped
- 1 tablespoon butter
- Salt and black pepper, to taste
- 6 mushrooms, chopped
- 3.5 oz. cream cheese

Directions

1. Preheat the oven to 400°F and grease a baking dish lightly.
2. Mix bacon with butter, cream cheese, salt and black pepper in a bowl.
3. Stuff this mixture inside the mushrooms and arrange on a baking dish.
4. Transfer to the oven and bake for about 20 minutes.
5. Remove from the oven and serve warm.

Thai Curry Cabbage

Serves: **5** | Prep Time: **20** mins

Ingredients

- 1 tablespoon Thai red curry paste
- 3 tablespoons coconut oil
- 30 oz. green cabbage, shredded
- 1 tablespoon sesame oil
- 1 teaspoon salt

Directions

1. Heat coconut oil in a wok over high heat and add Thai curry paste.
2. Cook for about 1 minute and add green cabbage.
3. Sauté for about 5 minutes until golden brown and lower the heat.
4. Season with salt and drizzle with sesame oil.
5. Sauté for 2 more minutes and dish out to serve hot.

Low Carb Broccoli Mash

Serves: **4** | Prep Time: **15** mins

Ingredients

- 4 tablespoons fresh parsley, finely chopped
- 25 oz. broccoli florets, boiled and drained
- 3 oz. butter
- Salt and black pepper, to taste
- 1 garlic clove

Directions

1. Blend broccoli with other ingredients in an immersion blender.
2. Blend until smooth and serve.

Creamy Lemon Green Beans

Serves: **4** | Prep Time: **25** mins

Ingredients

- 3 oz. butter
- 1 cup heavy whipping cream
- 10 oz. fresh green beans
- Sea salt and black pepper, to taste
- ½ lemon zest

Directions

1. Heat butter on medium heat in a frying pan and add green beans.
2. Sauté for about 4 minutes over medium high heat and lower the heat.
3. Season with sea salt and black pepper and cook for about 1 minute.
4. Stir in the heavy cream and lemon zest and cook for about 3 minutes.
5. Dish out to a bowl and serve hot.

Oven Baked Tofu

Serves: **2** | Prep Time: **50** mins

Ingredients
- 1 tablespoon soy sauce
- 15 ounces extra firm tofu, pressed and dried
- 1 tablespoon sesame oil
- 2 tablespoons rice wine vinegar
- 2 teaspoons garlic, minced

Directions
1. Preheat the oven to 350°F and line a baking sheet with parchment paper
2. Mix together soy sauce, sesame oil, garlic and rice wine vinegar in a bowl.
3. Marinate tofu in this mixture for about 2 hours and arrange on the baking sheet. Transfer into the oven and bake for about 35 minutes.
4. Remove from the oven and serve hot.

Cauliflower Mac and Cheese

Serves: **7** | Prep Time: **30** mins

Ingredients
- 6 ounces cream cheese, cubed
- Salt and black pepper, to taste
- 2 pounds cauliflower florets, boiled
- 8 ounces cheddar cheese, shredded
- 1 teaspoon Dijon mustard

Directions
1. Put the cream cheese in a bowl and bring to a simmer.
2. Stir in Dijon mustard, 6 ounces of the cheddar cheese, salt and black pepper and mix until the cheese is melted. Add cauliflower to the cheese sauce and coat well.
3. Top with the remaining 2 ounces of cheddar cheese and stir well until the cheese is melted. Dish out to a bowl and serve hot.

Avocado Walnut Pesto

Serves: **4** | Prep Time: **10** mins

Ingredients
- 2 cups fresh basil leaves
- 1 large avocado
- ½ cup walnuts
- ½ cup parmesan cheese, grated
- 4 garlic cloves, peeled

Directions
1. Put avocado with all other ingredients into the food processor and process until smooth.
2. Dish out to a bowl and serve.

Cheesy Hearts of Palm Dip

Serves: **4** | Prep Time: **35** mins

Ingredients
- 3 stalks green onions, chopped
- 1 (14 ounce) can hearts of palm, drained
- ¼ cup mayonnaise
- ½ cup parmesan cheese, shredded
- 2 tablespoons Italian seasoning

Directions
1. Preheat the oven to 350°F and grease a small baking dish.
2. Mix together green onions, hearts of palm, mayonnaise, Italian seasoning and parmesan cheese in the food processor.
3. Pulse until well chopped and transfer into prepared baking dish.
4. Bake for about 20 minutes and remove from the oven to serve.

Zucchini Parmesan Chips

Serves: **4** | Prep Time: **30** mins

Ingredients
- ¾ cup parmesan cheese
- 4 small zucchinis, sliced into small rounds
- ¾ cup cheddar cheese
- Salt and black pepper, to taste
- ¼ teaspoon turmeric powder

Directions
1. Preheat the oven to 425°F and grease a small baking sheet.
2. Season the zucchini with turmeric powder, salt and black pepper.
3. Arrange the sliced zucchini rounds on the baking sheet and sprinkle evenly with parmesan cheese and cheddar cheese.
4. Transfer to the oven and bake for about 20 minutes until the cheese turns golden brown.
5. Remove from the oven and serve warm.

Buttery Bacon and Cabbage Stir Fry

Serves: **4** | Prep Time: **15** mins

Ingredients
- ¼ cup butter
- 2½ cups Chinese cabbage, shredded
- 2 rashers bacon
- 1 pinch salt
- 1 pinch cayenne pepper

Directions
1. Heat half the butter in a pan and add bacon.
2. Cook until the bacon becomes crispy and add cabbage.
3. Cook for about 3 minutes and add the rest of the butter, salt and cayenne pepper. Dish out to a bowl and serve hot.

Vegan Recipes

Vegan Tofu Scramble

Serves: **2** | Prep Time: **20** mins

Ingredients
- 1½ tablespoons olive oil
- 1 block firm tofu, drained, pressed and chopped
- Black salt and black pepper, to taste
- ¼ cup dairy free milk, unsweetened
- 2 teaspoons ground turmeric

Directions
1. Heat olive oil in a skillet over medium heat and add tofu, turmeric, black salt and black pepper.
2. Cook for about 7 minutes and stir in the dairy free milk.
3. Cover the skillet and cook for about 5 more minutes.
4. Dish out to a bowl and serve hot.

Vegan Porridge

Serves: **4** | Prep Time: **10** mins

Ingredients
- 3 tablespoons golden flaxseed meal
- 2 tablespoons coconut flour
- 2 tablespoons vegan vanilla protein powder
- 1 scoop Stevia
- 1½ cups almond milk, unsweetened

Directions
1. Mix together the golden flaxseed meal, coconut flour and vanilla protein powder in a bowl.
2. Put this mixture in the saucepan along with almond milk and cook for about 10 minutes over medium heat.
3. Stir in the Stevia and dish out to a bowl and serve hot.

Vegan Sesame Tofu and Eggplant

Serves: **4** | Prep Time: **25** mins

Ingredients
- 4 tablespoons toasted sesame oil
- 1 pound block firm tofu
- 1 whole eggplant, peeled and julienned
- ¼ cup sesame seeds
- Salt and black pepper, to taste

Directions
1. Put the sesame seeds on a plate and coat both sides of tofu with them.
2. Heat sesame oil in a skillet and add eggplant.
3. Cook for about 5 minutes and season the coated tofu with salt and black pepper.
4. Cover with lid and cook for about 10 minutes on medium low heat.
5. Dish out to a bowl and serve hot.

Coconut Bacon

Serves: **4** | Prep Time: **5** mins

Ingredients
- 2 tablespoons liquid smoke
- 3½ cups flaked coconut, unsweetened
- 1 tablespoon Braggs liquid aminos
- 3 tablespoons heavy whipping cream
- 1 tablespoon water

Directions
1. Preheat the oven to 325°F and grease a baking sheet lightly.
2. Mix together coconut flakes, liquid smoke, liquid aminos, water and cream in a bowl. Pour this mixture onto a baking sheet and place in the oven.
3. Bake for about 25 minutes, flipping every 5 minutes.
4. Dish out to a plate and serve.

Dark Saltwater Truffles

Serves: **2** | Prep Time: **30** mins

Ingredients
- 1 scoop Stevia
- 150g dark chocolate, broken into small pieces
- 55ml water
- Cocoa powder, for dusting
- Pinch of salt

Directions
1. Heat water and salt in a pot and bring to a boil.
2. Remove from heat and add chocolate pieces and Stevia.
3. Stir well until the chocolate is dissolved and ladle into a bowl. Refrigerate for about 4 hours.
4. Put cocoa powder in a bowl and dust it on your hands.
5. Make small balls out of the chocolate mixture and roll into cocoa powder.
6. Put these truffles in the fridge for 1 more hour then serve and enjoy.

Zucchini Noodles with Avocado Sauce

Serves: **2** | Prep Time: **20** mins

Ingredients
- 1¼ cups basil
- 1 zucchini, spiralized with noodles
- 4 tablespoons pine nuts
- 1 avocado
- 2 tablespoons lemon juice

Directions
1. Put basil, pine nuts, avocado and lemon juice in a blender along with 1/3 cup water. Blend until smooth and dish into a bowl. Add zucchini noodles to the avocado sauce and serve.

Mushroom Brussels Sprouts

Serves: **6** | Prep Time: **30** mins

Ingredients
- 3 tablespoons olive oil
- 2 cups brown mushrooms, thinly sliced
- 2 tablespoons sour cream
- 1½ pounds Brussels sprouts, trimmed and outer leaves removed
- Salt and smoked paprika, to taste

Directions
1. Mix together mushrooms, sour cream, salt and smoked paprika in a bowl.
2. Heat 1 tablespoon of olive oil in a skillet on medium high heat and add mushrooms mixture. Cook for about 10 minutes and dish out.
3. Heat the rest of the oil in a saucepan and add the Brussels sprouts.
4. Coat well and add ¼ cup hot water.
5. Cover with a lid and cook on medium heat for about 8 minutes.
6. Stir in the mushrooms mixture and cook for about 2 minutes. Dish out and serve hot.

Vegan Almond and Cinnamon Cookies

Serves: **5** | Prep Time: **30** mins

Ingredients
- ⅔ cup coconut sugar
- 2 cups ground almonds
- 2 tablespoons chia seeds
- 3 tablespoons orange juice
- 2 tablespoons cinnamon

Directions
1. Preheat the oven to 360°F and grease a baking sheet.
2. Put chia seeds and coconut sugar in a food processor and process until smooth. Dish into a bowl and add almonds and cinnamon. Stir in orange juice and mix well to form a dough.
3. Form small balls out of this mixture and transfer to a baking sheet. Press with a fork and place in the oven. Bake for about 15 minutes until golden brown and remove from baking sheet to serve.

Vegan Mashed Cauliflower

Serves: **4** | Prep Time: **15** mins

Ingredients
- 1 cup vegetable broth
- 1 large head cauliflower, cored and roughly chopped
- ¼ cup vegan parmesan
- Sea salt and black pepper, to taste
- 2 tablespoons non-dairy butter

Directions
1. Put cauliflower and vegetable broth in the pressure cooker and close the lid.
2. Cook on High Pressure for about 5 minutes. Quickly release the pressure and drain well.
3. Transfer to a food processor and add parmesan, butter, salt and black pepper.
4. Process until smooth and dish into a bowl and serve immediately.

Crispy Tofu and Cauliflower Stir Fry

Serves: **4** | Prep Time: **15** mins

Ingredients
- 3 tablespoons toasted sesame oil
- 12 ounces extra firm tofu, pressed
- 1 small head cauliflower, riced
- ¼ cup low sodium soy sauce
- 2 garlic cloves, minced

Directions
1. Preheat the oven to 400°F and grease a baking sheet.
2. Put the tofu on the baking sheet and place in the oven. Bake for about 25 minutes and dish into a bowl.
3. Heat sesame oil in a large skillet over medium high heat and add garlic.
4. Sauté for about 1 minute and add tofu and soy sauce. Sauté for about 5 minutes and stir in cauliflower rice. Cover the skillet and cook on medium low heat for about 6 minutes. Dish out to a bowl and serve warm.

Tofu in Purgatory

Serves: **2** | Prep Time: **30** mins

Ingredients
- 1 can diced tomatoes
- 2 teaspoons dried herbs
- 2 tablespoons olive oil
- Garlic powder, salt and black pepper, to taste
- 1 block unpressed medium tofu, cut into rounds

Directions
1. Heat olive oil in a skillet on medium heat and add tofu. Sauté for about 3 minutes and add tomatoes.
2. Sauté for about 2 minutes and sprinkle with dried herbs, garlic powder, salt and black pepper.
3. Lower the heat and let it simmer for about 15 minutes.
4. Dish into a bowl and serve hot.

Low Carb Maple Oatmeal

Serves: **4** | Prep Time: **40** mins

Ingredients
- ¼ cup sunflower seeds
- 1 cup nuts (walnuts and pecans)
- ¼ cup coconut flakes
- 2 scoops Stevia
- 4 cups unsweetened almond milk

Directions
1. Put nuts and sunflower seeds in a food processor and pulse until crumbled.
2. Transfer this mixture into a large pot along with rest of the ingredients.
3. Allow to simmer for about 30 minutes, stirring occasionally.
4. Dish into a bowl and allow it to cool down before serving.

Crackers

Serves: **8** | Prep Time: **3 hours 25** mins

Ingredients
- 3 tablespoons chia seeds
- 1 cup whole flaxseeds
- 3 tablespoons hemp hearts
- ½ teaspoon sea salt
- 3 tablespoons dried rosemary

Directions
1. Preheat the oven to 200°F and line a baking tray with parchment paper.
2. Combine the chia seeds and flaxseeds with water in a bowl.
3. Mix well and allow it to sit for about 20 minutes.
4. Stir in the rest of the ingredients and spread in a thin layer on the baking tray.
5. Bake for about 1½ hours and then flip over the cracker mixture.
6. Bake for another 1½ hours and turn off the oven.
7. Allow to stay in the warmed oven for about 20 minutes.
8. Remove from oven and allow the crackers to cool and serve.

Mushroom Spaghetti Squash

Serves: **6** | Prep Time: **20** mins

Ingredients
- 8 ounces mushrooms, sliced
- 6 cups spaghetti squash, cooked and shredded
- ¼ cup pine nuts, toasted
- Kosher salt and black pepper, to taste
- 3 tablespoons olive oil

Directions
1. Heat olive oil over medium heat in a large pan and add mushrooms.
2. Sauté for about 4 minutes and add cooked spaghetti squash. Cook for about 2 minutes and stir in pine nuts, salt and black pepper. Mix well and dish into a bowl to serve.

Garlic Roasted Radishes

Serves: **3** | Prep Time: **30** mins

Ingredients
- ½ cup low sodium vegetable broth
- 3 garlic cloves, minced
- 3 radish bunches, chopped
- ½ teaspoon dried rosemary
- Himalayan pink sea salt and black pepper, to taste

Directions
1. Preheat the oven to 400°F and grease a medium sized casserole dish.
2. Put vegetable broth, garlic cloves, dried rosemary, pink sea salt and black pepper in a bowl.
3. Put the radishes in the casserole and top with the broth mixture.
4. Transfer to the oven and bake for about 20 minutes.
5. Dish into a platter and serve hot.

Mashed Cauliflower with Garlic and Herbs

Serves: **3** | Prep Time: **20** mins

Ingredients
- 1 tablespoon olive oil
- 1 head cauliflower, boiled
- 2 garlic cloves, minced
- Salt and black pepper, to taste
- 2 teaspoons fresh herbs, chopped

Directions
1. Heat olive oil on medium heat in a small pan and add garlic.
2. Sauté for about 1 minute and add boiled cauliflower and fresh herbs.
3. Season with salt and black pepper and cook for about 3 minutes.
4. Mash the cauliflower with a potato masher and dish into a bowl to serve.

Roasted Cabbage with Lemon

Serves: **4** | Prep Time: **40** mins

Ingredients
- 2 tablespoons olive oil
- 1 large head green cabbage, cut into 8 wedges
- 3 tablespoons lemon juice, freshly squeezed
- 6 lemon slices, for serving
- Sea salt and black pepper, to taste

Directions
1. Preheat the oven to 450°F and grease a roasting pan with olive oil.
2. Whisk together lemon juice and olive oil in a bowl and brush onto the cabbage wedges.
3. Season generously with salt and black pepper and arrange the cabbage wedges on a roasting pan.
4. Roast for about 30 minutes, flipping once after 15 minutes.
5. Dish onto a platter and top with lemon slices to serve.

Balsamic Glazed Mushrooms

Serves: **6** | Prep Time: **3 hours 15 minutes**

Ingredients
- ¼ cup extra-virgin olive oil
- 2 pounds portobello mushrooms
- 2 tablespoons balsamic vinegar
- 2 tablespoons tamari
- Sea salt and black pepper, to taste

Directions
1. Put the portobello mushrooms along with rest of the ingredients in a slow cooker.
2. Mix well and cover with lid.
3. Cook on low for about 3 hours and dish out to serve hot.

Vegan Garlic Aioli

Serves: **4** | Prep Time: **10** mins

Ingredients
- 3 fresh garlic cloves, minced
- ¾ cup vegenaise
- 2½ tablespoons fresh lemon juice
- ¼ teaspoon black pepper
- ¼ teaspoon pink sea salt

Directions
1. Put all the ingredients in a bowl and mix well until combined.
2. Cover and refrigerate for about 1 hour before serving.

Basil Pesto

Serves: **6** | Prep Time: **5** mins

Ingredients
- 2 cups fresh organic basil leaves
- 1 large garlic clove, peeled
- 1/3 cup extra virgin olive oil
- Sea salt and black pepper, to taste
- 1/3 cup pine nuts, toasted

Directions
1. Place garlic in a food processor and pulse until chopped.
2. Add basil leaves, olive oil, pine nuts, salt and black pepper and process until smooth. Dish into a bowl and serve with your favorite dish.

Mexican Spiced Chocolate

Serves: **4** | Prep Time: **20** mins

Ingredients
- ¼ teaspoon chili powder
- 25 drops liquid Stevia
- ½ cup cocoa powder
- 1 pinch fine sea salt, black pepper and cinnamon
- ¼ cup cacao butter, melted

Directions
1. Whisk together cocoa powder and salt in a small bowl.
2. Microwave cacao butter for about 30 seconds on high until melted.
3. Mix chili powder and liquid Stevia with cacao butter.
4. Stir in the cocoa powder mixture and mix well.
5. Pour the mixture into greased mini loaf pans and allow to set until firm.

BLT Sushi

Serves: **5** | Prep Time: **35** mins

Ingredients
- 1 cup tomatoes, chopped
- 10 bacon slices
- ½ avocado, diced
- Kosher salt and black pepper, to taste
- 1 cup romaine lettuce, shredded

Directions
1. Preheat the oven to 400°F and put a wire rack over a baking sheet.
2. Make a weave with the bacon slices and place on the baking sheet.
3. Bake for about 20 minutes until bacon is cooked.
4. Put tomatoes, avocado and romaine lettuce on the bacon weave and season with salt and black pepper.
5. Roll up tightly and slice crosswise into "sushi rolls".

Roasted Mushrooms

Serves: **4** | Prep Time: **30** mins

Ingredients
- ½ cup tomato puree
- 18 ounces whole mushrooms, quartered
- 4 tablespoons olive oil
- Salt and black pepper, to taste
- 2 teaspoons ginger garlic paste

Directions
1. Heat olive oil over medium high heat in a nonstick frying pan and add whole mushrooms and ginger garlic paste.
2. Sauté for about 5 minutes and add tomato puree, salt and black pepper.
3. Sauté for about 3 minutes until crisp and tender then dish into a bowl and serve hot.

Vegan Cauliflower Pizza Crust

Serves: **5** | Prep Time: **1 hour**

Ingredients
- 1½ pounds frozen cauliflower rice, thawed
- ½ cup almond flour
- ½ teaspoon dried oregano
- 3 tablespoons flax seeds
- Salt and garlic powder, to taste

Directions
1. Preheat the oven to 390°F and line a baking sheet with parchment paper.
2. Mix together cauliflower rice with rest of the ingredients and add a little water to make a dough.
3. Press this dough on the baking sheet to form a thin crust and transfer into the oven. Bake for about 45 minutes and dish out.
4. Top with your favorite toppings and bake again.

Curried Spinach Stuffed Portobello Mushrooms

Serves: **6** | Prep Time: **25** mins

Ingredients
- 1 cup coconut cream
- 1 cup spinach
- 4 cups Portobello mushroom caps, stems removed
- Salt and red pepper, to taste
- ¼ cup oil and vinegar salad dressing

Directions
1. Preheat the grill to medium high heat.
2. Rub salad dressing on the Portobello mushrooms and arrange in a pan.
3. Season with salt and black pepper and cover with a plastic wrap.
4. Marinate for at least an hour and then place on the grill, stem side down.
5. Grill for about 10 minutes on both sides and dish out.
6. Mix spinach with coconut cream and fill in the grilled portobellos.
7. Broil for about 5 minutes in the oven and dish out to serve.

Tabbouleh

Serves: **4** | Prep Time: **15** mins

Ingredients
- ¼ cup lemon juice
- ½ cup extra-virgin olive oil
- ½ teaspoon gray sea salt
- 1⅓ cups Manitoba Harvest Hemp Hearts
- 1 cup fresh parsley, chopped

Directions
1. Whisk together lemon juice, olive oil and sea salt in a large bowl until combined. Stir in Hemp Hearts and fresh parsley to serve.

Green Coffee Shake

Serves: **4** | Prep Time: **10** mins

Ingredients
- 1½ cups chilled brewed coffee
- 8 ice cubes, for serving
- 1¾ cups full fat coconut milk
- 2 tablespoons almond butter, unsweetened
- 1 tablespoon vegan greens

Directions
1. Put all the ingredients in a blender and blend until smooth.
2. Pour into 4 glasses and serve immediately.

Vanilla Overnight Oats

Serves: **2** | Prep Time: **5** mins

Ingredients
- ½ cup Manitoba Harvest Hemp Hearts
- ⅔ cup full fat coconut milk
- 1 tablespoon chia seed
- ½ teaspoon vanilla extract
- 4 drops liquid Stevia

Directions
1. Put all the ingredients in a large container and stir well.
2. Cover and refrigerate for at least 6 hours. Dish into a bowl and serve.

Harissa Portobello Mushrooms Tacos

Serves: **6** | Prep Time: **30** mins

Ingredients
- ¼ cup spicy harissa
- 1 pound portobello mushrooms, sliced
- 3 tablespoons olive oil, divided
- 6 collard green leaves, rinsed and chopped
- 1 teaspoon ground cumin

Directions
1. Mix together harissa, 1½ tablespoons olive oil and cumin in a bowl.
2. Rub each portobello mushroom with the harissa mixture and allow the mushrooms to marinade for 15 minutes.
3. Heat remaining olive oil in a pan and add portobello mushrooms.
4. Cook for about 6 minutes on both sides and lower the heat.
5. Allow the mushrooms to rest for about 3 minutes.
6. Fill the portobello mushrooms slices in a collard green leaf and serve.

Side Dishes Recipes

Brie with Apple

Serves: **3** | Prep Time: **10** mins

Ingredients
- 1 tablespoon unsalted butter
- 2 oz. pecans, chopped
- ¼ teaspoon cinnamon
- 4 oz. brie cheese, thinly sliced
- 1 small gala apple, thinly sliced

Directions

Mix together apple and brie in a bowl and top with butter, pecans and cinnamon.Serve over low carb crepes.

Oven Baked Brie Cheese

Serves: **4** | Prep Time: **15** mins

Ingredients
- 2 oz. pecans, chopped
- 9 oz. Brie cheese
- 1 tablespoon fresh rosemary
- Salt and black pepper, to taste
- 1 tablespoon olive oil

Directions
1. Preheat the oven to 400ºF and grease a small baking dish.
2. Mix together pecans with olive oil, fresh rosemary, salt and black pepper.
3. Place Brie cheese on the baking dish and top with pecans mixture.
4. Transfer to the oven and bake for about 10 minutes.
5. Remove from the oven and serve warm.

Pan Fried Radishes with Bacon

Serves: **8** | Prep Time: **30** mins

Ingredients
- 3 pounds radishes, quartered
- 20 oz. bacon, chopped
- 2 garlic cloves, pressed
- 2 tablespoons olive oil
- Salt and black pepper, to taste

Directions
1. Heat olive oil in a large nonstick skillet and add bacon.
2. Fry until crispy and add garlic and radishes.
3. Fry for about 12 minutes, stirring occasionally and season with salt and black pepper to serve.

Lemon and Dill Butter

Serves: **6** | Prep Time: **10** mins

Ingredients
- 5½ oz. butter
- 2 tablespoons cream cheese
- 3 tablespoons fresh dill, finely chopped
- Salt and black pepper, to taste
- 1 tablespoon lemon juice

Directions
1. Put all the ingredients in a blender and blend until smooth and fluffy.
2. Dish into a bowl to serve with snacks.

Herb Butter

Serves: **6** | Prep Time: **10** mins

Ingredients
- 2 garlic cloves, pressed
- 5 oz. butter
- 4 tablespoons fresh parsley, finely chopped
- ½ teaspoon salt
- 1 teaspoon lemon juice

Directions
1. Mix together butter with all other ingredients in a small bowl until well combined.
2. Set aside for about 15 minutes and allow the flavors to infuse well to serve.

Low Carb Salsa Dressing

Serves: **4** | Prep Time: **5** mins

Ingredients
- 4 tablespoons olive oil
- ½ cup low carb salsa
- 4 tablespoons sour cream
- 1 teaspoon chili powder
- 3 tablespoons cider vinegar

Directions
1. Mix together salsa with the rest of the ingredients in a bowl until well combined and smooth. Serve over your favorite salad.

Ginger Asian Slaw

Serves: **8** | Prep Time: **15** mins

Ingredients
- 2 cups carrots, shredded
- 6 cups red cabbage, thinly sliced
- 1 cup cilantro, roughly chopped
- 4 tablespoons almond butter
- ¾ cup green onions, sliced

Directions
1. Mix together carrots, cabbage, cilantro and green onions in a large mixing bowl.
2. Top with almond butter and toss to coat well and serve.

Strawberry Matcha Chia Pudding

Serves: **4** | Prep Time: **15** mins

Ingredients
- 1½ cups coconut milk
- 1 teaspoon matcha powder
- 3 tablespoons chia seeds
- 4 scoops Stevia
- 4 strawberries, diced small

Directions
1. Whisk together coconut milk with chia seeds, matcha powder and Stevia.
2. Pour mixture into 4 glasses and refrigerate for about 4 hours.
3. Stir the strawberries into the pudding and serve chilled.

Eggplant Hole in the Head

Serves: **6** | Prep Time: **30** mins

Ingredients
- 2 tablespoons extra-virgin olive oil
- 2 eggplants, sliced half lengthwise
- 2 teaspoons salted butter
- Salt and black pepper, to taste
- 8 eggs, whole

Directions
1. Preheat the grill to high heat.
2. Drizzle eggplant slices with olive oil and season with salt and black pepper.
3. Transfer to the grill and grill for about 4 minutes on each side.
4. Cut a hole in the center of each slice of eggplant and place in the frying pan.
5. Sauté for about 4 minutes with butter over medium heat.
6. Crack egg in the eggplant hole and cook for about 3 minutes.
7. Flip carefully and cook for 3 more minutes.
8. Season with salt and black pepper and serve immediately.

Bagels

Serves: **6** | Prep Time: **55** mins

Ingredients
- ½ cup tahini
- ¾ cup ground flax seed
- 1/8 cup psyllium husks
- 1 teaspoon baking powder
- 1 cup water

Directions
1. Preheat the oven to 375°F and grease a baking tray.
2. Mix together ground flax seed, psyllium husks and baking powder in a bowl until combined.
3. Whisk together tahini with water and pour into the flax seed mixture.
4. Knead well to make the dough and form patties out of this mixture.
5. Arrange the patties on the baking tray and place in the oven.
6. Bake for about 40 minutes until golden brown and remove from the oven to serve.

Hemp Heart Porridge

Serves: **4** | Prep Time: **5** mins

Ingredients
- 1 cup nondairy milk
- 3 tablespoons flax seed, freshly ground
- ½ cup Manitoba Harvest Hemp Hearts
- ¼ cup almonds, crushed
- 5 drops Stevia

Directions
1. Put the milk, flax seed, Hemp Hearts and Stevia in a saucepan and mix well.
2. Heat over medium heat until boiling and allow to simmer for about 2 minutes.
3. Dish into a bowl and top with almonds to serve.

Kelp Noodles with Avocado Pesto

Serves: **4** | Prep Time: **20** mins

Ingredients
- ½ cup extra-virgin olive oil
- 1 Hass avocado
- 1¼ cups fresh baby spinach leaves
- 1 package kelp noodles, soaked in water for at least 30 minutes
- 1 teaspoon salt

Directions
1. Put avocado, olive oil, baby spinach leaves and salt in a blender.
2. Blend until smooth and dish out in a bowl.
3. Stir in the kelp noodles and mix well to serve.

Parmesan Zucchini Pasta

Serves: **6** | Prep Time: **20** mins

Ingredients
- 1 pint cherry tomatoes, halved
- 2 pounds zucchini, spiralized
- ¼ cup extra virgin olive oil
- ½ cup parmesan cheese, shredded
- Salt and black pepper, to taste

Directions
1. Heat olive oil over medium low heat in a large pot and add cherry tomatoes.
2. Cook for about 3 minutes and stir in the zucchini noodles.
3. Season with salt and black pepper and cover the lid.
4. Cook for about 4 minutes on low heat and stir in the parmesan cheese.
5. Cook for about 2 minutes and dish out to serve hot.

Crack Slaw

Serves: **4** | Prep Time: **20** mins

Ingredients
- ½ cup macadamia nuts, chopped
- 3 tablespoons liquid aminos
- 4 cups green cabbage, shredded
- 1 teaspoon Sriracha paste
- 1 tablespoon sesame oil

Directions
1. Mix together cabbage with sesame oil, Sriracha paste and liquid aminos in a bowl.
2. Top with macadamia nuts and serve immediately.

Crumbly Almond Feta

Serves: **3** | Prep Time: **40** mins

Ingredients
- 3 tablespoons lemon juice
- 1 cup almonds, soaked for at least 8 hours and skins removed
- 3 tablespoons olive oil
- ½ teaspoon salt
- 1 garlic clove

Directions
1. Preheat the oven to 400°F and grease a baking sheet.
2. Put almonds, lemon juice, olive oil, salt and garlic in a high powered blender and blend until smooth.
3. Place a colander over a bowl and cover with a few layers of cheesecloth.
4. Pour the pureed nut cheese into the colander and fold the cloth around the cheese to squeeze.
5. Allow to sit for about 24 hours at room temperature and place the cheese on the baking sheet.
6. Transfer to the oven and bake for about 30 minutes until firm and golden brown.
7. Allow it to cool and refrigerate for about 2 hours to serve.

Creamy Spinach with Dill

Serves: **4** | Prep Time: **25** mins

Ingredients
- 1 pound spinach, large stems removed, coarsely chopped
- 1 tablespoon unsalted butter
- 1/3 cup heavy cream
- 1/3 cup fresh dill, coarsely chopped
- Salt, black pepper and nutmeg, to taste

Directions
1. Heat butter over medium heat in a large pot and add the spinach.
2. Cover and cook for about 3 minutes, stirring occasionally.
3. Dish into a bowl and drain the spinach.
4. Return to the pot over medium heat and stir in the cream and nutmeg.
5. Cook on low heat for about 4 minutes and season with salt and black pepper.
6. Sprinkle with fresh dill and cook for about 3 minutes. Dish out and serve hot.

Cheese Bread

Serves: **2** | Prep Time: **15** mins

Ingredients
- 2 large eggs
- 2 tablespoons olive oil
- 4 tablespoons coconut flour
- ½ teaspoon baking powder
- ½ cup cheddar cheese, grated

Directions
1. Whisk together eggs, coconut flour, 1 tablespoon olive oil, cheddar cheese and baking powder in a small bowl.
2. Stir well and pour into a microwave safe mug.
3. Microwave for about 1 minute 30 seconds and invert the mug onto a cutting board. Cut the bread crosswise into ½ inch thick slices.
4. Heat the rest of the oil over medium heat in a small skillet and add slices.
5. Toast for about 30 seconds on each side until golden brown and serve.

Saucy Chili Garlic Cucumber Noodles

Serves: **3** | Prep Time: **15** mins

Ingredients
- 1 tablespoon sesame oil, toasted
- 3 tablespoons rice vinegar
- 2 teaspoons Asian chili garlic sauce
- 2 teaspoons sesame seeds, toasted
- 1½ pounds English cucumbers, spiralizes into noodles

Directions
1. Whisk together sesame oil, rice vinegar and chili garlic sauce in a large bowl.
2. Put the cucumber noodles in a bowl and drizzle with the dressing.
3. Top with the sesame seeds and immediately serve.

Garlic Butter Mushrooms

Serves: **6** | Prep Time: **25** mins

Ingredients
- 2 pounds white button mushrooms, stems trimmed but not removed
- 6 tablespoons unsalted butter
- Salt and black pepper, to taste
- 4 teaspoons fresh thyme leaves
- 4 garlic cloves, minced

Directions
1. Heat butter over medium heat in a large skillet and add button mushrooms.
2. Season with salt and black pepper and cook for about 10 minutes until browned on both sides.
3. Stir in the thyme and garlic and sauté for about 1 minute.
4. Dish into a bowl and serve immediately.

Kale with Lemon and Garlic

Serves: **6** | Prep Time: **20** mins

Ingredients
- 3 tablespoons olive oil
- 6 cups kale, coarsely chopped
- 4 cloves garlic, thinly sliced
- 2 teaspoons lemon juice
- Red pepper flakes, salt and black pepper, to taste

Directions
1. Heat olive oil over medium heat in a large pan and add garlic and red pepper flakes.
2. Sauté for about 1 minute and add kale and season with salt and black pepper.
3. Cover with lid and cook for about 5 minutes, stirring occasionally.
4. Stir in the lemon juice and dish out to serve warm.

Oven Roasted Frozen Broccoli

Serves: **4** | Prep Time: **25** mins

Ingredients
- 2 tablespoons olive oil
- ¼ cup parmesan cheese, grated
- 1 (16 ounce) bag frozen broccoli florets
- Salt and black pepper, to taste
- 1 medium lemon, halved

Directions
1. Preheat the oven to 450°F and grease a baking sheet lightly.
2. Mix together broccoli, olive oil, salt and black pepper in a bowl until well coated.
3. Arrange the broccoli on the baking sheet and transfer to the oven.
4. Bake for about 15 minutes and top with lemon halves and Parmesan cheese.
5. Place in the oven and bake for about 3 minutes until melted. Remove from the oven and serve hot.

Roasted Cabbage with Bacon

Serves: **6** | Prep Time: **40** mins

Ingredients
- 4 tablespoons olive oil
- 1 head green cabbage, outer leaves removed and quartered into wedges
- Kosher salt and black pepper, to taste
- 3 tablespoons sesame seeds
- 8 ounces thick cut bacon slices

Directions
1. Preheat the oven to 450°F and grease a large roasting pan. Arrange on the baking sheet and drizzle with olive oil. Season with salt and black pepper and top with bacon slices.
2. Place in the oven and roast for about 30 minutes. Remove from the oven and serve hot.

BLT Dip

Serves: **8** | Prep Time: **2s0** mins

Ingredients
- ¼ cup mayonnaise, salted
- 12 oz. cream cheese
- 1/3 cup cheddar cheese, shredded and divided
- 2/3 cup tomatoes, chopped
- 2 cups lettuce, chopped

Directions
1. Mix together mayonnaise and cream cheese in a bowl until combined.
2. Add half of the cheddar cheese and top with tomatoes, lettuce and rest of the cheddar cheese.
3. Dish out to a serving bowl and serve.

Crispy Baked Garlic Parmesan Wings

Serves: **8** | Prep Time: **1 hour 20** mins

Ingredients
- ½ cup butter, melted
- 2 pounds chicken wings
- ½ cup parmesan cheese, grated
- Sea salt, black pepper, garlic powder and onion powder
- 1 garlic clove, minced

Directions
1. Preheat the oven to 250°F and grease a baking sheet lightly.
2. Season the chicken wings with salt and arrange on the baking sheet.
3. Bake for about 20 minutes and increase the temperature to 425°F.
4. Transfer the baking sheet to the middle upper rack.
5. Bake for 45 more minutes until crispy and remove from the oven.
6. Mix together butter, garlic, black pepper, parmesan cheese, garlic powder and onion powder in a bowl.
7. Stir until well combined and serve with the wings.

Cheesy Zucchini

Serves: **3** | Prep Time: **20** mins

Ingredients
- 1 zucchini, spiralized into noodles
- ½ cup water
- 1 tablespoon salted butter
- 2 tablespoons coconut milk
- 1 cup cheddar cheese, shredded

Directions
1. Put zucchini noodles and water in a saucepan and bring to a boil.
2. Reduce heat to low and add butter, coconut milk and cheddar cheese to the pan. Stir well and dish into a bowl to serve.

Bacon Wrapped Maple Parmesan Asparagus Bundles

Serves: **8** | Prep Time: **55** mins

Ingredients
- ½ cup salted butter
- ½ cup sugar free maple syrup
- 2 pounds fresh asparagus, washed, ends chopped off
- ¼ cup parmesan cheese, grated
- 8 slices thick cut bacon

Directions
1. Preheat the oven to 425°F and grease a casserole dish lightly.
2. Heat butter over medium low heat in a small pot and add maple syrup.
3. Bring to a boil and remove from heat.
4. Wrap bacon slices around the asparagus stalks and secure with a toothpick.
5. Place these in the casserole dish and top with butter maple sauce and parmesan cheese.
6. Transfer in the oven and bake for about 40 minutes.
7. Turn on the oven broiler and broil for about 2 minutes. Remove from the oven and serve hot.

Garlic Broccoli

Serves: **6** | Prep Time: **15** mins

Ingredients
- ¼ cup olive oil
- 1½ pounds broccoli florets, steamed and drained
- 1/8 cup fresh lemon juice
- 1 teaspoon salt
- 1 teaspoon garlic powder

Directions
1. Mix together lemon juice, olive oil, salt and garlic powder in a small blender and blend until creamy.
2. Drizzle the broccoli with the lemon garlic dressing and serve.

Snacks Recipes

Niçoise toasts

Serves: **4** | Prep Time: **20** mins

Ingredients
- 3 tablespoons olive oil
- 2 garlic cloves, crushed
- 1½ cups tomatoes, chopped
- 2 tablespoons mini capers, drained
- 12 pitted black olives, drained and halved
- Baby basil leaves, to serve
- 1 (¾ cup) part-baked baguette, cut into 24 circles
- 6 anchovy fillets in olive oil, drained
- ½ medium red onion, finely chopped
- 2 tablespoons tomato purée
- ½ teaspoon chili flakes
- 2 tablespoons parmesan, finely grated

Directions
1. Preheat the oven to 375 degrees F and grease a baking sheet.
2. Arrange the bread slices on the baking sheet and drizzle with a tablespoon of olive oil.
3. Bake for about 12 minutes and keep aside.
4. Heat the rest of the oil in a nonstick skillet and add onion, garlic, and anchovies.
5. Sauté for about 4 minutes and add puree, tomatoes, caper, and chili flakes.
6. Cook this mixture with occasional stirring and spoon out this mixture over the baked slices. Divide half of the olives over each piece and top with parmesan cheese. Cover the slices and refrigerate overnight.
7. Place the pizza toasts in the oven and bake for about 8 minutes.
8. Serve garnished with basil leaves and enjoy.

Herbed Olives

Serves: **6** | Prep Time: **5** mins

Ingredients
- 2 teaspoons extra-virgin olive oil
- ⅛ teaspoon dried basil
- Black pepper, to taste
- 3 cups olives
- ⅛ teaspoon dried oregano
- 1 garlic clove, crushed

Directions
1. Toss the olives with all other ingredients in a bowl.
2. Insert a toothpick into each olive and serve.

Stuffed tomatoes

Serves: **6** | Prep Time: **30** mins

Ingredients
- 2 mozzarella balls, sliced
- 6 large tomatoes, heads chopped and seeds removed
- 12 basil leaves, fresh
- 2 tablespoons red pesto
- 4 pieces red peppers, cooked

Directions
1. Preheat the oven to 375 degrees F and grease a baking sheet.
2. Arrange the tomatoes on a baking sheet with their cut side up.
3. Top the tomato bases with chopped mozzarella cheese, red peppers, and basil leaves. Repeat the layers and top each base with a dollop of pesto. Cover the tomato bases with their chopped off heads.
4. Transfer into the oven and bake for about 20 minutes. Dish out and serve immediately.

Crispy Squid with Capers

Serves: **6** | Prep Time: **25** mins

Ingredients
- 7 oz. whole wheat flour
- 1 garlic clove, crushed
- 10 oz. baby squid, cleaned and sliced into thick rings
- 2 tablespoons caper, drained and finely chopped
- 5 tablespoons mayonnaise
- Lemon wedges, to serve
- Vegetable oil, for frying

Directions
1. Mix together squid, capers and whole wheat flour in a shallow bowl.
2. Heat oil in a wok and deep fry capers and squids.
3. When fried to a golden color, dish out the capers and squid in a plate.
4. Serve with garlic, mayonnaise, and lemon wedges.

Spiced Tortilla

Serves: **4** | Prep Time: **25** mins

Ingredients
- 1 onion, sliced
- 2 teaspoons curry spice
- 1 pound cooked potatoes, sliced
- 8 eggs, beaten
- 1 tablespoon sunflower oil
- 1 red chili, deseeded and shredded
- 1½ cups cherry tomatoes
- 1 bunch coriander, finely chopped

Directions
1. Heat oil in a skillet and add half of the chili and onion.
2. Sauté for about 5 minutes and add the spices, potatoes, coriander stalks, and tomatoes. Whisk the eggs with seasoning and pour it into the pan.
3. Cook for about 10 minutes until it is set.
4. Preheat the grill and transfer the pan into the grill.
5. Grill for about 2 minutes and garnish with the remaining chilies and coriander leaves. Slice and serve to enjoy.

Crustless Vegetable Quiche

Serves: **4** | Prep Time: **40** mins

Ingredients
- 1 small yellow onion, diced
- ½ cup red bell pepper, diced
- ½ cup zucchini, sliced
- 1 tablespoon olive oil
- 2 garlic cloves, minced
- ½ cup green bell pepper, diced
- 6 broccoli florets
- 3 large eggs
- 2 tablespoons coconut milk
- ½ teaspoon black pepper
- ¼ cup low-fat parmesan cheese
- ¼ cup sun-dried tomatoes, diced
- 4 large egg whites
- 1 teaspoon dried oregano
- Sea salt, to taste

Directions
1. Preheat the oven to 425 degrees F and grease a 9-inch pie dish.
2. Heat oil in a large skillet over medium heat and add onion and garlic.
3. Sauté for about 4 minutes and add zucchini, broccoli, bell pepper, and dried tomatoes.
4. Sauté for about 2 minutes and dish out in a bowl.
5. Whisk eggs with spices, milk, egg whites, and ¼ cup parmesan cheese.
6. Stir in sautéed egg mixture and transfer the batter into a pie dish.
7. Place in the oven and bake for about 10 minutes.
8. Reduce the heat to 350 degrees F and bake for about 20 minutes.
9. Top with parmesan cheese and serve.

Ditalini Minestrone

Serves: **4** | Prep Time: **30** mins

Ingredients
- 1 onion, chopped
- 2 celery stalks, chopped
- 1 teaspoon salt
- 2 cups water
- ½ cup tomato sauce
- ¼ cup olive oil
- 2 carrots, chopped
- 3 garlic cloves, minced
- ¼ teaspoon black pepper
- 4 cups chicken stock
- 3 sprigs fresh thyme
- 2 cups swiss chard, chopped
- 1 can cannellini beans
- 1 pinch red pepper flakes
- Olive oil, to drizzle
- 1 bay leaf
- 1 cup Napa cabbage, chopped
- ⅔ cup ditalini pasta
- Parmesan cheese ribbons, for garnish

Directions
1. Heat olive oil in a cooking pot and add celery, onions, and carrots.
2. Sauté until soft and stir in salt, black pepper, and garlic.
3. Cook for about 1 minute and pour in the stock, water, tomato sauce, thyme, and bay leaf.
4. Boil the soup and add spinach, red pepper flakes, and cabbage.
5. Cook until the veggies turn soft and add pasta.
6. Cook until al dente and garnish with lemon juice, parmesan cheese, and olive oil.
7. Dish out and serve immediately.

Baked Kale and Eggs with Ricotta

Serves: **4** | Prep Time: **30** mins

Ingredients
- 1 tablespoon olive oil
- ¼ cup ricotta cheese, fat-free
- 6 cups kale, stems removed and chopped
- 2 garlic cloves, chopped
- ¼ cup fat-free feta cheese, crumbled
- 1/3 cup grape tomatoes, cut in half
- ½ teaspoon salt
- 4 large eggs
- ¼ teaspoon black pepper

Directions
1. Preheat the oven to 350 degrees F and grease a casserole dish.
2. Heat a skillet on medium heat and stir in garlic and kale.
3. Sauté for about 30 seconds and transfer garlic mixture to a bowl.
4. Mix feta cheese and ricotta cheese in another bowl.
5. Spread the kale mixture in the casserole dish and make about 4 wells in the kale mixture.
6. Crack one egg into each well and spread cheese mixture spoon by spoon on top.
7. Top with tomatoes and sprinkle with salt and black pepper.
8. Bake for about 20 minutes until golden brown and dish out to serve hot.

Ham and Poached Egg English Muffin

Serves: **4** | Prep Time: **10** mins

Ingredients
- 3 teaspoons olive oil
- 2 whole wheat English muffins, halved
- Black pepper, to taste
- 1 tomato, quartered
- 4 ham slices
- 4 eggs, poached

Directions
1. Heat 2 teaspoons of olive oil in a skillet and add ham and tomatoes.
2. Sauté until the meat turns golden and place the ham over the English muffin and tomatoes.
3. Top these muffins with poached eggs and drizzle with olive oil.
4. Season with black pepper and serve.

Caprese Snack

Serves: **4** | Prep Time: **5** mins

Ingredients
- 8 oz. mozzarella, mini cheese balls
- 8 oz. cherry tomatoes
- 2 tablespoons green pesto
- Salt and black pepper, to taste
- 1 tablespoon garlic powder

Directions
1. Slice the mozzarella balls and tomatoes in half.
2. Stir in the green pesto and season with garlic powder, salt and pepper to serve.

Almond Flour Crackers

Serves: **6** | Prep Time: **25** mins

Ingredients
- 2 tablespoons sunflower seeds
- 1 cup almond flour
- ¾ teaspoon sea salt
- 1 tablespoon whole psyllium husks
- 1 tablespoon coconut oil

Directions
1. Preheat the oven to 350°F and grease a baking sheet lightly.
2. Mix together sunflower seeds, almond flour, sea salt, coconut oil, psyllium husks and 2 tablespoons of water in a bowl.
3. Transfer into a blender and blend until smooth.
4. Form a dough out of this mixture and roll it on the parchment paper until 1/16 inch thick.
5. Slice into 1 inch squares and season with some sea salt.
6. Arrange the squares on the baking sheet and transfer to the oven.
7. Bake for about 15 minutes until edges are crisp and brown.
8. Allow to cool and separate into squares to serve.

Crispy Baked Zucchini Fries

Serves: **4** | Prep Time: **30** mins

Ingredients
- ¾ cup parmesan cheese, grated
- 2 medium zucchinis, chopped into small sticks
- 1 large egg
- ¼ teaspoon black pepper
- ¼ teaspoon garlic powder

Directions
1. Preheat the oven to 425°F and grease a baking sheet lightly.
2. Whisk egg in one bowl and mix together parmesan cheese, black pepper and garlic powder in another bowl.
3. Dip each zucchini stick in the egg and then dredge in the dry mixture.
4. Transfer to the baking sheet and place in the oven.
5. Bake for about 20 minutes until golden and broil for 3 minutes to serve.

Low Carb Onion Rings

Serves: **6** | Prep Time: **30** mins

Ingredients
- 2 medium white onions, sliced into ½ inch thick rings
- ½ cup coconut flour
- 4 large eggs
- 4 oz pork rinds
- 1 cup parmesan cheese, grated

Directions
1. Preheat an Air fryer to 390°F and grease a fryer basket.
2. Put coconut flour in one bowl, eggs in the second bowl and pork rinds and parmesan cheese in the third bowl.
3. Coat the onion rings through the three bowls one by one and repeat.
4. Place the coated onion rings in the fryer basket and cook for about 15 minutes.
5. Dish out to a platter and serve with your favorite low carb sauce.

Broccoli Fritters with Cheddar Cheese

Serves: **4** | Prep Time: **20** mins

Ingredients
- 1 cup cheddar cheese, shredded
- 8 ounces broccoli, chopped, steamed and drained
- 2 large eggs, beaten
- 1 tablespoon avocado oil
- 2 tablespoons oat fiber

Directions
1. Mix together broccoli with cheddar cheese, eggs and oat fiber in a bowl.
2. Heat avocado oil over medium heat in a nonstick pan and add the broccoli mixture in small chunks.
3. Cook for about 5 minutes on both sides until browned and dish onto a platter to serve.

Cheesy Low Carb Creamed Spinach

Serves: **8** | Prep Time: **25** mins

Ingredients
- 2 (10 oz) packages frozen chopped spinach, thawed
- 3 tablespoons butter
- 6 ounces cream cheese
- Onion powder, salt and black pepper
- ½ cup parmesan cheese, grated

Directions
1. Mix together 2 tablespoons of butter with cream cheese, parmesan cheese, salt and black pepper in a bowl.
2. Heat the rest of the butter on medium heat in a small pan and add onion powder. Sauté for about 1 minute and add spinach.
3. Cover and cook on low heat for about 5 minutes.
4. Stir in the cheese mixture and cook for about 3 minutes.
5. Dish into a bowl and serve hot.

Jicama Fries

Serves: **2** | Prep Time: **20** mins

Ingredients
- 2 tablespoons avocado oil
- 1 Jicama, cut into fries
- 1 tablespoon garlic powder
- ½ cup parmesan cheese, grated
- Salt and black pepper, to taste

Directions
1. Preheat the Air fryer to 400°F and grease the fryer basket.
2. Boil jicama fries for about 10 minutes and drain well.
3. Mix jicama fries with garlic powder, salt and black pepper in a bowl.
4. Place in the fryer basket and cook for about 10 minutes.
5. Dish onto a platter and serve warm.

Spicy Tuna Rolls

Serves: **2** | Prep Time: **15** mins

Ingredients
- 1 pouch StarKist Selects E.V.O.O. Wild Caught Yellowfin Tuna
- 1 medium cucumber, thinly sliced lengthwise
- 1 teaspoon hot sauce
- 2 slices avocado, diced
- Cayenne, salt and black pepper

Directions
1. Mix together tuna with hot sauce, cayenne, salt and black pepper in a bowl until combined.
2. Put the tuna mixture on the cucumber slices and top with avocado.
3. Roll up the cucumber and secure with 2 toothpicks to serve.

Cheesy Radish

Serves: **5** | Prep Time: **1 hour**

Ingredients
- 16 oz. Monterey jack cheese, shredded
- 2 cups radish
- ½ cup heavy cream
- 1 teaspoon lemon juice
- Salt and white pepper, to taste

Directions
1. Preheat the oven to 300ºF and lightly grease a baking sheet.
2. Heat heavy cream in a small saucepan and season with salt and white pepper.
3. Stir in Monterey jack cheese and lemon juice.
4. Place the radish on the baking sheet and top with the cheese mixture.
5. Bake for about 45 minutes and remove from the oven to serve hot.

Parmesan Garlic Oven Roasted Mushrooms

Serves: **6** | Prep Time: **30** mins

Ingredients
- 3 tablespoons butter
- 12 oz. baby Bella mushrooms
- ¼ cup pork rinds, finely ground
- Pink Himalayan salt and black pepper, to taste
- ¼ cup parmesan cheese, grated

Directions
1. Preheat the oven to 400ºF and lightly grease a baking sheet.
2. Heat butter in a large skillet over medium high heat and add mushrooms.
3. Sauté for about 3 minutes and dish out.
4. Mix together pork rinds, parmesan cheese, salt and black pepper in a bowl.
5. Put the mushrooms in this mixture and mix to coat well.
6. Place on the baking sheet and transfer to the oven.
7. Bake for about 15 minutes and dish out to immediately serve.

Garlicky Green Beans Stir Fry

Serves: **4** | Prep Time: **25** mins

Ingredients
- 2 tablespoons peanut oil
- 1 pound fresh green beans
- 2 tablespoons garlic, chopped
- Salt and red chili pepper, to taste
- ½ yellow onion, slivered

Directions
1. Heat peanut oil in a wok over high heat and add garlic and onions.
2. Sauté for about 4 minutes add beans, salt and red chili pepper.
3. Sauté for about 3 minutes and add a little water.
4. Cover with lid and cook on low heat for about 5 minutes.
5. Dish out into a bowl and serve hot.

Collard Greens with Burst Cherry Tomatoes

Serves: **4** | Prep Time: **25** mins

Ingredients
- 1 pound collard greens
- 3 strips bacon, cooked and crisped
- ¼ cup cherry tomatoes
- Salt and black pepper, to taste
- 2 tablespoons chicken broth

Directions
1. Put the collard greens, cherry tomatoes and chicken broth in a pot and stir gently.
2. Cook for about 8 minutes and season with salt and black pepper.
3. Cook for about 2 minutes and stir in the bacon.
4. Cook for about 3 minutes and dish out into a bowl to serve hot.

Basil Parmesan Tomatoes

Serves: **6** | Prep Time: **30** mins

Ingredients
- ½ teaspoon dried oregano
- 4 Roma tomatoes
- Spices: onion powder, garlic powder, sea salt and black pepper
- ½ cup parmesan cheese, shredded
- 12 small fresh basil leaves

Directions
1. Preheat the oven to 425°F and grease a baking sheet lightly.
2. Mix together dried oregano, onion powder, garlic powder, sea salt and black pepper in a small bowl.
3. Arrange the tomato slices on a baking sheet and sprinkle with the seasoning blend.
4. Top with parmesan cheese and basil leaves and transfer to the oven.
5. Bake for about 20 minutes and remove from the oven to serve.

Roasted Spicy Garlic Eggplant Slices

Serves: **4** | Prep Time: **35** mins

Ingredients
- 2 tablespoons olive oil
- 1 eggplant, sliced into rounds
- 1 teaspoon garlic powder
- Salt and red pepper
- ½ teaspoon Italian seasoning

Directions
1. Preheat the oven to 400°F and line a baking sheet with parchment paper.
2. Arrange the eggplant slices on a baking sheet and drizzle with olive oil.
3. Season with Italian seasoning, garlic powder, salt and red pepper.
4. Transfer to the oven and bake for about 25 minutes. Remove from the oven and serve hot.

Egg Fast Fettuccini Alfredo

Serves: **2** | Prep Time: **20** mins

Ingredients
- 1 oz. cream cheese
- 2 eggs
- Garlic powder, salt and black pepper
- 1 tablespoon butter
- 2 oz. Mascarpone cheese

Directions
1. Preheat the oven to 325°F and grease a baking pan lightly.
2. Put the cream cheese, eggs, garlic powder, salt and black pepper in a blender.
3. Pour this mixture into the baking pan and transfer to the oven.
4. Bake for about 8 minutes and remove from the oven.
5. Allow to slightly cool and roll up the baked sheet.
6. Mix together butter and Mascarpone cheese in a small bowl.
7. Microwave for about 1 minute on high and whisk well until smooth.
8. Put the baked sheet in the butter cheese mixture and immediately serve.

Braided Garlic Breadsticks

Serves: **4** | Prep Time: **35** mins

Ingredients
- 1 egg
- 2 garlic cloves, crushed
- 10 oz. mozzarella cheese, shredded
- 1 cup ground flax seed
- 2 tablespoons salted butter, melted

Directions
1. Preheat the oven to 400°F and lightly grease a cookie sheet.
2. Mix together garlic and butter in a bowl and set aside.
3. Melt the cheese in microwave and stir in flax seed and egg.
4. Mix well and press into a rectangle and cut lengthwise into small strips.
5. Braid the dough with 3 strips and brush with half of the garlic butter.
6. Transfer onto the cookie sheet and bake for about 15 minutes.
7. Remove from the oven and brush with the rest of the garlic butter.
8. Bake for another 10 minutes and dish out to serve warm.

Stir Fried Bok Choy

Serves: **4** | Prep Time: **15** mins

Ingredients
- 1 tablespoon oyster sauce
- 2 teaspoons soy sauce
- 1 tablespoon butter
- 2 heads bok choy, ends trimmed and cut crosswise into strips
- 2 tablespoons sesame oil

Directions
1. Mix together soy sauce, oyster sauce, sesame oil and 2 tablespoons water in a bowl and set aside. Heat butter in a wok on medium heat and add bok choy.
2. Sauté for about 3 minutes and stir in the soy sauce mixture.
3. Stir fry for about 2 more minutes and dish out onto a platter to serve.

Black and White Fat Bombs

Serves: **8** | Prep Time: **45** mins

Ingredients
- 1 cup extra-virgin coconut oil
- 2 cups almonds, slivered
- 2 scoops Stevia
- 2 tablespoons unsweetened cocoa powder
- 2 teaspoons sugar free vanilla extract

Directions
1. Put mini liners in 8 cup mini muffin tin.
2. Put the coconut oil, almonds, Stevia and vanilla extract in a food processor and process until coarsely smooth.
3. Dish out half of this mixture into a bowl and add cocoa powder.
4. Put almond mixture in half of the muffin tin and top with the cocoa mixture.
5. Transfer the muffin tray in the freezer and freeze for about 30 minutes before serving.

Cheddar Taco Crisps

Serves: **5** | Prep Time: **15** mins

Ingredients
- ¼ cup parmesan cheese, shredded
- ¾ cup full fat sharp cheddar cheese, finely shredded
- ¼ teaspoon chili powder
- 1 pinch cayenne pepper
- ¼ teaspoon ground cumin

Directions
1. Preheat the oven to 400°F and grease a baking sheet lightly.
2. Mix together parmesan cheese, cheddar cheese, chili powder, cayenne pepper and cumin in a bowl.
3. Spoon the cheese mixture 1 inch apart on the baking sheet and transfer to the oven.
4. Bake for about 5 minutes until the cheese is golden brown and remove from the oven to serve.

Cheesy Cauliflower Breadsticks

Serves: **6** | Prep Time: **30** mins

Ingredients
- ½ teaspoon dried Italian seasoning
- 4 cups cauliflower, riced
- 2 large eggs, beaten
- Kosher salt and black pepper, to taste
- 3 cups cheddar cheese, shredded

Directions
1. Preheat the oven to 475°F and grease a baking sheet lightly.
2. Mix together cauliflower, Italian seasoning, eggs, cheddar cheese, salt and black pepper in a bowl.
3. Spread this mixture on the prepared baking sheet and transfer to the oven.
4. Bake for about 20 minutes and remove from the oven to serve.

Citrus Marinated Olives

Serves: **4** | Prep Time: **20** mins

Ingredients
- ¼ lemon, zest and juice
- ¼ cup extra virgin olive oil
- ¼ orange, zest and juice
- 1 cup Castelvetrano olives
- Kosher salt, black pepper and red chili pepper, to taste

Directions
1. Heat olive oil over medium heat in a small saucepan and add olives.
2. Sauté for about 3 minutes and stir in the lemon zest, orange zest, salt, black pepper and red chili pepper.
3. Sauté for about 2 minutes and stir in the lemon juice and orange juice.
4. Dish into a bowl and serve warm.

Spicy Edamame Dip

Serves: **5** | Prep Time: **30** mins

Ingredients
- 1 cup edamame beans, shelled
- 2 tablespoons olive oil
- Salt and cayenne pepper, to taste
- ¼ cup fresh lime juice
- ¼ cup fresh cilantro, finely chopped

Directions
1. Boil edamame beans in water and reserve ¾ cup of the cooking water.
2. Put the boiled beans, reserved cooking water, olive oil, lime juice, cilantro, salt and cayenne pepper in the food processor.
3. Process until smooth and serve with your favorite snacks.

Crab and Avocado Duet

Serves: **4** | Prep Time: **10** mins

Ingredients
- 3 tablespoons lemon juice
- 1 ripe avocado, chunked
- Salt and white pepper, to taste
- ½ pound lump crabmeat
- 2 teaspoons Dijon mustard

Directions
1. Mix the avocado chunks with half of lemon juice and some salt.
2. Mix together remaining lemon juice, Dijon mustard, white pepper and lump crabmeat in another bowl.
3. Put the avocado mixture on the plate and top with the crabmeat mixture. Serve immediately.

Bacon Wrapped Scallops

Serves: **4** | Prep Time: **25** mins

Ingredients
- 1 lime, juiced and zested
- 8 slices center cut smoked bacon, cut in half
- 8 large sea scallops, trimmed and well drained
- 1 tablespoon sesame oil, toasted
- Salt, red pepper flakes and black pepper

Directions
1. Preheat the oven to 425°F and lightly grease a baking pan.
2. Mix together scallops, lime juice, sesame oil, salt, red pepper flakes and black pepper in a bowl.
3. Wrap the scallops with bacon slices and transfer to the baking pan.
4. Bake for about 15 minutes and remove from the oven to serve.

Teriyaki Ginger Tuna Skewers

Serves: **8** | Prep Time: **15** mins

Ingredients
- 3 ounces sesame oil
- 2 pounds fresh tuna steak, cut into 1 inch cubes
- 15 ounces teriyaki sauce
- 2 tablespoons ginger garlic paste
- 1 lemon, juiced

Directions
1. Preheat the grill to high heat.
2. Soak bamboo skewers in water for about 1 hour.
3. Mix together all the ingredients except tuna steak in a bowl.
4. Marinate tuna in this mixture for about 1 hour.
5. Thread the tuna on the skewers and transfer to the grill.
6. Grill for about 4 minutes and serve hot

Cinnamon and Cardamom Fat Bombs

Serves: **5** | Prep Time: **15** mins

Ingredients
- ½ cup unsweetened coconut, shredded
- 3 oz. unsalted butter
- ¼ teaspoon ground cardamom
- ¼ teaspoon ground cinnamon
- ½ teaspoon vanilla extract

Directions
1. Heat a nonstick pan and add shredded coconut.
2. Roast for about 3 minutes until brown and mix half of coconut with butter, cardamom, cinnamon and vanilla extract.
3. Form small balls out of this mixture and roll in the rest of the shredded coconut.
4. Transfer to the freezer for about 2 hours and serve chilled.

Pistachio Truffles

Serves: **3** | Prep Time: **15** mins

Ingredients
- ¼ teaspoon vanilla extract
- 1 cup mascarpone cheese, softened
- 3 scoops Stevia
- 1 pinch cinnamon
- ¼ cup pistachios, chopped

Directions
1. Mix together mascarpone cheese, cinnamon, vanilla extract and Stevia in a bowl.
2. Mix thoroughly until well blended and form small balls out of this mixture.
3. Place pistachios in a plate and roll the balls in it.
4. Place in the freezer for about 3 hours and dish out to serve.

Dessert Recipes

Banana Greek Yogurt Bowl

Serves: **4** | Prep Time: **10** mins

Ingredients
- 2 medium bananas, sliced
- 4 cups vanilla Greek yogurt
- ¼ cup creamy natural peanut butter
- 1 teaspoon nutmeg
- ¼ cup flax seed meal

Directions
1. Put yogurt in the serving bowls and stir in melted butter, flaxseeds and nutmeg.
2. Top equally with banana slices and serve immediately.

Popped Quinoa Bars

Serves: **6** | Prep Time: **10** mins

Ingredients
- 1 cup dry quinoa
- 4 (4 oz.) semi-sweet chocolate bars, chopped
- ½ teaspoon vanilla
- 1 tablespoon peanut butter

Directions
1. Toast quinoa in a pan until golden and stir in vanilla, chocolate, and peanut butter.
2. Spread this mixture evenly in a baking sheet and refrigerate for about 3 hours.
3. Break it into small pieces and serve to enjoy.

Honey yogurt cheesecake

Serves: **8** | Prep Time: **1 hour 15** mins

Ingredients
- 3 tablespoons almonds, flaked
- 1 cup Greek yogurt
- 2 eggs
- 1 orange, zested
- Fresh fruit, to serve
- 4 oz. amaretti biscuits
- 3 tablespoons almond butter, melted
- 26 oz. mascarpone
- 1 lemon, zested
- 1 cup honey

Directions
1. Preheat the oven to 280 degrees F and grease a baking dish.
2. Seal almonds and biscuits in a ziplock bag and crush them with a rolling pin.
3. Toss this mixture with butter and crumbs and transfer evenly into a baking dish.
4. Bake for about 10 minutes and dish out.
5. Whisk eggs, yogurt and mascarpone with a beater and stir in honey, orange and lemon zest.
6. Transfer the batter to the baked crust and cover the pan with a foil tent.
7. Bake for about 1 hour and garnish with honey and almonds to serve.

Almond Orange Pandoro

Serves: **6** | Prep Time: **10** mins

Ingredients
- 1¼ cups mascarpone
- 1 large orange, zested
- ¼ cup almonds, whole
- 1¼ cups coconut cream
- 4 tablespoons sherry
- 1 pandoro, diced

Directions
1. Whisk cream with mascarpone, icing sugar, ¾ zest and half sherry in a bowl.
2. Place the bottom slice of pandoro in a plate and top with remaining sherry.
3. Spoon the mascarpone mixture over the slice and top with almonds.
4. Place another pandoro slice over and continue adding layers of pandoro slices and cream mixture to serve.

Fruity Almond cake

Serves: **8** | Prep Time: **2 hours 10** mins

Ingredients

- 2 large oranges, zested and juiced
- 1¼ cups butter, softened
- 5 oz. whole wheat flour
- 2 teaspoons mixed spice
- 5 oz. whole almond
- 2 pounds mixed dried fruit
- ½ cup sherry
- 1¼ cups light muscovado sugar
- 1 vanilla pod, seeds scraped
- 4 oz. ground almond
- 4 large eggs, beaten

Directions

1. Preheat the oven to 280 degrees F and grease a baking dish.
2. Mix fruits, sherry, orange juice and zest in a bowl and refrigerate overnight.
3. Grease a cake pan with butter and spread brown paper in it.
4. Beat sugar and vanilla seeds in butter until smooth and creamy.
5. Add spices, flour and ground almond and mix well until smooth.
6. Fold in marinated fruits and whole almonds.
7. Pour the batter in the baking dish and bake it for 1 hour 30 minutes.
8. Reduce the heat of the oven to 250 degrees F and bake for 1 hour and 30 minutes to enjoy.

Honey Glazed Pears

Serves: **3** | Prep Time: **35** mins

Ingredients

- ¼ cup pear nectar
- 2 tablespoons almond butter
- Dollop of cream
- 3 ripe medium pears, peeled, halved and cored
- 3 tablespoons honey
- 1 teaspoon orange zest
- ½ cup mascarpone cheese
- 1/3 cup salted pistachios, roasted and chopped

Directions

1. Let your oven preheat at 4000 F (2040 C)
2. Spread the sliced pear in a baking pan with their cut sides down.
3. Pour honey, butter, nectar and orange zest on top.
4. Roast these pears for 25 mins in the preheated oven.
5. Mix sugar with mascarpone and top the baked pears with it.
6. Garnish with honey and pistachios. Enjoy.

Compote Dipped Berries Mix

Serves: **4** | Prep Time: **20** mins

Ingredients

- 3 orange pekoe tea bags
- 1 cup fresh strawberries, hulled and halved lengthwise
- 1 cup fresh red raspberries
- ½ cup water
- 34-inch sprigs fresh mint
- 1 cup fresh golden raspberries
- 1 cup fresh blackberries
- 1 cup fresh sweet cherries, pitted and halved
- ½ cup pomegranate juice
- Fresh mint sprigs
- 1 cup fresh blueberries
- 1 ml bottle Sauvignon Blanc
- 1 teaspoon vanilla

Directions

1. Preheat the oven to 280 degrees F and grease a baking dish.
2. Soak 3 mint sprigs and tea bags in hot boiled water for 10 minutes in a covered bowl.
3. Mix together all the berries and cherries in another bowl and keep aside.
4. Stir cook wine with pomegranate juice in a saucepan.
5. Add the strained tea liquid to the saucepan.
6. Toss in the mixed berries and mix them well to serve and enjoy.

Eggs and Dairy Recipes

Breakfast Meaty Quiche

Yield: 6 | Total Time: 40 Mins | Prep Time: 10 Mins | Cook Time: 30 Mins

Ingredients

- 2 cups chopped green onions
- ¼-pound diced ham
- ¼-pound ground turkey
- 4 tablespoons olive oil
- 6 slices cooked bacon, crumbled
- 1 cup milk
- 4 large eggs
- 1 cup shredded cheese
- 1/4 tsp. salt
- 1/8 tsp. pepper

Directions

1. Set your instant pot to manual high; heat oil and cook in ground turkey until browned. Mix green onions, ham, cooked turkey, bacon and cheese. Whisk together milk, eggs, salt and pepper in a large bowl until well blended and pour over the meat and stir to mix well.
2. Lock lid and cook for 30 Mins. When ready, let pressure come down on its own.
3. Remove from the pot and sprinkle with more cheese. Broil until cheese is melted and serve.

Breakfast Eggs de Provence

Yield: 4 | Total Time: 20 Mins | Prep Time: 10 Mins | Cooking Time: 10 Mins

Ingredients

- 1 ½ cups cream cheese
- 3 large eggs
- ½-pound cooked ham, diced
- 1 red onion, chopped
- 1 cup cheddar cheese
- 1 ½ cup chopped kale leaves
- 1 tsp Herbes de Provence
- 1/8 tsp. sea salt
- 1/8 tsp. pepper

Directions

1. In a bowl, beat cream cheese and eggs until well blended; stir in the remaining ingredients and pour the mixture into an instant pot. Lock lid and set it to manual high setting. Cook for 10 Mins and then release the pressure naturally. Serve hot with a glass of fresh orange juice.

Instant Pot Bacon-Spinach Frittata

Yield: 4 | Total Time: 37 Mins | Prep Time: 10 Mins | Cook Time: 27 Mins

Ingredients

- 2 tablespoons butter
- 8 eggs
- 1 cup fresh spinach
- 5 ounces diced bacon
- 1 cup heavy whipping cream
- salt & pepper
- ¾ cup shredded cheese

Directions

1. Set your instant pot to manual high; melt in butter and the fry bacon for about 7 Mins. Stir in spinach until wilted and remove the pan from heat; set aside.
2. In a small bowl, whisk together cream and eggs until well combined and then pour in the pot; top with spinach, bacon and cheese. Lock lid and cook for 15 Mins. When ready, let pressure come down on its own.

Roasted Veggie Breakfast Frittata

Yield: 8 | Total Time: 1 Hour 20 Mins | Prep Time: 30 Mins | Cook Time: 50 Mins

Ingredients

- 4 tbsp. extra virgin olive oil
- 1 cup fresh cremini mushrooms, sliced
- 20 egg whites, beaten
- 1 cup cheddar cheese
- 1/2 cup chopped fresh baby spinach
- 1 cup sweet red pepper strips
- 1 cup thin red onion wedges
- Olive oil cooking spray
- 2 tbsp. fresh oregano, snipped
- 1/4 tsp. black pepper
- 1/4 tsp. sea salt

Directions

1. Set your instant pot to manual high. Toss together extra virgin olive oil, sweet pepper, mushrooms, onion, salt and pepper in a large bowl until well combined. Spoon the mixture evenly into the pot and roast for about 20 Mins or until the veggies are tender. Toss together the roasted veggies and spinach; spread the mixture in the pot and sprinkle with pieces of cheese and pour the egg whites on top. Lock lid and cook for 30 Mins. When ready, let pressure come down on its own. Serve sprinkled with oregano.

Instant Pot Avocado Shrimp Omelet

Yields: 2 | Total Time: 40 Mins | Prep Time: 10 Mins | Cook Time: 30 Mins

Ingredients

- 150g shrimp, peeled and deveined
- 4 large free-range eggs, beaten
- 1 medium avocado, diced
- 1 large tomato, diced
- 2 tablespoons coconut oil
- 1/8 tsp. freshly ground black pepper
- 1/4 tsp. sea salt
- 1 tbsp. freshly chopped cilantro

Directions
1. Set your instant pot to manual high; cook shrimp until it turns pink; chop the cooked shrimp and set aside. In a small bowl, toss together avocado, tomato, and cilantro; season with sea salt and pepper and set aside. In a separate bowl, beat the eggs and set aside.
2. Melt coconut oil in the pot and then add in the egg mixture. Arrange the shrimp on top of the egg and lock lid; cook for 5 Mins and then let pressure come down on its own.

Healthy Frittata w/ Scallions & Smoked Salmon
Yield: 6 | Total Time: 30 Mins | Prep Time: 10 Mins | Cook Time: 20 Mins

Ingredients
- 2 tablespoons extra virgin olive oil
- 4 scallions, trimmed and chopped
- 3 large eggs
- 3 large egg whites
- ½ teaspoon finely chopped fresh tarragon
- ¼ cup water
- ½ teaspoon salt
- 2 ounces smoked salmon, sliced into small pieces
- 2 tablespoons black olive tapenade

Directions
1. Set your instant pot to manual high; add extra virgin olive oil and heat until hot, but not smoking; stir in scallions and sauté until fragrant. In a bowl, beat together eggs, egg whites, tarragon, water, and salt; season with black pepper and pour into the pot. Arrange the salmon onto the egg mixture. Cook, stirring frequently, for about 2 Mins or until almost set. Lock lid and cook for 14 Mins. When ready, let pressure come down on its own. Remove the frittata from the pot and transfer to a serving plate; slice and serve with tapenade.

Instant Pot Cheesy Green Omelet
Yield: 4 | Total Time: 30 Mins | Prep Time: 10 Mins | Cook Time: 20 Mins

Ingredients
- 4 tbsp. extra virgin olive oil
- 8 large eggs
- 1 red onion, finely chopped
- 2 tsp. chopped parsley
- ½ cup cheddar cheese
- Handful rocket leaves
- Salt and pepper

Directions
1. Set your instant pot to manual high; add extra virgin olive oil and heat until hot, but not smoking; stir in the red onion and fry for about 5 Mins. Whisk the eggs well and add to the pot with the onion; evenly distribute the egg mixture and sprinkle with grated cheese. Lock lid and cook for 15 Mins and then let pressure come down on its own. Remove the omelet from the pot and sprinkle with parsley and rocket; season with salt and pepper and roll up the omelet. Serve right away.

Instant Pot Sausage & Broccoli Quiche
Yield: 6 | Total Time: 1 Hour 10 Mins | Prep Time: 15 Mins | Cook Time: 55 Mins

Ingredients
- 4 cups broccoli
- 300g breakfast sausage
- 3 cups almond flour
- 1 tablespoon sea salt
- 8 eggs
- 2 tablespoons coconut oil
- 2 tablespoons water

Directions
1. Steam the broccoli and set aside.
2. Set your instant pot to manual high and cook the sausage until browned; set aside.
3. Blend almond flour and sea salt in a food processor until well combined; add one egg and coconut oil and continue processing to form a ball. Spread the dough in the pot and top with broccoli and sausage.
4. In a bowl, whisk the remaining eggs with water and pour over the broccoli and sausage.
5. Lock lid and cook for 35 Mins. Release the pressure naturally and serve warm.

Instant Pot Salmon Omelet
Yield: 1 | Total Time: 25 Mins | Prep Time: 10 Mins | Cook Time: 15 Mins

Ingredients
- 1 tablespoon extra virgin olive oil
- 1 oz. sliced smoked salmon
- 2 tablespoons capers
- 1 large egg
- 10g chopped rocket
- 1 teaspoon chopped parsley
- 1 red onion, chopped

Directions
1. Beat the egg in a large bowl; stir in salmon, rocket, capers, red onion, and chopped parsley.
2. Set your instant pot to manual high; add extra virgin olive oil and heat until hot, but not smoking; add the egg mixture and spread the mixture evenly in the bottom of the pot. Lock lid and cook for 15 Mins. When ready, let pressure come down on its own. With a spatula, roll the omelet in half and serve hot.

Low-Carb Instant Pot Egg Salad

Yield: 4 | Total Time: 10 Mins | Prep Time: 5 Mins | Cook Time: 5 Mins

Ingredients
- 6 eggs
- 1 tsp. lemon juice
- 1 tsp. Dijon mustard
- 2 tbsp. mayonnaise
- 1/8 tsp. kosher salt
- 1/8 tsp. pepper
- 2 lettuce leaves to serve

Directions
1. Add water to your instant pot and insert a trivet; place eggs in a metal dish and place on a trivet; lock lid and cook on high for 5 Mins and then let pressure come down on its own.
2. Transfer the eggs to a bowl of cold water and let cool completely; peel and add to a food processor. Pulse until chopped. Add lemon juice, mustard, mayonnaise, salt and pepper and continue pulsing until smooth. Spoon the egg mixture over lettuce leaves and wrap. Serve.

Instant Pot Jalapeno Omelettes

Yield: 4 | Total Time: 20 Mins | Prep Time: 10 Mins | Cook Time: 10 Mins

Ingredients
- ¼ cup heavy cream
- 1 cup cheddar cheese, shredded
- 4 jalapeno peppers, chopped
- 8 slices bacon, chopped
- 12 large eggs
- ¼ tsp. sea salt
- 1/8 tsp. pepper

Directions
1. Grease jars with oil and set aside.
2. In a skillet set over medium heat, cook bacon until crispy and then set aside on a plate; add jalapenos in bacon fat and cook for about 2 Mins or until tender and then remove from fat to a plate.
3. In a bowl, whisk together heavy cream, eggs, salt and pepper and then fold in bacon, peppers and shredded cheese. Divide the egg mixture among four greased jars and place them on a trivet in an instant pot; add two cups of water and lock lid. Cook on high for 5 Mins and then let pressure come down on its own.

Instant Pot Mini Mushroom Quiche

Yield: 6 | Total Time: 17 Mins | Prep Time: 7 Mins | Cook Time: 10 Mins

Ingredients
- 4 eggs
- 1/2 cup shredded Swiss cheese
- 1 scallion, chopped
- 1/4 cup heavy cream
- 2 ounces chopped cremini mushrooms
- 1/2 tsp. salt
- 1 cup water

Directions
1. Press Swiss cheese in the bottom of a silicone mold and up the sides; divide chopped mushrooms among the molds and top with chopped scallions.
2. In a blender, blend together cream, eggs and salt; pour over the mushrooms.
3. Add a cup of water to your instant pot and place on the trivet; place the silicon tray over the trivet and lock lid. Cook on high for 5 Mins and then release pressure quickly. Broil for 5 Mins in oven until lightly browned and serve.

Breakfast Casserole

Yield: 6 | Total Time: 45 Mins | Prep Time: 15 Mins | Cook Time: 30 Mins

Ingredients
- 2 tablespoons coconut oil
- 1 ⅓ cups sliced leek
- 2 teaspoons minced garlic
- 1 cup chopped kale
- 8 eggs
- ⅔ cups sweet potato, peeled and grated
- 1 ½ cups breakfast sausage

Directions
1. Set your instant pot to sauté mode and melt coconut oil; stir in garlic, leeks, and kale and sauté for about 5 Mins or until tender; transfer the veggies to a plate and clean the pot.
2. Whisk together eggs, beef sausage, sweet potato and the sautéed veggies in a large bowl until well blended; pour the mixture in a heatproof bowl or pan. Add water to the instant pot and insert a trivet; place the bowl onto the trivet and lock lid. Cook on manual for 25 Mins and then let pressure come down on its own. Remove the casserole and cut into equal slices.

Healthy Veggie Frittata

Yields: 4 | Total Time: 30 Mins | Prep Time: 10 Mins | Cook Time: 20 Mins

Ingredients
- 8 free-range eggs, whisked
- ½ cup milk
- 2 tbsp. chopped green onions
- 2 tbsp. chopped leek
- 2 tbsp. chopped fresh chives
- 2 tbsp. chopped fresh dill
- 4 tomatoes, diced
- 1 tsp. red pepper flakes
- 2 garlic cloves, minced
- Coconut oil, for greasing the pan
- Sea salt
- Black pepper

Directions
1. Grease a cast iron skillet or saucepan and set aside.
2. In a large bowl, whisk together the eggs; beat in the remaining ingredients until well mixed.
3. Pour the egg mixture into the prepared pan and. Add water to the instant pot and insert a trivet; place the pan onto the trivet and lock lid. Cook on high for 20 Mins and then let pressure come down on its own. Remove the casserole and cut into equal slices.
4. Garnish the frittata with extra chives and dill to serve.

Instant Pot Frittata with Pesto

Yield: 4 | Total Time: 60 Mins | Prep Time: 10 Mins | Cook Time: 50 Mins

Ingredients
- 4 tbsp. extra virgin olive oil
- 3 cloves garlic, minced
- 1 cup white onion, diced
- 200g ground beef
- 8 eggs, beaten
- ¼ cup basil pesto
- 200g bottled roasted red peppers, drained then sliced
- 1 cup baby arugula, torn
- ¼ tsp freshly ground black pepper
- ½ tsp kosher salt
- 1 cup shredded cheddar cheese

Directions
1. Set your instant pot to manual high and then add in olive oil; sauté the onions for about 5 Mins or until tender. Add in the garlic and sauté for 1 minute until fragrant; stir in ground beef and cook until browned; stir in eggs, arugula, red peppers, pesto, and cheese, and salt and pepper until well combined. Lock lid and cook for 40 Mins and then naturally release the pressure. Enjoy!

Instant Pot Berry Omelet

Yield: 4 | Total Time: 20 Mins | Prep Time: 10 Mins | Cook Time: 10 Mins

Ingredients
- 8 eggs
- 1 cup milk
- 1 teaspoon cinnamon
- 4 tbsp. olive oil
- 1 cup grated cottage cheese
- 1 ½ cups chopped raspberries, blueberries, and strawberries

Directions
1. In a bowl, beat together the egg, milk and cinnamon until well blended.
2. Add oil to an instant pot set to manual high. Add the egg mixture and swirl to cover the base evenly. Lock lid and cook the egg mixture for 10 Mins. Let pressure come down on its own.
3. Transfer the omelet to a plate and sprinkle with cheese. Top with berries and roll up to serve.

Instant Pot Low Carb Casserole

Yield: 6 | Total Time: 35 Mins | Prep Time: 10 Mins | Cooking Time: 25 Mins

Ingredients
- 12 large eggs
- 1 1/4 pounds diced ham
- 1 cup olive oil
- 500 grams raw radishes, sliced thinly into strips
- 1/2 cup diced red onions
- 1 clove fresh garlic, minced
- 1/2 teaspoon sea salt
- 1/4 teaspoon pepper
- 1 teaspoon seasoning
- 1 ½ cups water
- 1 cup spinach
- ½ cup chopped green bell pepper
- 1 cup parmesan cheese, grated

Directions
1. Set your instant pot to manual high setting and heat in olive oil and add onions and radishes; sprinkle with salt and pepper and cook, stirring occasionally, for about 3 Mins or until tender.
2. Whisk eggs and seasoning in a bowl until frothy and then add to the pot; stir to combine. Stir in diced ham, chopped green pepper and spinach; top with grated cheese. Lock lid and cook for 20 Mins. Serve warm.

Asian Breakfast Eggs

Yield: 1 Serving | Total time: 10 Mins | Prep time: 5 Mins | Cook time: 5 Mins

Ingredients
- 1 large egg
- pinch of sesame seeds
- 1 tsp chopped scallions
- 1/3 cup cold water
- pinch of garlic powder
- pinch of salt
- pinch of pepper

Directions
1. In a small bowl, whisk together water and eggs until frothy; strain the mixture through a fine mesh into a heat proof bowl. Whisk in the remaining ingredients until well combined; set aside.
2. Add a cup of water to an instant pot and place a steamer basket or trivet in the pot; place the bowl with the mixture over the basket and lock lid. Cook on high for 5 Mins and then naturally release pressure. Serve hot with a glass of freshly squeezed orange juice.

Mexican Frittata

Yield: 4 | Total Time: 35 Mins | Prep Time: 10 Mins | Cook Time: 25 Mins

Ingredients
- 1 cup half and half
- 4 eggs
- 1 cup diced green chilis
- 1 cup shredded Mexican blend cheese
- 1/4 cup chopped cilantro
- 1/2 tsp. salt
- 1/2 tsp. ground cumin

Directions
1. In a bowl, whisk together half and half, eggs, green chilis, ½ cup shredded cheese, cumin and salt until well combined; pour the mixture into a greased metal pan and cover with foil.
2. Add two cups of water in an instant pot and place on a trivet; place the pan over the trivet and lock lid; cook on high for 20 Mins and then let the pressure come down on its own.
3. Remove lid and sprinkle with the remaining cheese and cilantro; broil for about 5 Mins or until cheese is bubbly and browned.

Low Carb Instant Pot Egg Cups

Yield: 4 | Total Time: 18 Mins | Prep Time: 5 Mins | Cook Time: 13 Mins

Ingredients
- 1/4 cup half and half
- 4 eggs
- 1/2 cup shredded cheddar cheese
- 1/4 cup each of diced red onions, bell peppers, mushrooms, and tomatoes)
- 2 tbsp. chopped cilantro
- Salt & Pepper
- 1/2 cup shredded parmesan

Directions
1. In a bowl, beat together half and half, eggs, cheddar, veggies, cilantro, salt and pepper; pour in half-pint jars and cover with lids.
2. Add two cups of water to an instant pot and place in a trivet; place the jars on trivet and lock lid; cook on high pressure for 10 Mins and then quickly release the pressure.
3. Top with parmesan cheese and broil for about 3 Mins or until cheese is bubbly and lightly browned. Enjoy!

Instant Pot Spiced Salmon Frittata

Yield: 2 | Total Time: 30 Mins | Prep Time: 10 Mins | Cook Time: 20 Mins

Ingredients:
- 1 tablespoon coconut oil
- 1 red onion, chopped
- 1 green pepper, chopped
- 2 garlic cloves, minced
- 1 ½ cups cherry tomatoes
- 1/2 teaspoon paprika
- 1 teaspoon cumin
- 1/2 cup wild-caught salmon
- 6 free-range eggs, beaten
- Pinch of sea salt
- Pinch of pepper
- 2 tablespoons chopped cilantro

Directions:
1. Set your instant pot to manual high and melt in butter; sauté red onion and green pepper; stir in garlic and cook for about 2 Mins or until fragrant. Stir in paprika, cumin, salt and pepper and cook for about 1 minute; stir in tomatoes and cook until soft. Sprinkle with salmon and cover with eggs; season with salt and pepper and lock lid. Cook on high for 15 Mins and then release the pressure naturally. Serve warm garnished with cilantro.

Korean Steamed Breakfast Eggs

Yield: 1 | Total time: 10 Mins | Prep time: 5 Mins | Cook time: 5 Mins

Ingredients
- 1 tablespoon melted butter
- 1 large egg
- pinch of sesame seeds
- 1 tsp. chopped scallions
- 1/3 cup cold water
- pinch of garlic powder
- pinch of salt
- pinch of pepper

Directions
1. In a small bowl, whisk together butter and eggs until frothy; strain the mixture through a fine mesh into a heatproof bowl. Whisk in the remaining ingredients until well combined; set aside.
2. Add a cup of water to an instant pot and place a steamer basket or trivet in the pot; place the bowl with the mixture over the basket and lock lid. Cook on high for 5 Mins and then naturally release pressure.
3. Serve hot with a glass of freshly squeezed orange juice.

Pressure Cooked Zucchini & Beef Frittata

Yield: 4 | Total Time: 35 Mins | Prep Time: 15 Mins | Cook Time: 20 Mins

Ingredients:
- 1 tablespoon butter
- 1/2 red onion, minced
- 1 clove garlic, minced
- 8 ounce ground beef, crumbled
- 4 zucchinis, thinly sliced
- 6 free-range eggs
- Pinch of sea salt
- Pinch of pepper

Directions
1. Set your instant pot to manual high and melt in butter; sauté red onion for about 3 Mins or until tender; add garlic, beef, and zucchini and cook for about 7 Mins or until zucchini is tender and beef is cooked through. Season with salt and pepper and pour in the egg. Lock lid and cook on high for 10 Mins and then release the pressure naturally. Serve warm.

Instant Pot Breakfast Casserole

Yield: 6 | Total Time: 45 Mins | Prep Time: 15 Mins | Cook Time: 30 Mins

Ingredients
- 2 tbsp. coconut oil
- 1 ⅓ cups sliced leek
- 2 tsp. minced garlic
- 1 cup chopped kale
- 8 eggs
- ⅔ cups sweet potato, peeled and grated
- 1 ½ cups breakfast sausage,

Directions
1. Set your instant pot to sauté mode and heat coconut oil; stir in garlic, leeks, and kale and sauté for about 5 Mins or until tender; transfer the veggies to a plate and clean the pot.
2. Whisk together eggs, beef sausage, sweet potato and the sautéed veggies in a large bowl until well blended; pour the mixture in a heatproof bowl or pan. Add water to the instant pot and insert a trivet; place the bowl onto the trivet and lock lid. Cook on manual for 25 Mins and then let pressure come down on its own. Remove the casserole and cut into equal slices.

Easy Breakfast Casserole

Yields: 5 to 6 | Total Time: 55 Mins | Prep Time: 20 Mins | Cook Time: 35 Mins

Ingredients
- 1½ pounds breakfast sausage
- 1 large yam or sweet potato, diced
- 4 tbsp. melted coconut oil
- 10 eggs, whisked
- ½ tsp. garlic powder
- 2 cups chopped spinach
- ½ yellow onion, diced
- ½ tsp. sea salt

Directions
1. Coat a 9x12 baking dish with cooking spray.
2. Toss the diced sweet potatoes in coconut oil and sprinkle with salt. Set aside.
3. Set a sauté pan over medium heat; add yellow onion and sauté for about 4 Mins or until fragrant. Stir in breakfast sausage and cook for about 5 Mins or until the sausage is no longer pink.
4. Transfer the sausage mixture to the baking dish and add spinach and sweet potatoes. Top with eggs and sprinkle with garlic powder and salt. Mix until well combined and pour the mixture in a heatproof bowl or pan. Add water to the instant pot and insert a trivet; place the dish on the trivet and lock the lid. Cook on high for 25 Mins and then let pressure come down on its own. Remove the casserole and cut into equal slices.

Mini Mushroom Quiche

Yield: 6 | Total Time: 30 Mins | Prep Time: 10 Mins | Cook Time: 20 Mins

Ingredients
- 9 eggs
- 1 cup shredded Swiss cheese
- 1 cup scallion, chopped
- 1/2 cup heavy cream
- 1 cup chopped cremini mushrooms
- 2 tbsp. olive oil
- ½ tsp. black pepper
- 1/2 tsp. salt
- 1 cup water

Directions
1. Set your instant pot to manual high and then heat olive oil; sauté scallions until fragrant and add mushrooms; cook for a few Mins and then transfer to a plate. Press Swiss cheese in the bottom of the pot and up the sides; top with the cooked mushrooms and extra scallions.
2. In a blender, blend together cream, eggs, pepper and salt; pour over the mushrooms.
3. Lock lid and cook on high setting for 15 Mins. Release the pressure naturally and then broil in the oven for 5 Mins or until lightly browned.

Instant Pot Breakfast Eggs & Sausage

Yield: 6 | Total Time: 25 Mins | Prep Time: 10 Mins | Cook Time: 15 Mins

Ingredients
- 8 eggs
- 1-pound chorizo sausage, chopped
- ¼ cup Kalamata olives, pitted and coarsely chopped
- ½ cup roasted red peppers, drained and cut into long strips
- 2 tbsp. extra virgin olive oil
- ½ tsp harissa paste
- 1 tsp Stevia
- 1 tsp. salt
- ¼ cup tomato sauce
- 1 tbsp. freshly chopped parsley
- 1 cup grated parmesan cheese

Directions
1. Set your instant pot to manual high and heat olive oil; fry the sliced sausage until crispy. Stir in the tomato sauce, harissa, Stevia, salt and the roasted peppers. Simmer for 10 Mins then stir in the sliced olives. Make four wells in the sausage sauce and crack the 4 eggs into each well. Lock lid and cook on high setting for 5 Mins; let pressure come down on its own.
2. Garnish with the chopped parsley and sprinkle with salt and freshly ground pepper if desired. Serve immediately with the crusty bread. Enjoy!

Green Eggs with Bacon

Yield: 6 | Total Time: 25 Mins | Prep Time: 10 Mins | Cook Time: 15 Mins

Ingredients
- 12 eggs
- 4 bacon strips, fried and crumbled
- 2 tbsp. milk
- ¼ cup Kalamata olives, pitted and chopped
- 3 tbsp. chopped roasted red peppers
- 2 cups fresh baby spinach
- 1 tbsp. extra virgin olive oil
- ¼ cup crumbled bacon
- ½ tsp kosher salt
- 1 cup crumbled feta cheese

Directions
1. Set your instant pot on manual high and heat olive oil; sauté spinach until wilted and then transfer to a plate. Beat the eggs together with the milk, salt and pepper in a medium bowl.
2. Add the remaining oil to the pot and pour in egg mixture; scramble the eggs using a rubber spatula being careful not to overcook them.
3. Stir in the spinach, olives, bacon, roasted peppers and feta cheese until well combined. Lock lid and cook on high for 3 Mins. Let pressure come down.
4. Serve the green eggs with freshly squeezed orange juice. Enjoy!

Instant Pot Egg Mug

Yield: 3 | Total Time: 20 Mins | Prep Time: 10 Mins | Cook Time: 10 Mins

Ingredients
- 4 large eggs
- 1 tomato, sliced
- 1 cup egg whites
- 3 fresh basil leaves
- 1 cup fresh mozzarella
- 1 tsp aged balsamic vinegar
- 2 tbsp. olive oil

Directions
1. Grease a mug with the olive oil and add all the ingredients apart from the egg, balsamic vinegar and egg whites and pop in the microwave for half a minute. Crack the egg and add to the mug together with the egg whites, stirring very gently with the other ingredients.
2. Insert a metal trivet in the instant pot and add in water; place the mug over the trivet. Lock lid and cook for 10 Mins on high. Remove from the pot and drizzle with the aged balsamic vinegar.
3. Let it stand for a minute or so and serve with crusty bread.

Instant Pot Greek Breakfast Sausage

Yield: 4 | Total Time: 16 Mins | Prep Time: 10 Mins | Cook Time: 6 Mins

Ingredients

- 450g minced lamb
- 4 tbsp. olive oil
- 450g minced pork
- ¼ cup ice water
- 4 cloves garlic, minced
- ¼ tsp cayenne pepper
- 1 tsp oregano
- 1 tsp fennel seed
- 1 tbsp. kosher salt
- 1 tsp ground coriander
- Finely grated zest of 2 oranges

Directions

1. Combine the minced meats in a large bowl.
2. In a small separate bowl, combine all the spices and add them to the meat. Also add the ice water and use your hands to mix everything up.
3. Cover the bowl with plastic wrap and refrigerate for at least one hour up to overnight.
4. Divide the meat mixture into 16 portions and flatten to form rounded disks.
5. Set your instant pot to manual high and heat oil; add in the disks and lock lid. Cook for 6 Mins and then let pressure come down on its own. Transfer to a plate lined with paper towels Enjoy!

Eggtastic Smoothie

Serves: **1** | Prep Time: **10** mins

Ingredients

- 2 tablespoons cream cheese
- 2 raw eggs
- 1 tablespoon vanilla extract
- ¼ cup heavy cream
- 3 ice cubes

Directions

1. Put all the ingredients in a blender and blend until smooth.
2. Pour into 1 glass and immediately serve.

Cheesy Ham Souffle

Serves: **4** | Prep Time: **30** mins

Ingredients

- ½ cup heavy cream
- 1 cup cheddar cheese, shredded
- 6 large eggs
- Salt and black pepper, to taste
- 6 ounces ham, diced

Directions

1. Preheat the oven to 375°F and lightly grease ramekins.
2. Whisk together ham with all other ingredients in a bowl.
3. Mix well and pour the mixture into the ramekins. Transfer to the oven and bake for about 20 minutes.
4. Remove from the oven and slightly cool before serving.

Mushroom and Cheese Scrambled Eggs

Serves: **4** | Prep Time: **20** mins

Ingredients

- 8 eggs
- 4 tablespoons butter
- 4 tablespoons parmesan cheese, shredded
- 1 cup fresh mushrooms, finely chopped
- Salt and black pepper, to taste

Directions

1. Whisk together eggs with salt and black pepper in a bowl until well combined.
2. Heat butter in a nonstick pan and stir in the whisked eggs.
3. Cook for about 4 minutes and add mushrooms and parmesan cheese.
4. Cook for about 6 minutes, occasionally stirring and dish out to serve.

Red Pepper Frittata

Serves: **3** | Prep Time: **15** mins

Ingredients

- 6 large eggs
- 2 red peppers, chopped
- Salt and black pepper, to taste
- 1¼ cups mozzarella cheese, shredded
- 3 tablespoons olive oil

Directions

1. Whisk together the eggs in a medium bowl and add red peppers, mozzarella cheese, salt and black pepper. Heat olive oil over medium high heat in an ovenproof skillet and pour in the egg mixture. Lift the mixture with a spatula to let the eggs run under.
2. Cook for about 5 minutes, stirring well and dish out onto a platter to serve.

Cream Cheese Pancakes

Serves: **4** | Prep Time: **25** mins

Ingredients
- ½ cup almond flour
- 2 scoops Stevia
- ½ teaspoon cinnamon
- 2 eggs
- 2 oz cream cheese

Directions
1. Put all the ingredients in a blender and blend until smooth.
2. Dish out the mixture to a medium bowl and set aside.
3. Heat butter in a skillet over medium heat and add one quarter of the mixture.
4. Spread the mixture and cook for about 4 minutes on both sides until golden brown. Repeat with rest of the mixture in batches and serve warm.

Spicy Chorizo Baked Eggs

Serves: **4** | Prep Time: **40** mins

Ingredients
- 5 large eggs
- 3 ounces ground chorizo sausage
- ¾ cup pepper jack cheese, shredded
- Salt and paprika, to taste
- 1 small avocado, chopped

Directions
1. Preheat the oven to 400°F. Heat a nonstick oven safe skillet and add chorizo.
2. Cook for about 8 minutes and dish into a bowl.
3. Break the eggs in the skillet and season with salt and paprika.
4. Add cooked chorizo and avocado and cook for about 2 minutes.
5. Top with pepper jack cheese and transfer to the oven.
6. Bake for about 20 minutes and remove from the oven to serve.

Cheesy Taco Pie

Serves: **6** | Prep Time: **45** mins

Ingredients
- 1 tablespoon garlic powder
- 1 pound ground beef
- 6 large eggs
- Salt and chili powder, to taste
- 1 cup cheddar cheese, shredded

Directions
1. Preheat the oven to 350°F and lightly grease a pie plate.
2. Heat a large nonstick skillet and add beef, garlic powder, salt and chili powder.
3. Cook for about 6 minutes over medium low heat and transfer to the pie plate.
4. Top with cheddar cheese and transfer to the oven.
5. Bake for about 30 minutes and remove from the oven to serve hot.

Sausage Egg Casserole

Serves: **8** | Prep Time: **40** mins

Ingredients
- 1 cup almond milk, unsweetened
- 6 large eggs
- Salt and black pepper, to taste
- 2 cups cheddar cheese, shredded
- 1 pound ground pork sausage, cooked

Directions
1. Preheat the oven to 350°F and lightly grease a casserole dish.
2. Whisk together eggs with almond milk, salt and black pepper in a bowl.
3. Put the cooked sausages in the casserole dish and top with the egg mixture and cheddar cheese.
4. Transfer to the oven and bake for about 30 minutes.
5. Remove from the oven and serve hot.

Egg Bites

Serves: **8** | Prep Time: **25** mins

Ingredients
- 12 large eggs
- 1 (8 ounce) package cream cheese, softened
- 8 slices bacon, cooked and crumbled
- 1 cup gruyere cheese, shredded
- Salt and paprika, to taste

Directions
1. Put eggs, cream cheese, salt and paprika in a blender and blend until smooth.
2. Grease 8 egg poaching cups lightly with cooking spray and put half the gruyere cheese, bacon and egg mixture in them. Put the cups in a large saucepan with boiling water and cover the lid.
3. Lower the heat and cook for about 10 minutes. Dish out the eggs into a serving dish and slice to serve.

Chorizo and Eggs

Serves: **2** | Prep Time: **20** mins

Ingredients
- ½ small yellow onion, chopped
- 1 teaspoon olive oil
- 2 (3 ounce) chorizo sausages
- Salt and black pepper, to taste
- 4 eggs

Directions
1. Open the sausage casings and dish the meat into a bowl.
2. Heat olive oil over medium high heat in a large skillet and add onions.
3. Sauté for about 3 minutes and stir in the chorizo sausage.
4. Cook for about 4 minutes and add eggs, salt and black pepper.
5. Whisk well and cook for about 3 minutes. Dish into a bowl and serve warm.

Egg in the Avocado

Serves: **6** | Prep Time: **25** mins

Ingredients
- 3 medium avocados, cut in half, pitted, skin on
- 1 teaspoon garlic powder
- ¼ cup parmesan cheese, grated
- 6 medium eggs
- Sea salt and black pepper, to taste

Directions
1. Preheat the oven to 350°F and grease 6 muffin tins.
2. Put the avocado half in each muffin tin and season with garlic powder, sea salt, and black pepper.
3. Break 1 egg into each avocado and top with the parmesan cheese.
4. Transfer into the oven and bake for about 15 minutes.
5. Remove from the oven and serve warm.

Egg, Bacon and Cheese Cups

Serves: **6** | Prep Time: **30** mins

Ingredients
- ¼ cup frozen spinach, thawed and drained
- 6 large eggs
- 6 strips bacon
- Salt and black pepper, to taste
- ¼ cup sharp cheddar cheese

Directions
1. Preheat the oven to 400° and grease 6 muffin cups.
2. Whisk together eggs, spinach, salt and black pepper in a bowl.
3. Put the bacon slices in the muffin cups and pour in the egg spinach mixture.
4. Top with sharp cheddar cheese and transfer to the oven.
5. Bake for 15 minutes and remove from the oven to serve warm.

Steak and Eggs

Serves: **4** | Prep Time: **25** mins

Ingredients
- 6 eggs
- 2 tablespoons butter
- 8 oz. sirloin steak
- Salt and black pepper, to taste
- ½ avocado, sliced

Directions
1. Heat butter in a pan on medium heat and fry the eggs.
2. Season with salt and black pepper and dish out onto a plate.
3. Cook the sirloin steak in another pan until desired doneness and slice into bite sized strips.
4. Season with salt and black pepper and dish out alongside the eggs.
5. Put the avocados with the eggs and steaks and serve.

Butter Coffee

Serves: **4** | Prep Time: **20** mins

Ingredients
- ½ cup coconut milk
- ½ cup water
- 2 tablespoons coffee
- 1 tablespoon coconut oil
- 1 tablespoon grass fed butter

Directions
1. Heat water in a saucepan and add coffee.
2. Simmer for about 3 minutes and add coconut milk.
3. Simmer for another 3 minutes and allow to cool down.
4. Transfer to a blender along with coconut oil and butter. Pour into a mug and serve immediately.

California Chicken Omelet

Serves: **1** | Prep Time: **20** mins

Ingredients
- 2 bacon slices, cooked and chopped
- 2 eggs
- 1 oz. deli cut chicken
- 3 tablespoons avocado mayonnaise
- 1 Campari tomato

Directions
1. Whisk together eggs in a bowl and pour into a nonstick pan.
2. Season with salt and black pepper and cook for about 5 minutes.
3. Add chicken, bacon, tomato and avocado mayonnaise and cover with lid.
4. Cook for 5 more minutes on medium low heat and dish out to serve hot.

Eggs Oopsie Rolls

Serves: **3** | Prep Time: **25** mins

Ingredients
- 3 oz cream cheese
- 3 large eggs, separated
- 1/8 teaspoon cream of tartar
- 1 scoop stevia
- 1/8 teaspoon salt

Directions
1. Preheat oven to 300°F and line a cookie sheet with parchment paper.
2. Beat the egg whites with cream of tartar until soft peaks form.
3. Mix together egg yolks, salt and cream cheese in a bowl.
4. Combine the egg yolk and egg white mixtures and spoon them onto the cookie sheet.
5. Transfer to the oven and bake for about 40 minutes.
6. Remove from the oven and serve warm.

Easy Blender Pancakes

Serves: **2** | Prep Time: **25** mins

Ingredients
- 2 eggs
- 2 oz. cream cheese
- 1 scoop Isopure Protein Powder
- 1 pinch salt
- 1 dash cinnamon

Directions
1. Mix together eggs with cream cheese, protein powder, salt and cinnamon in a bowl.
2. Transfer to a blender and blend until smooth.
3. Heat a nonstick pan and pour quarter of the mixture.
4. Cook for about 2 minutes on each side and dish out.
5. Repeat with the remaining mixture and dish out in a platter to serve warm.

Shakshuka

Serves: **2** | Prep Time: **25** mins

Ingredients
- 1 chili pepper, chopped
- 1 cup marinara sauce
- 4 eggs
- Salt and black pepper, to taste
- 1 oz. feta cheese

Directions
1. Preheat the oven to 390°F.
2. Heat a small oven proof skillet on medium heat and add marinara sauce and chili pepper. Cook for about 5 minutes and stir in the eggs.
3. Season with salt and black pepper and top with feta cheese.
4. Transfer into the oven and bake for about 10 minutes.
5. Remove from the oven and serve hot shakshuka.

Rooibos Tea Latte

Serves: **1** | Prep Time: **20** mins

Ingredients
- 2 bags rooibos tea
- 1 cup water
- 1 tablespoon grass fed butter
- 1 scoop collagen peptides
- ¼ cup full fat canned coconut milk

Directions
1. Put the tea bags in boiling water and steep for about 5 minutes.
2. Discard the tea bags and stir in butter and coconut milk.
3. Pour this mixture into a blender and blend until smooth.
4. Add collagen to the blender and blend on low speed until incorporated.
5. Pour into a mug to serve hot or chilled as desired.

Feta and Pesto Omelet

Serves: **3** | Prep Time: **10** mins

Ingredients
- 3 eggs
- 2 tablespoons butter
- 1 oz. feta cheese
- Salt and black pepper, to taste
- 1 tablespoon pesto

Directions
1. Heat butter in a pan and allow it to melt. Whisk together eggs in a bowl and pour into the pan.
2. Cook for about 3 minutes until done and add feta cheese and pesto.
3. Season with salt and black pepper and fold it over.
4. Cook for another 5 minutes until the feta cheese is melted and dish out onto a platter to serve.

Eggs Benedict

Serves: **2** | Prep Time: **25** mins

Ingredients
- 4 oopsie rolls
- 4 eggs
- 4 Canadian bacon slices, cooked and crisped
- 1 tablespoon white vinegar
- 1 teaspoon chives

Directions
1. Boil water with vinegar and create a whirlpool in it with a wooden spoon.
2. Break an egg in a cup and place in the boiling water for about 3 minutes.
3. Repeat with rest of the eggs and dish out onto a platter.
4. Place oopsie rolls on the plates and top with bacon slices.
5. Put the poached eggs onto bacon slices and garnish with chives to serve.

Egg Clouds

Serves: **2** | Prep Time: **25** mins

Ingredients
- 6 strips bacon
- ¼ teaspoon cayenne pepper
- 2 eggs, separated
- Salt and black pepper, to taste
- ½ teaspoon garlic powder

Directions
1. Preheat oven to 350°F and grease a baking sheet lightly.
2. Whisk the egg whites in a bowl until fluffy and add garlic powder and salt.
3. Make 2 bacon weaves and spoon the egg white mixture on to it to form a cloud.
4. Make a hole in the egg cloud and put the egg yolks in it.
5. Season with cayenne pepper and black pepper and transfer to the oven.
6. Bake for about 10 minutes and dish out on a platter to serve.

Spicy Shrimp Omelet

Serves: **6** | Prep Time: **15** mins

Ingredients
- 6 eggs
- 10 large shrimp, boiled
- 4 grape tomatoes
- Sriracha salt and cayenne pepper, to taste
- 1 handful spinach

Directions
1. Whisk together eggs with all other ingredients in a bowl.
2. Heat a nonstick pan and pour the mixture in it.
3. Cook for about 5 minutes on medium low heat and flip the side.
4. Cook for another 5 minutes and dish out onto a platter to serve.

Egg Pizza Crust

Serves: **4** | Prep Time: **25** mins

Ingredients
- 4 eggs
- 2 tablespoons coconut flour
- 2 cups cauliflower, grated
- ½ teaspoon salt
- 1 tablespoon psyllium husk powder

Directions
1. Preheat the oven to 360°F and lightly grease a pizza tray.
2. Mix together all the ingredients in a bowl until well combined and set aside for about 10 minutes.
3. Pour this mixture into the pizza tray and place in the oven.
4. Bake for about 15 minutes until golden brown and remove from the oven.
5. Add your favorite toppings and serve.

Coffee Egg Latte

Serves: **2** | Prep Time: **15** mins

Ingredients
- 8 ounces black coffee
- 2 tablespoons grass fed butter
- 2 pasture raised eggs
- 1 scoop vanilla collagen protein
- ¼ teaspoon Ceylon cinnamon

Directions
1. Put eggs, butter and coffee in a blender.
2. Blend until smooth and stir in the collagen protein.
3. Blend on low and pour into 2 mugs.
4. Sprinkle with cinnamon and serve hot or chilled as desired.

Buttery Egg Waffles

Serves: **4** | Prep Time: **30** mins

Ingredients
- 4 tablespoons coconut flour
- 5 eggs, whites separated
- 4 scoops Stevia
- 1 teaspoon baking powder
- ½ cup butter, melted

Directions
1. Mix together coconut flour, egg yolks, Stevia and baking powder in a bowl.
2. Add butter and mix well to form a smooth batter.
3. Whisk egg whites in another bowl until fluffy and pour into the flour mixture.
4. Put this mixture into a waffle maker and cook until golden in color.
5. Dish out on plates to serve.

Egg and Bacon Breakfast Muffins

Serves: **4** | Prep Time: **40** mins

Ingredients
- 4 large eggs
- 4 bacon slices, cooked and crisped
- 1/3 cup green onions, chopped green stem only
- Salt and black pepper, to taste
- ¼ teaspoon paprika

Directions
1. Preheat the oven to 350°F and lightly grease muffin tin cavities.
2. Whisk together eggs in a bowl and add green onions, bacon, paprika, salt and black pepper. Pour this mixture into the muffin tin cavities and transfer to the oven.
3. Bake for about 25 minutes and remove from oven to serve.

Egg Bacon Fat Bombs

Serves: **6** | Prep Time: **15** mins

Ingredients
- ¼ cup butter, softened
- 4 large slices bacon, baked
- 2 large eggs, boiled
- 2 tablespoons mayonnaise
- Salt and black pepper, to taste

Directions
1. Preheat the oven to 375°F and lightly grease a baking tray.
2. Put the bacon on the baking tray and bake for about 15 minutes.
3. Remove from the oven, crumble it and set aside.
4. Mash together boiled eggs with butter, mayonnaise, salt and black pepper with a fork.
5. Refrigerate for about 1 hour and then form small balls out of this mixture.
6. Roll the balls into the bacon crumbles and refrigerate for an hour to serve.

Soft Boiled Eggs with Butter and Thyme

Serves: **3** | Prep Time: **20** mins

Ingredients
- 2 tablespoons butter, melted
- 3 large eggs
- ½ teaspoon black pepper
- 2 tablespoons thyme leaves
- ½ teaspoon Himalayan pink salt

Directions
1. Boil eggs in water for about 6 minutes and then put under cold water.
2. Peel the eggs and dip in the melted butter.
3. Top with thyme leaves and season with salt and black pepper to serve.

Soups Recipes

Red Barley Soup

Serves: **4** | Prep Time: **1 hour 10** mins

Ingredients
- ½ cup barley
- 2 small onions, diced
- 1 celery stalk
- 2 bay leaves
- 7 cups water
- 1 teaspoon salt
- 3 tablespoons red wine
- Brown bread cubes, to serve
- ½ pound small red lentils, dried
- ½ cup olive oil
- 2 medium carrots, diced
- 6 garlic cloves
- 1½ cups tomato sauce
- 2 teaspoons smoked paprika
- 1 tablespoon dried Greek oregano
- Black pepper, to taste
- Cheddar cheese, to serve

Directions
1. Put the lentils and water in a cooking pot and boil for 5 minutes.
2. Stir in barley along with all the other ingredients and 6 cups of water.
3. Cover and cook for about 45 minutes until it thickens.
4. Remove the bay leaves and garnish with cheddar cheese to serve.

Greek Meatball Soup

Serves: **4** | Prep Time: **40** mins

Ingredients
For the Meatballs
- ½ cup medium grain rice
- 1 pound lean ground beef
- 1 small onion, grated
- 3 tablespoons fresh dill, minced
- 1½ teaspoons salt

For the egg-lemon broth
- 2 egg yolks
- 1 whole egg

- 2 tablespoons olive oil
- ½ cup whole wheat flour
- ½ cup fresh parsley, minced
- ½ teaspoon black pepper
- 2 tablespoons water

- 4 tablespoons lemon juice
- 2 teaspoons cornstarch

Directions
1. Stir the meat with rice, salt, dill, parsley, water, olive oil, black pepper, and onion in a large bowl.
2. Cover this meat mixture and refrigerate for about 15 minutes. Make 30 meatballs of golf balls size out of this mixture. Prepare the soup by boiling 8 cups water in a large soup pot.
3. Add ½ teaspoon salt and 3 tablespoons olive oil. Place the meatballs in this soup and cover it partially.
4. Cook the soup for 30 mins approximately, on a simmer.
5. Beat egg with egg yolks in a suitable bowl until frothy.
6. Mix cornstarch with lemon juice, and pour this slurry into the soup.
7. Once the soup turns creamy, stir in the egg mixture. Garnish with olive oil and parsley to serve.

Zucchini Soup

Serves: **6** | Prep Time: **30** mins

Ingredients
- 8 oz. baby Bella mushrooms, sliced
- 1 bunch flat leaf parsley, chopped
- 2 celery ribs, chopped
- 2 golden potatoes, peeled and diced
- 1 teaspoon ground coriander
- ½ teaspoon thyme
- 1 (32 oz.) can whole peeled tomatoes
- 6 cups turkey bone broth
- 1 lime zest
- 1/3 cup pine nuts, toasted
- 2 tablespoons olive oil
- 2 medium-sized zucchinis, sliced
- 1 medium-sized yellow onion, chopped
- 2 garlic cloves, chopped
- 2 carrots, peeled and chopped
- ½ teaspoon turmeric powder
- ½ teaspoon sweet paprika
- Salt and black pepper, to taste
- 2 bay leaves
- 1 (15 oz.) can chickpeas, rinsed and drained
- 1 lime, juiced

Directions
1. Preheat 1 tablespoon olive oil in an iron cooking pot on medium heat.
2. Stir in mushrooms and sauté for about 4 minutes. Transfer the mushrooms into a flat plate and keep aside. Toss the sliced zucchini into the pot and sauté for about 5 minutes.
3. Dish out the sautéed zucchini into a plate. Heat more oil in that same pan and add celery, potatoes, garlic, and onion. Cook these veggies for about 7 minutes and season the mixture with pepper, salt, and other spices. Stir in bay leaves, tomatoes and broth and bring to a boil. Cover the soup with a lid and allow it to simmer for about 5 minutes. Uncover the soup and add chickpeas, sautéed mushrooms, and zucchini. Let the soup cook for 5 more minutes and garnish with pine nuts to serve.

Napoletana Hoki Soup

Serves: **4** | Prep Time: **30** mins

Ingredients
- 2 cups fish stock
- 1 bulb fennel, finely sliced
- 1 handful basil leaves, torn
- 5 tablespoons half-fat crème Fraiche, to serve
- 1 pound Napoletana pasta sauce
- 2 zucchinis, finely sliced
- 1 pound hoki fillet, defrosted
- 1 teaspoon chipotle chili in adobo sauce or chili paste, to serve

Directions
1. Boil pasta sauce and stock in a large cooking pan.
2. Let it simmer for about 3 minutes and stir in zucchinis and fennel.
3. Cook for about 2 minutes and add the hoki fillets.
4. Cook for about 3 minutes on low heat and add seasoning and basil.
5. Mix crème Fraiche with chili paste and season in a small bowl.
6. Garnish the soup with this seasoned crème Fraiche and serve.

Passata Cream Soup

Serves: **4** | Prep Time: **40** mins

Ingredients
- ½ onion, finely chopped
- 1 celery stick, finely chopped
- 4 large ripe tomatoes
- 2 tablespoons cream
- Shaved parmesan, chopped basil or pesto
- 2 tablespoons olive oil
- 1 small carrot, finely chopped
- ½ cup passata
- ½ vegetable stock
- 4 oz. soup pasta, cooked

Directions
1. Heat oil in a saucepan on low heat and add onion, celery, and carrots.
2. Sauté for about 10 minutes until soft and add the passata sauce and tomatoes.
3. Add water, stock, seasoning and sugar and cook for about 20 minutes.
4. Stir in boiled pasta and cream with gentle stirring.
5. Garnish with parmesan, basil, and pesto to serve.

Instant Pot Turkey & Coconut Soup

Yield: 2 | Total Time: 40 Mins | Prep Time: 10 Mins | Cook Time: 30 Mins

Ingredients
- 1 tsp. coconut oil
- 1 red onion, finely sliced
- 1 ginger, finely chopped
- 1 clove garlic, finely chopped
- 1 lemon grass, bashed with a rolling pin
- 2 sticks celery, diced
- 1/4 cup coconut milk
- ½ cup vegetable stock
- 8 oz. turkey, cooked, roughly chopped
- 1/8 tsp. sea salt
- 1/8 tsp. black pepper
- 1 cup coriander, finely chopped
- 1 cup spinach, roughly chopped
- 2 tbsp. fresh lime juice

Directions
1. Add coconut oil to your instant pot and set it on sauté mode; stir in red onions and sauté for about 5 Mins or until translucent. Add ginger and garlic and sauté for about 3 Mins or until garlic is golden.
2. Stir in lemon grass, celery, coconut milk, vegetable sock, turkey, salt and pepper and then lock lid. Cook on high for 15 Mins and then quick release the pressure. Stir in spinach and coriander and serve into soup bowls and sprinkle with a squeeze of lime juice and coriander.

Instant Pot Detox Veggie Soup

Yield: 1 Serving | Total Time: 15 Mins | Prep Time: 5 Mins | Cook Time: 10 Mins

Ingredients
- 1 medium cauliflower
- 8 cups water
- 1 tsp. lemon juice
- 3 tsp. ground flax seeds
- 3 cups spinach
- 1 tsp. cayenne pepper
- 1 tsp. black pepper
- 1 tsp. soy sauce

Directions:
1. Core cauliflower and cut the florets into large pieces; reserve stems for juicing.
2. Add cauliflower to an instant pot and add water; lock lid and cook on high pressure for 10 Mins. Release pressure naturally and then transfer the cauliflower to a blender along with 2 cups of cooking liquid; blend until very smooth. Add the remaining ingredients and continue blending until very smooth. Serve hot or warm.

Instant Pot Spicy Green Soup

Yield: 2 | Total Time: 30 Mins | Prep Time: 15 Mins | Cook Time: 15 Mins

Ingredients
- 2 tablespoons olive oil
- 5 cups water
- 1 cup chickpeas
- 1 green bell pepper, chopped
- 1 red onion, chopped
- 4 celery stalks, chopped
- 2 cups chopped spinach
- 1 tsp. dried mint
- 1/2 tsp. ground cumin
- 1/2 tsp. ground ginger
- 1/2 tsp. cardamom
- 2 cloves of garlic
- 1 tbsp. coconut milk
- Pinch of sea salt
- pinch of pepper

Directions:
1. Combine all ingredients, except spinach and coconut milk, in your instant pot and lock lid; cook on high pressure for 15 Mins and then release the pressure naturally. Stir in spinach; let sit for about 5 Mins and then blend the mixture until very smooth.
2. Serve the soup in soup bowls and add coconut milk. Season with salt and more pepper and enjoy!

Instant Pot Easy Everyday Chicken Soup

Yield: 3 | Total Time: 1 Hour 10 Mins | Prep Time: 10 Mins | Cook Time: 1 Hour

Ingredients:
- 3 skinned, bone-in chicken breasts
- 6 skinned and boned chicken thighs
- 1 tsp salt
- ½ tsp freshly ground pepper
- ½ tsp chicken spice seasoning
- 3-4 carrots sliced
- 4 celery ribs, sliced
- 1 sweet onion, chopped
- 2 cans evaporated milk
- 2 cups chicken stock

Directions
Prepare Chicken: Rub chicken pieces with salt, pepper, and chicken spice seasoning. Place breasts in an instant pot, top with thighs.
Add carrots and next 3 ingredients. Whisk evaporated milk and stock until smooth. Pour soup mixture over vegetables. Lock lid and cook on high for 1 hour. Let pressure come down on its own. Remove chicken; cool 10 Mins. Debone and shred chicken. Stir chicken into soup-and-vegetable mixture. Cook on manual high for 1 hour before serving.

Comforting Chicken Soup w/ Avocado

Yield: 2 | Total Time: 40 Mins | Prep Time: 10 Mins | Cook Time: 30 Mins

Ingredients
- 200g boneless skinless chicken breast, cooked
- 3 ounces coarsely chopped celery
- 3 cloves garlic
- 1 ½ cups vegetable broth
- 1 tablespoon onion, dehydrated
- ½ teaspoon parsley
- ½ teaspoon basil
- White pepper
- Sea salt
- 1 avocado, for serving

Directions:
1. In a food processor, combine all ingredients and process until chunky. Set your instant pot on manual high and add the mixture. Lock lid and cook on high for 30 Mins. Let pressure come down on its own. Serve the soup topped with diced avocado.

Creamy Instant Pot Chicken & Tomato Soup

Yield: 4 | Total Time: 1 Hour 10 Mins | Prep Time: 10 Mins | Cook Time: 1 Hour

Ingredients:
- 8 frozen skinless boneless chicken breasts
- 2 tbsp. Italian Seasoning
- 1 tbsp. dried basil
- 2 cloves garlic, minced
- 1 large onion, chopped
- 2 cups coconut milk (full fat) to avoid separation
- 2 cans diced tomatoes and juice
- 2 cups chicken stock
- 1 small can of tomato paste
- sea salt & pepper

Directions
1. Put all the above ingredients into the instant pot and cook on high setting for 1 hour. Let pressure come down on its own. Shred the chicken, cover the pot until ready to serve.

Instant Pot Flat-Belly Soup

Yield: 4 | Total Time: 34 Mins | Prep Time: 15 Mins | Cook Time: 19 Mins

Ingredients

- 2 tbsp. extra virgin olive oil
- 1 red onion, sliced
- 2 jalapeño peppers, seeds removed and diced
- 4 cups sliced green cabbage
- 1 carrot, peeled and chopped
- 4 cups crushed tomatoes
- 2 cups diced tempeh
- 4 cups vegetable broth
- 3 tbsp. apple cider vinegar
- 2 tbsp. brown sugar
- ½ tsp. salt
- ¼ tsp. black pepper

Directions

1. Heat extra virgin olive oil in an instant pot set on sauté mode and stir in red onion, jalapenos, cabbage, and carrot; sauté for about 7 Mins or until almost tender.
2. Stir in tomatoes, tempeh, broth, apple cider vinegar, and brown sugar, salt and pepper until well combined. Lock lid and cook on high pressure for 12 Mins. Let pressure come down naturally. Serve hot.

Instant Pot Tomato Basil Soup

Yield: 6 | Total Time: 40 Mins | Prep Time: 10 Mins | Cook Time: 20 Mins

Ingredients

- 2 cloves fresh garlic
- 4 cups tomato puree
- 2 cups vegetable broth
- ¼ cup coconut oil
- ¼ cup coconut cream
- ½ cup fresh basil leaves
- pinch of Stevia, if desired
- 1 teaspoon sea salt

Directions

1. Blend together garlic and tomatoes in a blender until very smooth; pour into your instant pot and add broth, coconut oil and salt. Lock lid and cook on high pressure for 20 Mins. When done, release pressure naturally and then stir in chopped basil and coconut cream. Blend the mixture with an immersion blender until smooth and then serve. Enjoy!

Instant Pot Seafood Soup

Yield: 3 | Total Time: 1 Hour 40 Mins | Prep Time: 10 Mins | Cook Time: 1 Hour 30 Mins

Ingredients:

- 12 slices bacon, chopped
- 2 cloves garlic, minced
- 6 cups chicken stock
- 3 stalks celery, diced
- 2 large carrots, diced
- ground black pepper to taste
- ½ teaspoon red pepper flakes
- 2 cups onions
- 2 cup uncooked prawns, peeled and deveined
- 500g white fish fillet, cut into bite-size pieces
- 1 can evaporated milk

Directions

1. Set your instant pot to manual high; fry bacon in coconut oil or olive oil, add onion and garlic.
2. Pour chicken stock into the pot and stir celery, and carrots into the stock. Season with black pepper and red pepper flakes. Lock lid and cook on high for 1 hour. Let pressure come down naturally. Stir prawns and fish into the soup and cook 30 Mins on manual high. Stir evaporated milk into chowder, heat thoroughly, and serve.

Instant Pot Detox Veggie Soup

Yield: 1 Serving | Total Time: 15 Mins | Prep Time: 5 Mins | Cook Time: 10 Mins

Ingredients

- 1 tablespoon olive oil
- 1 medium cauliflower
- 8 cups water
- 1 tsp. lemon juice
- 3 tsp. ground flax seeds
- 3 cups spinach
- 1 tsp. cayenne pepper
- 1 tsp. black pepper
- 1 tsp. soy sauce

Directions:

1. Core cauliflower and cut the florets into large pieces; reserve stems for juicing.
2. Add cauliflower to an instant pot and add water; lock lid and cook on high pressure for 10 Mins. Release pressure naturally and transfer the cauliflower to a blender along with two cups of cooking liquid; blend until very smooth. Add the remaining ingredients and continue blending until very smooth. Serve hot or warm.

Instant Pot Spicy Green Soup

Yield: 2 | Total Time: 30 Mins | Prep Time: 15 Mins | Cook Time: 15 Mins

Ingredients
- 5 cups water
- 1 cup chickpeas
- 1 green bell pepper, chopped
- 1 red onion, chopped
- 4 celery stalks, chopped
- 2 cups chopped spinach
- 1 tsp. dried mint
- 1/2 tsp. ground cumin
- 1/2 tsp. ground ginger
- 1/2 tsp. cardamom
- 2 cloves of garlic
- 1 tbsp. coconut milk
- 2 tablespoons olive oil
- Pinch of sea salt
- pinch of pepper

Directions:
1. Combine all ingredients, except spinach and coconut milk, in your instant pot and lock lid; cook on high pressure for 15 Mins and then release the pressure naturally. Stir in spinach; let sit for about 5 Mins and then blend the mixture until very smooth.
2. Serve the soup in soup bowls and add coconut milk. Drizzle with olive oil and season with salt and more pepper and enjoy!

Lemony Veggie Soup w/ Cayenne

Yield: 4 | Total Time: 40 Mins | Prep Time: 15 Mins | Cook Time: 25 Mins

Ingredients
- 1-pound curly kale, torn
- 12 ounces baby spinach
- ¼ cup brown Arborio rice, rinsed
- 2 yellow onions, chopped
- 4 tablespoons olive oil
- 3 cups plus 2 tablespoons water
- 4 cups homemade vegetable broth
- 1 tablespoon fresh lemon juice
- 1 large pinch of cayenne pepper
- Salt, to taste

Directions
1. Add the two tablespoons of olive oil in a large pan and cook the onions over medium heat. Sprinkle with salt and cook for 5 Mins until they start browning.
2. Lower the heat and pour in two tablespoons of water. Cover and lower the heat and cook for 25 Mins until the onions caramelize, stirring frequently.
3. Meanwhile, add the remaining water, broth, and some salt to an instant pot and stir in the rice. Lock the lid and cook on high pressure for 5 Mins. Naturally release the pressure and then stir in kale, onions, spinach and cayenne and lock the lid. Let sit for about 5 Mins.
4. Use an immersion blender to puree the rice mixture until smooth then stir in the lemon juice. Serve in soup bowls and drizzle each with some olive oil.

Instant Pot Black Bean Chipotle Soup

Yield:6 | Total Time: 28 Mins | Prep Time: 10 Mins | Cook Time: 18 Mins

Ingredients:
- 4 tbsp. extra virgin olive oil
- 2 medium red onions, diced
- 1 red bell pepper, diced
- 1 green bell pepper, diced
- 4 tsp. ground cumin
- 4 garlic cloves, minced
- 16 ounces dried black beans
- 7 cups hot water
- 1 tbsp. chopped chipotle chilies
- 2 tsp. coarse kosher salt
- 2 tsp. fresh lime juice
- 1/4 tsp. ground black pepper
- Optional toppings: coconut cream and avocado

Directions:
1. In a large skillet set over medium high heat, heat olive oil until hot but not smoky; sauté bell peppers and onion for about 8 Mins or until brown. Stir in cumin and garlic for about 1 minute; transfer the mixture to your instant pot and then stir in 7 cups water, chipotles and beans and lock lid; cook on high pressure for 10 Mins and then release the pressure naturally.
2. Transfer about 4 cups of the mixture to a blender and blend until very smooth; return the puree to the pot and stir in salt, lime juice and pepper until well combined. Ladle the soup into serving bowls and top with coconut cream and avocado.

Instant Pot Spicy Coconut Cauliflower Soup

Yield: 4 | Total Time: 24 Mins | Prep Time: 10 Mins | Cook Time: 14 Mins

Ingredients
- 1 ⅓ tablespoons olive oil
- 2 cups diced cauliflower
- ⅔ cups diced carrot
- 1 cup diced red onion
- ⅛ teaspoons dried thyme
- 1 ⅓ tablespoons curry powder
- 2 ⅔ cups vegetable broth
- ⅛ teaspoons salt
- ⅛ teaspoons pepper

Directions

1. Heat oil in your instant pot and sauté red onion, cauliflower and carrots for 4 Mins; stir in spices and stock and lock lid. Cook on manual for 10 Mins and then let pressure come down naturally. Stir in coconut milk and then blend with an immersion blender until smooth. Serve topped with toasted cashews.

Farmhouse Veggie Soup

Yield: 4 | Total Time: 25 Mins | Prep Time: 10 Mins | Cook Time: 15 Mins

Ingredients

- 3 tablespoon olive oil
- 1 cup dried porcini mushrooms
- 6 large button mushrooms, sliced
- 1 cup chopped kale leaves
- 1 brown onion, diced
- 4 cloves garlic, diced
- 2 medium carrots, diced
- Chopped parsley and lemon zest for garnish
- 2 celery sticks, sliced
- 1 cup tinned chopped tomatoes
- 1 small zucchini, diced
- ½ long red chili, sliced
- ¼ teaspoon of salt
- 1 bay leaf
- 4 cups vegetable

Directions

1. Turn your instant pot on sauté mode and heat coconut oil; sauté onion, carrots, celery for about 2 Mins; stir in salt. Add dried porcini mushrooms, garlic, mushrooms, and chili and cook for about 2 Mins. Stir in zucchini, kale, stock, tomatoes, and bay leaves. Press the cancel button and lock the lid and set to manual high for 10 Mins.
2. When done, let pressure release naturally and then serve in serving bowls garnished with chopped parsley and lemon zest.

Hot Instant Pot Vegetable Soup

Yield: 4-6 | Total Time: 45 Mins | Prep Time: 15 Mins | Cook Time: 30 Mins

Ingredients

- 1 pound curly kale, torn
- 12 ounces baby spinach
- ¼ cup brown Arborio rice, rinsed
- 2 yellow onions, chopped
- 4 tablespoons olive oil
- 3 cups plus 2 tablespoons water
- 4 cups homemade vegetable broth
- 1 tablespoon fresh lemon juice
- 1 large pinch of cayenne pepper
- Salt, to taste

Directions

1. Add the two tablespoons of olive oil in a large pan and cook the onions over medium heat. Sprinkle with salt and cook for 5 Mins until they start browning.
2. Lower the heat and pour in two tablespoons of water. Cover and lower the heat and cook for 25 Mins until the onions caramelize, stirring frequently.
3. Meanwhile, add the remaining water, broth, and some salt to an instant pot and stir in the rice. Lock the lid and cook on high pressure for 5 Mins. Naturally release the pressure and then stir in kale, onions, spinach and cayenne and lock the lid. Let sit for about 5 Mins.
4. Use an immersion blender to puree the rice mixture until smooth then stir in the lemon juice. Serve in soup bowls and drizzle each with some olive oil.

Chicken Enchilada Soup

Yield: 6 | Total Time: 30 Mins | Prep Time: 10 Mins | Cook Time: 20 Mins

Ingredients

- 1 ½ pounds chicken thighs, boneless, skinless
- 3 cloves garlic, minced
- 1 bell pepper, thinly sliced
- 1 onion, thinly sliced
- 1 can roasted crushed tomatoes
- 1/2 cup water
- 2 cups bone broth
- 1/2 tsp smoked paprika
- 1 tsp oregano
- 1 tbsp. chili powder
- 1 tbsp. cumin
- 1/2 tsp sea salt
- 1/2 tsp pepper

For garnish:

- fresh cilantro
- 1 avocado

Directions

1. Combine all ingredients in your instant pot, except garnishes; lock lid and cook on high pressure for 20 Mins. Release pressure naturally and shred the chicken with fork. Serve in soup bowls garnished with cilantro and avocado.

Instant Pot Spicy Green Soup

Yield: 2 | Total Time: 30 Mins | Prep Time: 15 Mins | Cook Time: 15 Mins

Ingredients
- 2 tablespoons olive oil
- 5 cups water
- 1 cup chickpeas
- 1 green bell pepper, chopped
- 1 red onion, chopped
- 4 celery stalks, chopped
- 2 cups chopped spinach
- 1 tsp. dried mint
- 1/2 tsp. ground cumin
- 1/2 tsp. ground ginger
- 1/2 tsp. cardamom
- 2 cloves of garlic
- 1 tbsp. coconut milk
- Pinch of sea salt
- pinch of pepper

Directions:
1. Combine all ingredients, except spinach and coconut milk, in your instant pot and lock lid; cook on high pressure for 15 Mins and then release the pressure naturally. Stir in spinach; let sit for about 5 Mins and then blend the mixture until very smooth.
2. Serve the soup into soup bowls and add coconut milk. Season with salt and more pepper and enjoy!

Yummy Minestrone Soup

Yield: 2 | Total Time: 1 Hour 15 Mins | Prep Time: 15 Mins | Cook Time: 1 Hour

Ingredients
- 2 Italian chicken sausage links, sliced
- 2 cups low-sodium chicken stock
- 1 cup canned navy beans, rinsed
- 2 celery stalks, sliced
- 2 carrots, sliced
- 1 onion, diced
- 1 cup canned diced tomatoes
- 2 zucchinis, sliced
- 1/2 cup pasta
- 1/2 tsp. dried thyme
- 1/2 tsp. dried sage
- 2 bay leaves
- 1/4 cup grated Parmesan
- Salt

Directions
1. Set your instant pot to manual high, stir together onions, tomatoes, beans, celery, carrots, sausage, stock, sage, thyme, and bay leaves; lock lid and cook on high for 30 Mins. Let pressure come down naturally.
2. Stir in zucchini and orzo and cook on manual high for 30 Mins. Season with sea salt and divide the soup among 8 serving bowls, discard bay leaves and top each serving with a tablespoon of grated Parmesan cheese. Enjoy!

Instant Pot French Onion Soup

Yield: 2 | Total Time: 1 Hour 20 Mins | Prep Time: 10 Mins | Cook Time: 1 Hour 10 Mins

Ingredients:
- 4 cups organic beef broth
- 1 large red onion, thinly sliced
- 1/2 tsp. garlic powder
- 2 tbsp. Worcestershire Sauce
- 4 tbsp. grated Parmesan cheese
- 2 packets Stevia
- 1/2 tsp. dried thyme
- sea salt & pepper
- 4 slices thin Swiss cheese

Directions
1. Set your instant pot to manual high and heat oil; cook in onion until caramelized and then stir in 1 cup beef broth and garlic powder. Stir in the remaining ingredients; cook on high for 1 hour. Let pressure come down naturally. Ladle the soup into an ovenproof bowl and stir in Swiss cheese; place in a preheated oven at 150°F and cook for about 5 Mins or until cheese is melted.

Pressure Cooked Vegetable Soup

Yield: 2 Serving | Total Time: 1 Hour 10 Mins | Prep Time: 10 Mins | Cook Time: 1 Hour

Ingredients
- 1 head cauliflower
- 8 cups water
- 1 tsp. lemon juice
- 3 tsp. ground flax seeds
- 2 cups spinach
- 1 tsp. cayenne pepper
- 1 tsp. black pepper
- 1 tsp. soy sauce

Directions:
1. Core cauliflower and cut the florets into large pieces; reserve stems for juicing.
2. Add cauliflower to a slow cooker and add water; cook on low for about 3 hours.
3. Transfer the cauliflower to a blender along with 2 cups of cooking liquid; blend until very smooth. Add the remaining ingredients and continue blending until very smooth. Serve hot or warm.

Healthy Hot & Sour Soup

Yield: 6 | Total Time: 1 Hour 15 Mins | Prep Time: 15 Mins | Cook Time: 60 Mins

Ingredients
- 1 pound curly kale, torn
- 12 ounces baby spinach
- 1 pound ground turkey
- 2 yellow onions, chopped
- 2 tablespoons olive oil
- 3 cups plus 2 tablespoons water
- 4 cups homemade vegetable broth
- 1 tablespoon fresh lemon juice
- 1 large pinch of cayenne pepper
- Salt, to taste
- 2 avocados, diced, to serve
- 1 cup chopped toasted almonds to serve

Directions
1. Add the two tablespoons of olive oil in a large pan and cook the onions over medium heat. Sprinkle with salt and cook for 5 Mins until they start browning.
2. Lower the heat and pour in two tablespoons of water. Cover and lower the heat and cook for 25 Mins until the onions caramelize, stirring frequently.
3. Meanwhile, add the remaining water, broth, and some salt to an instant pot and stir in the turkey. Lock the lid and cook on high pressure for 5 Mins. Naturally release the pressure and the stir in kale, onions, spinach and cayenne and lock the lid. Let sit for about 5 Mins.
4. Serve in soup bowls and topped with avocado and toasted almonds. Enjoy!

Creamy Chicken Soup with Sautéed Cauliflower Rice

Yield: 1 Serving | Total Time: 45 Mins | Prep Time: 10 Mins | Cook Time: 35 Mins

Ingredients
- 1 tablespoon olive oil
- 1 red onion
- 150g boneless skinless chicken breast, cooked
- ¼ cup coarsely chopped celery
- 2 cloves garlic
- 1 ½ cups vegetable broth
- 1 tablespoon onion, dehydrated
- ½ teaspoon parsley
- ½ teaspoon basil
- White pepper
- Sea salt
- 1 cup riced cauliflower
- 2 tablespoon butter
- 1 red onion

Directions
1. Prepare cauliflower by melting butter in a skillet and then sautéing red onion. Stir in cauliflower and cook for about 4 Mins or until tender. Set aside until ready to serve.
2. In a food processor, combine the remaining ingredients, except oil and onion and process until chunky. Heat oil in your instant pot set over manual high; sauté onion until fragrant and then add the mixture. Lock lid and cook on high for 30 Mins and then let pressure come down on its own. Serve soup with creamy cauliflower.

Instant Pot Spiced Turkey Soup

Yield: 2 | Total Time: 40 Mins | Prep Time: 10 Mins | Cook Time: 30 Mins

Ingredients
- 6 ounces ground turkey, cooked
- 2 (15-ounce) can crushed or skewed tomatoes
- 3 cloves garlic, crushed
- 2 teaspoons red wine vinegar
- Pinch of parsley
- Pinch of cumin
- Pinch of basil
- Pinch of rosemary
- Pinch of red pepper flakes
- 2 cups steamed broccoli to serve

Directions:
1. Set your instant pot on manual high, add in vinegar, tomatoes, and seasonings; cook for 5 Mins and then stir in ground turkey; lock lid and cook on high for 30 Mins and then let pressure come down on its own. Serve warm over steamed broccoli.

Instant Pot Cream of Carrot Soup

Yield: 4 | Total Time: 1 Hour 25 Mins | Prep Time: 10 Mins | Cook Time: 1 Hour 15 Mins

Ingredients:
- 1 onion, diced
- 2 stalks celery, diced
- 1 large sweet potato, diced
- 8 whole carrots, sliced
- 1 liter chicken broth stock
- 1 whole bay leaf
- salt and pepper, to taste
- 4 dashes tabasco (or other hot sauce)
- 1 cup heavy cream
- 1 teaspoon parsley

Directions
1. Add all ingredients (except heavy cream and parsley) to an instant pot. Cook on high setting for 1 hour and the let pressure come down on its own. Remove bay leaf. Using a hand blender, puree the vegetables. (You may also puree in batches using a standard blender.) Set instant pot on manual high and stir in heavy cream and parsley. Check seasoning and adjust to taste. Cook for an additional 15 Mins to allow heavy cream to heat thoroughly.

Instant Pot Broccoli & Blue Cheese Soup

Yield: 3 | Total Time: 2 Hours 20 Mins | Prep Time: 10 Mins | Cook Time: 2 Hours

Ingredients:
- 2 red onions, diced
- 4 stick celery, sliced
- 4 leeks, sliced (white part only)
- 2 tbsp. butter
- 1 liter chicken stock
- 2 large heads of broccoli, cut into florets
- 140g (1 1/4 cups) crumbled blue cheese
- 125ml cream

Directions
1. Combine all ingredients in an instant pot; lock lid and cook on stew setting for 2 hours. Let pressure come down on its own. Using a hand blender, blitz the soup until smooth. Ladle into bowls and top with extra crumbles of blue cheese (if desired).

Italian Meatball Zoodle Soup

Yield: 4 | Total Time: 1 Hour 50 Mins | Prep Time: 10 Mins | Cook Time: 1 Hour 40 Mins

Ingredients:
- 8 cups beef stock
- 1 medium zucchini – spiralled
- 2 ribs celery – chopped
- 1 small onion – dice
- 1 carrot – chopped
- 1 medium tomato – diced
- 1 ½ tsp. garlic salt
- 1 ½ lb. ground beef
- ½ cup parmesan cheese – shredded
- 6 cloves garlic – minced
- 1 egg
- 4 tbs. fresh parsley – chopped
- 1 ½ tsp. sea salt
- 1 ½ tsp. onion powder
- 1 tsp. Italian seasoning
- 1 tsp. dried oregano
- ½ tsp. black pepper

Directions
1. Set your instant pot on manual high; mix in beef stock, zucchini, celery, onion, carrot, tomato, and garlic salt. Cook until veggies are tender.
2. In a large mixing bowl, combine ground beef, Parmesan, garlic, egg, parsley, sea salt, onion powder, oregano, Italian seasoning, and pepper. Mix until all ingredients are well incorporated. Form into approximately 30 meatballs. Heat olive oil in a large skillet over medium-high heat. Once the pan is hot, add meatballs and brown on all sides. No need to worry about cooking them all the way through as they will be going into the instant pot. Add meatballs to the pot and lock lid. Cook on high for 1 ½ hours. Let pressure come down on its own.

Instant Pot Indian Curried Vegetable Soup

Yield: 4 | Total Time: 1 Hour 10 Mins | Prep Time: 10 Mins | Cook Time: 1 Hour

Ingredients:
- 1 head cauliflower
- 2 cups chicken stock
- 3 cloves garlic
- 1 can coconut milk
- 1 cup plain yogurt
- 1 tablespoon curry powder
- salt and pepper to taste
- 1/4 cup roasted pine nuts
- 3/4 teaspoon garam masala
- 1/2 cup xylitol
- 1/2 tsp salt
- 1 tbsp. water

Directions
1. Cut cauliflower from stalk, place in an instant pot and add in chicken stock and garlic. Lock lid and cook on high for 1 hour.
2. Quick release the pressure and stir in coconut milk and yogurt and cook on manual high for an additional hour. Using a hand blender, blend until pureed. Sprinkle with toasted pine nuts and some fresh mint.

Three- Ingredient Instant Pot Veggie Beef Soup

Yield: 2 | Total Time: 40 Mins | Prep Time: 10 Mins | Cook Time: 30 Mins

Ingredients:
- 500g ground beef mince
- 500ml tomato-vegetable juice cocktail
- 2 packages frozen mixed vegetables

Directions
1. Place ground beef mince in your instant pot; cook on manual high until browned. Stir in juice cocktail and mixed vegetables. Lock lid and cook on high for 30 Mins and then let pressure come down on its own.

Low Carb Italian Gnocchi Soup

Yield: 3 | Total Time: 40 Mins | Prep Time: 10 Mins | Cook Time: 30 Mins

Ingredients:
- 500g ground spicy Italian sausage
- 1 small onion, diced
- 2 cloves garlic, minced
- 4 cups chicken stock or bone broth
- 1 red medium pepper, diced
- 1 cup chopped fresh or frozen spinach
- ½ cup heavy cream
- sea salt and black pepper
- optional garnish: Parmesan cheese, crumbled bacon

Directions
1. Set your instant pot on manual high; fry sausage, onion and garlic until the sausage is completely browned; stir occasionally and break up the sausage with a spoon. Add in the bone broth or chicken stock and diced red peppers and lock lid. Cook on high for 30 Mins and then let pressure come down naturally. Stir in spinach and cook on manual high for an additional 5 Mins. Stir in gnocchi & cream and season to taste with salt and pepper.

Instant Pot Bolognese Mince Soup

Yield: 6 | Total Time: 1 Hour 15 Mins | Prep Time: 10 Mins | Cook Time: 1 Hour 5 Mins

Ingredients:
- 1kg beef mince
- 2 brown onions, diced
- 4 cloves garlic, crushed
- 1 cup tomato paste
- 2 tbsp. chicken stock powder or 2 Knorr Jelly pots
- 1 tin tomato soup
- 1 thin diced tomato
- 1/4 cup sweet chili sauce
- 1 tbsp. oregano
- 2 bay leaves
- 2 cups water
- 1 cup finely grated carrot
- 3-4 finely chopped sticks of celery
- 2 cups finely chopped mushrooms

Directions
1. In an instant pot, add the olive oil and set on manual high. Brown the beef and add the onions and garlic. Cook for 2 Mins more. Mix the tomato paste into the pot and cook for another 2 Mins. Mix in the remaining ingredients and lock lid. Cook on high for 1 hour and then release the pressure naturally.

Low Carb Curried Vegetable Soup

Yield: 2 | Total Time: 20 Mins | Prep Time: 10 Mins | Cook Time: 10 Mins

Ingredients:
- 1 tablespoon olive oil
- 1 medium spring onion
- 1 cup cauliflower, steamed
- 1 cup beef stock
- 125ml coconut milk
- 10 cashew nuts
- ½ teaspoon coriander
- ½ teaspoon turmeric
- ½ teaspoon cumin
- 2 tablespoons fresh parsley, finely chopped
- salt and pepper, to taste

Directions
1. Place the cauliflower and onion in an instant pot and add chicken stock. Stir in coriander, turmeric, cumin and a pinch of salt. Lock lid and cook high for 10 Mins. Quick release the pressure. Using a hand blender, puree the ingredients in the pot until smooth. Stir in the
2. coconut milk. Serve with roasted cashew nuts and top with parsley.

Smoky Pork Cassoulet Soup

Yield: 4 | Total Time: 2 Hour 15 Mins | Prep Time: 10 Mins | Cook Time: 2 Hours 5 Mins

Ingredients:
- 1 pack bacon, fried and crumbled
- 2 cups chopped onion
- 1 tsp dried thyme
- 1/2 tsp dried rosemary
- 3 garlic cloves, crushed
- 1/2 teaspoon salt
- 1/2 teaspoon freshly ground black pepper
- 2 cans diced tomatoes, drained
- 500g boneless pork loin roast, cut into 2cm cubes
- 250g smoked sausage, cut into 1cm cubes
- 8 teaspoons finely shredded fresh Parmesan cheese
- 8 teaspoons chopped fresh flat-leaf parsley

Directions
1. Set your instant pot on manual high and fry bacon, onion, thyme, rosemary, and garlic, then
2. add salt, pepper, and tomatoes. Add in the remaining ingredients and cook on high for 2 hours. Let the pressure come down on its own. Sprinkle with Parmesan cheese and parsley when cooked

South African Cabbage & Boerewors Soup

Yield: 3 | Total Time: 1 Hour 40 Mins | Prep Time: 10 Mins | Cook Time: 1 Hour 30 Mins

Ingredients:
- 2 cups sweet potatoes, cubed and peeled
- 4 cups cabbage and carrot coleslaw mix
- 1 large onion, chopped
- 500g boerewors cooked, halved lengthwise and cut into thick slices
- 4 cups chicken stock

1. **Directions**

Place potatoes, coleslaw mix, onion, caraway seeds and sausage in an instant pot. Pour stock in pot and cook on high for 1 1/2 hours. Let pressure come down naturally.

Spicy Red Curry Roasted Cauliflower Soup

Serves: **6** | Prep Time: **50** mins

Ingredients
- 4 tablespoons Thai red curry paste
- 1 large cauliflower, cut into florets
- 4 cups vegetable broth, low sodium
- ¼ teaspoon Himalayan pink salt
- 14 oz. can coconut milk, unsweetened

Directions
1. Preheat the oven to 400°F and grease a baking tray.
2. Arrange the cauliflower florets on the baking tray and bake for about 20 minutes.
3. Put the roasted cauliflower and vegetable broth in a blender and blend until smooth.
4. Pour this mixture in the pot and add Thai red curry paste, vegetable broth, coconut milk and pink salt.
5. Mix well and allow to cook for about 20 minutes on low heat.
6. Dish out into a bowl and serve hot.

Cream of Mushroom Soup

Serves: **4** | Prep Time: **40** mins

Ingredients
- 3 cups unsweetened almond milk
- 4 cups cauliflower florets
- Onion powder, salt and black pepper, to taste
- 3 cups diced white mushrooms
- 1 teaspoon extra-virgin olive oil

Directions
1. Put almond milk, cauliflower florets, onion powder, salt and black pepper in a saucepan. Cover the lid and bring to a boil.
2. Lower the heat and allow to simmer for about 10 minutes.
3. Transfer into a food processor and process until smooth.
4. Meanwhile, heat olive oil in a saucepan and add mushrooms.
5. Cook for about 7 minutes and stir in the cauliflower puree.
6. Bring to a boil and allow to simmer, covered for about 10 minutes.
7. Dish out into a bowl and serve immediately.

Broccoli Cheese Soup

Serves: **8** | Prep Time: **30** mins

Ingredients
- 4 garlic cloves, minced
- 4 cups broccoli, cut into florets
- 1 cup heavy cream
- 3 cups cheddar cheese, shredded
- 3½ cups chicken broth

Directions
1. Sauté garlic in a nonstick saucepan for about 1 minute and add broccoli, heavy cream and chicken broth.
2. Bring to a boil and cook on low heat for about 12 minutes.
3. Stir in the cheddar cheese and cook for about 8 minutes.
4. Dish out into a bowl and serve hot.

Taco Soup

Serves: **4** | Prep Time: **40** mins

Ingredients
- 2 tablespoons taco seasoning
- ½ pound ground beef
- 4 cups beef bone broth
- 4 tablespoons Ranch dressing
- ¼ cup tomatoes, diced

Directions
1. Brown the ground beef over medium high heat in the large pot for about 10 minutes.
2. Add taco seasoning and bone broth and cook on low heat for about 8 minutes.
3. Stir in the tomatoes and simmer for about 10 minutes.
4. Remove from heat and allow to cool. Add ranch dressing and mix well to serve.

Tomato Soup

Serves: **6** | Prep Time: **25** mins

Ingredients
- 1 medium white onion, chopped
- 3 (14 oz.) cans diced tomatoes, with their juices
- 3 garlic cloves, minced
- 3 cups heavy cream
- 1 handful basil leaves, julienned

Directions
1. Put onion, tomatoes, garlic and basil in a saucepan and stir well.
2. Cook over medium high heat for about 10 minutes and transfer into an immersion blender.
3. Puree until smooth and mix in the heavy cream. Dish out into a bowl and serve hot.

Cheesy Cauliflower Soup

Serves: **6** | Prep Time: **30** mins

Ingredients
- 1 yellow onion
- 3 tablespoons butter
- 6 cups chicken broth
- 1½ cups cheddar cheese, shredded
- 6 cups cauliflower, cut into florets

Directions
1. Heat butter in a heavy pot and add onions.
2. Sauté for about 3 minutes and add chicken broth and cauliflower.
3. Allow to simmer for about 10 minutes and transfer into an immersion blender.
4. Blend until smooth and return to the pot. Stir in the cheddar cheese and cook for about 3 minutes until the cheese is melted. Dish out into a bowl and serve hot.

Hot Mushroom Clear Soup

Serves: **1** | Prep Time: **10** mins

Ingredients
- ½ cup mushrooms, finely chopped
- 2 cups water
- 2 teaspoons butter
- Salt, to taste
- Black pepper, to taste

Directions
1. Heat butter in a heavy pot and add mushrooms.
2. Cook on low heat for about 5 minutes and add water.
3. Season with salt and black pepper and cook for about 6 minutes, stirring occasionally.
4. Ladle out into a bowl and serve hot.

Mushrooms and Spinach Clear Soup

Serves: **3** | Prep Time: **20** mins

Ingredients
- 3 cups clear vegetable stock
- 1 cup spinach, torn into small pieces
- ½ cup mushrooms, chopped
- Salt and black pepper, to taste
- 1 tablespoon olive oil

Directions
1. Heat olive oil on medium heat in a nonstick wok and add garlic.
2. Sauté for about 1 minute and add mushrooms and spinach.
3. Sauté for about 2 minutes and pour in clear vegetable stock.
4. Season with salt and black pepper and cook for about 4 minutes, stirring occasionally.
5. Ladle out in a bowl and serve hot.

Creamy Garlic Chicken Soup

Serves: **4** | Prep Time: **25** mins

Ingredients
- 1 large chicken breast, cooked and shredded
- 2 tablespoons salted butter
- 5 ounces cream cheese, cubed
- 2 tablespoons garlic seasoning
- 14.5 oz chicken broth

Directions
1. Heat butter in a saucepan over medium heat and add chicken.
2. Sauté for about 3 minutes and add garlic seasoning and cream cheese.
3. Cook for about 2 minutes and stir in the chicken broth.
4. Cook for about 7 minutes until boiled and reduce the heat to low.
5. Simmer on low heat for about 5 minutes and serve hot.

Cream of Zucchini Soup

Serves: **4** | Prep Time: **30** mins

Ingredients
- 1½ cups parmesan cheese, freshly grated
- 2 medium zucchinis, cut into large chunks
- 2 tablespoons sour cream
- Salt and black pepper, to taste
- 32 oz chicken broth

Directions
1. Mix together zucchini and chicken broth over medium heat in a pot and bring to a boil.
2. Lower the heat and simmer for about 18 minutes until tender.
3. Remove from heat and transfer into an immersion blender.
4. Stir in the sour cream and purée until smooth.
5. Add cheese and season with salt and black pepper to serve.

Cream of Asparagus Soup

Serves: **6** | Prep Time: **30** mins

Ingredients
- 6 cups reduced sodium chicken broth
- 4 tablespoons unsalted butter
- 2 pounds asparagus, cut in half
- Salt and black pepper, to taste
- ½ cup sour cream

Directions
1. Heat butter in a large pot over medium low heat and add asparagus.
2. Sauté for about 3 minutes and stir in the chicken broth, salt and black pepper.
3. Bring to a boil, cover and cook for about 20 minutes on low heat.
4. Remove from heat and transfer into blender along with sour cream.
5. Pulse until smooth and ladle out in a bowl to serve.

Cream of Brown Butter Mushroom Soup

Serves: **6** | Prep Time: **25** mins

Ingredients
- ½ cup heavy cream
- 4 cups chicken stock
- 6 tablespoons butter
- Salt and black pepper, to taste
- 1 pound mushrooms, sliced

Directions
1. Heat butter in a large pot over medium heat and add mushrooms.
2. Sauté for about 4 minutes and stir in the chicken stock.
3. Allow it to simmer for about 10 minutes and transfer to food processor.
4. Blend until smooth and return to the pot.
5. Stir in the heavy cream and season with salt and black pepper to serve.

Butternut Squash Soup

Serves: **4** | Prep Time: **1 hour 30** mins

Ingredients
- 4 cups chicken broth
- 1 small onion, chopped
- 1 butternut squash
- Nutmeg, salt and black pepper, to taste
- 3 tablespoons coconut oil

Directions
1. Heat coconut oil in a large pot and add onion.
2. Sauté for about 3 minutes and stir in the chicken broth and butternut squash.
3. Let it simmer for about 45 minutes on medium low heat and transfer into an immersion blender.
4. Pulse until smooth and season with nutmeg, salt and black pepper.
5. Return to the pot and cook for about 35 minutes. Dish out into a bowl and serve hot.

Spring Soup

Serves: **4** | Prep Time: **20** mins

Ingredients
- 4 tablespoons butter
- 4 eggs
- 8 cups chicken broth
- Salt, to taste
- 2 heads romaine lettuce, chopped

Directions
1. Boil the chicken broth over high heat and lower the flame.
2. Poach the eggs in the chicken broth for about 5 minutes and remove the eggs into a bowl.
3. Stir the chopped romaine lettuce into the broth and cook for about 10 minutes.
4. Ladle out into a bowl and season with salt and top with butter to serve.

Leek, Cauliflower and Bacon Soup

Serves: **4** | Prep Time: **1 hour 30** mins

Ingredients
- ½ cauliflower head, chopped
- 4 cups chicken broth
- 1 leek, chopped
- 5 bacon strips, cooked and chopped
- Salt and black pepper, to taste

Directions
1. Put the leek, cauliflower and chicken broth into the pot and cook on medium heat for about 45 minutes.
2. Transfer into an immersion blender and puree until smooth.
3. Return the soup into the pot and add the bacon.
4. Season with salt and black pepper and cook for about 30 minutes on low heat.
5. Dish out into a bowl and serve hot.

French Onion Soup

Serves: **6** | Prep Time: **40** mins

Ingredients
- 1 pound brown onions
- 5 tablespoons butter
- 4 drops liquid Stevia
- 3 cups beef stock
- 4 tablespoons olive oil

Directions
1. Heat butter and olive oil in a large pot over medium low heat and add onions.
2. Sauté for about 4 minutes and stir in beef stock and Stevia.
3. Cook for about 5 minutes and reduce the heat to low.
4. Allow to simmer for about 25 minutes and ladle out into soup bowls to serve hot.

Green Chicken Enchilada Soup

Serves: **5** | Prep Time: **20** mins

Ingredients
- ½ cup salsa verde
- 4 oz. cream cheese, softened
- 1 cup cheddar cheese, shredded
- 2 cups chicken stock
- 2 cups cooked chicken, shredded

Directions
1. Put cheddar cheese, salsa verde, cream cheese and chicken stock in an immersion blender.
2. Blend until smooth and pour this mixture into a medium saucepan.
3. Cook for about 5 minutes on medium heat and add the shredded chicken.
4. Cook for another 5 minutes and dish out into a bowl to serve hot.

Cheesy Mushroom Shrimp Soup

Serves: **8** | Prep Time: **30** mins

Ingredients
- 24 oz. extra small shrimp
- 8 oz cheddar cheese, shredded
- 2 cups mushrooms, sliced
- 1 cup butter
- 32 oz. chicken broth

Directions
1. Put chicken broth and mushrooms in a large soup pot and bring to a boil.
2. Lower the heat and stir in butter and cheddar cheese.
3. Mix well and add shrimp to the soup pot.
4. Allow it to simmer for about 15 minutes and dish out into a bowl to serve hot.

Bacon and Pumpkin Soup

Serves: **6** | Prep Time: **8 hours 15** mins

Ingredients
- 3 cups bacon hock, diced
- 400g pumpkin, diced
- Boiling water
- Salt, to taste
- 2 tablespoons butter

Directions
1. Pour some boiling water in the slow cooker. Add pumpkin and bacon hock and cover the lid.
2. Cook on low for about 8 hours and pull the meat away from the bones.
3. Return the meat to the slow cooker along with salt and butter.
4. Allow it to simmer for about 5 minutes and ladle out into a bowl to serve hot.

Mint Avocado Chilled Soup

Serves: **2** | Prep Time: **10** mins

Ingredients
- 1 medium ripe avocado
- 2 romaine lettuce leaves
- 1 cup coconut milk, chilled
- Salt, to taste
- 20 fresh mint leaves

Directions
1. Put mint leaves with the rest of the ingredients in a blender and blend until smooth.
2. Refrigerate for about 20 minutes and remove to serve chilled.

Chilled Zucchini Soup

Serves: **5** | Prep Time: **15** mins

Ingredients
- 4 cups chicken broth
- 1 medium zucchini, cut into ½ inch pieces
- 8 oz. cream cheese, cut into cubes
- Salt and black pepper, to taste
- ½ teaspoon ground cumin

Directions
1. Put chicken broth and zucchini in a large stockpot and bring to a boil.
2. Lower the heat and allow to simmer for about 10 minutes.
3. Stir in the cream cheese and transfer into an immersion blender.
4. Blend until smooth and season with cumin, salt and black pepper.
5. Refrigerate to chill for about 2 hours and remove from the fridge to serve chilled.

Chilled Cantaloupe Soup

Serves: **8** | Prep Time: **10** mins

Ingredients
- 6 tablespoons butter
- 2 cantaloupes, cut into chunks
- 2/3 cup plain, nonfat Greek yogurt
- 6 tablespoons fresh basil leaves, for garnish
- Pinch of kosher salt and nutmeg

Directions
1. Put all the ingredients except basil in a food processor and pulse until smooth.
2. Refrigerate for at least 3 hours and garnish with fresh basil leaves to serve.

Turmeric Beef Broth Soup

Serves: **3** | Prep Time: **10** mins

Ingredients
- 2 cups beef bone broth
- 2 tablespoons ginger, finely grated
- ½ teaspoon ground turmeric
- 1 cup coconut cream
- Himalayan salt and black pepper, to taste

Directions
1. Put all the ingredients except salt in a saucepan and allow it to simmer over medium heat.
2. Cook for about 5 minutes, stirring occasionally and season with salt and black pepper.
3. Dish out into a bowl and serve hot.

Chicken Feet Soup

Serves: **8** | Prep Time: **12 hours**

Ingredients
- 1 teaspoon salt
- 12 chicken feet
- 2 tablespoons raw apple cider vinegar
- 1 (½ inch) piece of fresh ginger
- 1 sprig of rosemary

Directions
1. Put chicken feet with apple cider vinegar and water in a stock pot.
2. Bring to a boil and then reduce to a simmer for about 12 minutes.
3. Allow to cool by blanching the feet in cold water.
4. Return the chicken to the stock pot along with some water.
5. Bring to a boil and reduce the heat to low.
6. Simmer for about 5 minutes and add salt, rosemary and ginger.
7. Simmer for about 10 hours and allow to cool.
8. Dish out the liquid into glass jars through strainers and immediately serve.

Savory Pumpkin Soup

Serves: **6** | Prep Time: **30** mins

Ingredients
- 2 cups chicken bone broth
- 1 cup full fat coconut milk
- 6 cups pumpkin, baked
- Sea salt and black pepper, to taste
- ½ cup sour cream

Directions
1. Heat a soup pan over medium heat and add the chicken bone broth, coconut milk, pumpkin, sea salt and black pepper.
2. Stir well and allow the mixture to simmer for about 15 minutes.
3. Transfer into an immersion blender and blend until smooth.
4. Dish out into a bowl and stir in the sour cream to serve.

Hearty Green Soup

Serves: **3** | Prep Time: **20** mins

Ingredients
- 1 medium head broccoli
- 3 zucchinis, chopped
- ¾ cup butter, salted
- 3 leeks, chopped
- 1 cup chicken bone broth

Directions
1. Put broccoli, leeks and zucchinis in a large saucepan and mix well.
2. Stir in the butter and chicken broth and cook for about 10 minutes on medium low heat.
3. Transfer the mixture into a blender and blend until smooth.
4. Dish out into a bowl and serve hot.

Queso Chicken Soup

Serves: **4** | Prep Time: **35** mins

Ingredients
- 3 cups chicken broth
- 1 pound chicken breast
- 10 ounces cream cheese
- 1 tablespoon taco seasoning
- Salt, to taste

Directions
1. Put all the ingredients in a wok over medium heat except cream cheese and cover with lid.
2. Simmer for about 25 minutes and transfer into an immersion blender.
3. Stir in the cream cheese and dish out into a bowl to serve.

Chilled Cucumber Soup

Serves: **5** | Prep Time: **10** mins

Ingredients
- 4 cups chicken broth
- 2 cucumbers, cut into ½ inch pieces
- 8 oz cream cheese, cut into cubes
- Salt and black pepper, to taste
- 1/3 cup plain, nonfat Greek yogurt

Directions
1. Mix together chicken broth and zucchini in a large stockpot.
2. Bring to a boil and reduce the heat to low.
3. Allow to simmer for about 10 minutes and add cream cheese and yogurt.
4. Stir well and transfer to an immersion blender.
5. Blend until smooth and season with salt and black pepper.
6. Refrigerate to chill for about 3 hours and serve chilled.

INSTANT POT STEWS

Instant Pot Spiced Coconut Fish Stew

Yield: 4 | Total Time: 35 Mins | Prep Time: 5 Mins | Cook Time: 30 Mins

Ingredients
- 1 1/2 lb. fish fillets
- 1 cup coconut milk
- 2 tbsp. coconut oil
- 1 cup onion chopped
- 1 tbsp. garlic
- 1 tbsp. ginger
- 1/2 serrano or jalapeno
- 1 cup tomato chopped
- 1 tsp ground coriander
- 1/4 tsp ground cumin
- 1/2 tsp turmeric
- 1 tsp lime juice
- 1/2 tsp black pepper and salt

Directions
1. Set your instant pot on sauté mode; heat in oil and cook onion, garlic and ginger until fragrant. Add in fish and cook for 5 Mins per side or until browned and then stir in the remaining ingredients. Lock lid. Cook on meat/stew setting for 20 Mins and then let pressure come down on its own.

Instant Pot Chicken and Vegetable Stew

Yield: 4-6 | Total Time: 45 Mins | Prep Time: 15 Mins | Cook Time: 30 Mins

Ingredients

- 4 tablespoons olive oil
- 2 red onions, chopped
- 1 pound diced chicken
- 1 pound curly kale, torn
- 12 ounces baby spinach
- 3 cups plus 2 tablespoons water
- 4 cups homemade vegetable broth
- 1 tablespoon fresh lemon juice
- 1 large pinch of cayenne pepper
- Salt, to taste

Directions

1. In an instant pot, heat oil on sauté setting and then sauté onion and salt until fragrant. Add in diced chicken and cook for 5 Mins or until browned. Stir in the remaining ingredients; lock lid and cook on high pressure for 20 Mins. Release pressure naturally.

Ground Beef and Vegetable Stew

Yield: 6 | Total Time: 40 Mins | Prep Time: 10 Mins | Cook Time: 30 Mins

Ingredients

- 2 tablespoons olive oil
- 1 ½ pounds ground beef
- 1 onion, thinly sliced
- 3 cloves garlic, minced
- 1 bell pepper, thinly sliced
- 1 can roasted crushed tomatoes
- 1/2 cup water
- 2 cups bone broth
- 1/2 tsp smoked paprika
- 1 tsp oregano
- 1 tbsp. chili powder
- 1 tbsp. cumin
- 1/2 tsp sea salt
- 1/2 tsp pepper

Directions

1. In an instant pot, heat oil on sauté setting and then sauté onion and garlic until fragrant. Add in beef and cook for 5 Mins or until browned. Stir in the remaining ingredients; lock lid and cook on high pressure for 20 Mins. Release pressure naturally.

Instant Pot Spiced and Creamy Vegetable Stew with Cashews

Yield: 4 | Total Time: 29 Mins | Prep Time: 10 Mins | Cook Time: 19 Mins

Ingredients

- 2 tablespoons olive oil
- 1 cup diced red onion
- ⅔ cups diced carrot
- 2 cups diced cauliflower
- ⅛ teaspoons dried thyme
- 1 ⅓ tablespoons curry powder
- 2 ⅔ cups vegetable broth
- ½ cup coconut cream
- ⅛ teaspoons salt
- ⅛ teaspoons pepper
- Toasted cashews for serving

Directions

1. Heat oil in your instant pot and sauté red onion, cauliflower and carrots for 4 Mins; stir in spices and stock and lock lid. Cook on manual for 10 Mins and then let pressure come down naturally. Stir in coconut cream and cook on manual high for 5 Mins. Serve the stew topped with toasted cashews.

Coconut Fish Stew with Spinach

Yield: 2 | Total Time: 25 Mins | Prep Time: 5 Mins | Cook Time: 20 Mins

Ingredients

- 300g firm white fish, cubed
- 450g spinach, roughly chopped
- 100g coconut cream
- 2 ½ tbsp. Thai curry paste
- 2 tbsp. coconut oil
- 100ml water
- Kosher salt and pepper, to taste

Directions

1. Add the oil to an instant pot set on manual high. Stir in the curry paste and cook for 3 Mins to bring the spices to life. Pour in the coconut cream and water and bring the sauce to a boil.
2. Add in the fish cubes and lock lid. Cook on high for 15 Mins and then let pressure come down on its own. Gently stir in the spinach and cook for 3 Mins until it wilts. Serve hot!

Filling Herbed Turkey Stew

Yield: 2 | Total Time: 35 Mins | Prep Time: 10 Mins | Cook Time: 25 Mins

Ingredients

- 6 ounces ground turkey, cooked
- 2 (15-ounce) can crushed or skewed tomatoes
- 3 cloves garlic, crushed
- 2 teaspoons red wine vinegar
- Pinch of parsley
- Pinch of cumin
- Pinch of basil
- Pinch of rosemary
- Pinch of red pepper flakes
- 1 Avocado for serving

Directions:

Set your instant pot on manual high, add in vinegar, tomatoes, and seasonings; cook for about 5 Mins. Stir in ground turkey and cook on high for 20 Mins and the let pressure come down on its own. Serve warm.

Low Carb Bouillabaisse Fish Stew

Yield: 6 | Total Time: 50 Mins | Prep Time: 10 Mins | Cook Time: 40 Mins

Ingredients

- 1 cup dry white wine
- Juice and zest of 1 orange
- 2 tbsp. olive oil
- 1 large onion, diced
- 2 cloves garlic, minced
- 1 tsp dried basil
- 1/2 tsp dried thyme
- 1/2 tsp salt
- 1/4 tsp ground black pepper
- 4 cups fish stock, chicken stock can also be used
- 1 can diced tomatoes, drained
- 1 bay leaf
- 400g boneless, skinless white fish fillet (ex. cod)
- 400g prawns peeled and deveined
- 400g mussels in their shells
- Juice of 1/2 lemon
- 1/4 cup fresh Italian (flat leaf) parsley

Directions

1. Set your instant pot on manual high and heat oil; add the onion and fry all the vegetables until almost tender; add the garlic, basil, thyme, salt, and pepper. Pour in the wine and bring to a boil. Add the fish stock, orange zest, tomatoes, and bay leaf and stir to combine. Lock lid and cook on high for 1 hour. Quick release the pressure and set on manual high; toss the fish and prawns with the lemon juice and stir into the broth in the pot. Cook for about 20 Mins and then add in the mussels right at the end and allow to steam for 20 Mins with the lid on.

Instant Pot Thai Nut Chicken

Yield: 4 | Total Time: 2 Hours 10 Mins | Prep Time: 10 Mins | Cook Time: 2 Hours

Ingredients

- 8 boneless skinless chicken thighs (about 2 pounds)
- ½ cup coconut flour
- 3/4 cup creamy nut butter
- 1/2 cup orange juice
- 1/4 cup diabetic apricot jam
- 2 tablespoons sesame oil
- 2 tablespoons soy sauce
- 2 tablespoons teriyaki sauce
- 2 tablespoons hoisin sauce
- 1 can coconut milk
- 3/4 cup water
- 1 cup chopped roasted almonds or any of the other
- nuts on green list

Directions

1. Place coconut flour in a large resealable plastic bag. Add chicken, a few pieces at a time, and shake to coat. Transfer to a greased instant pot. In a small bowl, combine the nut butter, orange juice, jam, oil, soy sauce, teriyaki sauce, hoisin sauce and 3/4 cup coconut milk; pour over chicken. Lock lid and cook on high for 2 hours. Let pressure come down on its own Sprinkle with nuts before serving.

Tasty Instant Pot Greek Fish Stew

Yield: 5 | Total Time: 30 Mins | Prep Time: 10 Mins | Cook Time: 20 Mins

Ingredients

- 5 large white fish fillets
- 1 large red onion, chopped
- 4 cloves of garlic
- 1 leek, sliced
- 1 carrot, chopped
- 3 sticks celery, chopped
- 1 can tomatoes
- 1/2 tsp. saffron threads
- 8 cups fish stock
- 2 tbsp. fresh lemon juice
- 1 tbsp. lemon zest
- handful parsley leaves chopped
- handful mint leaves chopped

Directions

1. Combine all ingredients in your instant pot and lock lid; cook on high for 20 Mins and then release pressure naturally. Serve with gluten-free bread.

Pressure Cooker Vegetable and Fish Stew

Yield: 4 | Total Time: 34 Mins | Prep Time: 15 Mins | Cook Time: 19 Mins

Ingredients

- 2 tbsp. extra-virgin olive oil
- 1 red onion, sliced
- 2 jalapeño peppers, seeds removed and diced
- 4 cups sliced green cabbage
- 1 carrot, peeled and chopped
- 4 cups crushed tomatoes
- 2 cup diced white fish filet
- 4 cup vegetable broth
- 3 tbsp. apple cider vinegar
- 2 tsp. Stevia
- ½ tsp. salt
- ¼ tsp. black pepper

Directions

1. Heat extra virgin olive oil in an instant pot set on sauté mode and stir in red onion, jalapenos, cabbage, and carrot; sauté for about 7 Mins or until almost tender.
2. Stir in tomatoes, fish, broth, apple cider vinegar, and Stevia, salt and pepper until well combined. Lock lid and cook on high pressure for 12 Mins. Let pressure come down naturally. Serve hot.

Easy Cheesy Turkey Stew

Yield: 5 | Total Time: 30 Mins | Prep Time: 5 Mins | Cook Time: 25 Mins

Ingredients
- 2 tbsp. coconut oil
- 1/2 red onion
- 1 lb. ground turkey
- 2 cups coconut milk
- 2 garlic cloves
- 1 tbsp. mustard
- 2 cups riced cauliflower
- 1 tsp salt
- 1 tsp. black pepper
- 1 tsp. thyme
- 1 tsp. celery salt
- 1 tsp. garlic powder

Directions
1. Melt coconut oil in an instant pot, add garlic and onion and cook until fragrant. Stir in ground turkey until crumbled. Stir in cauliflower and spices until well mixed. Cook until meat is browned. Stir in coconut milk and lock lid. Cook on high for 20 Mins and then let pressure come down on its own. Stir in shredded cheese and serve.

Instant Pot Beef and Sweet Potato Stew

Yield: 6 | Total Time: 35 Mins | Prep Time: 10 Mins | Cook Time: 25 Mins

Ingredients
- 4 tablespoons olive oil
- 2 pounds ground beef
- 3 cups beef stock
- 2 sweet potatoes, peeled and diced
- 1 clove garlic, minced
- 1 onion, diced
- 1 (14-oz) can petite minced tomatoes
- 1 (14-oz) can tomato sauce
- 3-4 tbsp. chili powder
- ¼ tsp. oregano
- 2 tsp. salt
- ½ tsp. black pepper
- Cilantro, optional, for garnish

Directions
1. Brown the beef in a pan over medium heat; drain excess fat and then transfer it to an instant pot. Stir in the remaining ingredients and lock lid; cook on high for 25 Mins and then release pressure naturally. Garnish with cilantro and serve warm.

Instant Pot Coconut Fish Stew

Yield: 1 Serving | Total Time: 52 Mins | Prep Time: 10 Mins | Cook Time: 42 Mins

Ingredients
- 1 tablespoon olive oil
- 1 red onion
- 1 tablespoon onion powder
- 150g tilapia filet
- ¼ cup coarsely chopped celery
- 2 cloves garlic
- 1 ½ cups vegetable broth
- ½ teaspoon parsley
- ½ teaspoon basil
- White pepper
- Sea salt

Directions
1. Heat oil in your instant pot set over manual high heat; sauté onion until fragrant and then add in the fish. Cook for about 6 Mins per side or until browned. Add in the remaining ingredients and lock lid; cook on high for 30 Mins and then let pressure come down on its own.

Instant Pot Loaded Protein Stew

Yields: 2 | Total Time: 1 Hour 5 Mins | Prep Time: 5 Mins | Cook Time: 1 Hour

Ingredients
- 1-pound ground chicken
- 2 minced cloves garlic
- 2 large carrots, grated
- 1 medium red bell pepper, diced
- 1 teaspoon Stevia
- 1/4 cup low-sodium soy sauce
- 1/4 tsp. crushed red pepper flakes
- 1/4 cup ketchup

Directions: Combine all ingredients in your instant pot and cook on high setting for 1 hour. Shred the chicken and return to the pot.

Instant Pot Low Carb Mussel Stew

Yield: 4 | Total Time: 1 Hour 40 Mins | Prep Time: 10 Mins | Cook Time: 1 Hour 30 Mins

Ingredients:
- 1kg fresh or frozen, cleaned mussels
- 3 tbsp. olive oil
- 4 cloves garlic, minced
- 1 Large onion, finely diced
- 1 punnet mushrooms, diced
- 2 cans diced tomatoes
- 2 tbsp. oregano
- ½ tbsp. basil
- ½ tsp. black pepper
- 1 tsp. paprika
- dash red chili flakes
- 3/4 cup water

Directions
1. Set your instant pot on manual high and fry in onions, garlic, shallots and mushrooms; stir in the remaining ingredients, except mussels. Lock lid and cook on high for 1 hour; let pressure come down and then set on manual high. Add cleaned mussels to the pot and cook for 30 more Mins
2. Ladle your mussels into bowls with plenty of broth. If any mussels didn't open up during cooking, toss those as well. Enjoy!

Scrumptious Beef Stew

Yield: 6 | Total Time: 30 Mins | Prep Time: 5 Mins | Cook Time: 25 Mins

Ingredients
- 2 pounds beef stew meat
- 4 tbsp. extra virgin olive oil
- 3 cloves garlic, minced
- 1/4 cup tomato paste
- 4 large carrots, diced
- 2 medium potatoes, diced
- 2/3 cup chopped red onion
- 1 tsp. oregano
- 1 cup beef broth
- 1 ½ cups cooked peas

Directions
1. Heat oil u sauté mode in your instant pot; stir in meat and garlic and cook until browned. Add tomato paste, carrots, potato, onion, oregano and broth and lock lid. Cook on manual for 20 Mins and then release pressure naturally. Stir in cooked peas to serve.

Turkish Split Pea Stew

Yield: 4 | Total Time: 25 Mins | Prep Time: 10 Mins | Cook Time: 15 Mins

Ingredients
- 1 red onion, chopped
- 1½ tablespoons olive oil
- 4-5 cloves garlic, chopped
- ½ cup chopped tomatoes
- 2 cups split peas, rinsed
- 1 celery stick, chopped
- 1 medium carrot, chopped
- 1½ teaspoons cumin powder
- 1 teaspoon paprika powder
- ¼ teaspoon chili powder
- ¼ teaspoon cinnamon
- 6 cups vegetable stock
- 2 tablespoons lemon juice
- 1 bay leaf
- ½ teaspoon sea salt
- Chopped scallions and chives for garnish

Directions
1. Turn your instant pot on sauté mode and heat oil; add onion, celery and carrots and sauté for 4 Mins. Stir in the remaining ingredients and press the cancel or warm button. Lock lid and press manual high for 10 Mins. When done, let pressure release naturally and then serve topped with chopped scallions or chives and lemon wedge.

Delicious Seafood Stew

Yield: 6 | Total Time: 35 Mins | Prep Time: 15 Mins | Cook Time: 20 Mins

Ingredients:
- 3 tablespoons olive oil
- 2 pounds seafood (1 pound large shrimp & 1 pound scallops)
- 1/2 cup chopped white onion
- 3 garlic cloves, minced
- 1 tbsp. tomato paste
- 1 can (28 oz.) crushed tomatoes
- 4 cups vegetable broth
- 1 pound yellow potatoes, diced
- 1 tsp. dried basil
- 1 tsp. dried thyme
- 1 tsp. dried oregano
- 1/8 tsp. cayenne pepper
- 1/4 tsp. crush red pepper flakes
- 1/2 tsp. celery salt
- salt and pepper
- handful of chopped parsley

Directions:
1. Mix all ingredients, except seafood, in your instant pot and lock lid; cook on high for about 15 Mins. Quick release the pressure and then stir in seafood and continue; lock lid and cook on high for five Mins and then let pressure come down on its own. Serve hot with crusty gluten-free bread and garnished with parsley.

Curried Chicken Stew

Yield: 2 | Total Time: 2 Hours | Prep Time: 20 Mins | Cook Time: 1 Hour 40 Mins

Ingredients:
- 2 bone-in chicken thighs
- 2 tbsp. olive oil
- 3 carrots, diced
- 1 sweet onion, chopped
- 1 cup coconut milk
- 1/4 cup hot curry paste
- Toasted almonds
- Coriander
- Sour cream to serve

Directions
1. Set your instant pot to manual high setting; heat oil and cook chicken for 8 Mins or until browned. Stir in carrots and onion and cook for about 3 Mins.
2. In a bowl, combine curry paste and coconut milk; whisk until well blended and pour over chicken mixture.
3. Lock lid and cook on high for 1 ½ hours and then let pressure come down naturally.
Serve the stew topped with toasted almonds, coriander, fresh chili and a dollop of sour cream.

Beef Chuck & Green Cabbage Stew

Yield: 2 | Total Time: 9 Hours 20 Mins | Prep Time: 20 Mins | Cook Time: 3 Hours

Ingredients
- 1 packet frozen baby carrots
- 2 onions, roughly chopped
- 1 cup chopped cabbage
- 4 garlic cloves, smashed
- 2 bay leaves
- 4 pieces of beef chuck with marrow
- Salt & pepper
- 1 thin diced tomato, drained
- 1 cup chicken stock

Directions
1. Place the baby carrots and chopped onions into the bottom of your instant pot. Layer the cabbage wedges on top and add the crushed garlic cloves and bay leaves.
2. Season the beef shanks generously with salt and pepper then add them on top of the veggies.
3. Pour in the diced tomatoes and broth before putting on the lid. Set the pot on high for 3 hours. Let pressure come down naturally.
4. Once ready, allow to cool then pack in freezer friendly bags or jars and freeze until when you are ready to eat.

Madras Lamb Stew

Yield: 2 | Total Time: 2 Hours 25 Mins | Prep Time: 25 Mins | Cook Time: 2 Hours

Ingredients:
- 3 fatty lamb chops
- 3 tbsp. coconut milk
- 2 cups water
- 3 tbsp. Red Curry Paste
- 2 tbsp. Thai fish sauce
- 1 tbsp. dried onion flakes
- 2 tbsp. fresh red chilies, minced
- 1 tbsp. sugar
- 1 tbsp. ground cumin
- 1 tbsp. ground coriander
- 1/8 tsp. ground cloves
- 1/8 tsp. ground nutmeg
- 1 tbsp. ground ginger

Toppings when ready to serve:
- 2 tbsp. coconut milk powder
- 1 tbsp. red curry paste
- 2 tbsp. sugar
- 1/4 cup cashews, roughly chopped
- 1/4 cup fresh cilantro, chopped

Directions
1. Place the raw lamb chops in an instant pot; add the coconut milk, water, red curry paste, fish sauce, onion flakes, chilies, cumin, coriander, cloves, nutmeg, and ginger. Cover and cook on high for 2 hours.
2. Let the lamb curry cool completely then pack in freezer friendly bags or jars.
3. After thawing and heating, just before serving, whisk the coconut milk powder, curry paste and sweetener into the sauce
4. Break the meat into pieces and stir into the sauce together with the chopped cashews.
5. Garnish with fresh coriander.

Curried Goat Stew

Yield: 4 | Total Time: 1 Hour 5 Mins | Prep Time: 5 Mins | Cook Time: 1 Hour

Ingredients
- 4 goat chops
- 2 tbsp. olive oil
- 3 carrots, cut in 2-inch pieces
- 1 sweet onion, cut in thin wedges
- 1/2 cup unsweetened coconut milk
- 1/4 cup mild curry paste
- Toasted almond
- Coriander
- Fresh green or red chili

Directions
1. Combine all ingredients in an instant pot and lock lid. Cook on high for 1 hour and let pressure come down on its own. Serve topped with toasted almonds and a dollop yogurt.

Instant Pot Lemon Chicken Stew

Yield: 2 | Total Time: 1 Hour 40 Mins | Prep Time: 10 Mins | Cook Time: 1 Hour 30 Mins

Ingredients:
- 2 carrots, chopped
- 2 ribs celery, chopped
- 1 onion, chopped
- 10 large green olives
- 4 cloves garlic, crushed
- 2 bay leaves
- ½ tsp. dried oregano
- ¼ tsp. salt
- ¼ tsp. pepper
- 6 boneless skinless chicken thighs
- ¾ cup chicken stock
- ¼ cup almond flour
- 2 tbsp. lemon juice
- ½ cup chopped fresh parsley
- grated zest of 1 lemon

Directions
1. In your instant pot, combine carrots, celery, onion, olives, garlic, bay leaves, oregano, salt and pepper. Arrange chicken pieces on top of vegetables. Add broth and ¾ cup water. Lock lid and cook on high setting for 1 ½ hours. Let pressure come down naturally. Discard bay leaves.

2. In a small bowl, whisk together a cup of cooking liquid and flour until very smooth; whisk in lemon juice and pour the mixture into your pot. Cook on manual high for about 15 Mins or until thickened.
3. In a small bowl, mix together lemon zest and chopped parsley; sprinkled over the chicken mixture and serve. Enjoy!

Hearty Lamb & Cabbage Stew
Yield: 4 | Total Time: 2 Hours 45 Mins | Prep Time: 15 Mins | Cook Time: 2 hours 30 Mins

Ingredients
- 2 tbsp. coconut oil
- 200g lamb chops, bone in
- 1 lamb or beef stock cube
- 2 cups water
- 1 cup shredded cabbage
- 1 onion, sliced
- 2 carrots, chopped
- 2 sticks celery, chopped
- 1 tsp. dried thyme
- 1 tbsp. balsamic vinegar
- 1 tbsp. almond flour

Directions
1. Set your instant pot to manual high and heat in oil; brown in the lamb chops and then add in the remaining ingredients. Cook on high for 2 hours and then let pressure come down naturally. Remove bones from the meat.
2. To thicken your sauce, ladle ¼ cup of sauce into a bowl and whisk in almond flour. Return to the pot and stir well; lock lid and cook for 30 Mins on manual high.

Rosemary-Garlic Beef Stew
Yield: 2 | Prep Time: 15 Mins | Cook Time: 2 Hours

Ingredients:
- 3 medium carrots
- 3 sticks celery
- 1 medium onion
- 2 tbsp. olive oil
- 4 cloves garlic, minced
- 200g beef chuck
- Salt and pepper
- ¼ cup almond flour
- 2 cups beef stock
- 2 tbsp. Dijon mustard
- 1 tbsp. Worcestershire sauce
- 1 tbsp. soy sauce
- 1 tbsp. xylitol
- ½ tbsp. dried rosemary
- ½ tsp. thyme

Directions
Combine all ingredients in an instant pot and cook on high setting for 2 hours. Let pressure come down naturally.

Instant Pot Oxtail Stew
Yield: 2 | Prep Time: 10 Mins | Cook Time: 2 Hours

Ingredients
- ½ pound oxtail
- 1 cup grated cabbage
- 1/2 cup grated carrots
- 2 large red onions, chopped
- 1 large bunch celery, chopped
- 1/2 cup diced tomatoes
- 2 jelly stock cubes
- 4 cups water
- 1 tbsp. crushed garlic
- 1 branch rosemary
- 2 bay leaves
- Grated cheese to serve

Directions
1. Place all ingredients except cheese into an instant pot and cook on high setting for 2 hours. Let pressure come down naturally. Serve sprinkled with grated cheese.

Pressure Cooked Lamb-Bacon Stew
Yield: 2 | Prep Time: 20 Mins | Cook Time: 2 Hours

Ingredients
- 2 cloves garlic, minced
- 1 leek, sliced
- 2 celery ribs, diced
- 1 cup sliced button mushrooms
- 2 Vidalia onions, thinly sliced
- 2 tbsp. butter
- 2 cups chicken stock
- 200g lamb, cut in cubes
- 4 oz. cream cheese
- 1 cup heavy cream
- 1 packet bacon – cooked crisp, and crumbled
- 1 tsp. salt
- 1 tsp. pepper
- 1 tsp. garlic powder
- 1 tsp. thyme

Directions
1. Set your instant pot on manual high setting and melt in butter; sear lamb meat until browned. Add in garlic, leeks, celery, mushrooms, onions, and cook for about 5 Mins; stir in the remaining ingredients and lock lid. Cook on high for 2 hours and then let pressure come down on its own.

Instant Pot Low Carb Vegetable Stew

Yield: 1 Serving | Total Time: 15 Mins | Prep Time: 5 Mins | Cook Time: 10 Mins

Ingredients
- 1 medium cauliflower
- 8 cups water
- 1 tsp. lemon juice
- 3 tsp. ground flax seeds
- 3 cups spinach
- 1 tsp. cayenne pepper
- 1 tsp. black pepper
- 1 tsp. soy sauce

Directions:
1. Core cauliflower and cut the florets into large pieces; reserve stems for juicing.
2. Add cauliflower to an instant pot and add water; lock lid and cook on high pressure for 10 Mins. Release pressure naturally and then transfer the cauliflower. Stir in the remaining ingredients and serve hot or warm.

Best Beef Stew for a King!

Yield: 2 | Total Time: 2 Hours 25 Mins | Prep Time: 15 Mins | Cook Time: 2 Hours 10 Mins

Ingredients
- 200g beef meat, cubed
- 1 tsp. Salt
- 1 tsp. pepper
- 1 medium onion, finely chopped
- 2 celery ribs, sliced
- 2 cloves of garlic, minced
- 1 can tomato paste
- 3 cups beef stock
- 2 tbsp. Worcestershire sauce
- 1 cup frozen mixed veggies
- 1 tablespoon almond flour
- 1 tablespoon water

Directions
1. Combine all ingredients except flour, frozen veggies, and water in your instant pot.
2. Cook on high setting for 2 hours. Let pressure come down on its own.
3. Stir together water and flour; stir into the pot and then add in veggies; lock lid and cook for 10 Mins.

Sandwiches and Wraps Recipes

Avocado and Egg Sandwich

Serves: **4** | Prep Time: **15** mins

Ingredients
- 2 tablespoons olive oil
- 1 teaspoon lemon juice
- 1 whole wheat bagel, sliced
- 1 avocado, mashed
- 2 eggs
- ¼ teaspoon black pepper
- ¼ teaspoon salt

Directions
1. Scoop out some material from inside of the bagel slices to make 1-inch wide hole.
2. Brush the prepared slice with olive oil and sear in a heated pan.
3. Meanwhile, mix avocado flesh with lemon juice.
4. Spread the avocado mixture in the hole of the toasted bagel.
5. Crack an egg at the center of each slice and season it with salt and black pepper.
6. Place them in the baking sheet and bake for about 4 minutes to serve.

Mediterranean Veggie Wrap

Serves: **2** | Prep Time: **15** mins

Ingredients
- ¼ cup red onions, sliced
- ½ small zucchini, sliced
- ¼ cup hummus
- 2 tablespoons feta cheese, crumbled
- 1 tablespoon black olives, sliced
- ½ teaspoon olive oil
- ½ medium red bell pepper, sliced
- 2 whole grain tortillas
- ½ cup baby spinach
- 1 teaspoon dried oregano

Directions
1. Heat oil in a small skillet and add zucchini, red onions, and bell pepper.
2. Sauté for about 5 minutes and keep aside.
3. Heat tortillas in another skillet and spread half of the hummus in each tortilla.
4. Equally divide spinach between wraps and layer with sautéed vegetables.
5. Sprinkle with olives, feta cheese, and oregano.
6. Fold the edges of the tortillas to roll up and serve warm.

Loaded Mediterranean Veggie Sandwich

Serves: **4** | Prep Time: **25** mins

Ingredients
- 6 tablespoons cilantro jalapeno hummus
- ½ cup sprouts
- 4 slices whole wheat bread
- 2 whole leaves fresh lettuce
- 4 whole tomatoes, thinly sliced
- 2 red onions, thinly sliced
- 4 Peppadew peppers, chopped
- 4 whole cucumbers, thinly sliced
- 4 tablespoons feta cheese, crumbled

Directions
1. Toast the bread and spread hummus on both the slices.
2. Layer with sprouts, lettuce, tomato, feta cheese, red onion, cucumber, and peppadew peppers. Slice the sandwich and serve immediately.

Couscous and Chicken Tender Wrap

Serves: **4** | Prep Time: **40** mins

Ingredients
- ⅓ cup couscous, whole-wheat
- ½ cup water
- 1 cup fresh parsley, chopped
- ¼ cup lemon juice
- 2 teaspoons garlic, minced
- ½ cup fresh mint, chopped
- 3 tablespoons extra-virgin olive oil
- Salt, to taste

Directions
1. Boil water in a pan and add couscous.
2. Remove from heat and fluff with a fork.
3. Meanwhile, mix together mint, parsley, lemon juice, garlic, oil, salt, and black pepper in a small bowl.
4. Mix together chicken tenders, 1 tablespoon of the mint mixture and some salt in a medium bowl.
5. Cook chicken tenders in a large nonstick skillet and cook for about 4 minutes on each side. Dish out and cut into bite-sized pieces.
6. Stir in the remaining parsley mixture, tomato and cucumber into the couscous to serve.

Mediterranean Grilled Cheese Sandwich

Serves: **1** | Prep Time: **15** mins

Ingredients
- 1 tablespoon extra-virgin olive oil, divided
- 1 oz. Feta cheese, crumbled
- 2 sourdough bread slices
- 2 oz. whole milk Mozzarella cheese, shredded
- 2 cups fresh spinach
- 2 teaspoons fresh basil, chopped
- Black pepper, to taste
- 4 Roma tomatoes, sliced
- 2 tablespoons black olives, diced
- 1 tablespoon red onion, finely chopped
- ¼ teaspoon garlic, finely minced

Directions
1. Heat half of olive oil in a non-stick skillet and add spinach and garlic.
2. Sauté for about 30 seconds and stir in basil.
3. Spread feta and Mozzarella cheese over one slice of bread.
4. Layer with tomatoes, followed by spinach mixture, olives, and red onions.
5. Sprinkle with black pepper and top with the other slice of bread.
6. Heat remaining olive oil in the skillet and add sandwich.
7. Cook for about 4 minutes on each side until bottom is golden brown.
8. Dish out and serve immediately.

Mediterranean Fish Wraps

Serves: **4** | Prep Time: **15** mins

Ingredients
- 4 ounces feta cheese, crumbled
- ½ cup jarred roasted red peppers, chopped
- 4 cups fish, cooked and shredded
- ½ cup plain Greek yogurt
- ½ cup black olives, chopped
- 2 teaspoons fresh lemon juice
- ¼ teaspoon black pepper
- 4 cups baby arugula
- 1 teaspoon fresh lemon zest
- ½ teaspoon salt
- 4 (12-inch) flour tortillas, whole wheat

Directions
1. Mix together chicken, yogurt, feta, lemon juice, red peppers, lemon zest, olives, salt, and black pepper in a bowl. Divide the baby arugula in the tortillas and spoon the chicken mixture in the center of the tortilla. Tightly roll up and cut in half to serve.

Pita Sandwich

Serves: **2** | Prep Time: **25** mins

Ingredients
- 4 tablespoons hummus
- 2 pita breads
- 2 tablespoons pesto
- ¼ cup cucumber, sliced and quartered
- ¼ cup parsley, chopped
- 4 tablespoons feta cheese, crumbled
- 10 black olives, sliced
- 10 cherry tomatoes, halved

Directions
1. Heat Pita bread in a pan and dish out. Spread hummus on the top of each pita and top with pesto.
2. Layer with cherry tomatoes, parsley, black olives, feta cheese, and cucumber.
3. Fold and cut in slices to serve.

Mushroom Veggies Wrap

Serves: **4** | Prep Time: **35** mins

Ingredients
- 1 zucchini, sliced
- ¼ pound fresh mushrooms, sliced
- 1 red onion, sliced
- 1 eggplant, sliced
- 1 red bell pepper, sliced
- Salt and black pepper, to taste
- ¼ cup goat cheese
- 1 large avocado, sliced
- 1 tablespoon olive oil
- 4 whole grain tortillas
- ¼ cup basil pesto

Directions
1. Put the onions, eggplant, zucchini, bell pepper and mushrooms in a bowl.
2. Drizzle with the olive oil and season with salt, and black pepper.
3. Heat a skillet and add the seasoned vegetables.
4. Cook for about 10 minutes and spread 1 tablespoon each of pesto and goat cheese in each tortilla. Put the sliced avocados and mixed veggies in the tortillas. Roll tightly into a wrap and serve.

Mediterranean Pressed Sandwich

Serves: **4** | Prep Time: **10** mins

Ingredients
- 1 garlic clove, cut lengthwise
- 8 kalamata olives, pitted
- ¼ pound green beans, blanched
- 2 small baguettes, cut in half lengthwise
- 2 sundried tomatoes
- ½ medium red bell pepper, roasted
- 1 tomato, cored and seeded
- 1 tablespoon olive oil
- Salt and black pepper, to taste
- 2 anchovy fillets
- 1 teaspoon lemon juice

Directions
1. Mix together all the ingredients in a food processor and pulse until chunky.
2. Stir in the lemon juice, olive oil, salt and black pepper.
3. Spread the mixture in each baguette and wrap each sandwich in waxed paper tightly.
4. Place a heavy object on top of the sandwiches and press down firmly for one hour before serving.

Pizza and Pasta Recipes

Garlic Bread Pizzas

Serves: **4** | Prep Time: **25** mins

Ingredients
For the dough
- 1 sachet fast-action yeast
- 1 pound strong whole wheat flour, plus extra for rolling
- 1 teaspoon salt
- 2 tablespoons olive oil

For the topping:
- 2 garlic cloves, crushed
- ¼ cup almond butter, softened
- 1½ cups mozzarella, drained
- 1 handful basil leaves, roughly chopped
- 1 teaspoon balsamic vinegar
- 4 tomatoes, roughly chopped
- 1 tablespoon extra-virgin olive oil

Directions
1. Preheat the oven to 320 degrees F and grease 2 baking sheets.
2. Knead together all the ingredients for the dough in a bowl and roll out into eight equal pieces. Mix together garlic and melted butter in a bowl and pour over the dough.
3. Arrange these pieces into the baking sheets and top with mozzarella cheese.
4. Transfer into the oven and bake for about 15 minutes.
5. Top with the remaining ingredients and immediately serve.

Mediterranean Olive Oil Pasta

Serves: **4** | Prep Time: **25** mins

Ingredients

- ½ cup olive oil
- Salt, to taste
- 1 pound thin spaghetti, boiled
- 4 garlic cloves, crushed
- 1 cup fresh parsley, chopped
- 3 scallions, chopped
- 6 oz. marinated artichoke hearts, drained
- ¼ cup feta cheese, crumbled
- 15 fresh basil leaves, torn
- 2 tablespoons red pepper flakes, crushed
- 12 oz. grape tomatoes, halved
- 1 teaspoon black pepper
- ¼ cup pitted olives, halved
- 1 lemon zest

Directions

1. Put olive oil in a skillet and add garlic and salt.
2. Sauté for 30 seconds and add tomatoes, parsley and scallions.
3. Cook for about 2 minutes and add boiled pasta. Toss well and season with black pepper.
4. Garnish with feta cheese and basil leaves to serve.

Easy Tomato Pizzas

Serves: **4** | Prep Time: **22** mins

Ingredients For the dough

- 1 sachet fast-action yeast
- 1½ cups warm water
- 1 pound bread flour, plus more to dust
- 2 tablespoons olive oil

For the topping

- 8 tomatoes
- ½ cup Parmesan cheese, grated
- 5 tablespoons roast tomato sauce
- ½ cup goat's cheese, grated

Directions

1. Preheat the oven to 390 degrees F and grease 2 baking sheets.
2. Mix yeast with flour in a bowl and stir in in water and oil.
3. Knead this dough well for 2 minutes and cover the dough with a plastic sheet.
4. Keep it at a warm place for 2 hours and knead the dough into eight equal balls.
5. Arrange these balls into 2 baking sheets and layer with sauce, tomato slices, parmesan, and seasoning. Transfer in the oven and bake for about 12 minutes. Dish out to serve and enjoy.

Mediterranean Whole Wheat Pasta

Serves: **4** | Prep Time: **20** mins

Ingredients

- 6 ounces whole wheat noodles
- 4 garlic cloves, minced
- 1 (14-ounce) can quartered artichoke hearts
- 3 tablespoons olive oil
- ½ teaspoon red pepper flakes, crushed
- ¼ cup fresh Italian parsley, chopped
- Salt, to taste
- 2 cups cherry tomatoes
- 1 (6-ounce) can whole black olives, pitted
- Black pepper, to taste
- ¼ cup lemon juice, freshly squeezed
- ¼ cup Parmesan cheese, freshly grated

Directions

1. Boil spaghetti pasta in salted water until al dente. Drain under cold water and keep aside.
2. Put olive oil to an iron skillet along with tomatoes, garlic, salt, black pepper and red pepper flakes. Sauté for about 2 minutes and add artichokes, olives and lemon juice.
3. Cook for another 2 minutes and add pasta. Adjust seasoning with salt and black pepper.
4. Garnish with parsley and parmesan cheese to serve.

Pasta with Sautéed Spinach and Garlic

Serves: **4** | Prep Time: **20** mins

Ingredients

- ½ cup extra-virgin olive oil
- 2 teaspoons oregano, dried
- ½ pound uncooked spaghetti
- 10 garlic cloves, chopped
- 1 teaspoon basil, dried
- 1 teaspoon balsamic vinegar
- ½ cup parmesan cheese, grated
- 10 ounces fresh spinach, stems removed
- Salt and black pepper, to taste

Directions

1. Boil spaghetti pasta in salted water until al dente.
2. Drain under cold water and keep aside.
3. Sauté garlic, basil and oregano in olive oil for about 1 minute.
4. Add spinach and sauté for another 3 minutes.
5. Turn off the heat and add balsamic vinegar.
6. Stir in pasta and garnish with parmesan cheese to serve warm.

Mediterranean Artichoke Pizza

Serves: **6** | Prep Time: **20** mins

Ingredients
- 1 cup pesto sauce
- 1 cup sun-dried tomato
- ½ cup kalamata olives
- 4 ounces mozzarella cheese
- 1 pizza dough crust
- 1 cup artichoke heart
- 1 cup spinach leaves, wilted
- 4 ounces feta cheese

Directions
1. Preheat the oven to 350 degrees F and grease a baking pan.
2. Spread the pizza dough crust in the baking pan and add pesto sauce.
3. Top with olives, artichoke hearts, spinach leaves and sun-dried tomatoes.
4. Sprinkle with cheese and transfer into the oven.
5. Bake for about 10 minutes and dish out to serve.

Mediterranean Cauliflower Pizza

Serves: **6** | Prep Time: **35** mins

Ingredients
- 1½ tablespoons olive oil, divided
- 1 lemon, sliced
- ⅓ cup black olives, pitted and sliced
- 1 cup mozzarella cheese, shredded
- ¼ cup fresh basil, slivered
- 1 medium head cauliflower, diced
- ¼ teaspoon salt
- 6 sun-dried tomatoes, chopped and drained
- 1 large egg, lightly beaten
- ½ teaspoon dried oregano
- Black pepper, to taste

Directions
1. Preheat the oven to 350 degrees F and grease a baking sheet.
2. Process cauliflower in a food processor until shredded.
3. Add 1 tablespoon oil and salt to a skillet and add cauliflower.
4. Sauté for about 10 minutes and dish out in a bowl.
5. Mix together olives, tomatoes, egg, oregano, cheese, and lemon slices in a bowl.
6. Add this mixture to the cooled cauliflower and pour into the baking sheet.
7. Transfer in the oven and bake for 14 minutes. Garnish with basil and serve warm.

Breakfast

Cauliflower Cheese Toast

Serves: **8** | Prep Time: **45** mins

Ingredients
- 2 cups cheddar cheese, shredded
- 10 cups cauliflower florets, finely chopped
- 2 large eggs, beaten
- ¼ teaspoon salt
- ½ teaspoon black pepper

Directions
1. Preheat the oven to 425°F and grease a large baking sheet.
2. Microwave the cauliflower on high for about 3 minutes and allow to cool.
3. Dish out into a bowl and stir in rest of the ingredients.
4. Divide the mixture into 8 portions and arrange on the baking sheet.
5. Transfer to the oven and bake for about 25 minutes until the toasts are browned and crispy.
6. Put the toasts between two layers of parchment paper and freeze for up to 3 months.

Vegetarian Breakfast Casserole

Serves: **6** | Prep Time: **50** mins

Ingredients
- 12 eggs
- 1/3 cup green olives
- 1 cup heavy whipping cream
- 3 oz. cherry tomatoes
- 8 oz. parmesan cheese, shredded

Directions
1. Preheat the oven to 400°F and lightly grease a casserole dish.
2. Whisk together eggs, cream and 6 oz. parmesan cheese in a bowl.
3. Arrange the olives on the casserole dish and top with the egg mixture.
4. Top with cherry tomatoes and remaining parmesan cheese.
5. Transfer to the oven and bake for about 40 minutes.
6. Remove from the oven and serve hot.
7. Refrigerate for up to 3 days and warm in microwave before serving.

Orange Peel and Ginger Smoothie

Serves: **3** | Prep Time: **10** mins

Ingredients
- 1 cup organic full fat Greek yogurt
- 2 cups ice cold water
- 1 tablespoon orange peel, freshly grated
- 2 packets Stevia
- 1 teaspoon organic ginger, freshly grated

Directions
1. Put all the ingredients in a blender and puree until smooth.
2. Pour into 3 glasses to serve immediately. Refrigerate for up to 2 days.

Cheese Crusted Omelet

Serves: **2** | Prep Time: **20** mins

Ingredients
- 1 tablespoon butter
- 2 eggs
- 2 tablespoons heavy whipping cream
- Salt and black pepper, to taste
- 3 oz. cheddar cheese, sliced

Directions
1. Whisk together eggs, heavy whipping cream, salt and black pepper in a bowl.
2. Heat butter in a nonstick pan and add cheese slices.
3. Cook for about 3 minutes on medium low heat until bubbly and stir in the egg mixture.
4. Cook for about 5 minutes on low heat without stirring and dish out to serve hot. Freeze for up to 3 days and warm in microwave before serving.

Italian Breakfast Casserole

Serves: **8** | Prep Time: **40** mins

Ingredients
- 2 oz. salted butter
- 8 oz. cheddar cheese, chopped
- 7 oz. cauliflower
- 12 oz. fresh Italian sausage
- 8 eggs

Directions
1. Preheat the oven to 375°F and lightly grease a baking dish.
2. Whisk together egg and cheddar cheese in a bowl and set aside.
3. Heat butter in a large skillet over medium high heat and add the cauliflower.
4. Cook for about 4 minutes and dish into the baking dish.
5. Put the sausage in the pan and fry until crumbled.
6. Transfer to the baking dish and top with the egg cheese mixture.
7. Transfer to the oven and bake for about 40 minutes.
8. Dish out into a bowl and serve hot.
9. Refrigerate for up to 2 days or freeze for up to a week and heat before serving.

Bacon and Mushroom Breakfast Casserole

Serves: **8** | Prep Time: **55** mins

Ingredients
- 10 oz. bacon
- 6 oz. mushrooms
- 2 oz. salted butter
- 1 cup heavy whipping cream
- 8 eggs

Directions
1. Preheat the oven to 400°F and lightly grease a casserole dish.
2. Heat butter in a skillet and add bacon and mushrooms.
3. Sauté for about 5 minutes until golden brown and place in the casserole dish.
4. Whisk together eggs and heavy whipping cream in a bowl.
5. Pour this mixture over the bacon and mushrooms and transfer to the oven.
6. Bake for about 40 minutes until golden brown and remove from the oven to serve. Refrigerate for up to 3 days and warm in microwave before serving.

Egg Chorizo Muffins

Serves: **8** | Prep Time: **20** mins

Ingredients
- 2 scallions, finely chopped
- 12 eggs
- 5 oz. air dried chorizo
- Salt and black pepper, to taste
- 6 oz. mozzarella cheese, shredded

Directions
1. Preheat the oven to 350ºF and grease 8 muffin tins.
2. Put the chorizo and scallions in the muffin tins.
3. Whisk together eggs with salt and black pepper in a bowl.
4. Pour this mixture into the muffin tins and top with mozzarella cheese.
5. Transfer to the oven and bake for 20 minutes.
6. Remove from the oven and serve warm.
7. Fold the muffins between parchment paper and freeze for up to 3 months.

Bacon Eggs Ham Muffin

Serves: **6** | Prep Time: **25** mins

Ingredients
- 12 eggs
- 2 oz. ham, cooked
- 3 oz. mozzarella cheese, shredded
- Salt and black pepper, to taste
- 2 oz. bacon, cooked

Directions
1. Preheat the oven to 400ºF and lightly grease 6 muffin tins.
2. Break 2 eggs in each muffin tin and season with salt and black pepper.
3. Top with ham, bacon and mozzarella cheese and place in the oven.
4. Bake for about 15 minutes and remove from the oven to serve warm.
5. Fold the muffins between parchment paper and freeze for up to 1 month.

Low Carb Chia Pudding

Serves: **1** | Prep Time: **15** mins

Ingredients
- 2 tablespoons chia seeds
- ¾ cup organic coconut milk
- ½ teaspoon vanilla extract
- 2 tablespoons almonds
- 2 scoops Stevia

Directions
1. Mix together all the ingredients in a glass jar and cover.
2. Refrigerate for at least 4 hours and remove from the fridge to serve chilled.
3. You can refrigerate this pudding for about 3 days.

Low Carb Seedy Oatmeal

Serves: **2** | Prep Time: **10** mins

Ingredients
- 2 tablespoons flaxseed, whole
- 2 cups organic coconut milk, full fat
- 2 tablespoons chia seeds
- 2 pinches salt
- 2 tablespoons sunflower seeds

Directions
1. Put all the ingredients in a small saucepan and bring to a boil.
2. Reduce the heat and allow it to simmer for about 20 minutes on low heat.
3. Dish out into a bowl and serve hot.
4. Let it cool down and refrigerate for about 3 days.

Salad Sandwich

Serves: **2** | Prep Time: **15** mins

Ingredients
- ½ oz. butter
- 2 oz. romaine lettuce
- 1 oz. edam cheese, shredded
- 1 cherry tomatoes
- ½ avocado

Directions
1. Spread butter on the lettuce leaves and top with avocado, cherry tomatoes and edam cheese. Top with the remaining lettuce leaves and serve.
2. Wrap in the plastic food wrap and store in the freezer for about 3 days.

Scrambled Eggs with Basil and Butter

Serves: **1** | Prep Time: **15** mins

Ingredients
- 2 tablespoons sour cream
- 2 eggs
- Salt, to taste
- 2 tablespoons fresh basil
- 1 oz. butter

Directions
1. Whisk together eggs, sour cream and salt in a bowl.
2. Heat butter on low heat in a pan and stir in the egg mixture.
3. Cook for about 3 minutes on medium low heat and dish onto a platter.Garnish with fresh basil and serve.
4. Store in the fridge for about 1 day and warm before serving.

Coffee with Cream

Serves: **1** | Prep Time: **10** mins

Ingredients

- ¾ cup water
- 1 tablespoon coffee
- 1 scoop Stevia
- 1 pinch cinnamon
- 4 tablespoons heavy whipping cream

Directions

1. Brew the coffee in water for about 5 minutes and add cinnamon and Stevia.
2. Heat heavy whipping cream in a saucepan until it is frothy.
3. Transfer into a large mug and top with the brewed coffee to serve.
4. Store in the fridge for about 1 day and warm before serving.

Cheese Roll Ups

Serves: **4** | Prep Time: **10** mins

Ingredients

- 2 oz. butter
- 8 oz. provolone cheese, in slices
- 2 tablespoons sour cream
- Red chili flakes, to taste
- 2 tablespoons basil

Directions

1. Divide and spread the butter and sour cream onto the cheese slices.
2. Sprinkle with basil and red chili flakes. Roll up the slices and serve.
3. Refrigerate for up to 2 days and freeze for up to 1 week.

Dairy Free Latte

Serves: **2** | Prep Time: **5** mins

Ingredients

- 1½ cups boiling water
- 2 eggs
- 2 tablespoons coconut oil
- 1 pinch vanilla extract
- 1 teaspoon ground ginger

Directions

1. Put all the ingredients in a blender and blend until smooth.
2. Pour into 2 mugs and serve hot.
3. Refrigerate for up to 1 day and heat before serving.

Chorizo and Spinach Frittata

Serves: **8** | Prep Time: **50** mins

Ingredients

- 8 oz. fresh spinach, chopped
- 5 oz. chorizo, diced
- 4 tablespoons salted butter
- 8 eggs
- 8 oz. cheddar cheese, shredded

Directions

1. Preheat the oven to 350ºF and lightly grease a baking dish.
2. Heat butter in a pan and add chorizo.
3. Cook for about 4 minutes and stir in the spinach.
4. Cook for about 3 minutes and add the eggs.
5. Mix well and cook for about 2 minutes.
6. Transfer into the baking dish and top with the cheddar cheese.
7. Bake for about 30 minutes until golden brown and remove from the oven to serve hot.

Put the frittata between two layers of parchment paper and freeze for up to 3 months.

Mushroom Omelet

Serves: **3** | Prep Time: **15** mins

Ingredients

- 1 oz. butter, for frying
- 3 eggs
- 1 oz. mozzarella cheese, shredded
- Salt and black pepper, to taste
- 3 mushrooms, sliced

Directions

1. Whisk together eggs, salt and black pepper in a bowl until frothy.
2. Heat butter over medium heat in a frying pan and stir in the egg mixture.
3. Cook for about 2 minutes and add mushrooms and mozzarella cheese.
4. Cook for about 4 minutes and dish out into a bowl to serve.
5. Freeze for up to 1 week and warm in microwave before serving.

Avocado Eggs with Bacon Sails

Serves: **4** | Prep Time: **20** mins

Ingredients
- ½ avocado
- 1 teaspoon olive oil
- 2 hardboiled eggs, cut in halves lengthwise and yolks scooped out
- 2 oz. bacon
- Salt and black pepper, to taste

Directions
1. Preheat the oven to 350°F and lightly grease a baking dish.
2. Arrange the bacon on the baking sheet and transfer to the oven.
3. Bake for about 7 minutes and dish out onto a platter.
4. Mix the egg yolks with the avocado and olive oil.
5. Mash well and season with salt and black pepper.
6. Fill this mixture into the egg whites and place on the platter alongside bacon.
7. Serve immediately. You can freeze the egg yolks mixture for up to 3 days.

Cauliflower Hash Browns

Serves: **4** | Prep Time: **30** mins

Ingredients
- ½ yellow onion, grated
- 1 pound cauliflower, grated
- 3 eggs
- Salt and black pepper, to taste
- 4 oz. butter, for frying

Directions
1. Mix together cauliflower with the remaining ingredients except butter and stir well.
2. Heat butter in the nonstick pan and add some mixture.
3. Cook for about 10 minutes on both sides and repeat with the rest of the mixture. Dish out onto a platter to serve. Put the hash browns between two layers of parchment paper and freeze for up to 3 months.

Western Omelet

Serves: **6** | Prep Time: **15** mins

Ingredients
- 4 oz. cheddar cheese, shredded
- 6 eggs
- 2 oz. salted butter
- 5 oz. smoked deli ham, diced
- ½ green bell pepper, finely chopped

Directions
1. Whisk together eggs and cheddar cheese in a bowl until fluffy.
2. Heat butter on medium heat in a frying pan and add ham and bell pepper.
3. Sauté for about 5 minutes and stir in the egg cheese mixture. Dish out onto a platter to serve.
4. Freeze for up to 3 days and warm in microwave before serving.

Low Carb Baked Eggs

Serves: **3** | Prep Time: **25** mins

Ingredients
- 3 tablespoons butter
- 3 oz. ground beef, cooked
- 2 eggs
- Salt and black pepper, to taste
- 2 oz. cheddar cheese, shredded

Directions
1. Preheat the oven to 400°F and lightly grease a baking dish.
2. Place the ground beef in the baking dish and create two holes with a spoon.
3. Crack the eggs into the holes and top with cheddar cheese.
4. Bake for about 15 minutes and remove from the oven to serve.
5. Put the baked eggs between two layers of parchment paper and freeze for up to 3 months.

Boiled Eggs with Mayonnaise

Serves: **4** | Prep Time: **15** mins

Ingredients
- 4 tablespoons mayonnaise
- 4 eggs, soft boiled
- 1 avocado, sliced
- Salt and black pepper, to taste
- 2 tablespoons fresh coriander

Directions
1. Place the boiled eggs on a plate and top with mayonnaise, avocado and fresh coriander. Season with salt and black pepper to serve.
2. You can freeze the boiled eggs and defrost when required to make this dish.

Scrambled Eggs with Halloumi Cheese

Serves: **3** | Prep Time: **25** mins

Ingredients
- 2 tablespoons olive oil
- 3 oz. halloumi cheese, diced
- 4 eggs
- Salt and black pepper, to taste
- ½ cup olives, pitted

Directions
1. Whisk together eggs with salt and black pepper in a small bowl.
2. Heat olive oil in a frying pan over medium high heat and add halloumi.
3. Sauté for about 3 minutes until nicely browned and stir in the whisked eggs.
4. Reduce the heat and stir in the olives.
5. Cook for about 3 minutes and dish out into a bowl to serve.
6. Store in the fridge for about 1 day and warm before serving.

Deviled Eggs

Serves: **4** | Prep Time: **15** mins

Ingredients
- 1 teaspoon tabasco
- 4 hardboiled eggs, cut in half lengthwise and yolks scooped out
- ¼ cup mayonnaise
- 8 shrimp, cooked and peeled
- 1 pinch herbal salt

Directions
1. Put the egg yolks with tabasco, mayonnaise and herbal salt in a bowl and mash with a fork.
2. Arrange the egg whites on a plate and fill with the egg yolk mixture.
3. Top with shrimp and serve.
4. You can freeze the egg yolks mixture for up to 3 days.

Coconut Porridge

Serves: **1** | Prep Time: **20** mins

Ingredients
- 1 egg
- 1 oz. butter
- 1 tablespoon coconut flour
- 4 tablespoons coconut cream
- 1 pinch ground psyllium husk powder

Directions
1. Heat all the ingredients over low heat in a nonstick saucepan and mix well.
2. Stir continuously for about 10 minutes and dish out ino a bowl to serve.
3. You can refrigerate this porridge for up to 3 days.

Eggplant Hash with Eggs

Serves: **4** | Prep Time: **20** mins

Ingredients
- 8 oz. halloumi cheese, diced
- 2 eggplants, diced
- 1 yellow onion, finely chopped
- 4 tablespoons butter
- 4 eggs

Directions
1. Heat butter on medium heat and add onions.
2. Sauté for about 3 minutes and stir in eggplants and halloumi cheese.
3. Cook for about 6 minutes until golden brown and dish out onto a platter.
4. Half fry the eggs and serve with the eggplant hash.
5. Store in the fridge for about 1 day and warm before serving.

No Bread Breakfast Sandwich

Serves: **2** | Prep Time: **15** mins

Ingredients
- 4 eggs
- 2 tablespoons butter
- 1 oz. deli ham, smoked
- Salt and black pepper, to taste
- 2 oz. provolone cheese, cut in thick slices

Directions
1. Heat butter over medium heat in a pan and add eggs.
2. Season with salt and black pepper and sauté for about 2 minutes on each side.
3. Dish out onto a plate and place ham over fried egg.
4. Top with cheese and close with another fried egg to serve.
5. Store in the fridge for about 2 days and warm before serving.

Coconut Cream with Berries

Serves: **1** | Prep Time: **10** mins

Ingredients
- ¼ cup fresh strawberries
- ½ cup heavy cream
- ¼ cup fresh raspberries
- 1 tablespoon almonds
- 1 pinch vanilla extract

Directions
1. Put all the ingredients in an immersion blender and blend until smooth.
2. Dish out into a bowl and serve chilled.
3. You can refrigerate this for about 3 days and freeze for up to 1 month.

Blueberry and Almond Smoothie

Serves: **4** | Prep Time: **10** mins

Ingredients
- ½ cup frozen blueberries
- 8 oz heavy cream
- 4 tablespoons almond butter
- 3 scoops Stevia
- 28 oz almond milk, unsweetened

Directions
1. Put all the ingredients in an immersion blender and blend until smooth.
2. Pour into 4 glasses and immediately serve.
3. Refrigerate for up to 2 days and serve.

Lunch

Salmon Filled Avocados

Serves: **2** | Prep Time: **15** mins

Ingredients
- 2 avocados, halved and pits removed
- Salt and black pepper, to taste
- 2 tablespoons lemon juice
- 6 oz. salmon, smoked
- ¾ cup crème fraiche

Directions
1. Put a scoop of crème fraiche in the hole of the avocado and top with smoked salmon.
2. Sprinkle with lemon juice and season with salt and black pepper to serve.
3. You can freeze the salmon for up to 6 months and use the frozen salmon to make this dish.

Tex Mex Casserole

Serves: **6** | Prep Time: **40** mins

Ingredients
- 2 oz. butter
- 1½ pounds ground beef
- 3 tablespoons Tex Mex seasoning
- 7 oz. Monterey Jack cheese, shredded
- 7 oz. tomatoes, crushed

Directions
1. Preheat the oven to 400°F and lightly grease a casserole dish.
2. Heat butter over medium heat and add ground beef.
3. Cook for about 5 minutes until brown and stir in tomatoes and Tex Mex seasoning.
4. Allow to simmer for about 6 minutes and transfer this mixture into the casserole dish.
5. Top with Monterey Jack cheese and place in the oven.
8. Bake for about 20 minutes until golden brown and remove from the oven to serve hot.
6. Refrigerate for up to 3 days and warm in microwave before serving.

Cilantro Lime Cauliflower Rice

Serves: **4** | Prep Time: **20** mins

Ingredients
- 3 tablespoons extra-virgin olive oil
- 1 medium lime, juiced
- 1 medium head cauliflower, coarsely chopped
- 2 green onions, chopped
- ¼ cup fresh cilantro, roughly chopped

Directions
1. Heat olive oil over medium heat in a pan and add green onions.
2. Sauté for about 2 minutes and add chopped cauliflower.
3. Cook for about 10 minutes on medium low heat and dish out into a bowl.
4. Sprinkle with the lime juice and garnish with cilantro to serve.
5. Refrigerate for up to 3 days and warm in microwave before serving.

Garlic Parmesan Roasted Cauliflower

Serves: **4** | Prep Time: **40** mins

Ingredients
- Salt and black pepper, to taste
- 1 tablespoon extra-virgin olive oil
- 1 large cauliflower head, cut into florets
- ½ cup parmesan cheese, grated
- 2 tablespoons garlic, minced

Directions
1. Preheat the oven to 400°F and lightly grease a baking sheet.
2. Mix together cauliflower florets with olive oil, garlic, salt and black pepper in a bowl.
3. Transfer to the baking sheet and place in the oven. Bake for about 15 minutes and flip the sides of the cauliflower. Top with parmesan cheese and bake for about 15 more minutes.
4. Remove from the oven and serve hot. Serve in a casserole and garnish with parsley.
5. Freeze for up to 1 week and warm in microwave before serving.

Mexican Street Broccoli Salad

Serves: **6** | Prep Time: **20** mins

Ingredients
- 2 cups yellow squash, chopped
- 3 teaspoons chili and lime seasoning
- 30 oz. broccoli, riced
- ½ cup Mexican crema
- ½ cup cotija cheese

Directions
1. Mix together Mexican crema, cotija cheese and chili and lime seasoning in a small bowl.
2. Place yellow squash and broccoli in a bowl and top with the crema mixture.
3. You can use both the frozen and fresh yellow squash and broccoli for this salad.

Parmesan Zucchini and Tomato Gratin

Serves: **6** | Prep Time: **50** mins

Ingredients
- 3 medium zucchinis, sliced
- 2 medium tomatoes, sliced
- ½ cup parmesan cheese, shredded
- 2 tablespoons olive oil
- Salt and garlic powder, to taste

Directions
1. Preheat the oven to 350°F and lightly grease a baking sheet.
2. Arrange the zucchini slices on the baking sheet and layer with tomato slices.
3. Layer again with zucchini slices and drizzle with olive oil.
4. Season with salt and garlic powder and top with parmesan cheese.
5. Transfer into the oven and bake for about 40 minutes. Remove from the oven and serve warm.
6. You can use both the fresh and frozen zucchinis and tomatoes.

Roasted Brussels Sprouts with Parmesan

Serves: **4** | Prep Time: **30** mins

Ingredients
- Salt and black pepper, to taste
- 1 tablespoon olive oil
- ½ cup parmesan cheese, shredded
- 13 oz. fresh Brussels sprouts, trimmed and halved
- ½ cup pork rinds, crushed

Directions
1. Preheat the oven to 400°F and lightly grease a baking dish. Arrange the Brussels sprouts in a baking dish and drizzle with olive oil. Season with salt and black pepper and top with crushed pork rinds.
2. Mix well and transfer, covered in the oven. Bake for about 15 minutes and uncover.
3. Top with the parmesan cheese and bake for 5 more minutes.
4. Remove from the oven and serve hot. Freeze the Brussels sprouts and thaw before baking.

Mixed Chicken and Veggies

Serves: **5** | Prep Time: **25** mins

Ingredients
- 1 carrot, chopped
- 2 pounds chicken, boiled
- ½ cup mushrooms, chopped
- Salt and black pepper, to taste
- 1½ tablespoons olive oil

Directions
1. Heat olive oil in a skillet over medium heat and add carrots and mushrooms.
2. Sauté for about 5 minutes and add chicken. Season with salt and black pepper and cover with lid.
3. Cook for about 7 minutes and dish out into a bowl to serve.
4. You can use the frozen as well as fresh chicken and veggies.

Oven Roasted Asparagus

Serves: **4** | Prep Time: **35** mins

Ingredients
- 3 tablespoons extra-virgin olive oil
- 2 pounds asparagus, stalks trimmed
- ¼ cup Monterey Jack Cheese
- ½ teaspoon black pepper
- ½ teaspoon kosher salt

Directions
1. Preheat the oven to 400°F and lightly grease a baking dish.
2. Arrange asparagus on the baking sheet and drizzle with olive oil.
3. Season with salt and black pepper and top with Monterey Jack Cheese.
4. Transfer to the oven and bake for about 25 minutes until slightly charred.
5. Refrigerate for up to 2 days and warm before serving.

Smashed Broccoli

Serves: **6** | Prep Time: **15** mins

Ingredients
- Kosher salt and crushed red pepper, to taste
- 1 large head broccoli, cut into florets
- 2 tablespoons olive oil
- 1 cup parmesan cheese, grated
- 2 garlic cloves, smashed

Directions
1. Blanch the broccoli in salted water for about 2 minutes and smash it.
2. Heat olive oil over medium heat in a large skillet and add garlic and smashed broccoli.
3. Season with salt and crushed red pepper and cook for about 3 minutes on each side.
4. Dish out into a bowl and top with parmesan cheese to serve.
5. You can use both the frozen and fresh broccoli, but fresh broccoli works better.

Chicken Noodle Soup

Serves: **6** | Prep Time: **30** mins

Ingredients
- 1 pound chicken, boiled and chopped
- ½ packet miracle noodles, boiled and rinsed
- 1 tablespoon olive oil
- Salt and black pepper, to taste
- ½ onion, chopped

Directions
1. Heat olive oil over medium heat in a pan and add onions. Sauté for about 3 minutes and add chicken, salt and black pepper. Cover with lid and cook for about 10 minutes.
2. Add miracle noodles with some water and cook for about 5 minutes. Dish out into a bowl and serve hot.
3. You can refrigerate this soup for up to 3 days and warm before serving.

Zoodle Alfredo with Bacon

Serves: **6** | Prep Time: **20** mins

Ingredients
- 1½ cups heavy cream
- ½ pound bacon, crisped and chopped
- ½ cup parmesan cheese, grated
- Kosher salt and black pepper, to taste
- 16 oz. zucchini noodles

Directions
1. Heat a nonstick pan and add bacon, heavy cream, salt and black pepper.
2. Bring to a boil and reduce the heat to low. Add parmesan cheese and cook for about 3 minutes.
3. Stir in the zucchini noodles and cook for about 2 minutes.
4. Dish out into a bowl and serve warm. Make the mixture without zucchini noodles and freeze for up to 1 month. Add zucchini noodles before serving.

Broiled Salmon

Serves: **4** | Prep Time: **20** mins

Ingredients
- 1 tablespoon grainy mustard
- 4 (4 oz.) salmon fillets
- 4 teaspoons fresh thyme leaves, chopped
- Kosher salt and black pepper, to taste
- Juice of 1 lemon

Directions
1. Preheat the broiler and lightly grease a baking sheet.
2. Mix together mustard, thyme, lemon juice, salt and black pepper in a bowl.
3. Arrange the salmon fillets on the baking sheet and top with this mixture.
4. Broil for about 8 minutes and remove from the oven to serve hot.
5. Refrigerate for up to 3 days and freeze for up to a week.

Cajun Parmesan Salmon

Serves: **4** | Prep Time: **25** mins

Ingredients
- Cajun seasoning and black pepper, to taste
- 4 (4 oz.) salmon fillets
- 4 tablespoons butter
- 2 tablespoons parmesan cheese, freshly grated
- 1/3 cup chicken broth, low sodium

Directions
1. Heat half of butter over medium high heat in a large skillet and add salmon fillets.
2. Season with Cajun seasoning and black pepper and cook for about 4 minutes on each side.
3. Dish out onto a plate and set aside.
4. Heat the remaining butter in the skillet and add broth and parmesan cheese.
5. Cook for about 5 minutes on high heat and return the salmon fillets.
6. Simmer for about 4 minutes and dish out to serve warm.
7. Refrigerate for up to 3 days and warm in microwave before serving.

Cheesy Bacon Butternut Squash

Serves: **8** | Prep Time: **40** mins

Ingredients
- 2 tablespoons olive oil
- 2 pounds butternut squash, peeled and cut into 1" pieces
- Kosher salt and black pepper, to taste
- 2 cups parmesan cheese, freshly grated
- ½ pound bacon, chopped

Directions
1. Preheat the oven to 425°F and lightly grease a baking dish.
2. Heat olive oil in a medium skillet and add butternut squash, bacon, salt and black pepper.
3. Sauté for about 2 minutes and then transfer into the baking dish.
4. Bake for about 25 minutes and remove from the oven.
5. Top with parmesan cheese and bake for another 10 minutes.
6. Remove the baking dish from the oven and serve warm.
7. Refrigerate for up to 3 days and warm in microwave before serving.

Bacon Avocado Bombs

Serves: **6** | Prep Time: **20** mins

Ingredients
- 1/3 cup cheddar cheese, shredded
- 2 avocados, halved and pits removed
- 8 bacon slices
- 2 tablespoons Dijon mustard
- 2 tablespoons butter

Directions
1. Preheat the broiler and lightly grease a baking sheet.
2. Put the cheddar cheese in the avocado halves and cover with the other halves.
3. Mix together butter and Dijon mustard and marinate stuffed avocados in it.
4. Wrap 4 slices of bacon around each avocado and transfer to the baking sheet.
5. Broil for about 10 minutes, flipping halfway through.
6. Remove from the oven, slice crosswise and serve immediately.
7. Refrigerate for up to 2 days and freeze for up to 1 week.

Lemon Ginger Shrimp

Serves: **4** | Prep Time: **15** mins

Ingredients
- 1 pound medium shrimp, peeled and deveined
- 3 tablespoons butter, divided
- 1 lemon, thinly sliced, plus juice of 1 lemon
- Kosher salt and crushed red pepper flakes, to taste
- 2 tablespoons ginger, minced

Directions
1. Heat butter over medium heat in a large skillet and add the rest of the ingredients.
2. Cook for about 3 minutes on each side and dish out into a bowl to serve.
3. You can freeze the shrimp for up to 6 months and use the frozen shrimp to make this dish.

Jalapeño Popper Stuffed Zucchini

Serves: **6** | Prep Time: **30** mins

Ingredients
- 6 oz. cream cheese, softened
- 3 medium zucchinis, ends removed and halved crosswise
- 1 cup mozzarella cheese, shredded and divided
- Garlic powder, kosher salt and black pepper
- 1 jalapeno, minced

Directions

1. Preheat the oven to 425°F and lightly grease a baking dish.
2. Arrange the zucchini on the baking sheet and bake for about 10 minutes.
3. Mix together cream cheese, ½ cup mozzarella cheese, jalapeño, garlic powder, kosher salt and black pepper in a bowl.
4. Remove zucchini from the oven and fill in the jalapeño mixture.
5. Bake again for about 8 minutes and remove from oven to serve.
6. Freeze up to 3 days but it is better to use fresh zucchini.

Baked Cajun Salmon

Serves: **4** | Prep Time: **30** mins

Ingredients

- 1 red bell pepper, thinly sliced
- ½ large white onion, thinly sliced
- Cajun seasoning, garlic powder, paprika, kosher salt and black pepper
- 4 (6 oz.) salmon fillets
- 4 tablespoons extra-virgin olive oil

Directions

1. Preheat the oven to 400°F and lightly grease a baking sheet.
2. Arrange onions and bell peppers on the baking sheet and season with salt and black pepper.
3. Whisk together Cajun seasoning, garlic powder and paprika in a bowl.
4. Put the salmon on the baking sheet and rub with seasoning blend.
5. Transfer to the oven and bake for about 20 minutes.
6. Refrigerate for up to 3 days and freeze for up to a week.

Cheesesteak Stuffed Portobellos

Serves: **4** | Prep Time: **35** mins

Ingredients

- 3 tablespoons extra-virgin olive oil, divided
- 4 medium portobello mushrooms, stems and gills removed
- Italian seasoning, kosher salt and black pepper
- 4 slices provolone cheese
- 1 pound sirloin steak

Directions

1. Preheat the oven to 350°F and lightly grease a baking sheet.
2. Mix together half of olive oil, salt and black pepper in a bowl and marinate mushrooms in it.
3. Heat the rest of the olive oil and add steak, salt and black pepper.
4. Cook for about 5 minutes on each side and stuff inside the portobello mushrooms.
5. Transfer onto the baking sheet and bake for about 20 minutes.
6. Remove from the oven and serve immediately. Freeze for about 5 days.

Turkey Carrot Roll Up

Serves: **2** | Prep Time: **15** mins

Ingredients

- 2 carrot sticks
- 2 thin slices of turkey breasts
- 2 teaspoons yellow mustard
- 2 cheddar cheese slices
- 2 tablespoons olive oil

Directions

1. Place turkey breast slices in a plate and spread mustard.
2. Put cheese slices in between and wrap around the carrot sticks.
3. Heat olive oil over medium heat in a skillet and add turkey carrot roll ups.
4. Sauté for about 3 minutes and dish out to serve.
5. Refrigerate for up to 3 days and warm in microwave before serving.

Sweet and Savory Grilled Chicken

Serves: **4** | Prep Time: **25** mins

Ingredients

- 2 teaspoons dry mustard
- 2 teaspoons light brown sugar
- 1 teaspoon onion powder
- 1¼ pounds boneless, skinless chicken breast
- Kosher salt and white pepper, to taste

Directions

1. Preheat the grill to medium high and grease the grill grate.
2. Mix together dry mustard, brown sugar, onion powder, kosher salt and white pepper in a small bowl.
3. Dredge chicken breasts in this mixture and coat well.
4. Transfer to the grill and grill for about 6 minutes on each side. Remove from the grill to serve hot.
5. You can use both the frozen and fresh chicken breasts. Frozen breasts need to be thawed.

Cheesy Cauliflower Casserole

Serves: **6** | Prep Time: **25** mins

Ingredients
- 4 oz. cream cheese
- 1 head cauliflower florets, boiled and drained
- 2 teaspoons Dijon mustard
- Garlic powder, salt and black pepper, to taste
- 2 cups cheddar cheese, shredded and divided

Directions
1. Preheat the oven to 375°F and grease glass baking dish.
2. Put cream cheese and Dijon mustard in a saucepan and cook for about 2 minutes.
3. Remove from the heat and stir in half of cheddar cheese, garlic powder, salt and black pepper. Mix well and stir in the boiled cauliflower. Transfer into the baking dish and top with the remaining cheese.
4. Move into the oven and bake for about 15 minutes. Remove from the oven and serve hot.
5. If you are using frozen cauliflower, thaw it thoroughly and drain the water.

Lemon Pepper Green Beans

Serves: **5** | Prep Time: **20** mins

Ingredients
- 3 tablespoons butter
- Crushed red pepper flakes, sea salt and black pepper, to taste
- 1½ pounds fresh green beans, trimmed and boiled
- 2 garlic cloves, minced
- 1½ teaspoons lemon pepper seasoning

Directions
1. Heat butter in a large skillet over medium high heat and add garlic, red pepper flakes and lemon pepper seasoning. Sauté for about 1 minute and add green beans.
2. Season with sea salt and black pepper and cook for about 5 minutes. Dish out into a bowl and serve hot.
3. You can store the green beans in the freezer for up to 3 months and they can be thawed before using.

Dinner

Fried Cabbage with Kielbasa

Serves: **5** | Prep Time: **20** mins

Ingredients
- 2 tablespoons red wine vinegar
- 6 tablespoons butter, divided
- 14 oz. kielbasa, thinly sliced
- Paprika, sea salt and black pepper, to taste
- 1 large head green cabbage, cored and sliced

Directions
1. Heat half of butter over medium heat in a large skillet and add kielbasa.
2. Sauté for about 3 minutes and add red wine vinegar.
3. Cook for about 2 minutes and stir in the green cabbage, paprika, sea salt and black pepper.
4. Cook for about 5 minutes and dish out into a bowl to serve.
5. You can prepare the kielbasa mixture but do not add cabbage. Add cabbage when you reheat it.

Garlic Butter Beef Sirloin Steak

Serves: **6** | Prep Time: **10** mins

Ingredients
- 1 teaspoon garlic powder
- Salt and black pepper, to taste
- 2 pounds beef top sirloin steaks
- 2 garlic cloves, minced
- ¼ cup butter

Directions
1. Heat butter in a wok and add beef top sirloin steaks. Sauté for about 3 minutes and stir in the rest of the ingredients. Cover the lid and cook on medium low heat for about 25 minutes.
2. Dish out into a bowl and serve hot. Thaw properly if you are using frozen beef steaks.

Beef Pot Roast

Serves: **6** | Prep Time: **45** mins

Ingredients
- ½ teaspoon garlic powder
- 2 pounds beef
- ½ teaspoon ginger powder
- Salt and black pepper, to taste
- 1 tablespoon avocado oil

Directions
1. Season the beef with ginger powder, garlic powder, salt and black pepper.
2. Heat avocado oil in a nonstick skillet and add beef. Sauté for about 6 minutes on each side and close the lid. Cook on medium low heat for about 30 minutes and dish out into a bowl to serve hot. You can store the leftovers in the freezer for up to 3 months.

Green Chile Pork Taco Bowl

Serves: **8** | Prep Time: **35** mins

Ingredients
- 4 tablespoons olive oil
- Garlic powder, salt and black pepper
- 2 pounds pork sirloin roast, thickly sliced
- 20 oz. green chile tomatillo salsa, without added sugar
- 2 teaspoons cumin powder

Directions
1. Mix together cumin powder, garlic powder, salt and black pepper in a bowl.
2. Coat this mixture on both the sides of pork.
3. Heat olive oil in a pressure cooker and add pork with green chile tomatillo salsa. Lock the lid and cook on High Pressure for about 25 minutes.
4. Naturally release the pressure and dish out into a bowl.
5. You can freeze the pork and defrost when required to make this dish.

Corned Beef

Serves: **4** | Prep Time: **45** mins

Ingredients
- 4 whole peppercorns
- 2 pounds corned beef, flat cut
- ½ small onion, quartered
- 1 cup low sodium chicken broth
- 2 large bay leaves

Directions
1. Put all the ingredients along with the beef in a pressure cooker.
2. Lock the lid and cook on High Pressure for about 35 minutes.
3. Naturally release the pressure and dish out into a bowl. You can freeze this dish for up to 3 months.

Thai Curry Insta Pork

Serves: **4** | Prep Time: **55** mins

Ingredients
- 1 cup coconut milk, canned
- 1 pound pork tenderloin
- 2 tablespoons Thai curry paste
- ½ cup water
- 1 tablespoon butter

Directions
1. Mix together coconut milk, butter, Thai curry paste and water in a bowl.
2. Put the pork meat in a nonstick skillet and pour the Thai curry sauce over it.
3. Cover with lid and cook on medium low heat for 40 minutes.
4. Naturally release the pressure and dish out to serve hot.
5. Wrap in the plastic food wrap and store in the freezer for about 3 months.

Lamb Roast

Serves: **6** | Prep Time: **8 hours 10** mins

Ingredients
- ¼ cup carrots
- 1 cup beef broth
- 2 pounds lamb roasted Wegman's
- 1 cup onion soup
- ¼ cup potatoes

Directions
1. Put all the ingredients in a slow cooker and mix well.
2. Cover the lid and cook on Low for about 8 hours.
3. Dish out into a bowl and serve hot.
4. You can use both the frozen and fresh lamb. Frozen lamb meat needs to be thawed.

Green Chili Adobo Turkey

Serves: **7** | Prep Time: **40** mins

Ingredients
- 1 tablespoon Goya adobo all-purpose seasoning with pepper
- 2 pounds turkey breasts
- 1 cup green chilies, diced
- 2 cups tomatoes, diced
- 2 tablespoons butter

Directions
1. Season the turkey breasts with adobo seasoning on both sides.
2. Heat butter in a wok and add seasoned turkey breasts.
3. Cook for about 5 minutes per side and stir in the green chilies and tomatoes.
4. Cover the lid and cook on medium low heat for about 25 minutes.
5. Dish out into a bowl and serve hot.
6. You can store the leftovers in the freezer for up to 3 months.

Mediterranean Turkey Cutlets

Serves: **4** | Prep Time: **25** mins

Ingredients
- 2 tablespoons olive oil
- 1 pound turkey cutlets
- ½ cup low carb flour mix
- 1 teaspoon Greek seasoning
- 1 teaspoon turmeric powder

Directions
1. Mix together turkey cutlets with low carb flour mix, turmeric powder and Greek seasoning in a bowl. Heat oil in a frying pan and add cutlets.
2. Cook on medium low heat for about 5 minutes on each side and dish out onto a platter to serve. Store these cutlets in the freezer for about 3 months.

Mustard Lemon Chicken

Serves: **6** | Prep Time: **30** mins

Ingredients
- 1 cup chicken broth
- 2 pounds chicken thighs, boneless
- Italian seasoning, salt and black pepper, to taste
- 3 tablespoons Dijon mustard
- ¼ cup lemon juice

Directions
1. Season the chicken thighs with salt and black pepper.
2. Mix together chicken broth, lemon juice and Dijon mustard in a bowl.
3. Transfer this mixture to a skillet and add seasoned chicken thighs.
4. Cover with lid and cook on medium low heat for about 20 minutes. Dish out onto a platter and serve hot.
5. Store in the fridge for about 1 day and warm before serving.

Citrus Turkey

Serves: **7** | Prep Time: **35** mins

Ingredients
- 1 cup scallions, thinly sliced
- 2 pounds turkey breasts
- 9 ounces mandarin oranges, canned and drained
- Poultry seasoning and crushed red pepper flakes, to taste
- 4 tablespoons butter

Directions
1. Mix together mandarin oranges, scallions, poultry seasoning and crushed red pepper flakes in a bowl.
2. Place turkey breasts in the pressure cooker and top with orange mixture.
3. Cover with lid and cook on High Pressure for about 25 minutes.
4. Dish out into a bowl and serve hot. You can store the leftovers in the freezer for up to 3 months.

Special Salsa Beef Steak

Serves: **6** | Prep Time: **45** mins

Ingredients
- 2 pounds beef steak
- 2 cups salsa
- 1 cup Monterey Jack cheese, shredded
- Garlic powder, salt and pepper, to taste
- ½ teaspoon hot pepper sauce

Directions
1. Season beef steak with garlic powder, salt and black pepper.
2. Mix together salsa and hot pepper sauce in a bowl. Heat a nonstick skillet and add seasoned beef steak.
3. Cook for about 6 minutes on each side and stir in the salsa mixture.
4. Cook covered for about 20 minutes and dish out to serve warm.
5. You can store the leftovers in the freezer for up to 3 months.

Enticing Chicken

Serves: **8** | Prep Time: **40** mins

Ingredients
- 1 tablespoon unsalted butter, melted
- 8 ounces fresh mushrooms, sliced
- 3 pounds boneless halved chicken breasts
- ¼ cup dry white wine
- Salt and black pepper, to taste

Directions
1. Mix together dry white wine, salt and black pepper in a bowl.
2. Heat butter in a skillet over medium heat and add chicken.
3. Sauté for about 6 minutes on both sides and stir in the mushrooms.
4. Cover with lid and cook for about 20 minutes. Dish out into a bowl and serve warm.
5. Refrigerate for up to 5 days and warm in microwave before serving.

Quick Beef

Serves: **6** | Prep Time: **8 hours 10** mins

Ingredients
- 2 pounds grass fed beef
- ¾ cup homemade beef broth
- 1 tablespoon olive oil
- ½ cup cilantro, chopped
- Salt, to taste

Directions
1. Put beef along with rest of the ingredients in a slow cooker and cover with lid.
2. Cook on low for about 8 hours.
3. Dish out into a bowl and serve hot.
4. You can use both the frozen and fresh beef. Frozen beef meat needs to be thawed.

Chicken Leg Quarters

Serves: **4** | Prep Time: **30** mins

Ingredients
- 1 cup homemade chicken broth
- 2 tablespoons olive oil
- 4 skinless chicken leg quarters
- Salt and black pepper, to taste
- 1 teaspoon turmeric powder

Directions
1. Heat olive oil in a skillet over medium heat and add chicken.
2. Sauté for about 4 minutes on each side and add chicken broth, turmeric powder, salt and black pepper.
3. Cover the lid and cook on medium low heat for about 20 minutes.
4. Dish out into a bowl and serve hot.
5. You can store the leftovers in the freezer for up to 3 months.

Whole Chicken

Serves: **8** | Prep Time: **40** mins

Ingredients
- 2 cups homemade chicken broth
- 3 pounds whole chicken, neck and giblet removed
- Salt and black pepper, to taste
- 2 tablespoons olive oil
- 1 tablespoon cayenne pepper

Directions
1. Season the chicken with cayenne pepper, salt and black pepper.
2. Heat olive oil in a skillet over medium heat and add chicken.
3. Sauté for about 4 minutes per side and stir in the chicken broth.
4. Cover with lid and cook on medium low heat for about 30 minutes.
5. Dish out into a bowl and serve hot.
6. Refrigerate for up to 5 days and warm in microwave before serving.

Moroccan Fish

Serves: **8** | Prep Time: **10** mins

Ingredients
- 3 pounds salmon fillets
- 1 pound cherry tomatoes, crushed slightly
- 1 tablespoon fresh basil leaves, torn
- 1 tablespoon butter
- Salt and crushed red pepper flakes, to taste

Directions
1. Heat butter in a skillet and add salmon fillets.
2. Sauté for about 4 minutes and stir in the rest of the ingredients.
3. Cover and cook for about 30 minutes. Dish out onto a platter and serve hot.
4. You can store the leftovers in the freezer for up to 3 months.

Quick Cod

Serves: **6** | Prep Time: **25** mins

Ingredients
- 3 lemon slices
- 2 pounds salmon fillets
- 3 teaspoons fresh lemon juice
- Salt and black pepper, to taste
- 1 tablespoon tamari

Directions
1. Preheat the oven to 350°F and lightly grease a baking sheet.
2. Season the salmon fillets with salt and black pepper and transfer onto the baking sheet.
3. Squeeze the lemon juice and tamari over the salmon fillets and top with lemon slices.
4. Bake for about 15 minutes and dish out onto a platter to serve.
5. Wrap in plastic food wrap and store in the freezer for about 3 months.

Easy Mahi Mahi Fillets

Serves: **5** | Prep Time: **25** mins

Ingredients
- 5 garlic cloves, minced
- 5 (8 ounce) mahi mahi fillets
- 5 tablespoons feta cheese
- Red pepper flakes, salt and black pepper, to taste
- 5 tablespoons fresh lime juice

Directions
1. Preheat the oven to 350°F and lightly grease a baking sheet.
2. Season mahi mahi fillets with salt and black pepper and arrange on the baking sheet.
3. Mix together garlic, red pepper flakes and lime juice in a bowl.
4. Pour this mixture over the fillets and place in the oven. Bake for about 15 minutes and dish out to serve.
5. You can store the leftovers in the freezer for up to 4 months.

Foolproof Cod Fillets

Serves: **6** | Prep Time: **20** mins

Ingredients
- 6 lemon slices
- 2 pounds cod fillets
- 2 tablespoons butter
- Garlic powder, salt and black pepper, to taste
- 3 fresh dill sprigs

Directions
1. Preheat the oven to 350°F and lightly grease a baking sheet.
2. Season the cod fillets with garlic powder, salt and black pepper.
3. Arrange on the baking sheet and top with lemon slices, dill and butter.
4. Transfer to the oven and bake for about 18 minutes. Dish out onto a platter and serve hot.
5. Wrap in the plastic food wrap and store in the freezer for about 3 months.

Low Carb Flavored Pork

Serves: **4** | Prep Time: **5** mins

Ingredients
- 4 (4 ounce) pork chops
- 2 tablespoons butter
- 1 (14 ounce) can sugar free diced tomatoes
- 2 tablespoons fresh lemon juice
- Salt and black pepper, to taste

Directions
1. Heat butter in a skillet and add pork chops. Sauté for about 3 minutes per side and season with salt and black pepper. Mix well and add tomatoes, lemon juice, salt and black pepper.
2. Cover the lid and cook for about 35 minutes. Dish out into a bowl and serve hot.
3. Store in the fridge for about 3 days and warm before serving.

Stuffed Chicken with Asparagus and Bacon

Serves: **8** | Prep Time: **50** mins

Ingredients
- ½ teaspoon salt
- 8 chicken tenders
- ¼ teaspoon black pepper
- 8 bacon slices
- 12 asparagus spears

Directions
1. Preheat the oven to 400°F and lightly grease a baking sheet.
2. Put 2 bacon slices on a baking sheet and top with 2 chicken tenders.
3. Season with salt and black pepper and drop in 3 spears of asparagus.
4. Wrap asparagus and chicken inside the bacon slices and make 3 more.
5. Transfer to the oven and bake for about 40 minutes.
5. You can store the leftovers in the freezer for up to 3 months.

Baked Sausage with Creamy Basil Sauce

Serves: **6** | Prep Time: **45** mins

Ingredients
- 1½ cups cream cheese
- 2 pounds Italian sausage
- 4 tablespoons basil pesto
- 1½ cups mozzarella cheese, shredded
- 4 tablespoons heavy cream

Directions
1. Preheat the oven to 400°F and lightly grease a casserole dish. Arrange sausage in the casserole dish and transfer to the oven. Bake for about 30 minutes and dish out into a bowl.
2. Whisk together cream cheese, heavy cream and basil pesto in a bowl.
3. Pour this cheese sauce over the sausages and transfer to the oven. Bake for about 10 minutes and remove from the oven to serve. You can store the leftovers in the freezer for up to 4 months

Low Carb Pork Medallions

Serves: **3** | Prep Time: **30** mins

Ingredients
- 3 medium shallots, finely chopped
- 1 pound pork tenderloin, cut into ½ inch thick slices
- ¼ cup olive oil
- Salt and black pepper, to taste
- 3 tablespoons basil

Directions

1. Press shallots on both sides of the pork. Heat oil over medium heat in a skillet and add pork and shallots. Season with salt and black pepper and cook for about 8 minutes on both sides. Dish out onto a platter and top with basils to serve.
2. Wrap in the plastic food wrap and store in the freezer for about 3 months.

Mozzarella and Pesto Chicken Casserole

Serves: **8** | Prep Time: **40** mins

Ingredients
- 2 cups cream cheese, softened
- ¼ cup pesto
- ½ cup heavy cream
- 2 pounds chicken breasts, cooked and cubed
- 2 cups mozzarella cheese, cubed

Directions: Preheat the oven to 400°F and lightly grease a large casserole dish.

1. Mix together cream cheese, pesto and heavy cream in a bowl.
2. Stir in the chicken cubes and mozzarella cheese. Move to the casserole dish and place in the oven. Bake for about 30 minutes and remove from the oven to serve warm. Refrigerate for up to 3 days and warm in microwave before serving

Spinach and Bacon Salad

Serves: **8** | Prep Time: **10** mins

Ingredients
- 2 eggs, boiled and sliced
- 8 pieces thick sliced bacon, cooked and chopped
- ½ medium red onion, thinly sliced
- 10 oz. organic baby spinach
- ½ cup mayonnaise

Directions: Mix together baby spinach and mayonnaise in a bowl. Fold in the rest of the ingredients and serve. Store in the fridge for about 2 days and warm before serving

Spicy Baked Chicken

Serves: **3** | Prep Time: **55** mins

Ingredients
- ½ cup salsa
- 1 pound boneless, skinless chicken breasts
- 4 ounces cream cheese, cut into large chunks
- Salt and black pepper, to taste
- 1 teaspoon parsley, finely chopped

Directions: Preheat the oven to 350°F and lightly grease a baking dish.

1. Heat salsa, cream cheese, salt and black pepper in a saucepan, stirring constantly. Place chicken in the baking dish and pour in the cream cheese sauce. Transfer to the oven and bake for about 45 minutes. Remove from the oven and garnish with parsley to serve.
2. You can store the leftovers in the freezer for up to 5 months.

Tortilla Pork Rind Wraps

Serves: **4** | Prep Time: **40** mins

Ingredients
- 3 ounces pork rinds, crushed
- 4 large eggs
- ½ teaspoon garlic powder
- ¼ cup coconut oil
- ¼ cup water

Directions: Put pork rinds, eggs, garlic powder and water in a food processor and process until smooth. Heat a little oil over medium low heat in a nonstick skillet and add 3 tablespoons of the batter. Cook for about 5 minutes on both sides and repeat with the remaining batter. Dish out onto a platter and serve hot. Store in the fridge for about 2 days and warm before serving.

Week 1 Meal Plan and Shopping List

Week 1 meal plan	Breakfast	Lunch	Dinner
Day 1	Breakfast Cheesy Sausage	Cheesy Bacon Butternut Squash	Browned Butter Asparagus
Day 2	Cauliflower Toast with Avocado	Jalapeño Popper Stuffed Zucchini	Roasted Brussels Sprouts
Day 3	Keto Avocado Toast	Turkey Carrot Roll Up	Mexican Taco Casserole
Day 4	Chocolate Chip Waffles	Sweet and Savory Grilled Chicken	Hamburger Patties
Day 5	Egg Crepes with Avocados	Lemon Pepper Green Beans	Keto Dinner Mussels
Day 6	Ham and Cheese Pockets	Cumin Spiced Beef Wraps	Thai Curry Insta Pork
Day 7	Clementine and Pistachio Ricotta	Mahi Mahi Stew	Mediterranean Turkey Cutlets

Shopping List for Week 1

Produce
1 small head cauliflower
3 avocados
4 oz. alfalfa sprouts
1 pint strawberries
2 Clementine oranges

1 small (1/2 lb.) butternut squash
1 medium zucchini
1 jalapeno
1 small bag carrots

½ lb. fresh green beans
1 onion
2 bundles (12 oz.) asparagus
8 oz. Brussels sprouts

Dairy
2 ½ cups shredded mozzarella cheese
12 oz. shredded parmesan cheese
1 pkg stick butter
1-8 oz. cream cheese
6 provolone cheese slices
12 oz. ricotta cheese

1 pkg cheddar cheese slices
8 oz. shredded cheddar cheese
8 oz. sour cream
1 small pkg (1 ½ oz.) feta cheese
1 pint coconut milk

Meat
1 small pkg (2 individual) pork sausage links
1 pkg (6 slices) turkey cold cuts
3 oz. pkg ham
1 pkg (2 oz.) bacon
¾ lb. skinless chicken breast

2 ½ lbs. ground beef
¾ lbs. Mahi Mahi
¾ lbs. mussels
8 oz. pork tenderloin
8 oz turkey cutlets

Miscellaneous
Sunflower Oil
Vanilla protein powder
12 oz. pkg sugar-free chocolate chips
Flax meal
12 oz. pistachio nuts
Yellow mustard

Light brown sugar
Coconut oil
1 cup fish broth
1 cup chicken broth
Low carb flour mix
8 oz. low carb salsa

Seasonings
Sea salt
Black pepper
Thyme
Sage
Pink Himalayan Sea Salt
Kosher Salt
Garlic powder
Onion Powder
White pepper
Crushed red pepper flakes

Fresh garlic cloves
Lemon pepper
Cumin
Cayenne pepper
Dried Rosemary
Taco Seasoning
Thai curry paste
Greek Seasoning
Turmeric powder
Dry mustard

Week 1 Breakfast Meal Plan

Breakfast Cheesy Sausage

Serves: 2 | Prep Time: 20 mins
Ingredients
- 2 pork sausage links, cut open and casing discarded
- Sea salt and black pepper, to taste
- ½ teaspoon thyme
- ½ teaspoon sage
- 1 cup mozzarella cheese, shredded

Directions
3. Mix sausage meat with thyme, sage, mozzarella cheese, sea salt and black pepper.
4. Shape the mixture into 2 equal-sized patties and transfer to a hot pan.
5. Cook for about 5 minutes per side and dish out to serve.

Cauliflower Toast with Avocado

Serves: 2 | Prep Time: 20 mins
Ingredients
- 1 large egg
- 1 small head cauliflower, grated
- 1 medium avocado, pitted and chopped
- ¾ cup mozzarella cheese, shredded
- Salt and black pepper, to taste

Directions
1. Preheat the oven to 420°F and line a baking sheet with parchment.
2. Place the cauliflower in a microwave-safe bowl and microwave for about 7 minutes on high.
3. Spread on paper towels to drain after the cauliflower has completely cooled and press with a clean towel to remove excess moisture.
4. Put the cauliflower back in the bowl and stir in the mozzarella cheese and egg.
5. Season with salt and black pepper and stir until well combined.
6. Spoon the mixture onto the baking sheet in two rounded squares, as evenly as possible.
7. Bake for about 20 minutes until golden brown on the edges. Mash the avocado with a pinch of salt and black pepper. Spread the avocado onto the cauliflower toast and serve.

Keto Avocado Toast

Serves: 2 | Prep Time: 20 mins
Ingredients
- 2 tablespoons sunflower oil
- ½ cup parmesan cheese, shredded
- 1 medium avocado, sliced
- Sea salt, to taste
- 4 slices cauliflower bread

Directions
3. Heat oil in a pan and cook cauliflower bread slices for about 2 minutes per side.
4. Season avocado with sea salt and place on the cauliflower bread.
5. Top with parmesan cheese and microwave for about 2 minutes.

Chocolate Chip Waffles

Serves: 2 | Prep Time: 30 mins
Ingredients
- 2 scoops vanilla protein powder
- 1 pinch pink Himalayan sea salt
- 50 grams sugar-free chocolate chips
- 2 large eggs, separated
- 2 tablespoons butter, melted

Directions
4. Mix together egg yolks, vanilla protein powder and butter in a bowl.
5. Whisk together egg whites thoroughly in another bowl and transfer to the egg yolks mixture.
6. Add the sugar-free chocolate chips and a pinch of pink salt.
7. Transfer this mixture to the waffle maker and cook according to manufacturer's instructions.

Egg Crepes with Avocados

Serves: 2 | Prep Time: 15 mins
Ingredients
- 4 eggs
- ¾ avocado, thinly sliced
- 2 teaspoons olive oil
- ½ cup alfalfa sprouts
- 4 slices turkey breast cold cuts, shredded

Directions
3. Heat olive oil over medium heat in a pan and crack in the eggs.
4. Spread the eggs lightly with the spatula and cook for about 3 minutes on both sides.
5. Dish out the egg crepe and top with turkey breast, alfalfa sprouts and avocado.
6. Roll up tightly and serve warm.

Ham and Cheese Pockets

Serves: 2 | Prep Time: 30 mins

Ingredients
- 1 oz cream cheese
- ¾ cup mozzarella cheese, shredded
- 4 tablespoons flax meal
- 3 oz provolone cheese slices
- 3 oz ham

Directions
7. Preheat the oven to 400°F and line a baking sheet with parchment paper.
8. Microwave mozzarella cheese and cream cheese for about 1 minute.
9. Stir in the flax meal and combine well to make the dough.
10. Roll the dough and add provolone cheese slices and ham.
11. Fold the dough like an envelope, seal it and poke some holes in it.
12. Place on the baking sheet and transfer to the oven.
13. Bake for about 20 minutes until golden brown and remove from the oven.
14. Allow it to cool and cut in half while still hot to serve.

Clementine and Pistachio Ricotta

Serves: 2 | Prep Time: 10 mins

Ingredients
- 4 teaspoons pistachios, chopped
- ¾ cup ricotta
- 4 strawberries
- 1 tablespoon butter, melted
- 2 clementine, peeled and segmented

Directions
3. Divide the ricotta into 2 serving bowls.
4. Top with clementine segments, strawberries, pistachios and butter to serve.

Week 1 Lunch Meal Plan

Cheesy Bacon Butternut Squash

Serves: 2 | Prep Time: 40 mins

Ingredients
- 1 tablespoon olive oil
- ½ pound butternut squash, peeled and cut into 1" pieces
- Kosher salt and black pepper, to taste
- ½ cup Parmesan cheese, freshly grated
- 2 oz. bacon, chopped

Directions
8. Preheat the oven to 425°F and lightly grease a baking dish.
9. Heat olive oil in a medium skillet and add butternut squash, bacon, salt and black pepper.
10. Sauté for about 2 minutes and then transfer to the baking dish.
11. Bake for about 25 minutes and remove from the oven.
12. Top with parmesan cheese and bake for another 10 minutes.
13. Remove the baking dish from the oven and serve warm.
14. Refrigerate for up to 3 days and warm in microwave before serving.

Jalapeño Popper Stuffed Zucchini

Serves: 2 | Prep Time: 30 mins

Ingredients
- 2 oz. cream cheese, softened
- 1 medium zucchini, ends removed and halved crosswise
- ¼ cup mozzarella cheese, shredded and divided
- Garlic powder, kosher salt and black pepper
- ½ of jalapeno, minced

Directions
7. Preheat the oven to 425°F and lightly grease a baking dish.
8. Arrange the zucchini on the baking sheet and bake for about 10 minutes.
9. Mix together cream cheese, ½ cup mozzarella cheese, jalapeño, garlic powder, kosher salt and black pepper in a bowl.
10. Remove zucchini from the oven and fill in the jalapeño mixture.
11. Bake again for about 8 minutes and remove from oven to serve.
12. Freeze up to 3 days but it is better to use fresh zucchini.

Turkey Carrot Roll Up

Serves: 2 | Prep Time: 15 mins
Ingredients
- 2 carrot sticks
- 2 thin slices of turkey breasts
- 2 teaspoons yellow mustard
- 2 cheddar cheese slices
- 2 tablespoons olive oil

Directions
6. Place turkey breast slices on a plate and spread mustard.
7. Put cheese slices in between and wrap around the carrot sticks.
8. Heat olive oil over medium heat in a skillet and add turkey carrot roll ups.
9. Sauté for about 3 minutes and dish out to serve.
10. Refrigerate for up to 3 days and warm in microwave before serving.

Sweet and Savory Grilled Chicken

Serves: 2 | Prep Time: 25 mins
Ingredients
- 1 teaspoon dry mustard
- 1 teaspoon light brown sugar
- ½ teaspoon onion powder
- ¾ pound boneless, skinless chicken breast
- Kosher salt and white pepper, to taste

Directions
6. Preheat the grill to medium high and grease the grill grate.
7. Mix together dry mustard, brown sugar, onion powder, kosher salt and white pepper in a small bowl.
8. Dredge chicken breasts in this mixture and coat well.
9. Transfer to the grill and grill for about 6 minutes on each side.
10. Remove from the grill to serve hot.
11. You can use both the frozen and fresh chicken breasts. Frozen breasts need to be thawed.

Lemon Pepper Green Beans

Serves: 2 | Prep Time: 20 mins
Ingredients
- 1 tablespoon butter
- Crushed red pepper flakes, sea salt and black pepper, to taste
- ½ pound fresh green beans, trimmed and boiled
- 1 garlic clove, minced
- ½ teaspoon lemon pepper seasoning

Directions
4. Heat butter in a large skillet over medium high heat and add garlic, red pepper flakes and lemon pepper seasoning. Sauté for about 1 minute and add green beans.
5. Season with sea salt and black pepper and cook for about 5 minutes. Dish out into a bowl and serve hot.
6. You can store the green beans in the freezer for up to 3 months and they can be thawed before using.

Cumin Spiced Beef Wraps

Serves: 2 | Prep Time: 30 mins
Ingredients
- ¾ pound ground beef
- Salt and black pepper, to taste
- 4 large cabbage leaves, boiled for 20 seconds and plunged in cold water
- 1½ tablespoons coconut oil
- 1 teaspoon cumin

Directions
5. Heat coconut oil in a pan on medium heat and add the ground beef.
6. Sauté for about 5 minutes and add cumin, salt and black pepper. Cook for about 5 minutes more.
Place the cabbage leaves on a plate and spoon the ground beef mixture on it. Fold into a roll and serve warm.

Mahi Mahi Stew

Serves: 2 | Prep Time: 45 mins
Ingredients
- 1½ tablespoons butter
- ¾ pound Mahi Mahi fillets, cubed
- ½ onion, chopped
- Salt and black pepper, to taste
- ¾ cup homemade fish broth

Directions
4. Season the Mahi Mahi fillets with salt and black pepper. Heat butter in a pressure cooker and add onion.
5. Sauté for about 3 minutes and stir in the seasoned Mahi Mahi fillets and fish broth.
6. Lock the lid and cook on High Pressure for about 30 minutes.
7. Naturally release the pressure and dish out to serve hot.

Week 1 Dinner Meal Plan

Browned Butter Asparagus

Serves: 2 | Prep Time: 25 mins
Ingredients
- ¼ cup sour cream
- 12 oz. green asparagus
- 1½ oz. parmesan cheese, grated
- Salt and cayenne pepper, to taste
- 1½ oz. butter

Directions
6. Season the asparagus with salt and cayenne pepper.
7. Heat 1 oz. butter in a skillet over medium heat and add seasoned asparagus.
8. Sauté for about 5 minutes and dish out into a bowl.
9. Heat the rest of the butter in a skillet and cook until it is light brown and has a nutty smell.
10. Add asparagus to the butter along with sour cream and parmesan cheese.
11. Dish out into a bowl and serve hot.

Roasted Brussels Sprouts

Serves: 2 | Prep Time: 30 mins
Ingredients
- 1 tablespoon olive oil
- 8 oz. Brussels sprouts
- ½ teaspoon dried rosemary
- 2 oz. parmesan cheese, shaved
- Salt and black pepper, to taste

Directions
5. Preheat the oven to 450°F and grease a baking dish with 2 tablespoons of olive oil.
6. Season the Brussels sprouts with dried rosemary, salt and black pepper.
7. Arrange the seasoned Brussels sprouts in a baking dish and sprinkle with olive oil and parmesan cheese.
8. Roast in the oven for about 20 minutes and remove from the oven to serve.

Mexican Taco Casserole

Serves: 2 | Prep Time: 35 mins
Ingredients
- 1/3 cup cheddar cheese, shredded
- 1/3 cup low carb salsa
- 1/3 cup cottage cheese
- ¾ pound ground beef
- ¾ tablespoon taco seasoning

Directions
6. Preheat the oven to 425°F and lightly grease a small baking dish.
7. Mix together the taco seasoning and ground beef in a bowl.
8. Stir in the cottage cheese, salsa and cheddar cheese.
9. Transfer the ground beef mixture to the baking dish and top with cheese mixture.
10. Bake for about 25 minutes and remove from the oven to serve warm.

Hamburger Patties

Serves: 2 | Prep Time: 30 mins
Ingredients
- ½ egg
- 12 oz. ground beef
- 1½ oz. feta cheese, crumbled
- 1 oz. butter, for frying
- Salt and black pepper, to taste

Directions
4. Mix together egg, ground beef, feta cheese, salt and black pepper in a bowl.
5. Combine well and form equal sized patties. Heat butter in a pan and add patties.
6. Cook on medium low heat for about 3-4 minutes per side. Dish out and serve warm.

Keto Dinner Mussels

Serves: 2 | Prep Time: 20 mins
Ingredients
- 1 tablespoon olive oil
- ¾ pound mussels, cleaned and debearded
- 1 garlic clove, minced
- Salt and black pepper, to taste
- ½ cup homemade chicken broth

Directions
6. Heat olive oil in a skillet over medium heat and add garlic.
7. Sauté for about 1 minute and add mussels.
8. Cook for about 5 minutes and stir in the broth, salt and black pepper.
9. Cover with lid and cook for about 5 minutes on low heat. Dish out to a bowl and serve hot.

Thai Curry Insta Pork

Serves: 2 | Prep Time: 55 mins

Ingredients
- ½ cup coconut milk, canned
- ½ pound pork tenderloin
- 1 tablespoon Thai curry paste
- ¼ cup water
- ½ tablespoon butter

Directions
6. Mix together coconut milk, butter, Thai curry paste and water in a bowl.
7. Put the pork meat in a nonstick skillet and pour the Thai curry sauce over it.
8. Cover with lid and cook on medium low heat for 40 minutes.
9. Naturally release the pressure and dish out to serve hot.
10. Wrap in plastic food wrap and store in the freezer for about 3 months.

Mediterranean Turkey Cutlets

Serves: 2 | Prep Time: 25 mins

Ingredients
- 1 tablespoon olive oil
- ½ pound turkey cutlets
- ¼ cup low carb flour mix
- ½ teaspoon Greek seasoning
- ½ teaspoon turmeric powder

Directions
3. Mix together turkey cutlets with low carb flour mix, turmeric powder and Greek seasoning in a bowl.
4. Heat oil in a frying pan and add cutlets.
5. Cook on medium low heat for about 5 minutes on each side and dish out onto a platter to serve.
6. Store these cutlets in the freezer for about 3 months.

Week 2 Meal Plan and Shopping List

Week 2 meal plan	Breakfast	Lunch	Dinner
Day 1	Chocolate Peanut Butter Smoothie	Tuscan Butter Salmon	Vegan Keto Porridge
Day 2	Cheesy Ham Soufflé	Keto Broccoli Pork	Citrus Cheesy Brussels Sprout Salad
Day 3	Cottage Cheese with Berries and Nuts	Beef with Green Olives and Prunes	Prosciutto Wrapped Salmon Skewers
Day 4	Cauliflower Cheese Toast	Cauliflower Turkey Casserole	Garlic Butter Broiled Lobster Tails
Day 5	Cheese Crusted Omelet	Paprika Mushroom Beef	Spicy Baked Chicken
Day 6	Keto Bacon Eggs Ham Muffin	Garlic Parmesan Roasted Cauliflower	Baked Sausage with Creamy Basil Sauce
Day 7	Low Carb Chia Pudding	Mixed Chicken and Veggies	Low Carb Flavored Pork

Shopping List for Week 2

Produce
1 small pkg prunes
1 jar green olives
1 cup of riced cauliflower
1 pint white mushrooms
1 carrot
1/3 lb. Brussels sprouts
3 lemons for juicing

1 bunch fresh basil
1 bunch fresh parsley
1 pint blueberries
1 pint blackberries
2 heads cauliflower
1 small bag baby spinach
1 bag broccoli florets

Dairy
1 pint heavy cream
1 pint almond milk
1 pint coconut milk
1 ½ cups shredded cheddar cheese
1 container cottage cheese
1 small bag mozzarella cheese shredded

1 small container parmesan-garlic cheese
1 small container parmesan cheese
8 oz. sour cream
1 block cream cheese
1 dozen eggs
1 box stick butter

Meat

4 oz. ham
1 small pkg bacon
¾ lb. Italian sausage
2-6 oz. salmon filets

½ lb. frozen salmon
2 lobster tails
½ lb. thin sliced pork
2-4 oz. pork chops

2-6 ox. Boneless skinless
chicken breasts
¾ lbs. chicken
1 cup cooked turkey

Miscellaneous

1 jar creamy peanut butter
1 small container cocoa powder
Stevia
1 pkg walnuts
Chia seeds
Vanilla extract

Cornstarch
Bone broth
Chicken broth
Extra virgin olive oil
Golden flax seed
Coconut flour

Vegan vanilla protein powder
Salsa
Basil pesto
14 oz. can sugar free diced
tomatoes

Spices

Sea salt
Black pepper
Kosher salt

Italian seasoning
Paprika
Garlic powder

Minced garlic
Smoked paprika
White pepper

Week 2 Breakfast Meal Plan

Chocolate Peanut Butter Smoothie

Serves: 2 | Prep Time: 5 mins
Ingredients
- ¼ cup creamy peanut butter
- 2 tablespoons cocoa powder
- 2 scoops Stevia
- 1 cup heavy cream
- 1 cup almond milk, unsweetened

Directions
1. Put all the ingredients in a blender and blend until smooth. Pour into two glasses and serve immediately.

Cheesy Ham Soufflé

Serves: 2 | Prep Time: 30 mins
Ingredients
- ¼ cup heavy cream
- ½ cup cheddar cheese, shredded
- 3 large eggs
- Salt and black pepper, to taste
- 3 ounces ham, diced

Directions
1. Preheat the oven to 375°F and lightly grease ramekins.
2. Whisk together ham with all other ingredients in a bowl.
3. Mix well and pour the mixture into the ramekins. Transfer to the oven and bake for about 20 minutes.
4. Remove from the oven and slightly cool before serving.

Cottage Cheese with Berries and Nuts

Serves: 2 | Prep Time: 10 mins
Ingredients
- ¼ cup blueberries
- ½ cup cottage cheese
- ¼ cup blackberries
- ¾ tablespoon almonds, chopped
- ¾ tablespoon walnuts, chopped

Directions
1. Put the blueberries and blackberries in 2 bowls followed by cottage cheese.
2. Top with almonds and walnuts to serve.

Cauliflower Cheese Toast

Serves: 2 | Prep Time: 45 mins
Ingredients
- ½ cup cheddar cheese, shredded
- 2½ cups cauliflower florets, finely chopped
- ½ of large egg, beaten
- Salt and black pepper, to taste

Directions
1. Preheat the oven to 425°F and grease a small baking sheet. Microwave the cauliflower on high for about 3 minutes and allow to cool. Dish out into a bowl and stir in rest of the ingredients.
2. Divide the mixture into 2 portions and arrange on the baking sheet.
3. Transfer to the oven and bake for about 25 minutes until the toasts are browned and crispy. Put the toasts between two layers of parchment paper and freeze for up to 3 months.

Cheese Crusted Omelet

Serves: 2 | Prep Time: 20 mins

Ingredients

- 1 tablespoon butter
- 2 eggs
- 2 tablespoons heavy whipping cream
- Salt and black pepper, to taste
- 3 oz. cheddar cheese, sliced

Directions

1. Whisk together eggs, heavy whipping cream, salt and black pepper in a bowl.
2. Heat butter in a nonstick pan and add cheese slices.
3. Cook for about 3 minutes on medium low heat until bubbly and stir in the egg mixture.
4. Cook for about 5 minutes on low heat without stirring and dish out to serve hot.
5. Freeze for up to 3 days and warm in microwave before serving.

Keto Bacon Eggs Ham Muffin

Serves: 2 | Prep Time: 25 mins

Ingredients

- 4 eggs
- ¾ oz. ham, cooked
- 2 oz. mozzarella cheese, shredded
- Salt and black pepper, to taste
- ¼ oz. bacon, cooked

Directions

1. Preheat the oven to 400°F and lightly grease 2 muffin holes of a tin.
2. Break 2 eggs in each muffin hole and season with salt and black pepper.
3. Top with ham, bacon and mozzarella cheese and place in the oven.
4. Bake for about 15 minutes and remove from the oven to serve warm.
5. Fold the muffins between parchment paper and freeze for up to 1 month.

Low Carb Chia Pudding

Serves: 2 | Prep Time: 15 mins

Ingredients

- 4 tablespoons chia seeds
- 1½ cup coconut milk
- 1 teaspoon vanilla extract
- 4 tablespoons almonds
- 2 scoops Stevia

Directions

1. Mix together all the ingredients in a glass jar and cover.
2. Refrigerate for at least 4 hours and remove from the fridge to serve chilled.
3. You can refrigerate this pudding for about 3 days.

Week 2 Lunch Meal Plan

Tuscan Butter Salmon

Serves: 2 | Prep Time: 35 mins

Ingredients

- 2 (6 oz) salmon fillets, patted dry with paper towels
- 1½ tablespoons butter
- 1/3 cup heavy cream
- Kosher salt and black pepper
- 1 cup baby spinach

Directions

1. Season the salmon with salt and black pepper.
2. Heat 1½ tablespoons butter over medium high heat in a large skillet and add salmon skin side up. Cook for about 10 minutes on both sides until deeply golden and dish out onto a plate.
3. Heat the rest of the butter in the skillet and add spinach. Cook for about 5 minutes and stir in the heavy cream. Reduce heat to low and simmer for about 3 minutes.
4. Return the salmon to the skillet and mix well with the sauce. Allow to simmer for about 3 minutes until salmon is cooked through. Dish out and serve hot.

Keto Broccoli Pork

Serves: 2 | Prep Time: 45 mins

Ingredients

- 1½ cups broccoli florets
- ½ pound pork, thinly sliced and chopped into 2 inch pieces
- 1 tablespoon butter
- 1 tablespoon cornstarch + 2 tablespoons cold water
- ½ cup bone broth

Directions

1. Heat butter on medium heat in a skillet and add pork. Sauté for about 3 minutes on each side and add broccoli and bone broth. Cook for about 30 minutes and stir in the cornstarch with water.
2. Cover the skillet and cook for about 4 minutes. Dish out and serve hot.

Beef with Green Olives and Prunes

Serves: 2 | Prep Time: 40 mins

Ingredients
- 1 tablespoon salted butter
- ¾ pound beef
- ½ cup reduced sodium chicken broth
- 2 tablespoons prunes, pitted and chopped
- 2 tablespoons green olives, pitted and chopped

Directions
1. Heat butter in a large nonstick skillet over medium high heat and add beef.
2. Cook for about 2 minutes per side until browned and add broth.
3. Bring to a simmer, stirring occasionally and add olives and prunes.
4. Reduce heat to low and cover with lid. Cook until the beef is tender and no longer pink in the center, 12-15 minutes. Transfer beef to a plate and serve hot.

Cauliflower Turkey Casserole

Serves: 2 | Prep Time: 35 mins

Ingredients
- ½ tablespoon Italian seasoning
- 1 cup cauliflower rice, uncooked
- 1 cup cooked turkey, diced
- 2 tablespoons heavy whipping cream
- ¼ cup parmesan and garlic cheese

Directions
1. Preheat the oven to 360°F and grease a small casserole dish with nonstick cooking spray.
2. Mix together cauliflower rice, Italian seasoning and turkey in a large bowl.
3. Transfer this mixture into the prepared casserole dish.
4. Combine cream, parmesan and garlic cheese in another bowl until mixed.
5. Pour over the cauliflower rice mixture and transfer to the oven.
6. Bake for about 20 minutes and remove from the oven to serve hot.

Paprika Mushroom Beef

Serves: 2 | Prep Time: 45 mins

Ingredients
- 1 tablespoon butter
- ½ pound boneless beef, cubed
- ¼ cup sour cream
- Paprika, salt and black pepper, to taste
- ½ cup white mushrooms, sliced

Directions
1. Season the beef with paprika, salt and black pepper. Put butter in a skillet and add seasoned beef.
2. Sauté for about 4 minutes and add mushrooms and sour cream.
3. Cover with lid and cook for about 30 minutes. Dish out and serve hot.

Garlic Parmesan Roasted Cauliflower

Serves: 2 | Prep Time: 40 mins

Ingredients
- Salt and black pepper, to taste
- ½ tablespoon extra-virgin olive oil
- ½ of large cauliflower head, cut into florets
- ¼ cup parmesan cheese, grated
- 1 tablespoon garlic, minced

Directions
1. Preheat the oven to 400°F and lightly grease a baking sheet.
2. Mix together cauliflower florets with olive oil, garlic, salt and black pepper in a bowl.
3. Transfer to the baking sheet and place in the oven. Bake for about 15 minutes and flip the sides of the cauliflower. Top with parmesan cheese and bake for about 15 more minutes.
4. Remove from the oven and serve hot. Serve in a casserole and garnish with parsley.
5. Freeze for up to 1 week and warm in microwave before serving.

Mixed Chicken and Veggies

Serves: 2 | Prep Time: 25 mins

Ingredients
- 1 small carrot, chopped
- ¾ pound chicken, boiled
- 1/3 cup mushrooms, chopped
- Salt and black pepper, to taste
- 1½ tablespoons olive oil

Directions
1. Heat olive oil in a skillet over medium heat and add carrots and mushrooms.
2. Sauté for about 5 minutes and add chicken. Season with salt and black pepper and cover with lid. Cook for about 7 minutes and dish out into a bowl to serve.
3. You can use the frozen as well as fresh chicken and veggies.

Week 2 Dinner Meal Plan

Vegan Keto Porridge

Serves: 2 | Prep Time: 10 mins

Ingredients
- 1½ tablespoons golden flaxseed meal
- 1 tablespoon coconut flour
- 1 tablespoon vegan vanilla protein powder
- ½ scoop Stevia
- ¾ cup almond milk, unsweetened

Directions
4. Mix together the golden flaxseed meal, coconut flour and vanilla protein powder in a bowl.
5. Put this mixture in the saucepan along with almond milk and cook for about 10 minutes over medium heat. Stir in the Stevia and dish out into a bowl and serve hot.

Citrus Cheesy Brussels Sprout Salad

Serves: 2 | Prep Time: 12 mins

Ingredients
- ¼ cup walnuts
- 1/3 pounds Brussels sprouts
- 1 tablespoon EVOO
- ¼ cup parmesan cheese, freshly grated
- 1 teaspoon fresh lemon juice

Directions
4. Put walnuts and Brussels sprouts in a food processor and process until chopped.
5. Transfer into a bowl and drizzle with EVOO and lemon juice.
6. Top with parmesan cheese and serve immediately.

Prosciutto Wrapped Salmon Skewers

Serves: 2 | Prep Time: 20 mins

Ingredients
- ½ pound salmon, frozen in pieces
- 2 tablespoons fresh basil, finely chopped
- Black pepper, to taste
- ½ tablespoon olive oil
- 1½ oz. prosciutto, in slices

Directions
5. Soak 4 skewers in water and season the salmon fillets with black pepper.
6. Mount the salmon fillets lengthwise on the skewers.
7. Roll the skewers in the chopped basil and wrap with prosciutto slices.
8. Drizzle with olive oil and fry in a nonstick pan for about 5-10 minutes on all sides.
9. Dish out and immediately serve.

Garlic Butter Broiled Lobster Tails

Serves: 2 | Prep Time: 25 mins

Ingredients
- 4 tablespoons butter
- 1 lemon, juiced
- 2 lobster tails, top removed and deveined
- ¼ cup garlic, minced
- Sea salt, smoked paprika and white pepper

Directions
6. Preheat the broiler to high and grease a baking sheet. Heat 4 tablespoons butter in a medium skillet and add garlic. Sauté for about 2 minutes and set aside.
7. Mix together sea salt, smoked paprika and white pepper in a bowl.
8. Arrange the lobster tails on the baking sheet and sprinkle with the spice mixture.
9. Drizzle with half the garlic butter and transfer to the oven.
10. Bake for about 10 minutes, drizzling rest of the garlic butter in between.
11. Remove from the oven and serve warm.

Spicy Baked Chicken

Serves: 2 | Prep Time: 55 mins

Ingredients
- 1/3 cup salsa
- 2 (6-ounce) boneless, skinless chicken breasts
- 2 ounces cream cheese, cut into large chunks
- Salt and black pepper, to taste
- 1 teaspoon parsley, finely chopped

Directions
3. Preheat the oven to 350°F and lightly grease a baking dish.
4. Heat salsa, cream cheese, salt and black pepper in a saucepan, stirring constantly.
5. Place chicken in the baking dish and pour in the cream cheese sauce.
6. Transfer to the oven and bake for about 45 minutes. Remove from the oven and garnish with parsley to serve. You can store the leftovers in the freezer for up to 5 months.

Baked Sausage with Creamy Basil Sauce

Serves: 2 | Prep Time: 45 mins

Ingredients

- 1/3 cup cream cheese
- ¾ pound Italian sausage
- 1½ tablespoons basil pesto
- ½ cup mozzarella cheese, shredded
- 2 tablespoons heavy cream

Directions

4. Preheat the oven to 400°F and lightly grease a casserole dish.
5. Arrange sausage in the casserole dish and transfer to the oven.
6. Bake for about 30 minutes and dish out into a bowl.
7. Whisk together cream cheese, heavy cream and basil pesto in a bowl.
8. Pour this cheese sauce over the sausages and transfer to the oven.
9. Bake for about 10 minutes and remove from the oven to serve.
10. You can store the leftovers in the freezer for up to 4 months

Low Carb Flavored Pork

Serves: 2 | Prep Time: 5 mins

Ingredients

- 2 (4 ounce) pork chops
- 1 tablespoon butter
- ½ of (14 ounce) can sugar free diced tomatoes
- 1 tablespoon fresh lemon juice
- Salt and black pepper, to taste

Directions

4. Heat butter in a skillet and add pork chops.
5. Sauté for about 3 minutes per side and season with salt and black pepper.
6. Mix well and add tomatoes, lemon juice, salt and black pepper.
7. Cover with lid and cook for about 35 minutes. Dish out into a bowl and serve hot.
8. Store in the fridge for about 3 days and warm before serving.

Week 3 Meal Plan and Shopping List

Week 3 meal plan	Breakfast	Lunch	Dinner
Day 1	Clementine and Pistachio Ricotta	Mexican Ground Beef	Brussels Sprouts with Caramelized Red Onions
Day 2	Banana Pancakes	Chicken Spinach Coconut Curry	Cottage Cheese with Cherry Tomatoes and Basil Salad
Day 3	Acai Almond Butter Smoothie	Sour Fish with Herbed Butter	Curried Spinach Stuffed Portobello Mushrooms
Day 4	Cream Cheese Pancakes	Turkey with Mozzarella and Tomatoes	Citrus Cheesy Brussels Sprout Salad
Day 5	Keto Salami and Brie Cheese Salad	Cheesy Bacon Ranch Chicken	Caesar Dressing Beef Salad
Day 6	Salad Sandwich	Buttery Beef Curry	Ground Pork with Zucchini
Day 7	No Bread Keto Breakfast Sandwich	Ice-Burgers	Chili Beef

Shopping List for Week 3

Produce

1 pint strawberries
2 Clementine oranges
1 medium banana
1 head iceberg lettuce
1 head Romain lettuce
1 pint cherry tomatoes
1 large Roma tomato
2 avocados
2 yellow onions

1 red onion
1 bunch fresh spinach
Celery
1 lb. Brussels sprouts
1 bunch fresh basil
2 Portabella mushroom caps
1 lemon for juicing
1 medium zucchini

Dairy

48 oz. Ricotta cheese
1 brick cream cheese
3 ½ oz. Brie cheese
1 oz. Edam cheese shredded
2 oz. provolone cheese

1 1/2 cups shredded cheddar cheese
2 slices cheddar cheese
4 slices mozzarella cheese
½ cup shredded mozzarella cheese

¼ cup parmesan cheese grated
1 small carton cottage cheese
1 box stick butter
Almond butter
Herbed butter

Meat

3 oz. salami
1 oz. smoked deli ham
½ lb. chicken
2 boneless chicken breasts

2 large turkey breasts
1 ½ lbs. ground beef
1 ½ lbs. grass fed beef
1 lb. (2 cups) beef

½ lb. lean ground pork
2 cod filets

Miscellaneous

Pistachios
Walnuts
Olive oil
Extra virgin olive oil
Avocado oil
Coconut cream

Red wine vinegar
Vinegar
Oil and vinegar salad dressing
Caesar dressing
Bone broth
Beef broth

Matcha powder
Almond flour
Stevia
2- 100g packs unsweetened acai puree
Sugar free maple syrup

Spices

Sea Salt
Black pepper
Cinnamon

Mexican seasoning
Curry paste
Lemon pepper

Kosher salt
Ranch seasoning
Red chili powder

Week 3 Breakfast Meal Plan

Clementine and Pistachio Ricotta

Serves: 2 | Prep Time: 10 mins
Ingredients.
- 4 teaspoons pistachios, chopped
- ¾ cup ricotta
- 4 strawberries
- 1 tablespoon butter, melted
- 2 clementine, peeled and segmented

Directions
5. Divide the ricotta into 2 serving bowls.
6. Top with clementine segments, strawberries, pistachios and butter to serve.

Banana Pancakes

Serves: 2 | Prep Time: 25 mins
Ingredients
- ½ medium banana
- 1 large egg
- 1 tablespoon butter
- ½ tablespoon sugar free maple syrup
- 2 tablespoons ricotta cheese

Directions
5. Put the banana and eggs in a blender and blend until smooth.
6. Heat ½ tablespoon of butter over medium heat in a large nonstick pan and pour in 2 tablespoons of the batter.
7. Cook for about 2 minutes until bubbles appear on the surface.
8. Flip the pancakes gently with a spatula and cook for 2 more minutes.
9. Dish out the pancakes to a plate and repeat with the remaining batter.

Acai Almond Butter Smoothie

Serves: 2 | Prep Time: 10 mins
Ingredients
- 1½ cups unsweetened almond milk
- 2 (100g) pack unsweetened acai puree
- 1 avocado
- 2 tablespoons almond butter
- 2 tablespoons matcha powder

Directions
1. Put all the ingredients in a blender and blend until smooth.
2. Pour into 2 glasses and serve instantly.

Cream Cheese Pancakes

Serves: 2 | Prep Time: 25 mins
Ingredients
- ¼ cup almond flour
- 1 scoops Stevia
- ¼ teaspoon cinnamon
- 1 egg
- 1 oz cream cheese

Directions
5. Put all the ingredients in a blender and blend until smooth.
6. Dish out the mixture to a medium bowl and set aside.
7. Heat butter in a skillet over medium heat and add half of the mixture.
8. Spread the mixture and cook for about 4 minutes on both sides until golden brown.
9. Repeat with rest of the mixture and serve warm.

Keto Salami and Brie Cheese Salad

Serves: 2 | Prep Time: 10 mins
Ingredients
- 3 oz. salami
- 1 oz. lettuce
- 2 tablespoons olive oil
- 3½ oz. Brie cheese
- ¼ cup macadamia nuts

Directions
3. Divide Brie cheese, lettuce, salami and macadamia nuts onto 2 plates.
4. Drizzle with olive oil and immediately serve.

Salad Sandwich

Serves: 2 | Prep Time: 15 mins
Ingredients
- ½ oz. butter
- 2 oz. romaine lettuce
- 1 oz. Edam cheese, shredded
- 1 pint cherry tomatoes
- ½ avocado

Directions
3. Spread butter on the lettuce leaves and top with avocado, cherry tomatoes and edam cheese.
4. Top with the remaining lettuce leaves and serve.
5. Wrap in the plastic food wrap and store in the freezer for about 3 days.

No Bread Keto Breakfast Sandwich

Serves: 2 | Prep Time: 15 mins
Ingredients
- 4 eggs
- 2 tablespoons butter
- 1 oz. deli ham, smoked
- Salt and black pepper, to taste
- 2 oz. provolone cheese, cut in thick slices

Directions
6. Heat butter over medium heat in a pan and add eggs.
7. Season with salt and black pepper and sauté for about 2 minutes on each side.
8. Dish out onto a plate and place ham over fried egg.
9. Top with cheese and close with another fried egg to serve.
10. Store in the fridge for about 2 days and warm before serving.

Week 3 Lunch Meal Plan

Mexican Ground Beef

Serves: 2 | Prep Time: 30 mins
Ingredients
- ¾ pound ground beef
- 1/3 cup cheddar cheese, shredded
- 3 tablespoons water
- Salt and black pepper, to taste
- 1 tablespoon Mexican seasoning

Directions
3. Put beef in a nonstick pan and season with salt and black pepper.
4. Cook for about 8 minutes until brown and pour in the water and Mexican seasoning.
5. Cook for about 5 minutes and dish out in a bowl to serve.

Chicken Spinach Coconut Curry

Serves: 2 | Prep Time: 5 hours 10 mins
Ingredients
- ¾ tablespoon curry paste
- ½ onion, finely sliced
- pped
- 200 ml coconut cream
- ½ pound chicken, cubed
- 400 g fresh spinach, cho

Directions
3. Put all the ingredients in a slow cooker and stir well.
4. Lock the lid and cook on High Pressure for about 5 hours.
5. Dish out in a serving bowl and serve hot.

Sour Fish with Herbed Butter

Serves: 2 | Prep Time: 45 mins
Ingredients
- 1½ tablespoons herbed butter
- 2 cod fillets
- 1 tablespoon vinegar
- Salt and black pepper, to taste
- 1 teaspoon lemon pepper seasoning

Directions
5. Preheat the oven to 375°F and grease a baking tray.
6. Mix together cod fillets, vinegar, lemon pepper seasoning, salt and black pepper in a bowl.
7. Marinate for about 3 hours and then arrange on the baking tray.
8. Transfer to the oven and bake for about 30 minutes.
9. Remove from the oven and serve with herbed butter.

Turkey with Mozzarella and Tomatoes

Serves: 2 | Prep Time: 1 hour 30 mins
Ingredients
- 1 tablespoon butter
- 2 large turkey breasts
- ½ cup fresh mozzarella cheese, thinly sliced
- Salt and black pepper, to taste
- 1 large Roma tomato, thinly sliced

Directions
6. Preheat the oven to 375°F and grease the baking tray with butter.
7. Make some deep slits in the turkey breasts and season with salt and black pepper.
8. Stuff the mozzarella cheese slices and tomatoes in the turkey slits.
9. Put the stuffed turkey breasts on the baking tray and transfer to the oven.
10. Bake for about 1 hour 15 minutes and dish out to serve warm.

Cheesy Bacon Ranch Chicken

Serves: 2 | Prep Time: 35 mins
Ingredients
- 2 boneless skinless chicken breasts
- 2 slices thick cut bacon, cooked and crisped
- Kosher salt and black pepper, to taste
- ¾ cup mozzarella cheese, shredded
- 1 teaspoon ranch seasoning

Directions
7. Preheat the oven to 390°F and grease a baking dish.
8. Season the chicken breasts with kosher salt and black pepper.
9. Cook chicken breasts in a nonstick skillet for about 5 minutes per side.
10. Top the chicken with mozzarella cheese and ranch seasoning and transfer to the oven.
11. Bake for about 15 minutes and dish out on a platter.
12. Crumble the crispy bacon and sprinkle over the chicken to serve.

Buttery Beef Curry

Serves: 2 | Prep Time: 30 mins
Ingredients
- ½ cup butter
- ½ pound grass fed beef
- ½ pound onions
- Salt and red chili powder, to taste
- ½ pound celery, chopped

Directions
4. Put some water in a pressure cooker and add all the ingredients.
5. Lock the lid and cook on High Pressure for about 15 minutes.
6. Naturally release the pressure and dish out the curry to a bowl to serve.

Ice-Burgers

Serves: 2 | Prep Time: 30 mins
Ingredients
- 2 slices bacon, cooked and crisped
- ½ large head iceberg lettuce, sliced into 8 rounds
- ½ pound ground beef
- 2 slices cheddar cheese
- Kosher salt and black pepper, to taste

Directions
4. Make 2 large patties out of ground beef and season both sides with salt and black pepper.
5. Grill for about 10 minutes per side and top with cheddar cheese slices.
6. Place one iceberg round on a plate and layer with grilled beef.
7. Place a slice of bacon and close with second iceberg round.
8. Repeat with the remaining ingredients and serve warm.

Week 3 Dinner Meal Plan

Brussels Sprouts with Caramelized Red Onions

Serves: 2 | Prep Time: 30 mins
Ingredients
- 2 oz. butter
- ½ red onion, cut into wedges
- ½ tablespoon red wine vinegar
- 12½ oz. Brussels sprouts
- Salt and black pepper, to taste

Directions
4. Heat butter in a medium skillet on low heat and add onions.
5. Sauté for about 10 minutes until the onions are caramelized.
6. Stir in the Brussels sprouts, vinegar, salt and black pepper and cover the skillet.
7. Cook on medium low heat for about 15 minutes and dish out into a bowl to serve hot.

Cottage Cheese with Cherry Tomatoes and Basil Salad

Serves: 2 | Prep Time: 10 mins
Ingredients
- ½ cup cherry tomatoes, quartered
- ½ cup cottage cheese
- 2 tablespoons basil, chopped
- Ground black pepper, to taste
- 4 tablespoons sour cream

Directions
3. Put the cherry tomatoes and basil in a bowl followed by cottage cheese.
4. Top with sour cream and season with black pepper to serve.

Curried Spinach Stuffed Portobello Mushrooms

Serves: 2 | Prep Time: 25 mins
Ingredients
- ½ cup coconut cream
- ½ cup spinach
- 2 Portobello mushroom caps, stems removed
- Salt and red pepper, to taste
- 2 tablespoons oil and vinegar salad dressing

Directions
8. Preheat the grill to medium high heat. Rub salad dressing on the Portobello mushrooms and arrange in a pan. Season with salt and black pepper and cover with plastic wrap.
9. Marinate for at least an hour and then place on the grill, stem side down.
10. Grill for about 10 minutes on both sides and dish out.
11. Mix spinach with coconut cream and fill in the grilled Portobellos.
12. Broil for about 5 minutes in the oven and dish out to serve.

Citrus Cheesy Brussels Sprout Salad

Serves: 2 | Prep Time: 12 mins

Ingredients
- ¼ cup walnuts
- 1/3 pounds Brussels sprouts
- 1 tablespoon EVOO
- ¼ cup parmesan cheese, freshly grated
- 1 teaspoon fresh lemon juice

Directions
7. Put walnuts and Brussels sprouts in a food processor and process until chopped.
8. Transfer into a bowl and drizzle with EVOO and lemon juice.
9. Top with parmesan cheese and serve immediately.

Caesar Dressing Beef Salad

Serves: 2 | Prep Time: 10 mins

Ingredients
- 1 large avocado, cubed
- 2 cups beef, cooked and cubed
- ¾ cup cheddar cheese, shredded
- Salt and black pepper, to taste
- ¼ cup Caesar dressing

Directions
3. Put avocado and beef in a bowl and season with salt and black pepper.
4. Top with cheese and Caesar dressing and refrigerate to serve chilled.

Ground Pork with Zucchini

Serves: 2 | Prep Time: 35 mins

Ingredients
- 1 medium zucchini, chopped
- ½ pound lean ground pork
- 1 tablespoon butter
- Salt and black pepper, to taste
- ¼ cup homemade bone broth

Directions
4. Put the butter and pork in a skillet and cook for about 5 minutes. Add the bone broth, zucchini, salt and black pepper. Cook for about 20 minutes and dish out to serve hot.

Chili Beef

Serves: 2 | Prep Time: 50 mins

Ingredients
- 1 celery rib, finely diced
- ¾ pound grass fed beef, ground
- 1 teaspoons chili powder
- ½ tablespoon avocado oil, divided
- ¾ cup beef broth

Directions
3. Heat avocado oil in a small skillet on medium heat and add beef.
4. Sauté for about 3 minutes on each side and stir in broth and chili powder.
5. Cover the lid and cook for about 30 minutes on medium low heat.
6. Add celery and dish out into a bowl to serve.